Collection
Science and technique of demo

The protection of minorities

Collected texts
- The protection of minorities at the international level : a European project
- The protection of minorities at the national level: diversity of legal models
- The protection of minorities in federal and regional states : specific solutions

**European Commission
for Democracy through Law**

Council of Europe Press, 1994

French edition:

La protection des minorités

ISBN 92-871-2646-1

Collection[1]

Science and technique of democracy

No. 1: Meeting with the presidents of constitutional courts and other equivalent bodies
Piazzola sul Brenta, 8 October 1990[2]

No. 2: Models of constitutional jurisdiction
by Helmut Steinberger[3]

No. 3: Constitution making as an instrument of democratic transition
Istanbul, 8-10 October 1992

No. 4: Transition to a new model of economy and its constitutional reflections
Moscow, 18-19 February 1993

No. 5: The relationship between international and domestic law
Warsaw, 19-21 May 1993

No. 6: The relationship between international and domestic law
by Constantin Economides[3]

No. 7: Rule of law and transition to a market economy
Sofia, 14-16 October 1993

No. 8: Constitutional aspects of the transition to a market economy
Collected texts of the European Commission for Democracy through Law

No. 9: The protection of minorities
Collected texts of the European Commission for Democracy through Law

No. 10: The role of the constitutional court in the consolidation of the rule of law
Bucharest, 8-10 June 1994

1. Also available in French
2. Speeches in the original language
3. Also available in Russian

Publishing and Documentation Service
Council of Europe
F-67075 Strasbourg Cedex

ISBN 92-871-2647-X
© Council of Europe, 1994
Printed in Germany

TABLE OF CONTENTS

INTRODUCTION

Although European States have been aware - to a varying degree - of the problem of protection of minorties, this subject only began to be of particular increasing interest in Europe at the end of the First World War. After a period of stagnation during and after the Second World War, the Council of Europe, set up in 1949, resumed discussion of this subject. However, until 1990, these were only isolated initiatives, which were not conclusive. It is only since 1990 that the protection of minorities has become one of the major points of interest and preoccupation of the Council of Europe, a European International Organisation which upholds the principles of democracy, respect for human rights and preeminence of law.

The European Commission for Democracy through Law - the Venice Commission - was, right from its creation in 1990, one of the first institutions to begin work on the considerable task of preparing an instrument guaranteeing minority rights at European level. It was an urgent choice : violent ethnic conflicts were beginning to rise up in several places on the new European map.

Its proposal for a European Convention for the Protection of Minorities, made public in 1991, represents an attempt to strike a fair balance between those minimum rights which should be granted to minorities and those duties which are incumbent on them. A system of control of the respect for the obligations undertaken by Contracting States under the proposed Convention was instituted: this was founded on three means of control, of which the first - periodical reports - was obligatory, while the two others - inter-State petition and individual petition - were optional.

European States very quickly recognised the need for an international instrument setting out the principles of effective protection of national minorities. At their Summit in Vienna on 8 and 9 October 1993, the Heads of States and Government of European States agreed to instruct the Committee of Ministers of the Council of Europe to "draft with minimum delay a framework Convention specifying the principles which contracting States commit themselves to respect, in order to assure the protection of national minorities" and to "begin work on drafting a protocol complementing the European Convention on Human Rights in the cultural field by provisions guaranteeing individual rights, in particular for persons belonging to national minorities". The first phase of this important work has just been accomplished by the adoption of the "Framework Convention for the Protection of National Minorities", on 8 November 1994.

The Venice Commission has been closely associated with the process of the first pan-European instrument regulating the explosive question of national minorities.

It participated in the work of the Ad Hoc Committee for the Protection of National Minorities (CAHMIN) established by the Committee of Ministers to draw up the Framework Convention for the protection of national minorities. It also participated in the activities in the Project Group "Human Rights and Genuine Democracy" (CAHDD), within the framework of which it presented, amongst others, two reports on the protection of minorities.

This publication aims to make the Venice Commission's work in the field of protection of minorities more available to the public.

It includes, on the one hand, the Proposal for a European Convention on the protection of minorities, as a reply to the heartfelt need for protection of minorities at the European level. The proposal and its explanatory report appear in the first chapter of the publication.

This publication includes, in addition, firstly the report on the protection of minorities at domestic law level which was drawn up within the framework of the Venice Commission and secondly the report concerning the special protection of which minorities can take advantage in States with a Federal or Regional structure.

The first of these reports, without being a study in comparative law, shows the extraordinary variety of models of protection adopted by European States, and also reveals - and this is an important point - that there are certain common aspects to this domestic protection and that these, accordingly, could serve to form a common basis for international and European protection of minorities. The report in question was established on the basis of replies provided by representatives of several European and non-European States to a questionnaire drawn up by the Commission ; the questionnaire, together with the replies, appears in an Appendix to the report. Perusal of the replies given by representatives of different States to the same question allows for a rapid appraisal of the solutions adopted in national laws to identical problems of protection of minorities.

The second summary report concerns the protection of minorities in federal and regional States ; it is followed by individual reports drawn up by members and Associate members of the Commission from Council of Europe member States which have a federal or regional structure, as well as a report from Canada.

The European Commission for Democracy through Law considers the question of the protection of minorities to be one of the most important fields of its activity. This publication is a modest contribution to the evolution of this protection which, nowadays, is considered as a particular but essential component of the protection of human rights as well as of democracy.

Franz MATSCHER
Chairman of the Sub-Commission
on the Protection of Minorities

The protection of minorities
at the international level:
a European Project

PROPOSAL FOR A EUROPEAN CONVENTION FOR THE PROTECTION OF MINORITIES

PREAMBLE

The member States of the Council of Europe and the other States, signatory hereto,

Considering that the aim of the Council of Europe is to achieve greater unity between its members, for the purpose of safeguarding and realising the ideals and principles which are their common heritage;

Considering that the dignity and equal worth of every human being constitute fundamental elements of these principles;

Considering that minorities exist in member States of the Council of Europe and in Central and Eastern European States;

Considering that minorities contribute to the pluriformity and cultural diversity within European States;

Having regard to the work carried out within the CSCE and in particular to the Declaration adopted during the Copenhagen meeting in June 1990, as well as the Charter of Paris for a new Europe, of 21 November 1990;

Having regard to Article 14 of the Convention for the Protection of Human Rights and Fundamental Freedoms and to Article 27 of the International Covenant on Civil and Political Rights;

Considering that an adequate solution to the problem of minorities in Europe is an essential factor for democracy, justice, stability and peace;

Being resolved to implement an effective protection of the rights of minorities and of persons belonging to those minorities,

Have agreed as follows :

CHAPTER I - GENERAL PRINCIPLES

Article 1

1.   The international protection of the rights of ethnic, linguistic and religious minorities, as well as the rights of individuals belonging to those minorities, as guaranteed by the present Convention, is a fundamental component of the international protection of Human Rights, and as such falls within the scope of international co-operation.

2.   It does not permit any activity which is contrary to the fundamental principles of international law and in particular of sovereignty, territorial integrity and political independence of States.

3.   It must be carried out in good faith, in a spirit of understanding, tolerance and good neighbourliness between States.

Article 2

1.   For the purposes of this Convention, the term "minority" shall mean a group which is smaller in number than the rest of the population of a State, whose members, who are nationals of that State, have ethnical, religious or linguistic features different from those of the rest of the population, and are guided by the will to safeguard their culture, traditions, religion or language.

2.   Any group coming within the terms of this definition shall be treated as an ethnic, religious or linguistic minority.

3.   To belong to a national minority shall be a matter of individual choice and no disadvantage may arise from the exercise of such choice.

CHAPTER II - RIGHTS AND OBLIGATIONS

Article 3

1.   Minorities shall have the right to be protected against any activity capable of threatening their existence.

2.   They shall have the right to the respect, safeguard and development of their ethnical, religious, or linguistic identity.

Article 4

1.   Any person belonging to a minority shall have the right to enjoy the same rights as any other citizen, without distinction and on an equal footing.

2.   The adoption of special measures in favour of minorities or of individuals belonging to minorities and aimed at promoting equality between them and the rest of the population or at taking due account of their specific conditions shall not be considered as an act of discrimination.

Article 5

With a view to promoting and reinforcing their common features, persons belonging to a minority shall have the right to associate and to maintain contacts, in particular with other members of their group, including across national borders. This right shall include notably the right to leave freely one's country and to go back to it.

Article 6

1.   Persons belonging to a minority shall have the right to freely preserve, express and develop their cultural identity in all its aspects, free of any attempts at assimilation against their will.

2.   In particular, they shall have the right to express themselves, to receive and to issue information and ideas through means of communication of their own.

Article 7

Any person belonging to a linguistic minority shall have the right to use his language freely, in public as well as in private.

Article 8

Whenever a minority reaches a substantial percentage of the population of a region or of the total population, its members shall have the right, as far as possible, to speak and write in their own language to the political, administrative and judicial authorities of this region or, where appropriate, of the State. These authorities shall have a corresponding obligation.

Article 9

Whenever the conditions of Article 8 are fulfilled, in State schools, obligatory schooling shall include, for pupils belonging to the minority, study of their mother tongue. As far as possible, all or part of the schooling shall be given in the mother tongue of pupils belonging to the minority. However, should the State not be in a position to provide such schooling, it must permit children who so wish to attend private schools. In such a case, the State shall have the right to prescribe that the official language or languages also be taught in such schools.

Article 10

Any person belonging to a religious minority shall have the right to manifest his religion or belief, either alone or in community with others and in public or private, in worship, teaching, practice or observance.

Article 11

Any person belonging to a minority whose rights set forth in the present Convention are violated shall have an effective remedy before a national authority.

Article 12

The rights set forth in Articles 5, 7 and 10 of this Convention shall be subject only to such limitations as are prescribed by law and are necessary in a democratic society in the interests of public safety, for the protection of public order, health or morals, or for the protection of the rights and freedoms of others.

Article 13

States shall refrain from pursuing or encouraging policies aimed at the assimilation of minorities or aimed at intentionally modifying the proportions of the population in the regions inhabited by minorities.

Article 14

1.   States shall favour the effective participation of minorities in public affairs in particular in decisions affecting the regions where they live or in the matters affecting them.

2.   As far as possible, States shall take minorities into account when dividing the national territory into political and administrative sub-divisions, as well as into constituencies.

Article 15

1.   Any person who belongs to a minority shall loyally fulfil the obligations deriving from his status as a national of his State.

2.   In the exercise of the rights set forth in this Convention, any person who belongs to a minority shall respect the national legislation, the rights of others, in particular those of the members of the majority and of other minorities.

Article 16

States shall take the necessary measures with a view to ensuring that, in any region where those who belong to a minority represent the majority of the population, those who do not belong to this minority shall not suffer from any discrimination.

Article 17

This Convention shall not prejudice the provisions of domestic law or any international agreement which provide greater protection for minorities or persons belonging to minorities.

CHAPTER III - CONTROL MACHINERY

Article 18

To ensure the observance of the undertakings by the Parties in the present Convention, there shall be set up a European Committee for the Protection of Minorities (hereinafter referred to as "the Committee").

Article 19

1.   The Committee shall consist of a number of members equal to that of the Parties. In principle, no two members of the Committee may be nationals of the same State.

2.   The members of the Committee shall be chosen from among persons known for their competence in the field of Human Rights and in particular in the fields covered by this Convention.

3.   The members shall serve in their individual capacity.

Article 20

1.   The members of the Committee shall be elected by the Committee of Ministers of the Council of Europe by an absolute majority of votes, from a list of names presented by the Bureau of the Consultative Assembly of the Council of Europe; each national delegation of the Parties shall put forward three candidates on this list.

2.   The same procedure shall be followed in filling casual vacancies.

3.   The members of the Committee shall be elected for a period of four years. They may be re-elected. However among the members elected at the first election, the terms of office of half of the members shall expire at the end of two years. The members whose terms of office are to expire at the end of the initial period of two years shall be chosen by lot by the Secretary General of the Council of Europe immediately after the first election has been completed.

4.   A member of the Committee elected to replace a member whose term of office has not expired shall hold office for the remainder of his predecessor's term.

5.   The members of the Committee shall hold office until replaced. After having been replaced, they shall continue to deal with such cases as they already have under consideration.

6.   Notwithstanding the provisions of this Article, members of the Committee in respect of the States Parties, non-members of the Council of Europe, shall be appointed by the Parties concerned; the other provisions of this Article shall apply mutatis mutandis.

Article 21

1.   The Committee shall meet in camera.

2.   A quorum shall be equal to the majority of its members. The decisions of the Committee shall be taken by a majority of the members present.

Article 22

1.   The Committee shall meet as the circumstances require, at least once a year. The meetings shall be convened by the Secretary General of the Council of Europe.

2.   The Committee shall draw up its own rules of Procedure.

3.   The Secretariat of the Committee shall be provided by the Secretary General of the Council of Europe.

Article 23

1.   In the application of this Convention, the Committee and the competent national authorities of the Party concerned shall co-operate with each other.

2.   Parties shall provide the Committee with the facilities necessary to carry out its task, in particular access to their territories, and the right to travel without restriction and to communicate freely with any person from whom it believes it can obtain relevant information.

Article 24

1.   The Parties shall submit to the Committee, through the Secretary General of the Council of Europe, reports on the measures they have adopted to give effect to their undertakings under this Convention, within one year of the entry into force of the Convention for the Party concerned. The Parties shall submit supplementary reports at three yearly intervals concerning any new measure adopted, as well as any other report requested by the Committee.

2.   Those reports shall be examined by the Committee who will forward them to the Committee of Ministers of the Council of Europe with its observations.

3.   By a majority of two-thirds of the members entitled to sit on the Committee, the Committee may make any necessary recommendations to a Party.

Article 25

1.   Provided that a Party has, by declaration addressed to the Secretary General of the Council of Europe, recognised the competence of the Committee to receive a State's request, the Committee may receive petitions from any Party which considers that another Party does not respect the provisions of this Convention.

2.   The declarations provided for in paragraph 1 may be made for a specified period. In this case, they shall be renewed automatically for the same period, unless withdrawn by previous notice of one year before the expiration of the period of validity.

3.   The Committee shall only exercise the powers provided for in this Article when at least five Parties are bound by declarations made in accordance with paragraph 1.

Article 26

1.   Provided that a Party has, by declaration addressed to the Secretary General of the Council of Europe, recognised the competence of the Committee to receive individual petitions, it may receive such petitions from any person, group of individuals or any international non-governmental organisation representative of minorities, claiming to be the victim of a violation by this Party of the rights set forth in this Convention.

2.   The declarations provided for in paragraph 1 may be made for a specific period. In this case, they shall be renewed automatically for the same period, unless withdrawn by previous notice of one year before the expiration of the period of validity.

3.   The Parties who have made the declaration provided for in paragraph 1 undertake not to hinder in any way the effective exercise of the right of individual petition.

4.   The Committee shall only exercise the powers provided for in this Article when at least five Parties are bound by declarations made in accordance with paragraph 1.

Article 27

1.   The Committee may only deal with the matter referred to it under Article 26 after all domestic remedies have been exhausted, according to the generally recognised rules of international law.

2.   The Committee shall declare inadmissible petitions submitted under Article 26 which :

a.   are anonymous;

b.   are substantially the same as a matter which has already been examined by the Committee;

c.   have already been submitted to another international body and do not contain any relevant new information;

d.   are incompatible with the provisions of this Convention, manifestly ill-founded or, an abuse of the right of petition;

e.   are submitted to the Committee more than six months from the final internal decision.

Article 28

In the event of the Committee accepting a petition referred to it :

a.   it shall, with a view to ascertaining the facts, undertake together with the representatives of the parties an examination of the petition and, if need be, an investigation.

b.   it endeavours to reach a friendly settlement of the matter on the basis of respect of this Convention. If it succeeds it shall draw up a report which shall contain a statement of the facts and of the solution reached and be sent to the State or States concerned.

Article 29

1.   If no friendly settlement has been reached, the Committee shall draw up a report as to whether the facts found disclose a breach by the State concerned of its obligations under this Convention and make such proposals as it thinks are necessary.

2.   The report shall be transmitted to the Committee of Ministers, to the State or States concerned and to the Secretary General of the Council of Europe.

3.   The Committee of Ministers may take any follow-up action it thinks fit in order to ensure respect of the Convention.

Article 30

This Convention shall not be construed as limiting or derogating from the competence of the organs of the European Convention on Human Rights or from the obligations assumed by the Parties under that Convention.

CHAPTER IV - AMENDMENTS TO THE ARTICLES OF THE CONVENTION

Article 31

1.   Amendments to the Articles of this Convention may be proposed by a Party or by the Committee of Ministers of the Council of Europe.

2.   Any proposal for amendment shall be communicated by the Secretary General of the Council of Europe to the States mentioned in Article 32 and to every State which has acceded to or has been invited to accede to this Convention in accordance with the provisions of Article 34.

3.   Any amendment proposed by a Party or the Committee of Ministers shall be communicated to the Committee which shall submit to the Committee of Ministers its opinion on the proposed amendment.

4.   The Committee of Ministers shall consider the proposed amendment and the opinion submitted by the Committee and may adopt the amendment, after having consulted the non-member States Parties to the Convention.

5.   The text of any amendment adopted by the Committee of Ministers in accordance with paragraph 4 of this Article shall be forwarded to the Parties for acceptance.

6.   Any amendment adopted in accordance with paragraph 4 of this Article shall come into force on the first day of the month following the expiration of a period of one month after all Parties have informed the Secretary General of their acceptance thereof.

CHAPTER V - FINAL PROVISIONS

Article 32

This Convention shall be open for signature by member States of the Council of Europe and non-member States which have participated in its elaboration. It is subject to ratification, acceptance or approval. Instruments of ratification, acceptance or approval shall be deposited with the Secretary General of the Council of Europe.

Article 33

1.   The Convention shall enter into force on the first day of the month following the expiration of a period of one month after the date on which five States, including at least four member States of the Council of Europe, have expressed their consent to be bound by the Convention in accordance with the provisions of Article 32.

2.   In respect of any signatory State which subsequently expresses its consent to be bound by it, the Convention shall enter into force on the first day of the month following the expiration of a period of one month after the date of signature or of the deposit of the instrument of ratification, acceptance or approval.

Article 34

1.   After the entry into force of this Convention, the Committee of Ministers of the Council of Europe, after consulting the Parties, may invite to accede to the Convention any European non-member State by a decision taken by the majority provided for in Article 20 d. of the Statute of the Council of Europe and by the unanimous vote of the representatives of the Contracting States entitled to sit on the Committee of Ministers.

2.   In respect of any acceding State, the Convention shall enter into force on the first day of the month following the expiration of a period of one month after the date of the deposit of the instrument of accession with the Secretary General of the Council of Europe.

Article 35

1.   Any State may, at the time of signature or when depositing its instrument of ratification, acceptance, approval or accession, specify the territory or territories to which this Convention shall apply.

2.   Any State may, at any later date, by a declaration addressed to the Secretary General, extend the application of this Convention to any other territory specified in the declaration. In respect of such territory the Convention shall enter into force on the first day of the month following the expiration of a period of one month after the date of receipt of such declaration by the Secretary General.

3.   Any declaration made under the two preceding paragraphs may, in respect of any territory mentioned in such declaration, be withdrawn by a notification addressed to the Secretary General. Such withdrawal shall become effective on the first day of the month following the expiration of a period of six months after the date of receipt of the notification by the Secretary General.

Article 36

1.   Any Party may, at any time, denounce this Convention by means of a notification addressed to the Secretary General of the Council of Europe.

2.   Such denunciation shall become effective on the first day of the month following the expiration of a period of six months after the date of receipt of the notification by the Secretary General.

Article 37

The Secretary General of the Council of Europe shall notify the Parties, the other member States of the Council of Europe, the non-member States which have participated in the elaboration of this convention and any State which has acceded or has been invited to accede to it of :

a.   any signature in accordance with Article 32 ;

b.   the deposit of any instrument of ratification, acceptance, or accession in accordance with Article 32 or 34 ;

c.   any date of entry into force of this Convention in accordance with Articles 33 et 34;

d.   any declaration made under the provisions of Articles 25 and 26 ;

e.   any report prepared in pursuance of the provisions of Article 24 ;

f.   any proposal for amendment or any amendment adopted in accordance with Article 31 and the date on which the amendment comes into force;

g.   any declaration made under the provisions of Article 35 ;

h.   any notification made under the provisions of Article 36 and the date on which the denunciation takes effect;

i.   any other act, notification or communication relating to this Convention.

In witness whereof the undersigned, being duly authorised thereto, have signed this Convention.

Done at ....., the ...., in English and French, both texts being equally authentic, in a single copy which shall be deposited in the archives of the Council of Europe. The Secretary General of the Council of Europe shall transmit certified copies to each member State of the Council of Europe, to the non-member States which have participated in the elaboration of this Convention and to any State invited to accede to it.

EXPLANATORY REPORT ON THE PROPOSAL FOR A EUROPEAN CONVENTION FOR THE PROTECTION OF MINORITIES

Introduction

1.   At the Hungarian, Italian and Yugoslavian authorities' request, the European Commission for Democracy through Law set up a Working Party on the protection of minorities chaired by Mr F. Matscher, member of the Commission in respect of Austria. At its first meeting (Strasbourg 4 May 1990), the Working Party held a general discussion in which participated experts and representatives of minorities. At its second meeting (Venice, 25 May 1990) the Working Party prepared a "set of principles on national minorities" on the basis of a report by Mr Malinverni, member of the Commission in respect of Switzerland. This set of principles, adopted by the Commission at its 4th meeting (Venice 25 - 26 May 1990), was presented by the President of the Commission, Mr La Pergola, at the CSCE meeting in Copenhagen in June 1990.

2.   At its third meeting (Paris 20-21 September 1990) the Working Party prepared a preliminary draft European Convention for the Protection of Minorities which was first discussed at the 5th meeting of the Commission (Venice 9 - 11 October 1990). This text took into account both the declaration adopted in copenhagen at the CSCE meeting and the Brincat report presented to the Parliamentary Assembly (AS/Jur (45) 5), which was the basis for Recommendation 1134 (1990). In addition to listing the rights recognised, the text included provision for control machinery to ensure fulfilment of the obligations accepted by the Parties.

3.   At its fourth meeting (Venice, 7 February 1991) the Working Party exchanged views with the Parliamentary Assembly members concerned and finalised the text which was submitted to the Commission at its meeting in Venice on 8 and 9 February 1991. The Commission adopted it and decided to forward it to the Committee of Ministers.

General considerations

4.   At the beginning of its works, the Working Party decided, despite the fact that problems vary from one country to another, that it would be preferable to examine the situation of minorities in Europe as a whole and not in a specific State or group of States. The purpose of this study was to set out general principles for inclusion in an international legal instrument.

5.   The Commission also examined proposals to supplement the European Convention on Human Rights with a provision extending the scope of Article 14 - which prohibits all discrimination in the exercise of the rights recognised by the Convention - by prohibiting all forms of discrimination.   While acknowledging the merits of such a proposal and the purpose it could serve, the Commission considered that the protection of the rights of minorities was a specific issue and it seemed wiser to deal with it by means of a specific legal instrument and control mechanism rather than by amending the European Convention on Human Rights or adopting an additional protocol thereto.

The Commission declared itself in favour of an overall solution to the problem of minorities rather than specifically protecting minorities according to their ethnic, religious or linguistic character. The fact is that minorities are usually ethnic, religious and linguistic at the same time. On the other hand, while both concentrated minorities and scattered minorities should be dealt with, these two categories may call for different solutions. In particular, territorial solutions can apply only to the first category.

Moreover, since the purpose of the proposal for a Convention is to proclaim fundamental rights, these rights must apply to all the minorities covered by the definition contained in this proposal.

6.   Solutions to the problems of minorities lie in, on the one hand, the respect of the principles of non-discrimination and, on the other, positive action such as proclaiming collective and individual rights. The rights which should be recognised include the right to identify, the right to preserve one's own culture, the right to education, the right to use one's own language and the right to practice one's own religion, but it is also important to regulate relations between the minority and the State.

7.   The drafters of the proposal took into account the rights proclaimed by the Committee on Local and Regional Authorities in Europe's Resolution 192, namely the right to dignity, to education, to cultural expression, to certain facilities in relations with administrative authorities, and to access to the mass media.

8.   The Commission also sought to remain consistent with the works on minority and regional languages being carried on within the Council of Europe. It is important to note that linguistic aspects occupy a central position in the approach adopted to the question of minorities and that, in this way, the draft European Charter on Regional and Minority languages deals, for example, with questions such as relations with the administrative and judicial authorities of the

States in which minorities live. On the other hand, the draft charter does not deal with other issues concerning minorities which are not directly related to linguistic problems, such as participation in political life.

9. The drafters of the proposal worked on the basis of the view that minorities should in no way be treated as nationalities and should exist within the territorial limits of States.

In this respect it is important to bear in mind the experience of the inter-war period and not to regard minorities as separate entities aspiring to emancipation but as groups entitled, because of their specific features, to special protection within the State. Minorities, for their part, should content themselves with the places in which they live and must remain. The solution to their problems does not lie in a change of frontiers, this being an essential factor for Europe's political stability. Minorities should not behave like "nationalities" seeking to fight against the State.

10. According to the Commission, the adoption of domestic law measures is a prerequisite to solving the problem of minorities: first of all, the structure of the State should guarantee the autonomy of minorities, through federal political systems, through regionalisation, or through the granting of a special status to certain territories. Next, domestic law should ensure that the fundamental rights proclaimed by the constitution are respected, particularly the principle of equality.

11. However, such measures could prove not to be sufficient and international law measures also need to be adopted, in the form of specific treaties, for example, between Italy and Austria or between Denmark and Germany, or through general human rights conventions, for example Article 14 of the European Convention on Human Rights or Article 27 of the International Covenant on Civil and Political Rights, or through a legal instrument concerning minorities exclusively.

12. The purpose of the proposal is not to replace domestic or international measures existing or being drafted but to provide an overall framework, a body of binding international rules to be applied as extensively as possible. To this end, it can and indeed must be supplemented by domestic measures in each State Party to it.

Observations on the articles of the proposal for a Convention

PREAMBLE

13.   The Preamble, modelled on those of the European Treaties, refers to the statutory aims of the Council of Europe: defence of democracy, respect for human rights and the principle of the rule of law.

14.   The proposal for a Convention contains five chapters:
     I   -   General Principles,
     II   -   Rights and Obligations,
     III   -   Control Machinery,
     IV   -   Amendments,
     V   -   Final Provisions.

CHAPTER I - GENERAL PRINCIPLES

Article 1

15.   The purpose of Article 1 of the proposal is to specify, just as with the protection of human rights, that the protection of minorities does not fall within the reserved domain of States (Article 2, paragraph 7 of the United Nations Charter).

16.   In addition, it seemed necessary to recognise rights as belonging not only to individual members of minorities but to the minorities as such, since minorities are not only the sum of a number of individuals but represent also a system of relations among them. Without the concept of collective rights the protection of minorities would be somewhat limited.

The drafters of the proposal acknowledged that such a principle did not reflect the present state of positive law: while this might be so for protection of the rights of individuals belonging to the minority, it is not the case with the rights of the minority as such (see Article 27 of the International Covenant on civil and political rights). They nevertheless considered that the proposal should go beyond a mere codification of international law and aim to develop it progressively.

It is important however not to exaggerate the difference between these two systems of protection. In the text of the proposal most of the rights recognised concern individuals. Only one article recognises rights for groups: Article 3 (right of minorities to be protected against any activity capable of threatening their existence; right to the respect, safeguard and development of their identity); moreover, two provisions place on States obligations in respect of minorities: Article 13 (obligation to refrain from forced assimilation) and Article 14 (obligation to favour the effective participation of minorities in public affairs in particular in decisions affecting the regions where they live or in the matters affecting them).

17.   Paragraphs 2 and 3 are designed to counterbalance paragraph 1. They stress the importance of the fundamental principles of international law and stipulate that the protection of the rights of minorities must comply with these principles.

Article 2

18.   The definition of minorities is a delicate problem and one solution might be not to include a specific definition in the text but to rely on the usual meaning of the word.

19.   However, the drafters of the proposal preferred to define the framework within which the rights set forth should be applied. According to the definition adopted, only persons possessing the nationality of the State on whose territory they reside are protected. It was noted that the question of migrant workers had already been dealt with in a Council of Europe Convention and that further works could be carried out in this matter.

20.   The proposal for a convention does not make enjoyment by minorities or their members of the rights set forth in the text conditional upon the obligation of previous acknowledgement. According to paragraph 2, any group meeting the definition of paragraph 1 must be treated as a minority; hence, all the provisions of the Convention must apply to it.

21.   For the remainder, paragraph 3 is identical in substance to the first sentence of paragraph 32 of the Copenhagen Declaration, which states that to belong to a national minority is a matter of individual choice and no disadvantage may arise from the exercise of such choice. Although the text of the proposal does not specifically say so it goes without saying that this principle applies also the choice not to belong to a minority.

CHAPTER II - RIGHTS AND OBLIGATIONS

Article 3

22.   The first right afforded to minorities is the right to continue to exist, in other words to be protected against any activity capable of threatening their existence. The provision applies equally to the activities of the State or of a group of individuals which could result in the disappearance of the minority.

Article 4

23.   This provision is central to the proposal for a Convention. Non-discrimination, within the meaning of the proposal is a general principle which applies to all the recognised rights of citizens.

24.   The second paragraph permits "positive discrimination" in favour of the minority. The fact is that while non-discrimination may appear to be sufficient to resolve many of the problems of minorities, the very nature of minorities implies that special measures should be taken in favour of persons belonging to them.

Therefore, non-discrimination within the meaning of the proposal does not denote formal equality between individuals belonging to the minority and the rest of the population, but rather substantive equality.

The term "rest of the population" was preferred to "majority" because the latter could be difficult to define in certain States where the population is composed of various minorities and no one group has an actual majority.

Article 5

25.   The freedom of association is afforded to all citizens and, by virtue of Article 4, persons belonging to minorities must also enjoy this right. However, it seemed necessary to make explicit reference to it in the proposal for a convention since it is an especially important right for minorities, with a view to promoting or strengthening their "common features". This expression refers to the definition of minorities as appearing in Article 2, paragraph 1.

26.   In addition to the right of association, Article 5 proclaims the right to maintain contacts with other members of the minority. As it is the case with the right to associate, the right to maintain contacts is aimed at promoting or strengthening common features.

27.   The right particularly concerns minorities scattered throughout the territory of one or more States. Persons belonging to such groups often account for an extremely small proportion of the population of the region they live in but at national level they may form a higher percentage.

28.   Moreover, this right applies to the many minorities which have settled close to frontiers and possess the same ethnic, religious and linguistic characteristics as the populations of the neighbouring States, including travelling regularly to those States, is of great importance for the life of the minority and its members.

29.   The rights provided for by this Article must be exercised in accordance with national legislation, under the terms of Article 15, paragraph 2 of the proposal. In particular this Article is not aimed at allowing minorities to form political parties on the mere basis of one's belonging to the minorities.

Article 6

30.   Article 6 of the proposal for a Convention is inspired by paragraph 32.2 of the Copenhagen Declaration. It proclaims the right to a cultural life and a cultural identity differing from that of the majority of the population. The provision is drafted in very general terms in order to cover all forms of safeguarding and developing the identity and culture of the persons concerned.

Article 7

31.   The use of their language is an important right for people belonging to minorities. For linguistic minorities it is the principal means of affirming their existence and preserving their identity.

It also enables people belonging to a minority to exercise their freedom of expression.

This Article states a general principle. The precise modalities for the exercise of this right are set forth in the Draft European Charter of Regional and Minority Languages.

Article 8

32.   Given the difficulties involved in recognising the right of a minority to use its own language in its relations with the administrative authorities, Article 8 of the proposal for a convention includes the wording "as far as possible" and does not proclaim an absolute right.

This proviso means that the right will not exist in particular when the financial means of the State concerned are insufficient or when the number of persons belonging to the minority concerned is too small.

The principle applies either in a particular region or in the whole State according to whether the minority forms a substantial percentage of the region's or of the State's population.

33.   It was considered preferable not to state a principle whereby, where the minority accounted for a certain percentage of the total population, the State would be obliged to declare the minority's language an official language throughout its territory or even in a part thereof.

34.   The proposal for a Convention deliberately avoids specifying the percentage above which people belonging to a minority shall be entitled to address administrative authorities in their own language. It seemed preferable to opt for flexible wording to take account of the individual circumstances of the State concerned, including its financial resources. The Committee referred to in Article 18 will have to interpret the notion of "'substantial percentage" when examining individual situations brought before it.

Article 9

35.   The principle set out in Article 9 is that "whenever a minority reaches a substantial percentage of the population of a region or of the total population, in State schools, obligatory schooling shall include, for pupils belonging to the minority, study of their mother tongue".

36.   The second and third sentences of Article 9 give the State an alternative: either to organise, in State schools, schooling in the mother tongue of the minority, or to allow children belonging to the minority to attend private schools in which schooling is given in their mother tongue. The drafters of the proposal for a Convention regard either of these solutions as sufficient to ensure schooling in the language of the minority. The State concerned will choose between the two options depending on its particular circumstances and financial resources.

The proposal for a convention nevertheless entitles the State to demand that, where the second alternative is chosen, the official language of the State be also taught in private schools, as it is in State schools.

Article 10

37.   Article 10 is based on Article 9 of the European Convention on Human Rights.

38.   It guarantees worship, practice and observance as well as religious teaching.

Article 11

39.   This principle is inspired by Article 13 of the European Convention on Human Rights.   It is important to stress that the effective remedy is not necessarily legal remedy.

Article 12

40.   This Article states the conditions under which the rights and freedoms set forth in Articles 5, 7 and 10 may be restricted.   It is inspired by sub-paragraph 2 of Articles 8 to 11 of the European convention on Human Rights. Restrictions must be prescribed by law, justified by an aim of public interest and must respect the principle of proportionality.

Article 13

41.   The aim of the provision is to prevent the assimilation of minorities by a modification of the proportions of the population. Although some thought that such a principle could threaten the sovereignty of the State and that citizens of the majority group were entitled to settle anywhere, this provision was regarded as essential by the drafters of the proposal for a Convention.

Moreover, the Article only prohibits States from conducting policies to populate areas or displace populations - regardless of whether they belong to a minority or the majority - with the aim of modifying the proportions of the population in a region inhabited by a minority, which would result in a dwindling minority.

Article 14

42.   The drafters of the proposal for a convention preferred not to include an obligation for the State to ensure proportional parliamentary representation of minorities since this principle seemed difficult to implement.

However, they decided to set forth the obligation for the State to favour the effective participation of minorities in decisions affecting the regions where they live or in the matters affecting them.

Moreover, it is necessary for States to take account of the presence of one or more minorities on their territory when dividing the territory into political and administrative sub-divisions, as well as into constituencies.

43.   This provision concerns the minority's obligations towards the State and towards the majority.

44.   The word "region" must be understood in this article and throughout the Convention in its geographical meaning of an entity of national territory rather than in its political, judicial or administrative meaning.

Article 15

45.   This provision concerns the obligations of people belonging to minorities towards the State and towards the majority. In this context the drafters of the proposal for a Convention considered that the equality which applies to rights also applies to obligations.

46.   Persons belonging to a minority are bound to observe the obligations to the State deriving from citizenship. The authors of the proposal for a convention decided not to lay down any specific obligation of loyalty for the minority.

47.   Persons belonging to minorities are also obliged to comply with national legislation. However, this does not mean that national legislation need not comply with the proposal's provisions. Indeed, one of the control machinery's objective is to ensure such compliance.

48.   Persons belonging to minorities must also respect the rights of others. Reference is made in this respect to a situation in which a minority group at national level is a majority group in one part of the State concerned.

Article 16

49.   The purpose of Article 16 of the proposal for a convention is to take account of a not infrequent situation in Europe, in which a minority section of the population of a State accounting for a small proportion of the national

population represents the majority of the population of one region of that State. In such a situation the population of the majority at national level - or that of another minority - becomes the minority in that region and it is therefore important to ensure that they do not suffer from any discrimination.

Article 17

50. The purpose of this article is to ensure that the implementation of the proposal for a convention does not interfere with the application of national or international legal texts relating to human rights which would be more favourable to minorities. This article sets out therefore the principle that the most favourable provisions shall apply, which is also present in other International Conventions (for example, Article 60 of the European Convention on Human Rights).

CHAPTER III - CONTROL MACHINERY

51. The solution adopted is that of an independent body of experts, regarded by the authors of the proposal for a Convention as preferable to a political committee composed of representatives of States or a judicial body.

Article 18

52. Article 18 sets up the body responsible for ensuring the observance of the obligations entered into by the parties in application of the proposal for a Convention. It is entitled the European Committee for the Protection of Minorities ("the Committee").

Article 19

53. To allow for the particular situation of small States, the expression "in principle" has been added to the general principle which states that no two members of the Committee may be nationals of the same State, the purpose of which is to allow exceptions where justified by the particular situation.

54. As regards the qualifications of the members of the Committee, paragraph 2 stipulates that they shall be chosen from among persons known for their competence or having experience in the field of Human Rights and in particular in the field covered by the proposal for a convention. It was not thought desirable to specify in detail the professional fields from which members

of the Committee might be drawn. It is clear that they do not have to be lawyers.

55.   Under paragraph 3, the Committee members serve in their individual capacity. This guarantees their independence and impartiality. Accordingly, it is expected that candidates who have a conflict of interests or who otherwise might encounter difficulties in satisfying the requirements of independence, impartiality and availability will not be proposed or elected. It is also expected that a member of the Committee who might have such difficulties with regard to an individual situation would not participate in any activity of the committee relating to that situation.

Article 20

56.   The procedure for the election of members of the committee is basically the same as that laid down in Article 21 of the European Convention on Human Rights for the election of members of the Commission.

It is considered appropriate that the same electoral procedure should be followed for filling casual vacancies (death or resignation).

The term of office has been fixed at 4 years, and members may be re-elected.

Provision is made for the partial renewal of the Committee after an initial period of two years. The procedure chosen is drawn from the corresponding versions of Articles 22 and 40 of the European Convention on Human Rights.

57.   Paragraph 6 contains the modalities for appointment of the members of the Committee in respect of States which are not members of the Council of Europe. The drafters of the proposal for a convention considered in fact that it was not possible for these members to be elected by the Committee of Ministers, on which only member States of the Council of Europe sit.

This solution is inspired by the procedure followed for the appointment of Ad hoc judges in international jurisdictions.

Article 21

58.   Having regard to the specific characteristics of the Committee's functions as provided for in the present proposal, it is specified that the committee shall meet in camera.

Article 22

59. This paragraph provides, in accordance with international practice, that the Committee shall draw up its own rules of procedure. They will regulate organisational matters normally found in such rules, including the election of the chairman.

Paragraph 3, specifying that the secretariat of the Committee shall be provided by the Secretary General of the Council of Europe, is inspired by the usual practice of this organisation.

Article 23

60. As a result of the solution opted for in Article 18, the Committee and the Parties must co-operate to ensure more effective protection of minorities and greater respect of the rights recognised by the proposal for a Convention. Article 23, paragraph 1 proclaims this principle of co-operation.

61. Paragraph 2 stipulates that the Parties shall afford the Committee the facilities necessary to carry out its tasks, namely free access to the territory of the Parties and the right to travel without restriction within it, and the right to communicate freely with any person in order to fulfil its tasks. The provision thus sets out some of the facilities the Committee is entitled to expect from the Parties but the latter must also offer any other forms of assistance necessary to its work.

Article 24

62. Article 24 stipulates that the Parties shall submit to the Committee reports on the application of the provisions of the proposal for a Convention. A first report must be submitted within one year of the entry into force of the proposal for a Convention for the Party concerned. Further reports must be submitted at three-yearly intervals or at the committee's request.

Despite the workload this represents for governments, the drafters of t(he proposal for a Convention regard this as a necessary procedure insofar as it is the only form of compulsory monitoring, since the acceptance of petitions from States and individuals is optional.

Article 25

63.   The drafters decided that State petitions should not be compulsory but optional. It was pointed out that in matters relating to minorities it was possible that a large number of State petitions would be introduced. The compulsory character of accepting State petitions might dissuade some States from ratifying the proposal for a Convention.

Article 26

64.   The right of individual petitions is also optional. An individual may only seize the Committee if the State concerned has accepted the competence of the committee to receive such petitions. Therefore States are entitled to ratify the proposal for a Convention without accepting the right of individual petition, as they are entitled not to accept the right of State petition.

Article 27

65.   Article 27 sets out the standard rule according to which all domestic remedies must be exhausted. The fact is that the control machinery set up by the proposal for a Convention is subordinate to and does not aim to supplant national machinery, but only to control their decisions with respect to the provisions of this proposal for a Convention.

66.   This provision sets out the classical conditions of admissibility of individual petitions, which are common to most of the international treaties for the protection of human rights.

Article 28

67.   Article 28 defines the procedure for examining petitions declared admissible by the Committee.

68.   The Committee initially attempts to ascertain the facts, for which purpose it may conduct an investigation and enjoys the facilities provided for by Article 23, paragraph 2.

69.   In accordance with the usual practice of international control bodies, the Committee endeavours to reach a friendly settlement of the matter. If it succeeds, the procedure ends with the sending of a report to the State or States concerned. The proposal for a convention does not specify whether this

document is public. This decision will be for the Committee to take, for each petition, when drawing up the friendly settlement.

Article 29

70.   If no friendly settlement is reached, the proposal for a Convention authorises the Committee to declare whether the facts in question disclose a breach of the proposal for a convention, and to make recommendations. These findings form a report to be sent to the Committee of Ministers, to the State or States concerned and to the Secretary General of the Council of Europe.

71.   The drafters of the proposal for a Convention considered it preferable not to precise the exact powers of the Committee of Ministers which will take such measures as it thinks fit.

Article 30

72.   Article 30 addresses the particular relationship between this proposal for a Convention and the European Convention on Human Rights which is referred to in the Preamble.   The obligations of the Parties under the European Convention on Human Rights are not affected.   Nor are the powers conferred by that Convention on the European Court and Commission of Human Rights and the Committee of Ministers.   Accordingly, the Committee set up by the present proposal for a Convention will not concern itself with matters raised in proceedings pending before them, and will not itself formulate interpretations of the provisions of the European Convention on Human Rights.

CHAPTER IV - AMENDMENTS TO ARTICLES OF THE PROPOSAL FOR A CONVENTION

Article 31

73.   As with other Council of Europe treaties, the proposal for a Convention contains a provision relating to amendments.   Amendments may be proposed by the Parties or by the Committee of Ministers.   They shall be communicated to all the member States of the Council of Europe, to all States invited to sign the proposal for a Convention in accordance with the provisions of Article 32 and

to all States which have acceded or have been invited to accede to the proposal for a Convention in accordance with the provisions of Article 34.

74.   The proposal shall also be submitted to the Committee which will give the Committee of Ministers its opinion on the amendment.

75.   The Committee of Ministers, which adopted the original text of this proposal for a Convention, is also competent to adopt any amendment.

76.   After its adoption by the Committee of Ministers, the amendment shall come into force after all the Parties have informed the Secretary General of their acceptance thereof.

CHAPTER V - FINAL PROVISIONS

77.   With a few exceptions, the provisions contained in this chapter are based on the "Model final clauses for conventions and agreements concluded within the Council of Europe", which was adopted by the Committee of Ministers of the Council of Europe at the 315th meeting of Ministers' Deputies in February 1980. Most of these articles do not therefore require any special comment, but the following points should be explained.

78.   The text of the proposal for a Convention contains no clause relating to reservations; in accordance with the Vienna Convention on the Law of Treaties, this means that reservations which are not contrary to the purpose and aim of the treaty shall be accepted. Such a solution seemed preferable to excluding the possibility of making any reservations at all insofar as it should render the proposal for a Convention more readily acceptable by a greater number of States.

Article 32

79.   The proposal for a Convention is open for signature by member States of the Council of Europe and non-member States which have participated in its elaboration. The purpose of this provision is to take account of the fact that some non-member States have played an active part in its elaboration.

Article 34

80.   Accession on the invitation of the Committee of Ministers is restricted
to European States, contrary to the rules applying to most of the conventions
drawn up within the Council of Europe, which are open for accession by all
States. It was thought that the very purpose of the proposal for a convention
and the restricting provisions contained therein applied at this stage only to
European States.

The protection of minorities
at the national level:
diversity of legal models

REPORT
ON THE REPLIES TO THE QUESTIONNAIRE
ON THE RIGHTS OF MINORITIES

PRELIMINARY REMARKS

This consolidated report is essentially based upon replies to the questionnaire on the rights of minorities formulated by the European Commission for Democracy through Law. It draws on a first analysis prepared by Mr Emmanuel Colla and Mrs Sylvie Marique, of the University of Liège, with reference to replies relating to eighteen countries.

In all, the Commission received replies from 26 European countries (Albania, Austria, Belgium, Croatia, Cyprus, Denmark, Finland, Germany, Greece, Hungary, Italy, Liechtenstein, Luxembourg, Malta, the Netherlands, Norway, Poland, Portugal, Romania, Russia, Slovakia, Slovenia, Spain, Sweden, Switzerland and Turkey) and two non-European States represented in the Venice Commission (Canada, Kyrgyzstan). The replies were given by members of the Commission.

The present report does not constitute an exhaustive study of comparative law in the matter of the protection of minorities. This is due partly to the fact that the Venice Commission received no reply to the questionnaire from some States. Its purpose is to demonstrate the diversity of legal models of protection which have been established, either independently or pursuant to obligations under an international treaty, a diversity which reflects the complexity of the situations in practice and, consequently, the variety of solutions adopted by different States to deal with the problem. This report might thereby serve as a concise repertoire of legislative practice in several European States.

I. · INTRODUCTION

The importance of the question of the protection of minorities is today beyond dispute. The currency of the issue is reflected on the international level, where the different types of initiatives (declarations, resolutions, conventions, etc.) designed to improve the protection of minorities have proliferated, as well as on the national level. In most of the States here considered, and especially in the countries of Central and Eastern Europe which have recently adopted democratic institutions, legislation relating to the rights of minorities has undergone important modifications in the course of the past few years.

It must nevertheless be borne in mind that every minority situation presents its own particular characteristics. There is consequently no standard means of resolving the multitude of concrete problems which each case throws up in a national context. Models which might be directly "exportable" from one national context to another are difficult to find. Yet each such context can serve as a source of inspiration for the resolution of the serious problems with which the international community is confronted in this domain.

If one sets aside the examples of the Principality of Liechtenstein and of the Republic of San Marino where, apparently, the question does nos arise, each of the States here considered acknowledges as a minimum, either in its Constitution or by way of ordinary legislation, the presence of minorities on its territory and the necessity of extending to such minorities a certain measure of protection. Yet it is important to understand what is meant by the term "minority" in the different countries and to see what is covered by the term or by the other terms employed to define these categories of persons (II). It is also necessary to examine the content and the extent of the rights or the measures of special protection granted to these groups or to their members, both at the international level (III) and nationally (IV), as well as the corresponding duties imposed upon them (V). The question of subminorities will then briefly be considered (VI). Finally, we must look to what mechanisms, if any, guarantee the effectiveness of this protection (VII).

II. DEFINITION OF THE CONCEPT OF "MINORITY"

There is no generally accepted definition of the concept of a "minority". Some elements thereof have certainly been identified as, for example, the standard if not universal classification of minorities into three groups: ethnic minorities, linguistic minorities and religious minorities; any one of these three criteria may be present or, more often, they may be in part cumulative. This (in part) threefold characterisation is adopted in Article 27 of the International Covenant on Civil and Political Rights and mentioned on section 5.1 of the General Comment adopted by the United Nations Human Rights Committee on 6 April 1994.(see also the Declaration on the Rights of Persons belonging to National or Ethnic, Religious and Linguistic Minorities of the United Nations of 18 December 1992). However, no generally accepted definition of minorities has been formulated in any international legal instruments or doctrine to date. While some authors have attempted to bear upon the question, others have preferred not to, considering either that such a definition is impossible or that it in any case serves no purpose. Thus, the CSCE High Commissioner for National Minorities acts, in a pragmatic manner, and without formulating any definition wherever he deems that a question affecting minorities exists.

These hesitations are naturally reflected in the replies to the questionnaire. While the concept of a minority is accepted in the various States concerned, the terms employed to describe it, whether in the Constitution or in legislation, differ.

A.   TERMS USED TO REFER TO MINORITIES

The laws of most of the States summarised in the replies to the questionnaire employ only the term "minority", combined in different cases with one or several terms of qualification: minorities are "linguistic", "ethnic", "religious", "cultural" or, more rarely, "national" (this is the case in Albania, in the Constitution of the German Land of Saxe, in Hungary, in Kyrgyzstan and in Poland). In Romania, rights are ensured to "persons (or citizens) belonging to national minorities", while Romanian law does not recognise minorities as distinct entities.

Other expressions are also used: in Austria the term "ethnic groups", since the passing of a 1976 law, is now employed; this term is also used in Hungary; in Canada, reference is made to minorities, indigenous peoples (Constitution), groups of individuals (Canadian Act on the Rights of the Individual), and to Catholic and Protestant groups (Constitutional Law of 1867). In Croatia and in Slovenia, the terms "communities" or "national and ethnic minorities" are used. In Slovakia the terms "national minority and ethnic group" (article 33 of the Constitution) and "national and ethnic minority" (articles 24-25 of the Charter of fundamental rights and freedoms) are used. In Finland, the terms "minorities" and "racial group, group of a national or ethnic origin, or religious group" are employed (Penal Code, Employment Contracts Act, etc.). Finally, the

Constitutions of certain German Länder use the terms "minorities and ethnic groups" (Schleswig-Holstein), and even "people".

In Russia, it is a question not only of national minorities but also "ethnic groups", "small ethnic communities" and the "small Northern populations".

It should be noted that the various terms used to designate a minority are largely synonymous.

In some States, no specific term is adopted at all ; such is the case in Denmark where the legislation speaks of the rights of the inhabitants of the Faroe Islands and of Greenland, as well as of certain Icelandic citizens, or in Finland, where legislation refers to "the Swedish speaking population", to "Sami" or to "Roma".

In Cyprus, the notion of a minority is rejected in favour of that of a community; there exist two communities, Greek (majority) and Turk (minority), the members of which have equal rights.

B.   ATTEMPTS TO DEFINE OR CIRCUMSCRIBE THE NOTION OF A MINORITY

Several States use the term "minority", or equivalent terms, in their Constitutions without ever defining them. This is, for example, the case in Albania, Belgium, Croatia, Finland, Hungary, Italy, Poland, Slovenia, Sweden, Switzerland and again in certain German Länder. There is therefore no definition of minorities in any of the States here considered which enjoys a constitutional underpinning.

The situation is similar in regard to certain international treaties having the status of constitutional law in domestic law (see, for example, Article 7 of the Treaty of Vienna, 1955, which refers to Austrian nationals belonging to the Slovene and Croatian minorities in Carinthia, Burgenland and Styria).

In several States, the term "minority" or a similar term is to be found in ordinary legislation, or in laws specifically concerning minorities (in Austria, Finland, Hungary, Italy, Portugal, Romania) or in other texts (Greece).

It is at this stage, at the legislative stage, that the only attempts at a direct definition of minorities are to be found.

In <u>Austria</u>, Article 1 of the 1976 Law on Ethnic Groups provides that such groups are constituted by:

> *"those groups of Austrian citizens permanently domiciled on the territory of the Republic, with a mother-tongue other than German and having their own cultural heritage".*

In <u>Hungary</u>, the scope of application of Law No. LXXVII of 1993 on the rights of national and ethnic minorities is delimited as follows:

Article 1. -

> *"1) The present law shall apply to all persons of Hungarian citizenship living on the territory of the Republic of Hungary who consider themselves as belonging to a national or ethnic minority, as well as to the communities formed by these persons.*
>
> *2) For the purposes of the present law, a national or ethnic minority (henceforth minority) is a whole population group living on the territory of the Republic of Hungary, for at least a decade, which constitutes a numerical minority in the population of the State, the members of which have Hungarian citizenship/nationality and who differ from the rest of the population by their mother-tongue, culture or traditions and who manifest at the same time a consciousness of inherent cohesion, which seeks the protection of these values and the expression and protection of the interests of their historically developed communities.*
>
> *3) The present law does not apply to refugees, immigrants and persons with the nationality of a foreign State but resident in Hungary on a long-term basis, nor to stateless persons".*

These are strictly speaking the only two definitions of minorities that are to be found in the legislation of the States here considered. Mention should nonetheless be made of the cases of three other countries, <u>Finland</u>, <u>Denmark</u> and <u>Norway</u> which, while not really defining the notion of "minority", do specify the characteristics that certain categories of persons must present if they are to obtain special protection.

This is the case, in <u>Finland</u>, of Samis and Roma (Gypsies). According to Section 2 of the Act on the Use of the Sami Language in Relations with Public Authorities, a Sami is any person who considers himself or herself to be Sami provided that such person or any parent or grandparent of such person learned the Sami language as his or her first language. The same situation is to e found in Norway. A Gypsy, according to Section 1 of the Finnish Act on the Improvement of the Housing Conditions of Gypsies, is a person who considers himself or herself to be a Gypsy, except when it is evident that he or she is not a Gypsy, as well as the spouse of such a person and his children living in the same household. Finally, the "citizens" of the autonomous province of Aland are Finnish citizens possessing the "home region right" of the province, which can at present only be acquired by "naturalisation" in the province.

In Denmark, a "Faroe" is defined as a Danish citizen domiciled in the Faroe Islands (Article 10, section 1 of the Faroe Islands Home Rule Act). The Greenland Home Rule Act, which recognises Greenland as a distinct society within the Kingdom of Denmark, simply provides that the special protection thereby conferred shall extend to all permanent residents of Greenland.

Even though legislation in the other States uses the term "minority" or other terms which cover more or less the same circumstance, they do not offer a definition of such terms. Nonetheless, and still setting aside the example of the Principality of Liechtenstein, where there are apparently no minorities, all such States accord rights to minorities or, at least, to persons who belong to them. Clearly, if these rights which are conceded to minorities are to be applied, those entitled to them must be identified. They must, therefore, fulfil certain conditions in order to enjoy them and it is in these conditions that the elements of definition are to be found. Such is the case in Slovakia (Article 34 of the Constitution) and in Croatia. In the latter case, the "Constitutional Law on Human Rights and Freedoms and the Rights of National and Ethnic Communities or Minorities" of 1992, in Articles 5 to 57, details the rights granted to minorities or to their members in the cultural field (the right to their own identity, culture, religion, the right to the public and private use of their own language, the right to their own education, the right to have their own public and cultural activities and to form societies in order to protect national and cultural identity), as well as in the educational field and in connection with their participation in the exercise of political power. According to the Croatian rapporteur, the Constitutional Law indirectly permits a definition of the term "minority"; within the meaning of Croatian law, minorities or their members are those groups and persons whose characteristics are the subject of the rights given to them by the Constitutional Law. The group and its members are thus defined by the content of their rights.

Thus, as a general rule, at the very least, the sine qua non for being granted special protection as a member of a minority is the possession of the nationality and/or residence on the territory of the State in question; in some countries such as Italy, the protection of those concerned is further restricted to certain well-defined geographical zones (Valle d'Aosta, the Trentino-Alto-Adige and the provinces of Trieste and Gorizia). Here, in the absence of a definition, only objective criteria have been taken into consideration.

It will be noticed that, as is moreover the case in the countries where they are defined, the only minorities granted special protection are those whose members possess the nationality of or have their residence in the State in question. It is extremely rare that specific measures of protection extend also to non-nationals. One example is the Finnish law on the use of the Sami language. By contrast, Hungarian legislation expressly excludes refugees, immigrants and stateless persons from their system of protection of minorities (cf. Article 1 of Law No. LXXVII cited above).

C.   THE FREE CHOICE TO BE TREATED AS A MINORITY

A further question to examine is the manner in which belonging to a minority is determined.

In theory this could be free, that is, a matter of personal choice for each individual who decides either to declare himself a member of a minority (provided that some objective criteria are also met) or, on the contrary, to decline to make such a declaration. This free choice was given expression for the first time at the international level in the CSCE Final Act of Copenhagen. This enshrines a subjective approach. It follows that such a choice will be practically free provided that no unwarranted harmful consequences nor unwarranted privileges result from its exercise.

Conversely, the choice itself may well not exist, in which case the authorities will intervene to determine themselves whether or not their citizens belong to a minority.

The replies given by the rapporteurs of the various States to this question all tend in the same direction: in each of them, belonging or not belonging to a minority is the result, in principle, of a personal choice. The choice is made by means of a periodic or special census of the population. Sometimes freedom of choice - including freedom not to declare oneself and the lack of harmful consequences of such a choice - are expressly provided by the law (this is the case for Austria in the 1976 Ethnic Groups Act). Indeed, States do not unilaterally impose on some of their citizens the quality of member of a minority. Similarly, none of them forbid them to renounce belonging to a minority. On the other hand, not everyone who would like to state that he or she belongs to a minority and consequently claim the enjoyment of specific rights may do so. The definition of a minority - inherently - implies the existence of objective criteria, usually together with subjective criteria. Thus, for example, in Austria and Hungary, one must be of a mother-tongue other than that of the majority of the population; in Finland, one can only describe oneself as Sami if one has, or has a parent or grand-parent who has Sami as one's mother-tongue, and it is not possible to claim to be Roma "if it is evident that one is not".

In Russia, whether an individual belongs to a national minority is determined by the authorities according to his ethnic and linguistic belonging.

In Kyrgyzstan, the choice of a "nationality" is restricted: it is not possible to opt for a nationality other than that of one's father or mother, and once the choice is made, it is definitive and irreversible.

The free choice of belonging to a minority does not, in general, have consequences for the acquisition or loss of nationality or the exercise of political rights. Of course, the fact of belonging to the majority race and speaking its language may actually constitute a factor facilitating the acquisition of nationality. In Finland, for example, when it is a question of granting Finnish nationality, and this decision is free, one's Finnish ethnic origin as well as one's knowledge of the Swedish or Finnish language can be taken into consideration in one's favour in the acquisition of nationality. But once nationality is acquired, it cannot be lost because one belongs to a minority.

D.   OBSERVATIONS

It is important to note that alongside the criteria of an objective nature employed by national laws to define minorities exist subjective criteria. In most cases, objective criteria are retained: nationality or citizenship of the State, residence on the territory of that State, a lasting presence, or even an ancient or historical presence, in the territory, the fact of constituting or being part of a numerical minority of the population, speaking a language distinct from that of the majority, or having their own cultural heritage, traditions or religion. In more recent legislation, criteria of a somewhat more subjective nature are preferred, whether it be "considering oneself Sami or Roma" (Finland) or "considering oneself as belonging to a minority", or again manifesting a "consciousness of inherent cohesion" (Hungary).

III. THE PROTECTION OF MINORITIES AT THE INTERNATIONAL LEVEL AND ITS INFLUENCE ON DOMESTIC LAW

The protection of minorities has been the subject of several international bilateral treaties and other international instruments.

The effects of international treaties (multilateral or bilateral) in the domestic legal order essentially depend upon the status conferred to international law in the State concerned. As regards provisions protecting minorities included in international instruments which are considered as being self-executing, these are directly applicable in the domestic legal order. Moreover, where the provisions protecting minorities are contained in international treaties which are not considered as being self-executing, a contracting state is expected, in accordance with Article 27 of the Vienna Convention on the Law of Treaties, to amend its legislation to make it compatible with the international treaty and with the international obligations deriving therefrom for the state concerned. The provisions protecting minorities in international law have thus a considerable influence on domestic law.

Among several international treaties and other international instruments, note must particularly be made of the conventions relating to human rights which, although looking to confer a first measure of protection on the individual as a human being, also confer protection on persons belonging to minorities. Work on instruments relating to minorities is under way in the CSCE and in the Council of Europe, while the UN adopted on 18 December 1992 a Declaration on the Rights of Persons Belonging to National or Ethnic, Religious and Lingistic Minorities. Yet, in express terms, the question of minorities is addressed only in the provisions set out below.

Article 27 of the 1966 International Covenant on Civil and Political Rights provides that persons belonging to ethnic, religious or linguistic minorities cannot be deprived of the right, in common with the other members of their group, to enjoy their own culture, to profess and practise their own religion, or to use their own language.

In addition, under Article 14 of the European Convention on Human Rights, and the similar provisions in Article 2 (1), of the 1966 International Covenant on Civil and Political Rights and Article 2 (2), of the 1966 International Covenant on Economic, Social and Cultural Rights, the enjoyment of the rights and freedoms set forth in these treaties must be secured without discrimination on any ground, including association with a national minority . But in contrast to the separate equality clause in the first International Covenant mentioned above (Art. 26), these provisions are not independent and can only be invoked in relation to the enjoyment of one of the rights and freedoms guaranteed by the Convention. The European Charter for regional or minority languages aims at protecting these languages mainly for cultural reasons. It should also be noted that the Austrian State Treaty (which is of a multilateral character), in its Articles 6-7, provides for the protection of the Slovenian minority.

As regards the CSCE, note must be particularly made of points 18 and 19 of the Concluding Document of the Vienna Meeting on the Follow-up to the Conference (15 January 1989), points 30-32 of the Document of the Copenhagen Meeting of the Conference on the Human Dimension of the CSCE (29 June 1990), the report of the meeting of experts of the CSCE on National Minorities of 19 July 1991 and the Charter of Paris for a New Europe (21 November 1990). In particular, the Copenhagen Document provides for the right of persons belonging to a national minority "to exercise fully and effectively their human rights and fundamental freedoms without any discrimination and in full equality before the law" (point 31), for a free choice in the matter of belonging to a national minority and for certain cultural linguistic and religious rights (point 32), and for the protection by States of the ethnic, cultural, linguistic and religious identity of national minorities on their territory (point 33).

In the States here considered, international treaties on human rights in general have not given rise to any significant jurisprudence on minority questions. Nor is there an abundance of international jurisprudence; see, however, European Court of Human Rights, Case "relating to certain aspects of the laws on the use of languages in education in Belgium"(Merits), judgment of 23 July 1968, Series A, Vol. 4, Case of Mathieu-Mohin and Clerfayt, judgment of 2 March 1987, Series A, Vol 113.

Alongside such treaties, there exist multilateral instruments which particularly aim at the protection of the rights of minorities. Examples are the 1948 Convention for the Prevention and Punishment of the Crime of Genocide - which does not refer expressly to minorities but which is applicable to them - the 1965 International Convention for the Elimination of all Forms of Racial

Discrimination, ILO Convention N°. 111 (1958) concerning Discrimination in
Respect of Employment and Occupation and the 1960 Unesco Convention
against Discrimination in Education. Bilateral agreements also address the
question of minorities. As examples one may note the Gruber-De Gasperi Pact
of 1946, which seeks to protect the German-speaking minority in Italy (in South
Tyrol), the 1954 Treaty of London between Italy and Yugoslavia on the Slovene
minority of Trieste, and the 1955 Declaration of Bonn and Copenhagen on the
protection of Danish and German minorities in Germany and Denmark
respectively.

Recently, Poland has concluded a series of bilateral treaties of friendship with
Germany, with Hungary and with the Czech and Slovak Federal Republic. These
treaties, inspired by certain documents of the CSCE in this area, contain a
comprehensive set of provisions for the protection of persons belonging to
minorities. In particular, they provide guarantees in respect of a set of
fundamental rights as well as the maintenance and development of ethnic,
cultural, linguistic and religious identity. Any attempt at forced assimilation is
expressly prohibited.

Russia has also recently concluded several treaties, in particular with the former
Republics of the USSR which now belong to the Community of Independent
States, containing clauses on the protection of minority rights.

For the Muslim minority in Greece and the Greek minority in Turkey (today
almost wholly disappeared), the provisions of the 1923 Treaty of Lausanne
relating to the protection of minorities (Arts. 37-45) retain a certain significance.
This Treaty is particularly concerned with guaranteeing civil and political rights,
with the use of one's own language and with the right to create and maintain
minority schools and charitable, religious and social institutions. These
guarantees are the more important in that the Treaty of Lausanne (in its Art. 37)
expressly provides that they cannot be abrogated by subsequent legislation. In
general, provisions relating to the protection of minorities contained in
international conventions cannot be amended unilaterally, which is a guarantee
of their continuance in force.

IV. THE PROTECTION OF MINORITIES AT THE DOMESTIC LEVEL

A. THE RECOGNITION OF MINORITIES BY THE STATE

Before examining those laws which protect minorities, it is necessary to know whether, in order to benefit from these laws, minorities must be recognised by the State, that is, recognised not simply as an entity, but recognised and identified precisely as groups who must be protected. If such recognition is not compulsory, then any minority can be protected: it is enough, in a concrete case, that the criteria used to define them are fulfilled. If, by contrast, such recognition is required, the fact of fulfilling these conditions is no longer sufficient: a positive act of recognition on the part of the State is additionally required.

In some countries, the Constitution or the law lays down restrictively the categories of persons who benefit from all or some of the safeguards provided. This is, for example, the case in Italy, (but the provisions adopted by central government in favour of recognised minorities do not operate to prevent the intervention of regional legislators in favour of other minority linguistic groups), in Belgium - where the protection granted to linguistic minorities by the law, for example on the use of languages, is limited exclusively to the categories of persons mentioned in the law, in Croatia and also in Hungary, where a procedure is further provided for which enables groups of citizens who so desire to have the fact that they constitute a minority certified and to thereby obtain this recognition (Law No. LXXVII, Article 61).

In Albania, the Constitutional laws in force expressly allow the State to recognise minorities, without however requiring it to do so. In most States, this possibility is not foreseen, but nor is it ruled out. This is the case in Greece, Poland, Denmark, Finland, Portugal, Kyrgyzstan, Slovenia, Switzerland and Germany. Finally, in Romania, the State does not recognise minorities as such, that is to say as a entity, because only individuals and not groups can be granted rights.

In Austria, there is no system for recognising minorities proper, but the minorities for which the ethnic group councils (III/D/U) are established are determined by decree (issued in implementation of the 1976 act, after consultation with the representatives of the minorities themselves): this results de facto in "recognition" of the minorities in question (at present, they are Croats, Slovenes, Hungarians, Czechs, Slovaks and Roma) and the term "recognised minority" has also entered everyday language. Nevertheless, granting of the special protection from which minorities benefit (use of their language in relations with the authorities, bilingual place names, teaching of the language) is regulated in a specific manner and formally without reference to the status of "recognised minority"; in addition, certain advantages may result from this status, such as the granting of subsidies.

The recognition of minorities may result in a different treatment of minorities, according to whether or not they are recognised by the State. This different treatment may take the form of a special status or of extra measures of help for certain minorities in respect of which the need for particular protection is recognised. Thus, in Slovenia, supplementary rights are accorded to certain native peoples. In Canada special rights are granted to the indigenous population. In Croatia, a special status has been accorded to two districts where the Serb minority represents more than 50% of the population. This minority enjoys privileges not granted to other minorities. Finally, in Hungary, privileges have been granted to some minorities only.

This holds good also for States having a federal structure, such as Switzerland and Belgium, where protection of language groups is essentially on a territorial basis.

B.   "INSTITUTIONAL" PROTECTION OF MINORITIES

One way of ensuring effective protection of minorities and of enabling them to best satisfy their claims is to take account of their existence in the State structure itself. Yet only three of the States here considered have opted for a federal model by reason of the heterogeneity of their populations and of the existence of minorities on their territory. These are Russia, Canada, and now Belgium, officially federal since the constitutional revision of 5 may 1993. The federal structure is an expression of the will to integrate the diverse cultural, linguistic and confessional elements which exist in these countries. While other States have chosen the same type of State structure, they do not justify having done so for the same reasons but rather for historical reasons.

The regional structure of a State also makes it possible to render the protection of minorities more effective. While Italian regionalism, for example, is the result of factors other than the presence of minorities, the two major linguistic minorities of Italy are nonetheless to be found in two regions, the Valle d'Aosta and Trentino-Alto-Adige, which both enjoy a particular autonomy for this reason. In addition, pursuant to Article 6 of the Constitution, the Republic protects linguistic minorities. Resort is often made to this provision as an interpretative aid in the case law of the Constitutional Court.

Yet, at all events, it is also possible to ensure an "institutional" protection of minorities in unitary States. For example, by adapting the administrative division of the territory to the presence of minorities, they can be guaranteed better participation in the political life of the country, and even a degree of autonomy, as, for example, in Greenland (Danish) and the Aland Islands (Finnish).

It will be noted at once, however, that these solutions (federalism, regionalism or others) can more easily be put into practice if the minorities are concentrated or grouped together; however, the institutional protection of minorities dispersed throughout the whole of the national territory, or a large part of it, must not be excluded a priori (see, for example, the election by the Finnish Samis of a Sami delegation which may freely use a part of the State budget in favour of the Sami population).

C.   PROTECTION BY THE GRANTING OF RIGHTS

1.   Fundamental rights and the principle of equality

Fundamental rights, whether recognised in the State's own Constitution or in the European Convention on Human Rights, are above all designed to protect every person, whoever he or she may be, as a human being. They also make it possible to provide, to some extent, protection for the members of minorities, notably through principles of equality and non-discrimination.

All the States here considered recognise the principles of equality and/or non-discrimination. The question of minorities is treated, sometimes explicitly, when they expressly forbid any discrimination on the grounds of belonging to a minority (Albania, Austria, Croatia, Slovakia), or more indirectly, when they simply prohibit any discrimination based upon grounds of nationality, race, language or religion (Canada, Germany, Hungary, Italy, Kyrgyzstan, Malta, the Netherlands, Poland, Portugal, Spain, Russia and Turkey). But often the constitutional provisions containing the principle of equality make no mention of these criteria, as is the case in Denmark, Finland, Liechtenstein, Luxembourg, Greece, Sweden and Switzerland, where on the contrary privileges of place or birth of persons or of families are forbidden. In Belgium, Article 6 of the Constitution simply proclaims the equality before the law of all Belgians, but Article 6bis forbids any discrimination affecting particularly ideological and philosophical minorities. It should also be remembered that most States here considered are bound by the European Convention on Human Rights, which provides expressly in Article 14 that the enjoyment of the rights and freedoms set forth in the Convention must be secured without discrimination on any ground, including language, religion, national origin or association with a national minority. The protection of minorities through these principles of equality and non-discrimination rests upon an approach to the question which is individual in character. The Grand Duchy of Luxembourg, for example, restricts itself purely and simply to this approach, protecting persons belonging to a minority only by means of rules of equality and non-discrimination.

However, the mere application of the principle of non-discrimination will not always make it possible to protect minority groups sufficiently, nor to take account of their particular characteristics or specific interests. It is even possible that a strict application of the principle of non-discrimination would result in discrimination against certain minorities. For this reason several States have introduced specific positive measures to be taken in favour of certain categories of individuals in order to redress the imbalances resulting from differences. According to the replies to the questionnaire, many States are to a greater or lesser extent familiar with this mechanism. This is, for example, the case in Albania, Austria, Canada, Croatia, in the Constitutions of certain German Länder, in Greece, Hungary, Italy, Norway and Slovenia. The use of this mechanism of positive discrimination indicates that we are passing from a strictly individual conception of the protection of minorities to a more collective conception, for individual protection alone, through classic fundamental rights, is no longer regarded as sufficient. The minority group is not simply the sum of its members but represents a distinct entity which itself enjoys rights. In fact, almost all the States provide for affirmative action and have adopted a collective approach to the problem.

In general, the evolution of the legal systems considered permits of a conclusion that an approach to minorities questions which is increasingly adopted simultaneously takes account of their individual and collective aspects (eg. Albania, Austria, Canada, Croatia, Germany and Poland). This is a positive evolution capable of making the protection granted more effective.

2. The specific rights accorded to minorities

Most States do not limit themselves to protecting minorities only by the application of the principle of equality, even if this is corrected by mechanisms of affirmative action. Most often, they seek to go further in the measures they take in favour of their minorities. Specific rights are then granted to them, these obviously differing in practice according to the needs of each type of minority and to the States' willingness to meet those needs.

a)   Linguistic rights

The countries where there are linguistic minorities (who often simultaneously constitute ethnic minorities), if they wish to protect these minorities, must establish regulations concerning the use of languages in order to guarantee a certain role to the minority language. Apart from Liechtenstein and Portugal, which have no linguistic minorities, virtually all States have regulated this question in domestic law. In Greece, Poland and Turkey the question of the right of minorities to use their mother-tongues is regulated neither in the Constitution nor by law, but by international treaties, which are, in principle, directly applicable in domestic law.

In general, all the States - without stating this expressly - accept the freedom of the individual to use the language he/she wishes in the private sphere. This right is rarely guaranteed expressly by the Constitution (Belgium), but is quite often safeguarded implicitly. In addition, this is a principle of general application which goes beyond the question of minority protection.

The question of the use of languages in the public sphere, that is, in relations between private individuals and public authorities, and between the latter, or in public signs of an official type, is much more complex.

Greece and Turkey have not provided for regulations governing the matter. The non-Muslim minorities in Turkey as well as the Muslim minority in Greece benefit from those provisions of the 1923 Treaty of Lausanne relating to minority languages (especially Articles 39 and 40) which concern private usage as well as usage in the judicial domain. In Romania, Article 13 of the Constitution makes Romanian the only official language of the Republic. However, Article 127 specifies that, in judicial proceedings, the members of national minorities and, more generally, all those who do not understand Romanian, have the right to an interpreter (free in criminal cases) and to a translation of procedural documents.

In Germany, German is the only official language of the country. According to federal law, only German may be used in the public sphere. However, the Sorban minority has the right to use its language in judicial and administrative matters at the level of the Land. The new Constitutions of the Länder of Brandenburg and Saxony, adopted in 1992, expressly protect the right of the

Sorban minority to preserve and develop its language and culture. In the regions occupied by this minority, all road signs are bilingual. In <u>Austria</u>, Article 8 of the Constitution also makes German the only official language of the Republic and confers on the ordinary legislature the duty to establish rules concerning the public use of minority languages. The laws in force (the 1976 Law on Ethnic Groups and its implementing decrees) guarantee to persons belonging to the Slovene and Croat minorities the right to use their language before the judicial and administrative authorities of the regions where they are represented, or before all the authorities in the districts where the largest proportion of the minorities resides, or before certain authorities in the whole region (Carinthia, Burgenland). In municipalities where the Slovene minority accounts for 25 per cent, place names are bilingual.

The case of the Grand Duchy of <u>Luxembourg</u> is rather particular since Luxembourgeois has been the official language of the country since 1984. Each citizen can thus address the authorities in this language. But, according to the Constitution, the use of languages is regulated by the law. Thus, French is used by the courts and generally by government departments in their communications with each other. In their communications with private individuals, they use Luxembourgeois, French or German, according to need. One cannot thus speak of a law which is aimed at linguistic minorities (in the current sense of the term), but of the regulation of the use of different languages used in the Grand Duchy.

In <u>Spain</u>, Castillian is the principal official language. The "other Spanish languages" enjoy official status on the territory of the Autonomous Communities whose Statutes of Autonomy provide for "coofficial" languages. The statement of "coofficiality" implies the right of every citizen to express himself or herself in Spanish or in the regional language in his or her relations with those public authorities which have defined competences applying to the Autonomous Community in question.

In <u>Belgium</u>, the three national languages, French, Dutch and German, have the status of official languages. Their use by, and in relations with, government departments, as well as in the fields of justice and social affairs, are the subject of very detailed and complex legislation which, based essentially on the principle of territoriality, does not always provide ideal protection for groups or linguistic minorities. This principle is also to be seen in <u>Switzerland</u>, where German, French, Italian and Romansh constitute the four national languages, the first three being official languages. Freedom of choice of language has been characterised by the Federal Court as an unenumerated constitutional right. But its practical weight is considerably limited by the principle of territoriality, which can justify cantonal measures which operate to maintain the traditional limits of linguistic regions and their homogeneity. It is therefore solely in relations with federal authorities that an individual enjoys a true right to use one of the three official languages of his choice. This is because, by contrast, the right of cantons to prescribe the use of a particular language in relations between individuals and the public administration is not disputed. In Canada, the use of languages in the official sphere has produced and is still producing abundant measures of regulation. English and French are the two official languages, and linguistic laws are tending to establish a generalised official bilingualism. In Cyprus, legislative, executive and administrative acts and documents must be written in the two official languages (Greek and Turkish). Texts published in the Official Gazette are written in the two languages. Official documents addressed to a Greek or to a Turk should be in the respective language. Legal proceedings take place and judgments are drawn up in Greek if the parties are Greek, in Turkish if the parties are Turkish and in both Greek and Turkish if one party is Greek and the other Turkish. Any person may address the authorities in Greek or in Turkish as he chooses. In Italy, while Italian is the only official language of the Republic, German enjoys exactly the same status as an official language in the region of Trentino-Alto-Adige, particularly in the province of Bolzano where the German-speaking minority which constitutes about two-thirds of the population is concentrated. It can therefore be used in the public sphere on the same basis as Italian. In the Valle d'Aosta, the principle is the same, this time in relation to French, except for the fact that Italian remains the only language employed in the judicial domain. In the provinces of Trieste and Gorizia, where there is a Slovene minority, an interpretation service is placed at the disposal of its members for communication with the authorities. Finally, in Finland, the Constitution gives both principal languages, Finnish and Swedish, exactly the same official status, which is itself elaborated by law. The Constitution provides that the right to use the Sami language in communications with the authorities is regulated by law, which states that Samis have the right to use their language before any administrative or judicial authority whose competence extends to the territory they occupy as well as before the national courts and certain national departments. In addition, they always have the right to an official translation of administrative documents in matters which concern them.

Article 6 of the Constitution of the Slovak Republic provides that Slovakian is the official language throughout the territory of the Slovak Republic. The Constitution, in its Article 34(2)(b), guarantees to persons belonging to a national minority, under the conditions provided by law, the right to use their language in official communications. This constitutional provision is elaborated upon in Law No. 428/1990 Coll. on the Official Language of the Slovak Republic, which provides in Article 6(2) for the right to use the language of a national minority in one's official communications with the organs of government, provided that the number of persons belonging to a national minority in a determined region constitutes at least 20% of the population of that region.

In the Russian Federation, legislation on languages is particularly complex.

In the whole of the territory of the Russian Federation, Russian, having the statute of official language, is the language of communication between countries through existing historical and cultural traditions (Article 68, paragraph 1, of the Constitution of the Russian Federation, Article 2, paragraph 2, of the Law on the languages of the peoples of the Russian Federation). At the same time, Article 68, paragraph 2, of the Constitution of the Russian Federation provides for the competence of the Republics within the Russian Federation to establish their official languages in their own rights, and the Law on the Languages of the Peoples of the Russian Federation provides for the right of the Republics to take decisions on the Statute of the languages of the peoples living in their territory. In regions of compact residence where a population does not have its own nation-state and nation-territory community or where it lives outside such a community, the language of the population of this region may be used simultaneously with the Russian language and the official languages of the Republics in official matters (Article 3, paragraph 4).

The Law on Languages of the Peoples of the Russian Federation obliges the organs of legislative, executive and judicial power of the Russian Federation to guarantee and to safeguard the social, economic and legal protection of all the languages of the peoples of the Federation of Russia.

The knowledge or lack of knowledge of the language cannot serve as a reason for limiting the linguistic rights of the citizens of the Russian Federation. Any violation of the linguistic rights of the peoples and of the individual has as a consequence the responsibility according to the law (Article 5, paras. 1 & 2).

According to the provisions, the Law establishes the modalities of the use of the languages of the peoples of the Federation of Russia in areas of legislation, administration and judicial procedure. In the higher legislative organs of the Russian Federation, work is carried out in the official language of the Russian Federation. The use of the official languages of the Republics within the Russian Federation is also allowed. The same modalities are observed for discussions of bills and other texts of a regulatory character (Article 11). In the activities of the organs, organisations, enterprises and establishments of the Russian Federation, the official language of the Russian Federation, the official languages of the Republics within the Russian Federation and the other languages of the peoples of the Russian Federation are used (Article 15). This principle forms the basis of the activities of the Constitutional Court of the Russian Federation, the Supreme Court and the Supreme Arbitration Court of the Russian Federation, other organs responsible for the protection of the laws of the Russian Federation as well as organs responsible for the protection of corresponding laws of the Republics within the Russian Federation (Article 18).

In other States, linguistic legislation seems to be less developed. The Constitutions are limited to affirming the right of linguistic minorities to express themselves freely, to preserve and to develop their cultural and linguistic identity (cf. Article 26 of the Constitution in Albania and Article 15 of Chapter 2 of the Instrument of Government in Sweden), or they even tend to place minority languages on an equal footing with the official language (Kyrgyzstan).

b)   Rights in the educational field

In the educational field, there are two principal aspects touching upon minorities that must be emphasised: the linguistic aspect, that is the question of education in the language or languages of minorities and also the teaching of these languages, and the religious aspect. The first aspect essentially concerns ethnic and linguistic minorities and is therefore intimately connected to the question of the use of languages discussed above. The second principally concerns religious minorities but possibly also ethnic minorities.

i)   Linguistic minorities

It may be noted that almost all States here considered provide, in their Constitutions or by law, for the teaching of minority languages, at least at primary and secondary level in State schools. In an increasing number of States, persons belonging to certain minorities can equally benefit from instruction in their respective languages (cf. the replies from Albania, Austria, Canada, Croatia, Finland, Greece, Hungary, Italy, Kyrgyzstan,Norway, Poland, Romania, Slovakia, Slovenia, Sweden, Switzerland and Turkey). However, the system and organisation of teaching of the languages of minorities, or in those languages, vary from country to country (schools and/or classes separate from or jointly with the majority;   influence of the minority on appointment of teachers and principals of the minority's schools, etc.).

Instruction in minority languages is generally restricted to certain regions where the minorities concerned are grouped together, as for example in Italy teaching is carried out in German only in the schools of the province of Bolzano (where there are also provisions for Ladin minorities) and in French in the Valle d'Aosta, where moreover it is for everyone half in French, half in Italian; teaching in Slovene is generally provided where that minority is present (in certain communes of the Friuli-Venezia Giulia region). In Canada teaching in the minority language is provided where numbers justify it. In Austria it is provided in Kärnten, where the Slovene minority is to be found, and in Burgenland, where the Croat and Hungarian minorities live. In Germany the teaching of Sorb takes place in Brandenburg and Saxony. The Belgian, and also the Swiss, system is similar: the principle of territoriality, which requires that teaching be carried out only in the official language of the linguistic region concerned, is tempered in some areas, exhaustively set out in the law, where teaching must be carried out in the language of the minority (in Belgium) or can be (in Switzerland) when there is a certain number of requests. In Spain, the scope of the rights of Autonomous Communities in respect of the teaching of regional languages is presently the subject of proceedings before the Constitutional Court. But teaching of the other languages is always provided.

In Russia, the level of education which can be reached in the mother-tongue is determined with respect to the numerical size of a given minority, the concentration of its residence and several other concrete factors.

Denmark confines itself to providing for the teaching of the minority language in State schools, but expressly allows parents to find other solutions if they want their children to be educated in their mother-tongue. In Sweden there is a mixed system: teaching is provided in the language of the Samis in their own region, but elsewhere only the teaching of languages other than Swedish is provided for. Similarly, in Poland, teaching at all levels may be in a minority language provided the number of pupils interested permits the creation of special classes. If not, teaching of the minority language will nonetheless be provided. In Switzerland, bilingual or trilingual cantons generally provide for instruction in minority languages. The local school administration in bilingual (Finnish and Swedish) municipalities in Finland is divided either between two separate school boards or between two distinct divisions of one common school board. Of the boards or divisions, the one administering schools for the Finnish-speaking population shall consist of members of this population, and conversely. In the Netherlands, part of the curriculum may be taught in Frisian. Furthermore, the study of Frisian is optional in the province of Friesland.

Finally, we must note that several States expressly make provision for the possibility of creating private schools where the use of languages is completely free. By way of example, one may cite Denmark, Poland, Slovenia and Sweden. In Germany, private schools of the Danish minority receive significant State subsidies.

ii)   Religious minorities

In regard to the teaching of religion (the catechism) in schools, the system varies from country to country, regardless of whether the religions concerned are the predominant ones in the country or the minority ones (although one cannot always speak of a "religious minority" per se).

In several countries, religious education is carried out in State schools, while in other countries (generally more secular), this education is left to religious institutions and is given outside State schools (or in private schools).

In State schools, parents can decide that their children will not attend religious education classes.   From a certain age, this decision resides in the pupils themselves.   For example, the following situations can be noted :

Canadian law provides for a guarantee of the confessional rights of Catholics and Protestants; schools of this persuasion must be financed out of public funds, funds which are also provided to other schools. In Germany and in Austria, private religious or confessional schools which guarantee an education similar to that of other establishments may be recognised and financed by the State. In Belgium, Article 17 of the Constitution guarantees freedom of education and the free choice of parents in respect of the religious education of their children. Official education is neutral and provides a guarantee of an optional choice of instruction in the major recognised religions or of non-confessional ethics. In the Netherlands Article 23 of the Constitution provides that in principle public and private (mostly religious based) education will be financed by the government on an equal footing.   Finally, in Romania, the State guarantees freedom of religious education and the organisation of religious instruction in State schools.

In Finland, religious instruction is in public schools provided according to the religion of the majority of the children in the school. However, if there are at least three Lutheran or Orthodox children in the school, instruction for them shall be provided according to their religion. Children belonging neither to the Lutheran nor to the Orthodox Church shall be exempted from the Lutheran or Orthodox religious instruction if so required by their parents. If there are at least three such children of another common denomination, they shall, upon request of their parents, be provided with instruction in their religion. Other children exempted from religious instruction shall be provided with instruction in ethical principles.

c)   Freedom of belief and worship

The rights of people belonging to religious minorities may be taken into consideration by States in various ways which result in varying degrees of protection.

Firstly, the problem can be approached from the point of view of non-discrimination, which means that individuals must be recognised as being able to enjoy and exercise freedom of thought, conscience and religion (rights which are guaranteed in the constitution without discrimination). This represents a minimum degree of protection for people belonging to religious minorities.

Another approach is for the State to take special measures to promote the material equality of religious groups. This is because some people may find themselves in a minority religious position and by reason thereof require special attention from the State.

i)   Freedom of thought, conscience and religion

All the States whose systems have been considered recognise this fundamental freedom, whatever the terminology employed. Reference is thus made to freedom of religion, conscience, belief, worship, etc. For States parties to the European Convention on Human Rights, the protection extended in domestic law is complemented by Article 9 thereof which guarantees to every person freedom of thought, conscience and religion. This right "includes freedom to change his religion or belief or freedom, either alone or in community with others and in public or in private, to manifest his religion or belief, in worship, teaching, practice and observance".

Freedom of thought, conscience and religion has implications at both the individual and the collective level, which means that everyone has the right to choose a religion and that individuals of the same religion may come together to worship. The right of persons to practise the religion of their choice, in both public and private, individually and collectively, is a right which is generally recognised.

This freedom also implies a freedom to decline to choose a religion. Few States explicitly recognise unbelief; we can, however, cite the example of Kyrgyzstan. Implicitly, this right is recognised in other countries (under the negative aspect of the freedom of religion).

Another important point is that no one can be obliged to practise a given religion: no country recognises such an obligation, all citizens being free to choose a religion, or to leave it and join another religious community.

There are persuasions which do not recognise the right of apostasy but this has no relevance for State law. Furthermore, in certain countries which have a "state religion", problems may arise in relation to payment of "ecclesiastical taxes" (treated like State taxes) which must be paid in principle by all persons domiciled in the country. In Switzerland, Article 49(6) of the Constitution provides that no person is bound to pay taxes which are specifically designed to offset the actual costs of the church of a religious community to which he or she does not belong.

Freedom of religion and conscience is not unlimited, certain restrictions thereon being accepted. As in the European Convention on Human Rights (Art.9 (2), these restrictions are appropriate to any democratic society. In the regulations of several States, the formula provided is that the exercise of this freedom cannot be contrary to public morality or to public order. By contrast, in the German Basic Law, freedom of thought, of conscience and of religion appears as a fundamental right without restriction. Restrictions on this right can therefore only result from other fundamental rights or constitutional values and then must respect the principle of proportionality.

ii) *The recognition of religious confessions*

In order to enjoy supplementary guarantees, some religious communities must be recognised by the public authorities. Thus in Portugal, in order to have a legal personality, religious communities must first obtain recognition.

The legislation of States such as Hungary require that certain specific conditions be fulfilled in order to create a religion. Among these conditions, it can be noted that it must not be contrary to the law or the Constitution and that it must be registered with a departmental or municipal court (see also Article 8 of Law No. IV of 1990).

Austrian legislation also has a system of "religious communities recognised by the State". This is not relevant to freedom of belief and worship but certain "privileges" are granted only to "recognised religions".

In Italy, relations between the minority religious communities and the State are regulated by law on the basis of special agreements between the State authorities and the representatives of the religious communities (Article 8 of the Constitution).

Other States grant a special degree of protection to some religions without any requirement of prior recognition. This is notably the case in Canada, where there is no State religion but where the confessional rights of Catholics and Protestants are protected in their schools by Article 93 of the Constitutional Law of 1867.

iii) The right to create educational establishments

There are several States which expressly recognise the right of religious communities to create their own educational establishments (see for example the replies of Canada and Germany). The new Constitution of Croatia provides that "religious communities are free, in conformity with the law, to .... open their own schools...".

In other countries, the establishment of private religious schools falls under either freedom of education and religion or public freedom in general, guaranteed under the Constitution. But there, too, the question arises of the extent to which these schools receive public subsidies and can award qualifications recognised by the State.

d) Cultural rights

It is generally accepted that the members of minorities have the right to preserve and develop their own culture. Thus, for example, Article 34(1) of the Slovak Constitution provides: "Citizens who, within the Slovak Republic, are members of national minorities or ethnic groups are guaranteed the right ... to develop their own culture ... and to maintain ... their cultural institutions". They are able to preserve their specificity in relation to the population of the country in which they form a minority by various means. Thus several countries allow minorities or persons belonging to minorities access to means of communication such as television and radio. They have the right to form associations to develop their cultural identity, through the press or other publications, through the theatre and a wide variety of cultural events, sometimes with the financial aid of the State.

It is exceptional for a Constitution to contain express rules for the promotion of the culture of ethnic minorities. The new Constitutions of the German Länder of Brandenburg and Saxony nonetheless stipulate a right in respect of the Sorban minority to the effect that its culture and language shall be preserved and promoted. According to a project for the revision of the Constitution which is now being discussed in Finland, the Samis and the Roma (in particular) should see the right to support and develop their language and culture recognised. Moreover, legislation concerning the promotion of minority cultures in certain specific domains exists in a certain number of States (for example, in Austria). Switzerland has adopted a law in favour of the culture of the Italophone and Romanche minorities.

i) **Radio and television**

An examination of the legal systems here considered reveals that there are several possible models of participation by minorities in radio broadcasting and television.

Various States give ethnic minorities the right to use national television channels or radio stations for a specified amount of time in order to produce programmes for the members of their minority in their own language. Examples of this are found in Austria, Finland, Hungary, Italy, Luxembourg, Norway, Portugal, Romania, Russia, Slovakia, Sweden and Switzerland, as well as other States. Sometimes, as in Switzerland or Finland, there are radio stations transmitting only in the minority language.

So as not to cut off all contact with their country of origin and their culture, Hungary and Italy, for example, have extended the practical possibility to minority groups to receive television or radio programmes from their mother countries, by means of appropriate technical equipment.

In general, the receiving of television and radio programmes from abroad is free to the extent that the geographical situtation and technical possibilities allow for it.

The various minority groups can also be involved in the management of national channels. Thus, in Finland, in Germany, and in Austria, linguistic and social groups are represented in the administrative bodies of the national channels.

ii) Press, theatre and publications

In many cases, States give aid to the minority press as well as to the theatre, notably in <u>Austria</u>, <u>Finland</u>, <u>Germany</u>, <u>Norway</u>, <u>Romania</u>, <u>Russia</u> and <u>Slovakia</u>.

iii) Encouragement of societies aiming to promote the culture and identity of minorities

In all countries where there are minorities there exist cultural societies founded by persons belonging to minorities, which aim at promoting the culture of these minorities. They have the status of private associations or enjoy a special status under the law. Often, they receive State subsidies.

D.   THE PARTICIPATION OF MINORITIES IN POLITICAL LIFE

As noted above in connection with the "institutional" dimension to the protection of minorities, a federal or regional State allows for the recognition of a certain autonomy in the minorities resident in the State territory. They can thereby be attributed their own territory in which they can conduct policy through autonomous institutions. (The federal or regional structure of certain States as a means of protecting minorities will be the subject of a separate study).

In addition, minorities participate in different ways in the political life of the State in which they are present. After having examined their right to form cultural and political groupings, we will look at the way in which States take account of the presence of minorities on their territory in the establishment in the country of political and administrative sub-divisions as well as in electoral policy.

1.   Freedom of association in general

a)   Do minorities enjoy this freedom?

In general, freedom of association is recognised either by the Constitution or by the law (see also Art. 11 of ECHR). But express references to minorities in this connection are not always to be found. In most countries, the general principle which applies to all citizens of the State is interpreted in a wide manner and extends to persons belonging to a minority. In any case, no State denies this freedom to persons belonging to a minority. Furthermore, it must be noted that some States go further and provide that this freedom is not limited only to nationals. This is the case in <u>Norway</u> and <u>Switzerland</u>, as well as in <u>Finland</u>, where "everyone, even a foreigner, is entitled to join an association". The criterion of nationality is therefore no longer relevant to the determination of entitlement to this freedom.

But even in the absence of specific provisions, it can be seen that nowhere is the right restricted to nationals.

b)   Conditions for the exercising of this freedom

Evidently, this freedom is subject to certain restrictions. These restrictions generally rely for their justification upon the safeguard of constitutionally recognised interests such as national security, public safety, the defence of public order, the prevention of crime, the protection of public health or morals, or the protection of the rights of others. Moreover, these restrictions apply to the right to freedom of association in general (see European Convention for the Protection of Human Rights, Article 11 (2) and are not specific to associations concerning minorities.

c)   Does this freedom have a transfrontier element?

Some States foresee the possibility of an extension of this right such that persons belonging to a minority can create associations open to persons domiciled in another country (Germany, Croatia, Slovenia). In general, there seems to be no problem in setting up associations open to persons domiciled abroad. The purpose of such a system is to encourage contacts with the country of origin. The case of Finland can also be cited, where the applicable legislation requires only that the President of the association and at least half the members of its governing body be domiciled in Finland, conditions which can also be fulfilled by foreign nationals.

2.   The right to form political parties

In general, States have not adopted specific rules on political parties representing minority rights. They must fulfil the same conditions as other political parties. In Germany, two Länder (Schleswig-Holstein and Saxony) have provisions in their Constitutions to facilitate the election of representatives of minorities, without guaranteeing them a minimum representation in the corresponding legislative body. Romania has specific rules on associations of citizens belonging to minorities in extending to them special guarantees in respect of election to Parliament.

In Turkey, it is forbidden to create a political party of a national minority which favours a language or culture other than Turkish. All political parties must abstain from putting national unity into question and from promoting regionalism.

3. Adaptations of electoral law in favour of minorities

Representation in political institutions tends to make participation by minorities in public affairs more effective and is one way of protecting minorities' interests. The problem arises both at national and at regional and municipal levels.

a)   The division of the country into electoral districts

In general, States do not proceed to the establishment of electoral districts by reference to the existence of minorities, whatever their nature. However, it may be noted that in Finland, the Province of Aland forms a special electoral district which elects a representative in parliamentary elections. In Hungary, a law specifies that when the boundaries of electoral districts are established, account must be taken of local ethnic particularities. In Switzerland, the cantons form the electoral districts for the election of the Federal Parliament and consequently minorities are represented.

In Russia, the electoral legislation of certain subjects of the Federation take into account the presence of minorities. Thus, Article 112 of the Constitution of the Republic of Sakha (Iakontie) provides that "in the areas of compact residence of the small Northern populations, electoral districts with the smallest number of electors may be created.

b)   The formation of minorities into political parties

Two solutions are possible here: either the interests of the minorities are defended by the political parties that they have formed to this end and which are composed only of representatives of the minorities, or the interests of minorities are defended by the traditional political parties which include in their lists some representatives of the minorities (this is notably the case of the German-speaking minority for federal elections in Belgium).

This question can be linked to whether or not minorities have their own electoral districts; if the division of the country into districts does not favour the vesting of a degree of autonomy to its minority components, minorities will evidently

- 73 -

have to merge with other political parties in order to ensure that they have a degree of representation in national institutions.

c)   Special measures for the attribution of seats to representatives of minorities interests

Some States have made provisions which make it possible to take account of the existence of minorities on their territory for electoral purposes.

Thus, in Croatia, if the members of an ethnic or national minority comprise more than 8% of the population, they can be represented proportionally in the national Parliament and in the Government, as well as in the superior courts. A number of seats in the national Parliament is also reserved for those minorities which do not reach this threshold. Similarly, in Denmark, legislation makes provision for two seats to be given to representatives from the Faroe Islands and two to representatives from Greenland. In the German Länder, the parties of the Danish and Sorban minorities are exempted from the rule according to which a political party must obtain more than 5% of the national vote in order to be represented in Parliament. Romania also makes special provision for associations of citizens belonging to national minorities, seats in the lower house being reserved for them on certain conditions. In Switzerland, linguistic criteria have had a certain influence on the mode of election of the principal confederal organs (the National Council, the Council of States, the Federal Council and the Federal Court). This is also applicable to certain bilingual Cantons.

It is evidently easier to give guarantees to minorities which are concentrated in a particular area than to minorities which are scattered throughout the national territory. In the latter case, other criteria have to be applied in order to ensure them some representation. Yet States can require that the minority constitutes a certain percentage of the total population in order to have seats in the political institutions.

It should be noted that the majority system can penalise candidates from the minority (when the latter is spread over several constituencies). The same is true of the proportional representation system combined with relatively small electoral constituencies, where minority lists can have difficulty in reaching the quorum required to obtain a seat in one constituency (this situation occurred in Austria when the regional election system was reformed in Carinthia). A similar effect (prejudicial for minorities) can occur when only the parties which obtained a certain percentage of the votes nationally in the first round are allowed to take part in the "second round" (as is the case under the new 1993 Italian electoral law in its proportional application).

4. Their representation in institutions

It is rare for States to establish a structure designed to guarantee in general the participation of minorities in political institutions. It is advisable in this respect to distinguish between concentrated minorities and dispersed minorities. In the former case, the minority will be represented in central institutions if the region where the minority is in the majority is in itself represented. The most concrete examples are Belgium and Switzerland. In Belgium, special measures have been taken both in the Constitution and by law to ensure the effective participation of minorities in political life. Such participation (and more particularly the francophone minority at the national level) is provided for at all levels of government - executive, legislative and judicial. In addition, this protection is not valid only for the federal government: the Flemish minority resident in the federated entity of the Region of Brussels also benefits from mechanisms quite similar to those used at federal level to protect the Francophone minority. In Switzerland, the mode of election to the principal confederal organs is influenced by the will to represent the various linguistic regions equitably. Proportional representation in the cantonal districts operates to provide a guarantee that all national languages will be represented in the National Council (lower chamber). In the Council of States (higher chamber), the rule of equal representation of each canton has the effect that the voice of a canton from a minority language group will be directly represented. In accordance with a customary rule, at least two representatives of latin cantons must sit on the Federal Council (the federal executive power). Finally, Article 107 of the Federal Constitution stipulates that the three official languages must be represented in the Federal Court. In Italy, in the province of Bolzano, in the Trentino-Alto-Adige, the membership of the provincial and local government executive bodies is corrected to ensure an adequate representation of the different linguistic communities, including the Ladin communities.

With regard to dispersed minorities, other States have adopted such concrete measures, but which do not reach every level of political life. They are rather concerned with one or other of the executive, legislative or judicial powers.

Finally, some States have created bodies for the management of problems relating to minorities. These bodies are generally confined to a consultative power. Thus, in Romania, there is the Council for National Minorities. Austria has a system of "Councils for ethnic groups" for each such group. In Finland, separate committees have been set up for Sami affairs and Roma affairs, as well as a delegation for the Province of Åland (a concentrated minority), whose function is to favour relations between the national Government and these various groups. Under the Constitution, Sami representatives have a right to be heard on matters concerning this minority. In Norway, a consultative Sami Parliament is established. In Hungary there is a national body for the self-management of minorities. In Cyprus, the Armenian, the Maronite and the Latin religious minorities each elect a representative to the Chamber of Representatives, which, however, has only a consultative vote. In the Netherlands, a national consultation Council in which all ethnic minority groups are represented discusses all major policy initiatives and can make recommendations with regard to them. In Slovakia, an advisory board for minority issues can be consulted by the executive.

V.   THE DUTIES OF MINORITIES

It is rare for a particular duty of loyalty to be imposed on minorities, beyond the general obligation to respect the laws in force applicable to all citizens. In the rare cases where such a duty exists, it is imposed upon all citizens independently of whether or not they belong to a minority. Thus, in Romania, all citizens including those belonging to national minorities have the same "duty of sacred fidelity to the country". Such appears also to be the case in Greece, where a special duty derives implicitly from the Constitution as well as from legislation. the non-respect of which can result, under certain conditions, in the loss of Greek nationality. In Spain, the Houses of Parliament, as well as some autonomous Assemblies, have imposed as a condition precedent to obtaining full parliamentary status the requirement of a vow or promise to respect the Constitution.

VI.   THE QUESTION OF SUBMINORITIES

The question of subminorities arises when, on a portion of the national territory, the members of the majority group at national level find themselves in the position of a minority. Only four of the States here considered have special regulations protecting subminorities, namely Belgium, Canada, Italy and Finland.

In Belgium, the Flemish linguistic group, which forms a majority at national level, is in a minority within one of the federal entities, the Region of Brussels. Here it enjoys a protective mechanism similar to that enjoyed by the Francophone minority at national level. In Canada, special protection in the field of education is accorded to the English-speakers of Quebec, where they are in a minority. In Finland, the members of the majority linguistic group at national level -those who speak Finnish - enjoy the same protection as the minority Swedish-speaking group when they find themselves in the position of a subminority; in the Province of Aland, this protection is limited to fundamental linguistic rights in order to protect the identity of the inhabitants of this province against a too great influence of Finnish-speaking immigrants. Finally, in Italy, the statute of the autonomous Trentino-Alto-Adige region provides special measures for the Italian-speaking subminority of the province of Bolzano.

VII.   PROTECTION MECHANISMS

Granting minorities a great number of specific rights and guaranteeing the broadest respect for their identity is one thing; it is also necessary that the effectiveness of these protective measures, as outlined above, be ensured.

A.   REMEDIES AVAILABLE TO MINORITIES

In general, the States here considered have been content to place in the hands of persons belonging to minorities the administrative and judicial remedies which are available to the population at large. However, in Italy, the region of Valle d'Aosta and the province of Trentino-Alto-Adige, along with the autonomous provinces of Bolzano and Trento and all regions having a special status, have the power to challenge before the Constitutional Court any legislative measures which are alleged to violate the rights, particularly those relating to the protection of minorities, guaranteed by their respective statutes of autonomy. Regional and provincial laws can also be challenged before the Constitutional Court by regional or provincial councillors who are members of a linguistic group.

While some States have created national organs whose task is to deal with affairs affecting minorities, these are generally not judicial organs whose decisions would bind State authorities. Thus, in Belgium there exists, in respect of linguistic minorities, the Permanent Commission for Linguistic Supervision and the Deputy Governor, and, in respect of ideological and philosophical minorities, a Permanent National Commission of the Cultural Covenant. In Austria, in the regional government of Kärnten, a special bureau has been created for problems of interest to the minority. In Hungary, one can note the institution of a Parliamentary Commissioner for the Rights of National and Ethnic Minorities and also that of local spokesperson for minorities. In Poland, a Commission for National Minorities has been established as a consultative body to the Council of Ministers. Furthermore, both Chambers of the Polish Parliament have instituted committees responsible for minority affairs. Finally, the minorities and their members are able to complain to the Ombudsman. Generally speaking, the function of the councils for minorities referred to in Part IV D 4 is to solve problems concerning minorities by way of negotiations with the authorities.

B. CRIMINAL LEGISLATION AGAINST RACIAL HATRED AND GENOCIDE

The criminal law of many States provides for post offences of incitement to racial hatred and to violence against minority groups such as ethnic and racial minorities. This special protection extends both to the groups themselves and to the individuals comprising them.

QUESTIONNAIRE ON THE
RIGHTS OF MINORITIES

(approved by the Commission during its 14th meeting, Venice, 5-6 February 1993)[1]

1. A)   Does the Constitution include a mention of the "unitary", "national" or "homogeneous" nature of the population or, on the contrary, does it indicate its "multiethnic", "multilingual" or "multireligious" nature?

    B)   If the State is organised on a federal or regional basis, is this structure justified by the heterogeneousness of the population (from the ethnic, linguistic or religious point of view)?

    C)   Does the Constitution put the State under the obligation to protect its own minorities outside the national territory?

2. A)   Is the term "minority" (or an equivalent term - please specify) used in
          a) the Constitution
          b) the law
          c) case-law?

    B)   Do these texts include a precise definition? Does this definition imply
          a) citizenship of the State in question
          b) and/or a lasting presence on the national territory or a portion of it?

---

[1]   *This questionnaire was drafted as a framework questionnaire to be adapted to each State. In particular, replies to one or another question may be more detailed according to the specific situation of the State concerned. Moreover, when a new legislation is being prepared, the replies should concern both the existing legislation and the draft legislation.*

C) Which minorities are covered by the texts referred to in A) and B)? Are they ethnic (or national?), linguistic or religious minorities?

D) Does the Constitution (or the Law) require or permit recognition of certain minorities (or all minorities) by the State? Which are the consequences of this? Does an individual's membership of a minority always depend on his free choice or can it be imposed on him by the public authorities?

E) Are the problems associated with minorities viewed in collective terms (groups) or in strictly individual terms (persons belonging to minorities)?

F) Can membership of a minority have an effect on the acquisition or loss of nationality and the exercise of political rights?

3. A) Are any international instruments (bilateral, multilateral or universal) relating to the protection of minorities applied in domestic law? What is their rank in the hierarchy of legal rules?

B) Has the implementation of these instruments resulted in legislative provisions or in decisions by national or international bodies?

4. A) Does the constitutional principle of equality refer to non-discrimination on the grounds of membership of a minority? Has there been any national or international case-law regarding this kind of issue?

B) Is the principle of positive discrimination in favour of minorities recognised by the Constitution, the law or case-law?

C) Are minority groups protected by the legislation restraining incitement to racial hatred, racial violence and xenophobia?

5. A) In what terms does the Constitution provide for freedom of belief and worship and for recognition of unbelief? To what extent do these provisions affect the rights of religious minorities (or unbelievers)?

B) Is there any national or international case-law illustrating the difficulties, if any, encountered by religious or philosophical minorities (in such fields as education, the labour market, military obligations, customs with regard to food or clothing, etc)?

6. A)   Does the Constitution (or the Law) contain any provisions restricting or protecting minorities' rights in the educational field?

   B)   If appropriate, please differentiate according to the type of minority and the type (state, grant-aided, private) or level of education.

   C)   Does the law provide for the study of the minority language or does it provide for all or part of the schooling in the minority language? If appropriate please differentiate according to the level of instruction and/or the different linguistic minorities.

   D)   Have these provisions given rise to any national or international case-law ?

7. A)   Does the Constitution (or the Law) contain any provisions relating to the official use of languages, the recognition and protection of minority languages, and the freedom of languages?

   B)   If appropriate, differentiate between official use (in the texts of laws and regulations, in the administration and in the legal system) and private use (in the broad sense).

   C)   Have these provisions given rise to any national or international case-law?

8.   Does the Constitution (or the Law) lay down any particular rules relating to minorities as regards the press, the theatre, the cinema, radio, Television and other media?

9.   Does the Constitution (or the Law) permit or require the application of any specific legal rules to certain minorities (e.g. in family law matters)?

10. A)   Is the right of association of persons belonging to minorities fully recognised, and does it extend across national borders? Or is it limited in one way or another?

B)   Are there any specific rules applying to political parties representing the interests of minorities?

11. A) Has the presence of minorities had any repercussions on the rules of electoral law?

B)   If so, what types of minority are involved? Are they confined to a particular area or scattered throughout the country?

C)   Has the presence of minorities had an effect on the country's division into electoral, administrative or judicial districts? Does this division tend to promote the autonomy of minorities or, on the contrary, does it tend to encourage their assimilation?

12. A) Have any special measures been taken to further the participation of minorities in political life?

B)   If so, please differentiate according to the type of body (legislative, executive or judicial) and the level of government (national, regional, local).

C)   Does the law provide for an official recognition of minorities' associations giving them public prerogatives?

13. A) Does the Constitution (or the Law) impose a special duty of loyalty or fidelity on persons belonging to minorities?

B)   If so, what practical consequences does this have?

14. A) Does the Constitution (or the Law) provide for protection of "sub-minorities", that is to say persons who, while they may or may not form a majority in the country as a whole, are in a minority position in a particular region?

B)   If so, are these "sub-minorities" treated in the same way as minorities at the level of the State as a whole?

15.   Besides the ordinary administrative or judicial remedies, are certain particular remedies available specifically to persons belonging to a minority?

Replies to the questionnaire
on the rights of minorities

Réponses au questionnaire
sur les droits des minorités

Albania	Albanie
Austria	Autriche
Belgium	Belgique
Canada	Canada
Croatia	Croatie
Cyprus	Chypre
Denmark	Danemark
Finland	Finlande
Germany	Allemagne
Greece	Grèce
Hungary	Hongrie
Italy	Italie
Kyrgyzstan	Kyrghyzstan
Liechtenstein	Liechtenstein
Luxembourg	Luxembourg
Malta	Malte
Netherlands	Pays-Bas
Norway	Norvège
Poland	Pologne
Portugal	Portugal
Romania	Roumanie
Russia	Russie
Slovakia	Slovaquie
Slovenia	Slovénie
Spain	Espagne
Sweden	Suède
Switzerland	Suisse
Turkey	Turquie

TABLE OF CONTENTS / TABLE DES MATIERES

ALBANIA

Albania has no complete and definitive Constitution. At present, there is in force a "small" constitution: Law No. 7491 dt. 29.04.1991 "On principal constitutional provisions", which is amended by some other laws. For that reason, we will use the term "Constitution" to mean this constitutional law.

1. A)   The Albanian Constitution does not use the term "unitary", "national" or "homogeneous" regarding the nature of the population.

   B)   The state is organised on a regional basis. The administrative separation is prefectura, districts, comuna. In some cases minorities are organised in the same comunas, but in others the population is mixed.

   C)   Yes, the Constitution puts the State under an obligation to protect its own minorities outside the national territory.

2. A)   Yes, the term "minority" is used in the Constitution, in the law and in the case-law.

   B)   The term minority usually includes nationality.

   C)   In Albania, there are two main national minorities: Greek and Macedonian, but there are some other smaller ones too.

   D)   Yes, the Constitution permits recognition of the other minorities by the state. Membership of a minority always depends on free choice and cannot be imposed by public authorities.

   E)   The problems associated with minorities are viewed both in collective terms and in individual ones.

   F)   Membership of a minority entails some special rights.

3. A)   At this point, there are no international instruments relating to the protection of minorities applicable in domestic law. But the

Albanian Constitution has a provision (Art. No. 4) which says: "The Republic of Albania shall recognise and respect the generally accepted norms in international law regarding fundamental freedoms, human rights and minorities."

B) In the Constitution, the chapter on "fundamental freedoms and human rights has a special article defending minorities (Art. 26).

4. A) Yes, the constitutional principle of equality refers to non-discrimination on the grounds of membership of a minority.

B) Yes, the principle of positive discrimination in favour of minorities is recognised.

C) Minority groups are protected by legislation (penal) from racial hatred, racial violence and xenophobia.

5. A) Article No. 26 of Law No. 7692 dt. 31.03.1993 on Fundamental freedoms and human rights says: "Individuals belonging to minorities shall enjoy, with no discrimination and in equality before the law, fundamental human rights and freedoms. They may freely express, preserve and develop their own ethnic, cultural, religious, and linguistic identity, teach and be taught in their mother tongue, and take part in organisations and societies to protect their interests and identity".

B) No.

6 A) Article 26 above mentioned

B) In Albania there is only state education

C) In Albania elementary education for minorities is in their mother tongue and in the middle school it is mixed. At this point in time there is no special high school education for minorities.

D) No.

7. A) Yes, Article 26 above mentioned.

B) In the tribunal the Albanian language is used (official). but members of minorities are guaranteed a translation.

C) No.

8. No.

9. No.

10. The right of association of persons belonging to minorities is fully recognised.

11. A) No.

B) Two types.

C) The country's division does not tend to encourage their assimilation.

12. A) The right of minorities to participate in the political life of the country has no limitation.

B) -

C) Yes.

13. A) The Constitution (or the law) does not impose a special duty on persons belonging to minorities.

B) No.

14. A) No.

B) No.

15. No.

AUTRICHE

1. A)   -

   B)   La République d'Autriche est un Etat fédéral, composé de 9 régions (Länder) "indépendants" (Art. 2 Loi constitutionnelle de 1920/29 = Bundesverfassungsgesetz "B-VG"). En principe (excepté Vienne et, en partie, aussi le Burgenland), cette structure répond aux régions historiques.

   C)   Non; voir cependant l'Accord Gruber-De Gasperi du 5 septembre 1946 sur lequel se base la prétention (juridico politique) de protéger la minorité de langue allemande au Tyrol du Sud.

2. A)   La Constitution comme telle ne parle pas de minorités ; seulement à l'art. 8, qui déclare que l'allemand est la langue officielle de la République, il est fait réserve des dispositions légales relatives à l'emploi des langues des minorités.

   La situation juridique des minorités existant en Autriche est réglée principalement dans la loi sur les groupes ethniques de 1976 (Volksgruppengesetz "VGG") ; depuis cette loi, on utilise de préférence le terme "groupe ethnique" au lieu de "minorité".

   B)   D'après l'art. 1 al 2 VGG sont considérés comme des groupes ethniques au sens de cette loi les groupes de citoyens autrichiens domiciliés en permanence (wohnhaft und beheimatet) sur le territoire de la République, de langue-mère autre que l'allemand et possédant un patrimoine culturel propre (eigenes Volkstum).

   C)   Les slovènes en Carinthie et en Styrie, les Croates et les Hongrois au Burgenland, les Tchèques, les Croates, les Hongrois et les Slovaques à Vienne ; il s'agit de minorités ethniques/historiques.

3. A)   Avant tout VGG ; voir également la loi de 1959 sur les écoles de la minorité en Carinthie (Minderheitenschulgesetz für Kärnten). En outre, il existe plusieurs décrets relatifs à l'établissement des

conseils des groupes ethniques, relatifs aux inscriptions topographiques, à l'usage des langues minoritaires.

B) Il y a une jurisprudence non particulièrement riche de juridictions de droit commun, de la Cour constitutionnelle (voir par ex. les arrêts VfSlg 9744/83, 9752/83, 11585/87), et de la Cour administrative en la matière ; en ce qui concerne les juridictions internationales, on peut mentionner certaines décisions (du reste isolées) de la Commission de Strasbourg déclarant irrecevables des requêtes provenant de personnes appartenant à la minorité slovène en Carinthie ; en général, la jurisprudence en question a trait à l'usage des langues minoritaires.

4. A) Les dispositions des art. 2 de la loi fondamentale 1867 (Staatsgrundgesetz) et de l'art. 7 VGG proclament le principe de l'égalité devant la loi pour tous les citoyens. Les art. 66 St. Germain et 7 Traité d'Etat de Vienne réaffirment le principe de l'égalité en ce qui concerne les citoyens autrichiens appartenant à une minorité.

B) Il est reconnu expressément par les art. 1 et 8 VGG et appliqué constamment (par ex. en ce qui concerne les mesures financières dans l'intérêt des groupes ethniques, l'établissement des conseils de la minorité, l'établissement d'écoles pour les minorités, etc... Dans son arrêt VfSlg 9224/81, la Cour constitutionnelle a reconnu expressément le devoir de l'action positive de l'Etat envers les minorités ; elle y a ajouté qu'un traitement égalitaire schématique et sans différenciation des personnes appartenant à la majorité et de celles appartenant à une minorité violerait le droit à l'égalité matérielle (et non seulement formelle), consacré par la Constitution.

C) L'art. 283 du Code pénal (Strafgesetzbuch) qui réprime l'incitation à la violence et à la haine ou l'insulte, mentionne expressément l'incitation à la violence et à la haine contre des groupes ethniques et l'insulte envers ceux-ci.

5. A) L'art. 14 de la loi fondamentale 1867 protège la liberté religieuse sans faire mention explicite des minorités religieuses. Que la liberté d'incroyance soit comprise dans la notion de la liberté de religion est hors de question.

B)   Certains rites islamiques peuvent violer les lois relatives à la protection des animaux. Pourtant, il ne s'agit là que des problèmes marginaux (il ne s'agit que de cas sporadiques qui ont été portés à l'attention des autorités), qui ne touchent pas sérieusement à la vie religieuse des minorités concernées. La loi sur l'exécution de peines 1969 (Strafvollzugsgesetz) ordonne à son art. 22 l'observation de la dignité humaine des détenus ; l'art. 38 ordonne d'avoir égard à la croyance de détenus en ce qui concerne leur alimentation ; les principes énoncés ci-dessus sont développés davantage dans les règlements internes des prisons. Il ne paraît pas qu'il y ait une jurisprudence à ce sujet.

6. A)B)C) La loi sur les écoles de la minorité slovène en Carinthie établit un système d'enseignement très développé au niveau primaire et secondaire (en principe, enseignement dans la langue de la minorité). Une loi analogue vaut pour l'enseignement de la langue croate (et hongroise) dans le Burgenland. L'obligation relative à l'enseignement pour certaines minorités dans leur langue nationale découle aussi des art. 68 du Traité de St. Germain de 1919 et de cet al. 2 du Traité d'Etat de Vienne de 1955.

D)   Un arrêt de la Cour constitutionnelle (VfSlg 12245/1989) a constaté que, en Carinthie, le droit à l'enseignement dans la langue slovène pour les personnes appartenant à cette minorité est protégé par la Constitution, de sorte qu'une réglementation qui fixerait d'une manière limitative (du point de vue géographique) les écoles auxquelles les personnes concernées auraient accès, serait contraire à la Constitution.

7. A)B) L'art. 8 B-VG stipule que l'allemand est la langue officielle de la République, sous réserve des dispositions légales relatives à l'emploi des langues des minorités. Des dispositions semblables se trouvent dans certaines constitutions régionales (Landesverfassungen) en ce qui concerne l'emploi des langues dans les régions.

L'emploi des langues des groupes ethniques dans les relations officielles avec les autorités administratives et judiciaires et en ce qui concerne les inscriptions publiques a trouvé une réglementation spécifique dans le VGG et dans plusieurs décrets d'exécution (voir également l'art. 7 du Traité d'Etat de Vienne précité).

L'usage privé de toutes langues n'est pas réglé par la loi ; cependant, ce droit fait partie des libertés civiques incontestées.

C)　　Voir 3/B/lit b

8.　　Il n'y a pas de dispositions légales particulières relatives à la presse ou aux médias e général et aux autres activités culturelles des minorités.

Les stations régionales de radio et de télévision consacrent des périodes d'émission variées aux programmes dans les langues de la minorité.

Les journaux des minorités participent aux subventions générales de la presse et jouissent de contributions particulières dans le cadre des subventions des activités culturelles des minorités.

9.　　Les lois civiles, pénales et administratives ne prévoient pas de dispositions spéciales applicables aux personnes appartenant à une minorité (en ce qui concerne les lois de caractère administratif tendant à la protection des minorités, voir supra, ad. 6, 7, 8).

10. A)　La loi relative au droit d'association ou d'assemblée (Vereinsgesetz 1951) ne fait aucune référence au critère de la nationalité ou de l'appartenance à une minorité. Dans le cadre des dispositions légales générales, toute personne peut fonder une association ou en devenir membre.

En ce qui concerne les manifestations publiques ou accessibles au public, la loi y relative (Versammlungsgesetz 1953) dispose que les étrangers ne peuvent pas agir en tant qu'organisateurs de telles manifestations.

Donc, en ce qui concerne le droit d'association et de manifestation, aucune règle spécifique en ce qui concerne les minorités.

B)　　-

11. A)　-

B)　　-

C)   Non; voir cependant, il convient d'observer que, d'après la Constitution de la Carinthie, toute la région avait formé une circonscription électorale unique, ce qui avait permis à la minorité slovène (vivant dispersée dans la région, avec son centre de gravité dans les districts du sud-est), d'obtenir le quorum nécessaire pour l'élection d'un candidat propre. Or, d'après un arrêt de la Cour constitutionnelle de 1978, la Constitution fédérale exige la division des régions en plusieurs districts électoraux.

L'adaptation nécessaire de la Constitution régionale de Carinthie à cet arrêt a été opérée en 1979, la région étant découpée en quatre districts électoraux. Depuis lors, il est presque impossible à une liste de la minorité d'obtenir le quorum nécessaire dans un seul district.

Toutefois, il faut ajouter que les listes électorales des partis politiques incluent en général des représentants de la minorité slovène pour les élections au niveau national et régional et que dans les conseils communaux ainsi que dans d'autres assemblées (chambres de commerce, de l'agriculture, du travail), il y a des représentants élus sur la base de listes propres à la minorité.

12. A)B)   Non; voir cependant le dernier alinéa de 11/C.

C)   En principe, il n'existe pas en droit autrichien une reconnaissance officielle des associations des minorités.

Cependant, on pourrait noter que pour certaines minorités "reconnues" (voir sub 2/C) au sujet desquelles des conseils de la minorité (Volksgruppenbeiräte) ont été établis, ces derniers possèdent le statut d'organe consultatif du gouvernement pour toutes les questions intéressant la minorité concernée.

13.   -

14.   La question ne se pose pas en Autriche ; il n'y a que quelques petites communes où les personnes appartenant à une minorité sont majoritaires ; mais cela n'a jamais causé de problèmes dignes de mention.

15. La prétendue violation d'une disposition légale ou réglementaire protégeant les minorités peut faire l'objet d'un recours, suivant le cas, de droit commun, administratif ou constitutionnel, mais il n'existe pas de dispositions spéciales à cet égard.

A mentionner qu'auprès du gouvernement régional (Landesregierung) de la Carinthie, il a été créé un bureau spécial (Bureau für Volksgruppenfragen) pour les problèmes intéressant la minorité, mais là il ne s'agit pas d'une instance "judiciaire" au sens strict du terme.

BELGIQUE

1. A)   La Constitution belge de 1831 a été conçue, à l'origine, comme la Constitution d'un état unitaire et homogène. Aucune mention n'est pourtant faite de ces qualités, qui allaient de soi, ni d'aucune autre.

    B)   L'Etat belge est, depuis le 8 mai 1993, officiellement un Etat fédéral. Cette structure, qui repose sur des communautés et des régions, imaginées dès 1970, s'explique essentiellement par le caractère hétérogène de la population au point de vue linguistique. En effet, les francophones de Belgique constituent une minorité au niveau de l'Etat fédéral, où ils représentent envirion 41 % de la population. Les plus ou moins 65.000 germanophones, regroupés dans la région linguistique de langue allemande, constituent l'autre minorité linguistique dotée par la Constitution d'un statut particulier (création en 1970 de la Communauté germanophone de Belgique), et protégée par un ensemble de règles protectrices particulièrement efficaces.

    C)   Non.

2. A)   <u>Dans la Constitution</u>

    Le terme "minorité" est utilisé une seule fois à l'article 6bis, qui énonce que *"La jouissance des droits et libertés reconnus aux Belges doit être assurée sans discrimination. A cette fin, la loi et le décret garantissent notamment les droits et libertés des minorités idéologiques et philosophiques"*.

    En dehors de cet article, aucune autre référence n'est faite, dans la Constitution, à quelqu'autre minorité. Cependant, certains mécanismes introduits par la réforme de l'Etat de 1970 ont pour finalité de protéger la minorité francophone au sein des institutions nationales (voir question 12B).

Dans la législation

La loi du 16/07/1973, dénommée "Pacte culturel", assure aux *minorités philosophiques et idélologiques* une protection toute particulière. L'artice 1er de cette loi précise que "les décrets pris par chacun des Conseils culturels ne peuvent contenir aucune discrimination pour des raisons philosophiques et idéologiques ni porter atteinte aux droits et libertés des minorités idéologiques et philosophiques".

Pour les minorités linguistiques, pour lesquelles la Constitution ne prévoit aucune garantie explicite, nous nous reportons essentiellement à la législation sur l'emploi des langues en matière administrative qui, en son article 8, comporte une référence à des minorités résidant dans des communes bénéficiant d'un statut linguistique spécial.

B)   Ces textes ne comportent pas de définition précise de ces minorités.

C)   Il existe en Belgique deux types de minorités ; il y a tout d'abord les **minorités philosophiques et idéologiques** qui ont été reconnues en Belgique à partir du début du processus de fédéralisation du pays (1970), qui risquait de bouleverser quelque peu l'équilibre philosophique, politique et idéologique existant jusqu'alors au niveau national. En effet, il existe deux grands courants philosophiques au sein de la population belge ; une tendance confessionnelle, catholique et un courant laïc qui s'équilibraient plus ou moins au niveau de l'Etat unitaire. L'influence du courant laïc est plus forte dans la Communauté française, tandis que l'influence chrétienne est dominante au sein de la Communauté flamande. A partir du moment où on reconnaissait les revendications autonomistes des deux communautés, cet équilibre pouvait être rompu et une protection de ces minorités s'imposait afin d'éviter que la minorité chrétienne en Communauté française et la minorité laïque en Flandre ne se retrouvent isolées au sein de communautés où étaient prépondérantes des tendances idéologiques et philosophiques opposées.

La Belgique connaît aussi des **minorités linguistiques**. On en distingue différents types :

Au niveau national

1. les francophones au niveau national ;
2. les germanophones, qui se sont vus reconnaître une véritable autonomie culturelle par la création d'une Communauté germanophone ;

Au niveau local

3. les francophones vivant dans les 6 communes périphériques de la Région de Bruxelles-Capitale (il s'agit des communes de Wezembeek-Oppem, Kraainem, Linkebeek, Wemmel, Drogenbos et Rhodes-Saint-Genèse) ;
4. les francophones établis dans des communes jouxtant la frontière linguistique mais situées en région linguistique de langue néerlandaise ;
5. les flamands dans les communes jouxtant la frontière linguistique, mais appartenant à la région de langue française;
6. les flamands de Bruxelles ;
7. les germanophones des communes malmédiennes qui sont situées en région de langue française (il s'agit des communes de Bellevaux-Ligneville, Béversé, Waimes, Faymonville, Robertville et Malmédy) ;
8. les francophones des communes de la région de langue allemande.

D) Sans objet.

E) Elle est envisagée à la fois sous l'aspect collectif (les francophones et les germanophones au niveau national) et sous l'aspect individuel (cf. tous les autres types de minorités linguistiques étudiées sous 2 C) en ce qui concerne les minorités linguistiques.

F) Non, aucune incidence.

3. A) Certains instruments internationaux relatifs à la protection des minorités sont d'application en Belgique. On peut citer essentiellement le **Pacte international relatif aux droits civils et politiques** (voy. l'article 27) et la **Convention européenne des droits de l'homme** (voy. l'article 14).

B) En ce qui concerne la jurisprudence, on citera essentiellement l'affaire Mathieu-Mohin et Clerfayt (*infra*, question 7 C), tranchée par la Cour européenne des Droits de l'Homme, où les protagonistes dénonçaient une discrimination fondée sur la langue et l'appartenance à une minorité nationale, et l'arrêt "Affaire linguistique belge", où les requérants dénonçaient, dans la législation sur l'enseignement, une discrimination fondée sur la langue (*infra*, question 6 D).

4. A) L'article 6 de la Constitution, qui n'a jamais été révisé depuis 1831 prévoit l'égalité juridique de tous les Belges devant la loi. Le constituant de 1970 a cependant quelque peu précisé la portée de cet article en insérant dans la Constitution un nouvel article 6bis qui pose quant à lui le principe général de l'interdiction de toute discrimination à l'égard des Belges. L'article 6bis, 2ème phrase prévoit une garantie supplémentaire pour les minorités philosophiques et idéologiques.

B) Non.

C) La loi du 30 juillet 1981 tendant à réprimer certains actes inspirés par le racisme et la xénophobie permet de condamner pénalement celui qui incite à la discrimination, la haine ou la violence à l'égard de *personnes* en raison de leur race, couleur, ascendance ou origine nationale ou ethnique. De même, on pourra poursuivre celui qui incite à la discrimination, ségrégation, haine ou violence à l'égard d'un *groupe*, d'une *communauté* ou de *leurs membres*, pour les mêmes motifs.

5. A) Les articles 14 et 15 de la Constitution belge garantissent la liberté des cultes. Chacun peut donc exercer publiquement le culte de son choix et manifester librement ses opinions, à ce sujet comme en toute matière (art. 14), et, corrélativement, personne ne peut être contraint d'en exercer un (art. 15). Les religions minoritaires sont ainsi mises sur le même pied que les autres, et les athées également protégés. On notera que l'article 17 de la Constitution prévoit que la Communauté doit organiser un enseignement *neutre*, c'est-à-dire qui respecte les conceptions philosophiques, idéologiques ou religieuses des parents et des élèves (§ 1er, al. 3), que les écoles publiques offrent le choix entre l'enseignement d'une des religions reconnues et celui de la morale non-confessionnelle (§ 1er, al. 4)

et que tous les élèves soumis à l'obligation scolaire ont droit à une éducation "morale ou religieuse" (§ 3). Enfin, l'article 117 de la Constitution met les traitements et pensions des ministres des cultes reconnus et ceux des délégués des organisations reconnues qui offrent une assistance morale selon une conception philosophique non-confessionnelle à charge de l'Etat.

B)   Il existe quelques cas de jurisprudence nationale assez caractéristiques, qui témoignent des difficultés rencontrées par certaines minorités religieuses. On les rencontre essentiellement dans deux domaines : en matière sociale et en matière d'enseignement. Dans ce dernier domaine, il existe une importante jurisprudence du Conseil d'Etat relative au choix, dans les écoles secondaires, entre l'enseignement de la morale laïque et celui d'une religion confessionnelle. Le Conseil d'Etat a eu à connaître à plusieurs reprises du refus exprimé par des témoins de Jéhovah de suivre l'un de ces cours, prétendument non conformes à leurs convictions.

6.   A)B)C) La Constitution ne prévoit rien de particulier quant à la protection des minorités linguistiques en matière d'enseignement. C'est une loi du 30 juillet 1963 qui fixe le *régime linguistique de l'enseignement,* qui est fondée sur le principe de la territorialité : il est organisé dans la langue de la région linguistique, donc dans les deux langues à Bruxelles. Il y a deux aspects différents de la question à envisager : les règles fixant la langue dans laquelle l'enseignement est organisé, puis la question de savoir si les parents d'élèves disposent du choix de la langue de l'enseignement que recevront leurs enfants.

a) La langue dans laquelle l'enseignement est organisé

En principe, l'enseignement est organisé uniquement dans la langue de la région. La loi du 30 juillet 1963 accorde toutefois une certaine protection aux minorités, mais qui ne concerne que les communes citées expressément dans la loi, à savoir les six communes périphériques, les communes de la frontière linguistique, les communes de la région de langue allemande, les communes malmédiennes et neuf autres communes contiguës à la région de langue allemande.

Dans ces communes, l'enseignement gardien et primaire peut être organisé dans la langue de la minorité, si certaines conditions (tenant au nombre d'enfants concernés, non-proximité d'une école de l'autre régime linguistique, ...) sont réunies.

b) Choix de la langue de l'enseignement par les parents

Dans ce domaine, la règle de la territorialité ne joue pas. Le principe est que les parents peuvent inscrire leurs enfants dans toute école de leur région linguistique, et même dans toute école d'une autre région linguistique, s'ils peuvent attester que l'enfant a suivi toute sa scolarité antérieure dans cette autre langue, ou, à défaut, qu'il s'agit de sa langue maternelle.

Néanmoins, la liberté reconnue aux parents n'est pas absolue. Il leur est interdit d'inscrire leurs enfants dans une école francophone de l'une des six communes périphériques ou d'une des communes de la frontière linguistique, sise en région flamande, s'ils ne sont pas domiciliés dans ces communes. De même, des parents néerlandophones ne peuvent pas inscrire leurs enfants dans une école flamande d'une commune de la frontière linguistique, située du côté francophone, s'ils n'y sont pas domiciliés.

D) La matière a donné lieu à un arrêt de la Cour européenne des Droits de l'Homme, l'arrêt "Affaire linguistique belge". Le 27 juillet 1968, la Cour décida que l'article 7 § 3 de la loi du 2 août 1963 sur l'emploi des langues en matière administrative, qui interdit aux enfants francophones non domiciliés dans une des communes périphériques de s'inscrire dans une école française de ces communes, comportait une discrimination fondée sur la langue. Cette disposition est toujours en vigueur. Cela se justifie sans doute par le fait qu'en 1970, la Belgique sera constitutionnellement divisée en régions linguistiques, et que dès lors, les communes périphériques deviendront des communes de la région de langue néerlandaise.

7. A)B) a) La Constitution, en son article 23, prévoit le principe de la *liberté des langues* : "L'emploi des langues usitées en Belgique est facultatif ; il ne peut être réglé que par la loi, et seulement pour les actes de l'autorité publique et pour les affaires judiciaires". Toutefois, l'article 59bis § 3 donne compétence aux communautés

pour régler par décret l'emploi des langues pour les matières administratives, l'enseignement et les relations sociales.

Actuellement, le principe est la liberté pure et simple de l'emploi d'une langue. Cependant, la portée de ce principe est restreinte dans une série de domaines : l'emploi des langues en matière administrative est réglé par des lois coordonnées du 18 juilllet 1966; l'emploi des langues en matière d'enseignement est réglé par la loi du 30 juillet 1963 ; l'emploi des langues en matière judiciaire est réglé par la loi du 15 juin 1935 (juridictions civiles et pénales), les lois coordonnées sur le Conseil d'Etat et la loi du 6 janvier 1989 sur la Cour d'arbitrage. Enfin, l'emploi des langues en matière sociale est réglé, pour la Flandre, par un décret du Conseil flamand du 19 juillet 1973, dit "décret de septembre", et pour la Communauté française par un décret du Conseil de la Communauté française du 30 juin 1982.

b) Les lois coordonnées sur l'emploi des langues en matière administrative et la loi sur le régime linguistique de l'enseignement prévoient expressément des mesures de protection des minorités. Pour l'enseignement, voir question n° 6 ; pour l'emploi des langues en matière administrative, on pourrait résumer les choses comme suit : la règle est l'unilinguisme dans les trois régions linguistiques unilingues, et le bilinguisme dans la région linguistique de Bruxelles-Capitale.

Cette règle n'est pas absolue : une certaine protection est accordée aux minorités. Ainsi, on déroge au principe de l'unilinguisme dans un certain nombre de communes, énumérées limitativement par la loi. Il s'agit des six communes périphériques, dotées par la loi d'un statut propre, et des communes de la frontière linguistique (notamment Fourons et Comines-Warneton), de la région de langue allemande (art. 8, 1° des lois coordonnées) et, enfin, des communes dites "malmédiennes", dotées, elles, d'un "régime spécial en vue de la protection de leurs minorités".

Dans ces communes donc, et dans celles-là exclusivement, des "facilités linguisitiques" sont, dans une série d'hypothèses, octroyées à la minorité - c'est-à-dire à ceux qui parlent une langue autre que celle de la région linguistique unilingue à laquelle appartient leur commune. Ces facilités peuvent être considérées sous deux angles : il s'agit d'une obligation faite à l'administration d'employer, pour certains types d'actes, soit les deux langues, soit la seule langue minoritaire, ou bien, si l'on adopte l'autre point de vue, d'une faculté offerte aux particuliers d'utiliser, toujours pour certains types de rapports avec l'administration locale, leur langue maternelle.

C)   De nombreux cas de jurisprudence nationale à propos de l'application de ces lois sur l'emploi des langues sont à relever. Les plus célèbres sont les arrêts rendus par le Conseil d'Etat à propos de la question des obligations linguistiques des mandataires politiques locaux (affaire "fouronnaise", du nom d'un petit village de la frontière linguistique, Fourons, situé du côté flamand de cette frontière, et dont le conseil communal est en majorité francophone, tout comme son bourgmestre), arrêts ayant suscité une importance polémique. Le problème s'est finalement résolu par le vote d'une loi du 9 juin 1988, dite de "pacification linguistique".

On signalera également un cas de jurisprudence internationale, l'arrêt de la Cour européenne des Droits de l'Homme, dans l'affaire très connue "Mathieu-Mohin et Clerfayt" (2 mars 1987). La Cour sera saisie d'un recours introduit contre l'article 29 § 1er de la loi spéciale de réformes institutionnelles du 8 août 1980, réglant la composition du Conseil flamand, texte qui permettait aux électeurs néerlandophones de l'arrondissement bilingue de Bruxelles-Hal-Vilvorde d'élire des conseillers au Conseil flamand - qui en réalité résulte de la fusion initiale des conseils communautaire *et régional*, alors que les électeurs francophones, s'ils pouvaient élire des représentants au Conseil de la Communauté française, n'avaient pas la possibilité d'être représentés au Conseil de la Région wallonne. La Cour refusera de suivre l'opinion de la Commission et décidera que cette règle, inachevée et transitoire, ne violait pas la Convention. Quoi qu'il en soit, la règle était bel et bien provisoire: avec la réforme de 1993 et l'élection directe des conseils sur une base strictement régionale, la situation critiquée ne pourra dorénavant plus se reproduire.

8.   Depuis 1970, date du début du processus de fédéralisation en Belgique, de nombreuses matières ont été transférées aux entités fédérées que sont les Communautés et Régions ; c'est le cas des matières culturelles qui relèvent désormais de la compétence du

législateur communautaire. Ce qui signifie que la culture - qui s'exprime par la presse, le théâtre, le cinéma, la radio, T.V. et autres médias - relève de la compétence des Communautés.

Pour la mise en oeuvre de leur politique culturelle, les différentes autorités publiques doivent respecter les principes du Pacte culturel (cf. la loi du 16 juillet 1973, garantissant la protection des tendances idéologiques et philosophiques) qui garantit les droits et libertés des minorités philosophiques et idéologiques. Celui-ci a pour but d'instaurer un pluralisme qui vise à éviter l'exclusion de certains représentants d'une idéologie, d'une philosophie, d'une confession. Chacun doit, de la sorte, obtenir les mêmes avantages que ceux accordés aux autres utilisateurs des moyens culturels à partir du moment où il répond aux mêmes critères. Le pluralisme est prévu par cette loi tant au niveau de la gestion des institutions culturelles qu'en ce qui concerne l'accès aux infrastructures culturelles dépendant d'une autorité publique.

A titre d'exemple, la R.T.B.F (télévision de la Communauté française) est gérée par un Conseil d'administration composé de membres élus au scrutin proportionnel par le conseil de la Communauté française, de sorte que les différentes tendances politiques présentes au sein de la Communauté ont un mot à dire quant à la gestion de cette institution culturelle.

9.   Sans objet.

10.   Sans objet.

11. A)B)   Oui ; les règles du droit électoral sont adaptées afin de prendre en compte l'existence de certaines minorités **linguistiques**. Le pays est divisé, pour les élections législatives, en arrondissements électoraux. Chaque arrondissement électoral est unilingue, en ce sens que les électeurs, quelle que soit leur langue maternelle, ne peuvent y voter que pour des listes flamandes dans les arrondissements électoraux de la région linguistique flamande, et pour des listes francophones dans les arrondissements situés en région linguistique française.

Néanmoins, il est dans une certaine mesure tenu compte de l'existence de minorités linguistiques, dans deux hypothèses :

a) A Bruxelles

La région de Bruxelles-Capitale étant bilingue, il est évidemment possible d'y voter au choix pour des listes flamandes ou francophones. Mais en-dehors des 19 communes qui forment la région bilingue de Bruxelles-Capitale, on se retrouve en région unilingue flamande. Toutefois, on a créé un arrondissement électoral mixte, qui regroupe Bruxelles, Hal et Vilvorde. Dans cet arrondissement, qui dépasse les limites géographiques de Bruxelles, il est possible de voter pour des listes de l'un ou l'autre régime linguistique. On notera qu'au lendemain de la réforme de l'Etat de 1993, cet arrondissement bilingue de Bruxelles-Hal-Vilvorde ne subsistera plus que pour les élections législatives ; pour l'élection directe des conseils de communauté et de région, la règle de la territorialité jouera pleinement et il ne sera plus possible, pour les personnes domiciliées en région linguistique flamande, de voter pour des listes francophones.

b) Dans les communes de Fourons et de Comines-Warneton

Pour ces communes de la frontière linguistique, situées respectivement en région linguistique flamande pour Fourons et francophone pour Comines-Warneton, et qui possèdent une minorité de personnes parlant une langue autre que celle de la région, la loi du 9 août 1988 a modifié le code électoral en permettant aux électeurs domiciliés dans ces communes d'aller voter, pour les élections législatives (et européennes, depuis la loi du 29 mars 1989), dans un arrondissement électoral faisant partie de l'autre région linguistique. Ainsi, les Fouronnais peuvent voter dans l'arrondissement électoral francophone de Verviers, à Aubel, et les Cominois dans l'arrondissement flamand d'Ypres, à Heuvelland. Une fois encore, pour l'élection directe des membres des conseils des entités fédérées, cette faculté disparaîtra.

C) Le découpage des circonscriptions électorales, administratives et judiciaires est tributaire de la frontière linguistique. Il n'a pas été tenu compte de l'existence des minorités linguistiques lorsque l'on a fixé cette frontière, en 1961. Une seule exception, c'est celle de l'arrondissement mixte de Bruxelles-Hal-Vilvorde, dont nous avons parlé ci-dessus.

12. A)   Oui, des mesures spéciales ont été prévues, tant dans la constitution que dans la législation, pour assurer une participation effective des minorités à la vie politique.

B)   <u>Au niveau fédéral</u>

1.   En ce qui concerne le *pouvoir législatif*, différents mécanismes ont été prévus afin de protéger essentiellement la minorité francophone au sein des institutions de l'Etat fédéral. On dénombre trois mécanismes qui ont cette finalité.

Tout d'abord, *l'article 32bis de la Constitution* crée deux groupes linguistiques, un français et un néerlandais, qui regroupent tous les élus des deux assemblées (le Sénat et la Chambre).

L'article 38bis crée une procédure inédite, appelée "sonnette d'alarme", qui permet à un groupe linguistique, lorsqu'un projet ou une proposition de loi est "de nature à porter gravement atteinte aux relations entre les communautés", d'introduire, à la majorité des trois quarts, une motion motivée avant le vote final du texte en séance publique, motion qui suspendra provisoirement la procédure parlementaire.

Enfin, *l'article 1er, al. 4 de la Constitution* instaure, à côté des mécanismes traditionnels de majorités connus en Belgique, une *majorité qualifiée* qui est requise pour les lois touchant à des matières déterminées. Ces lois, dont les cas sont en augmentation constante, doivent réunir la majorité des suffrages dans chaque groupe linguistique de chacune des Chambres, et le total des votes émis dans les deux groupes linguistiques doit atteindre les deux tiers des suffrages exprimés.

2.   Au niveau du *pouvoir exécutif*, un seul mécanisme peut être considéré comme une garantie pour la minorité francophone : *l'article 86bis de la Constitution* qui instaure la *parité linguistique au sein du Conseil des Ministres*, le Premier Ministre étant le cas échéant exclu du calcul (lorsque le Conseil des Ministres est en nombre impair).

3.   Au niveau des *juridictions*, l'organisation de la Cour de Cassation, de la Cour d'arbitrage et du Conseil d'Etat appartient

toujours à l'Etat central sans qu'aucune fédéralisation ne soit prévue mais certaines règles ont été introduites afin de tenir compte de la structure bipolaire de la Belgique. La Cour de Cassation, la Cour d'arbitrage et le Conseil d'Etat sont de la sorte composés de manière linguistiquement paritaire, la moitié des membres étant francophone et l'autre moitié néerlandophone.

Au niveau fédéré

La seule minorité reconnue au sein des entités fédérées est celle existant dans la Région de Bruxelles-Capitale. En effet les flamands, à Bruxelles, représentent plus ou moins 15 % de la population. Ils bénéficient d'une protection toute particulière qui est fort semblable à celle octroyée aux francophones au sein de l'Etat central (voir question 14).

Au *niveau du pouvoir législatif*, on retrouve les mêmes mécanismes que ceux déjà étudiés pour le pouvoir central. Les membres du Conseil de la Région de Bruxelles-Capitale sont répartis en groupes linguistiques, l'un francophone et l'autre néerlandophone. De plus, ils peuvent mettre en oeuvre un mécanisme fort semblable à la sonnette d'alarme (cf. l'art. 31 de la loi spéciale du 12 janvier 1989 relative aux institutions bruxelloises) prévu au niveau national.

Au *niveau du pouvoir exécutif*, on retrouve également la règle de parité au sein de l'exécutif de la Région de Bruxelles-Capitale. L'exécutif comprend 5 membres, 2 du groupe francophone et 2 du groupe néerlandophone et un président.

C)   Aucune.

13.   Sans objet.

14. A)   Comme nous avons déjà eu l'occasion de le signaler, la Constitution ne parle pas de "minorités", sauf le cas des minorités idéologiques et philosophiques. Toutefois, il existe un cas de "sous-minorité" : les flamands, majoritaires au niveau national, sont en minorité en Région de Bruxelles-Capitale (où ils représentent environ 15 % de la population bruxelloise).

B)   Les flamands à Bruxelles jouissent du même type de protection que les francophones au niveau national. On a d'ailleurs appelé Bruxelles le "miroir inversé de la Belgique" :

Au niveau du pouvoir législatif

Il est exercé par la Conseil de la Région de Bruxelles-Capitale. Les conseillers, élus sur des listes unilingues, sont *répartis en groupes linguistiques* ; la loi spéciale relative aux institutions bruxelloises prévoit un mécanisme semblable à celui de la *sonnette d'alarme*. Enfin, les flamands bénéficient d'une *garantie de présence dans tous les travaux du Conseil* : ils doivent être présents dans toutes les commissions et le bureau du Conseil doit compter un tiers de membres flamands.

Au niveau du pouvoir exécutif

Il est exercé par l'exécutif de la Région ; on y retrouve le mécanisme de la *parité*. L'exécutif comprend un président et deux membres de chacun des groupes linguistiques. La parité disparaît au niveau des secrétaires d'Etat régionaux, mais la loi prévoit qu'un d'entre eux au moins doit appartenir au groupe minoritaire.

15.   Pour les minorités linguistiques

Il existe, outre les recours classiques pour lésions des droits civils ou politiques devant les juridictions judiciaires ou administratives (Conseil d'Etat), des recours plus spécifiques :

- Tout particulier estimant que, par l'effet d'une loi ou d'un acte de nature législative, il a été victime d'une discrimination ou n'a pas été traité de la même manière qu'une autre personne se trouvant dans la même situation que lui, pourra introduire un recours devant la Cour constitutionnelle de Belgique, appelée *Cour d'arbitrage*. Celle-ci, depuis 1989, est compétente pour connaître de la violation des articles 6, 6bis et 17 de la Constitution, qui énoncent les principes d'égalité et de non-discrimination.

- Dans le domaine de la législation linguistique, dès le 1er janvier 1995, la fonction de "*gouverneur-adjoint*" sera créée dans la province du Brabant flamand (issue de la scission de l'actuelle province de Brabant, scission résultant de la réforme de l'Etat de 1993). Le gouverneur adjoint aura pour mission de surveiller l'application des lois et des règlements sur l'emploi des langues en matière administrative dans les 6 communes périphériques de Bruxelles ; en outre, il contrôlera le respect des lois sur le régime linguistique de l'enseignement. Les simples particuliers pourront déposer des plaintes devant lui. Il instruira ces plaintes, pourra imposer aux autorités administratives un délai de réponse contraignant à leur propos, et enfin, il pourra saisir, s'il l'estime nécessaire, la C.P.C.L. A Bruxelles même, le *vice-gouverneur* disposera des mêmes compétences, en vue de protéger la minorité flamande.

- La *Commission Permanente de Contrôle linguistique (C.P.C.L.)*, constituée par les lois coordonnées sur l'emploi des langues en matière administrative, a pour tâche de surveiller l'application de ces lois. Pour le moment, la C.P.C.L. a la possibilité de faire des observations, des suggestions ou d'adresser des avis, d'office ou sur demande, au gouvernement. Elle dispose de moyens d'investigation, et peut demander aux autorités et aux juridictions compétentes de constater la nullité d'actes contraires aux lois coordonnées. Mais dès le 1er janvier 1995, elle disposera de plus de pouvoirs. Elle pourra être saisie directement d'une plainte par des particuliers résidant dans une commune à statut spécial ; elle pourra demander aux autorités de prendre des mesures pour mettre fin à une illégalité et, si cela n'est pas fait dans un certain délai, s'y substituer.

En ce qui concerne les minorités philosophiques et idéologiques

La loi du 16 juillet 1973 a créé un organe particulier dénommé *Commission nationale permanente du pacte culturel*, auprès de laquelle tout particulier lésé peut introduire une plainte. La mission de cette commission est triple : elle sert à la fois d'organe d'instruction, d'organe de conciliation et d'organe d'avis.

Elle procède de la manière suivante :

1)   elle instruit les plaintes dont elle est saisie ; à cette fin, elle peut entendre la partie plaignante et l'autorité qui a pris la décision contestée ainsi que tous les témoins pouvant aider à la bonne

compréhension du litige. Elle peut aussi demander tous les documents et renseignements nécessaires à l'examen du litige.

2) après cette phase d'instruction, elle s'efforce d'obtenir une conciliation entre les différentes parties.

3) si cette procédure échoue, elle émettra un avis pouvant être accompagné d'une recommandation à l'autorité concernée lui demandant l'annulation de la décision prise ou de prendre toutes les mesures nécessaires pour assurer la bonne application de la loi.

CANADA

1. A)   Le Canada est un Etat fédéral bilingue sur le plan fédéral, multiculturel et hétérogène. La Constitution protège, de façon spéciale, les peuples autochtones (au paragraphe 91(24) de la Loi constitutionnelle de 1867, à l'article 25 de la Charte canadienne des droits et libertés et aux articles 35 et 35.1 de la Loi constitutionnelle de 1982). Elle protège les droits confessionnels des groupes catholiques et protestants aux articles 93 de la Loi constitutionnelle de 1867 et 29 de la Charte.

La liberté de conscience et de religion est garantie par l'alinéa 2a) de la Charte tandis que la promotion du multiculturalisme est assurée par l'article 27 de la Charte de 1982.

B)   La structure fédérale est justifiée par le caractère hétérogène de la population canadienne. Les francophones sont majoritaires au Québec, où ils forment 82 % de la population, mais minoritaires dans le reste du pays. Le Québec a une culture, un système d'éducation et un régime de droit (Code civil) qui le distinguent des autres provinces. Il est, de plus, à l'abri d'une modification visant à uniformiser le droit privé grâce à la protection offerte par l'article 94 de la Loi constitutionnelle de 1867. Dans la procédure de modification de la Constitution, il jouit d'une protection spéciale pour l'éducation et la culture (à l'article 40 de la Loi constitutionnelle de 1982).

C)   Non, pas directement. Sur le plan externe, seul le Parlement fédéral jouit de l'extraterritorialité.

2. A)   a)   A l'article 23 de la Charte canadienne des droits et libertés à propos du droit à l'instruction dans la langue de la minorité. La minorité de langue officielle a la gérance et le contrôle de ses écoles là où le nombre le justifie.

b)   Le paragraphe 16(1) de la Loi canadienne sur les droits de la personne emploie les mots "groupes d'individus". Ce paragraphe permet l'adoption de programmes de promotion sociale pour des groupes d'individus victimes de discrimination ou d'un ésavantage quelconque.

L'article 43 de la Charte des droits et libertés de la personne du Québec prévoit la promotion de la vie culturelle des minorités. Il se lit comme suit :

> 43. [Vie culturelle des minorités] Les personnes appartenant à des minorités ethniques ont le droit de maintenir et de faire progresser leur propre vie culturelle avec les autres membres de leur groupe.

    c)   L'arrêt Mahé, [1990] 1 R.c.s. 342, de la Cour suprême du Canada sur l'article 23 de la Charte de 1982.

B)   Il n'y a pas de définition précise du terme "minorité".

    a)   la citoyenneté de l'Etat en question.

La citoyenneté canadienne est requise pour bénéficier de l'article 23 de la Charte.

    b)   et/ou une présence durable sur le territoire national ou une portion de celui-ci ?

La citoyenneté implique, à tout le moins, une présence de trois ans au Canada. Cette présence est obligatoire avant de pouvoir revendiquer le statut de citoyen canadien. Tout citoyen canadien a le droit de demeurer au Canada, d'y entrer ou d'en sortir. Tout citoyen canadien et toute personne ayant le statut de résident permanent au Canada ont le droit de se déplacer dans tout le pays, d'établir leur résidence dans toute province et de gagner leur vie dans toute province (Article 6 de la Charte).

C)   Il s'agit des minorités de langues officielles, soit les francophones à l'extérieur du Québec et les anglophones au Québec.

D)   Outre les minorités de langues officielles, la Constitution favorise la promotion du multiculturalisme (article 27 de la Charte).

E)   Elle est envisagée en termes collectifs en ce qui concerne les peuples autochtones et les droits confessionnels. En ce qui concerne les droits linguistiques, le débat n'a pas encore été définitivement tranché par la Cour suprême du Canada. Dans ce dernier cas, il semblerait qu'il s'agit plutôt de droits individuels.

F)   Non.

3. A)   Les tribunaux, notamment la Cour suprême du Canada, interprètent et appliquent notre charte constitutionnelle, c'est-à-dire, la Charte canadienne des droits et libertés et aussi les lois quasi constitutionnelles des droits et libertés qui offrent une protection législative. Ils ont recours, au besoin, aux documents internationaux qui ont été ratifiés par le Canada, notamment le Pacte international relatif aux droits civils et politiques.

B)   Le Canada respecte ses engagements internationaux dans le domaine des droits et libertés. Un cas de jurisprudence très récent, l'arrêt Ballantyne et al. c. Canada, fut décidé sur la base du Pacte international relatif aux droits civils et politiques par le Comité des droits de l'homme des Nations unies. Cette contestation visait une loi québécoise (Loi 178) qui prescrivait l'unilinguisme français en matière d'affichage commercial en interdisant l'usage d'autres langues dont l'anglais. Cette loi brime la liberté d'expression des commerçants, a conclu le Comité.

4. A)   Oui. Le paragraphe 15(1) de la Charte consacre les droits à l'égalité. Il se lit comme suit :

15.   (1)   La Loi ne fait acceptation de personne et s'applique également à tous, et tous ont droit à la même protection et au même bénéfice de la loi, indépendamment de toute discrimination, notamment des discriminations fondées sur la race, l'origine nationale ou ethnique, la couleur, la religion, le sexe, l'âge ou les déficiences mentales ou physiques.

Nous bénéficions d'une jurisprudence abondante sur cette question. En traitent, notamment, les arrêts suivants : Andrews c. Law Society of British Columbia, [1989] 1 R.C.S. 143 ; Re Workers' Compensation Act, 1983 (T.-N.), [1989] 1 R.C.S. 922 ; R. c. Turpin, [1989] 2 R.C.S. 1296 ; Rudolf Wolff and Co/ Ltd. c.

- 111 -

Canada (P.G.), [1990] 1 R.C.S. 695 ; McKinney c. Université de
Guelph, [1990] 3 R.C.S. 229 ; Stoffman c. Vancouver General
Hospital, [1990] 3 R.C.S. 433 ; Douglas/Kwantlen Faculty
Association c. Douglas College, [1990] 3 R.C.S. 570 ; R. c. Swain,
[1991] 1 R.C.S. 933 ; Tétreault-Gadoury c. Canada (C.E.I.), [1991]
2 R.C.S. 22.

B)   Oui. Au paragraphe 15(2) de la Charte qui se lit comme suit :

15.   (2)   Le paragraphe (1) n'a pas pour effet d'interdire les
lois, programmes ou activités destinés à améliorer la situation
d'individus ou de groupes défavorisés, notamment du fait de leur
race, de leur origine nationale ou ethnique, de leur couleur, de leur
religion, de leur sexe, de leur âge ou de leurs déficiences mentales
ou physiques.

Nous n'avons pas encore de jurisprudence relative au paragraphe
15(2) de la Charte. Toutefois, on doit noter que la Cour suprême du
Canada a imposé des quotas en matière d'embauche au Canadien
National afin d'augmenter le nombre de femmes à l'emploi de cette
compagnie. Les critères d'embauche étaient discriminatoires. Cette
décision est fondée sur la Loi canadienne sur les droits de la
personne (Action Travail des Femmes c. C.N., [1987] 1 R.C.S.
1114).

C)   Oui. C'est principalement le Code criminel qui protège les groupes
minoritaires. Les dispositions qui prohibent la propagande haineuse
ont été jugées constitutionnelles par la Cour suprême du Canada
dans l'arrêt R. c. Keegstra, [1990] 3 R.C.S. 697.

5. A)   La liberté de conscience et de religion est expressément garantie
par l'alinéa 2a) de la Charte canadienne des droits et libertés. Il n'y
a pas de religion d'Etat au Canada. Chacun est libre de pratiquer
la religion de son choix. La liberté de religion implique le droit de
n'avoir aucune religion. Cependant, les droits confessionnels des
catholiques et des protestants sont protégés dans les écoles par
l'article 93 de la Loi constitutionnelle de 1867.

B)   Il existe une jurisprudence peu volumineuse sur les difficultés
rencontrées par les différentes minorités :

- Enseignement :

. Caldwell c. Stuart, [1984] 2 R.C.S. 603 (Professeur catholique dont le contrat de travail n'a pas été renouvelé parce qu'elle a épousé un homme divorcé. La Cour suprême a conclu qu'il n'y avait pas de discrimination car l'observance religieuse était une exigence réelle d'emploi dans cette école confessionnelle catholique).

- Marché du travail :

. Bhinder c. C.N., [1985] 2 R.C.S. 561 (Refus du port du casque protecteur sur les lieux de travail pour des motifs religieux. La Cour suprême a conclu, à la majorité (5-2), qu'il s'agissait d'une exigence réelle d'emploi).

. Commission ontarienne des droits de la personne et O' Malley c. Simpsons-Sears, [1985] 2 R.C.S. 536 (Refus de travailler le jour du Sabbat. Congé refusé par l'employeur. La Cour suprême fut d'avis que l'employeur n'avait pas pris de mesures raisonnables pour s'entendre avec son employée afin de respecter sa liberté de religion).

. Action Travail des Femmes c. C.N., [1987] 1 R.C.S. 1114 (Critères d'embauche discriminatoires à l'égard des femmes. LaCour suprême a imposé des quotas d'embauche afin de remédier à cette discrimination systémique. La Cour a parlé du critère de la masse critique à partir de laquelle l'injustice peut se corriger d'elle-même).

6. A)   Les droits confessionnels des catholiques et des protestants sont protégés par l'article 93 de la Loi constitutionnelle de 1867. L'article 23 de la Charte canadienne des droits et libertés garantit le droit à l'instruction dans la langue de la minorité de langue officielle (français ou anglais).

    B)   Les écoles catholiques et protestantes, aux niveaux primaire et secondaire, sont financées sur les fonds publics, selon la Constitution. Selon les lois, ce financement est assuré à d'autres écoles également.

C)   Le droit prévu à l'article 23 de la Charte pour les minorités de langues officielles s'applique là où le nombre le justifie.

D)   Oui, il y a trois arrêts majeurs de la Cour suprême du Canada sur le sujet :

. Québec Association of Protestant School Boards c. Québec (P.G.), [1984] 2 R.C.S. 66. (L'article 73 de la Charte de la langue française (Loi 101) fut jugé incompatible avec l'article 23 de la Charte canadienne).

. Mahé c. Alberta, [1990] 1 R.C.S. 342 (Portée de l'article 23 de la Charte : il confère le contrôle et la gestion des écoles à la minorité de langue officielle là où le nombre le justifie).

. Renvoi sur la Loi sur l'école publique du Manitoba, [1993] 1 R.C.S. ... (Confirme le jugement Mahé de 1990).

7. A)   Oui, l'article 133 de la Loi constitutionnelle de 1867 et les articles 16 à 22 de la Charte canadienne des droits et libertés. Ces articles se lisent comme suit :

Article 133 :
Dans les chambres du parlement du Canada et les chambres de la législature de Québec, l'usage de la langue française ou de la langue anglaise, dans les débats, sera facultatif ; mais dans la rédaction des archives, procès-verbaux et journaux respectifs de ces chambres, l'usage de ces deux langues sera obligatoire ; et dans toute plaidoirie ou pièce de procédure par-devant les tribunaux ou émanant des tribunaux de Québec, il pourra être fait également usage, à faculté, de l'une ou de l'autre de ces langues.

Les lois du Parlement du Canada et de la législature du Québec devront être imprimées et publiées dans ces deux langues.

16.   (1)   Le français et l'anglais sont les langues officielles du Canada ; ils ont un statut et des droits et privilèges égaux quant à leur usage dans les institutions du Parlement et du gouvernement du Canada.

(2) Le français et l'anglais sont les langues officielles du Nouveau-Brunswick ; ils ont un statut et des droits et privilèges égaux quant à leur usage dans les institutions de la Législature et du gouvernement du Nouveau-Brunswick.

(3) La présente charte ne limite pas le pouvoir du Parlement et des législatures de favoriser la progression vers l'égalité de statut ou d'usage du français et de l'anglais.

16. (1) La communauté linguistique française et la communauté linguistique anglaise du Nouveau-Brunswick ont un statut et des droits et privilèges égaux, notamment le droit à des institutions d'enseignement distinctes et aux institutions culturelles distinctes nécessaires à leur protection et à leur promotion.

(2) Le rôle de la législature et du gouvernement du Nouveau-Brunswick de protéger et de promouvoir le statut, les droits et les privilèges visés au paragraphe (1) est confirmé.

17. (1) Chacun a le droit d'employer le français ou l'anglais dans les débats et travaux du Parlement.

(2) Chacun a le droit d'employer le français ou l'anglais dans les débats et travaux de la Législature du Nouveau-Brunswick.

18. (1) Les lois, les archives, les comptes rendus et les procès-verbaux du Parlement sont imprimés et publiés en français et en anglais, les deux versions des lois ayant également force de loi et celles des autres documents ayant même valeur.

(2) Les lois, les archives, les comptes rendus et les procès-verbaux de la Législature du Nouveau-Brunswick sont imprimés et publiés en français et en anglais, les deux versions des lois ayant également force de loi et celles des autres documents ayant même valeur.

19. (1) Chacun a le droit d'employer le français ou l'anglais dans toutes les affaires dont sont saisis les tribunaux du Nouveau-Brunswick et dans tous les actes de procédure qui en découlent.

20. (1) Le public a, au Canada, droit à l'emploi du français ou de l'anglais pour communiquer avec le siège ou l'administration centrale des institutions du Parlement ou du gouvernement du Canada ou pour en recevoir les services ; il a le même droit à l'égard de tout autre bureau de ces institutions là où, selon le cas:

a) l'emploi du français ou de l'anglais fait l'objet d'une demande importante ;

b) l'emploi du français et de l'anglais se justifie par la vocation du bureau.

(2) Le public a, au Nouveau-Brunswick, droit à l'emploi du français ou de l'anglais pour communiquer avec tout bureau des institutions de la législature ou du gouvernement ou pour en recevoir les services.

21. Les articles 16 à 20 n'ont pas pour effet, en ce qui a trait à la langue française ou anglaise ou à ces deux langues, de porter atteinte aux droits, privilèges ou obligations qui existent ou sont maintenus aux termes d'une autre disposition de la Constitution du Canada.

22. Les articles 16 à 20 n'ont pas pour effet de porter atteinte aux droits et privilèges, antérieurs ou postérieurs à l'entrée en vigueur de la présente charte et découlant de la loi ou de la coutume, des langues autres que le français ou l'anglais.

B) Ces articles se rapportent au bilinguisme législatif, parlementaire et judiciaire. L'article 20 de la Charte permet aux administrés d'utiliser le français ou l'anglais dans leurs communications avec les institutions fédérales et les institutions du Nouveau-Brunswick.

C) Oui, il y a une jurisprudence assez volumineuse concernant ces dispositions : Québec (P.G.) c. Blaikie, [1979] 2 R.C.S. 1016 ; [1981] 1 R.C.S. 313 ; Manitoba (P.G.) c. Forest, [1979] 2 R.C.S. 1032 ; Renvoi sur les droits linguistiques au Manitoba, [1985] 1 R.C.S. 721 ; [1985] 2 r.c.s. 347 ; [1992] 1 r.c.s. 312 ; Bilodeau c. Manitoba (P.G.), [1986] 1 R.C.S. 449 ; Société des Acadiens du Nouveau-Brunswick c. Association of Parents, [1986] 1 R.C.S. 549 ; MacDonald c. Ville de Montréal, [1986] 1 R.C.S. 460 ; R. c.

Mercure, [1988] 1 R.C.S. 234 ; Sinclair c. Québec (P.G.), [1992] 1 R.C.S. 579.

8. Non, pas de façon particulière. L'alinéa 2b) de la Charte canadienne des droits et libertés est de portée générale et d'application globale. Il garantit la liberté de pensée, de croyance, d'opinion et d'expression, y compris la liberté de la presse et des autres moyens de communication.

9. Le droit de la famille (sauf les dispositions de fond en matière de mariage et sauf le divorce) relève de la compétence des provinces. Au Québec, les dispositions pertinentes se trouvent dans le Code civil.

10. A) La liberté d'association est garantie par l'alinéa 2d) de la Charte de 1982. Elle peut être revendiquée par tous. Mais, selon un jugement majoritaire (5-2) de la Cour suprême du Canada, la liberté d'association ne comprend pas le droit de négocier collectivement ni le droit de grève (Re Public Services Employee Relations Act, [1987] 1 R.C.S. 313). Le fédéral et les provinces peuvent réglementer le droit de grève et l'écarter même.

    B) Non.

11. A) Les règles du droit électoral tiennent compte de la présence, un peu partout au Canada, des peuples autochtones. La Loi électorale du Canada autorise certaines exceptions, notamment quant au déroulement du scrutin dans les réserves autochtones.

    B) Les peuples autochtones sont concentrés dans certaines réserves, mais ils sont aussi dispersés un peu partout au Canada.

    C) Non applicable au Canada.

12. A) Non.

    B) -

    C) Non.

13. A)   Non.

    B)   -

14. A)   La Constitution (ou la Loi) envisage-t-elle la protection des "sous-minorités", c'est-à-dire des personnes qui, majoritaires ou non dans l'ensemble du pays, sont dans une position de minorité dans une région déterminée ?

    Oui, l'article 23 de la <u>Charte canadienne des droits et libertés</u> confère le droit à l'instruction dans la langue de la minorité de langue officielle. Les anglophones, bien que majoritaires au Canada, bénéficient de ce droit au Québec car ils y forment la minorité de langue officielle.

    B)   Oui, en ce qui concerne les domaines qui relèvent de l'Etat central. Mais, en ce qui a trait aux domaines qui relèvent des provinces, la protection des minorités varie d'une province à l'autre.

15. Non.

CROATIA

1. A)   The Constitution of the Republic of Croatia ("Narodne novine" (Official Gazette) N° 56/90) does not include a mention of the nature of the population. Article 15 of the Constitution guarantees equal rights to all nations and minorities. Members of all nations and minorities are guaranteed freedom to express their nationality, freedom to use their language and script, as well as cultural autonomy.

   B)   The Croatian state is organised on regional lines. This structure is not justified by ethnic, linguistic or religious heterogeneousness, but rather based on historic development.

   C)   Article 10 of the Constitution obliges Croatia to protect Croatian minorities in other states : neighbouring, European and overseas. There is a Croatian national minority in Italy, Slovenia, Austria, Hungary, Slovakia, Romania, Serbia (Voivodina, Serbia proper, Kosovo) and Montenegro.

2. A)   The term "minority" is used in the Constitution and also in the Constitutional Law on Human Rights and Freedoms and the Rights of National and Ethnic Communities or Minorities in the Republic of Croatia ("Narodne novine" N° 34/92).

   B)   The texts of the Constitution and the Constitutional Law do not include a precise definition of the term "minority". However, the Constitutional Law in Articles 5 to 13 works out in detail the term "cultural autonomy" which includes most of cultural rights, such as : the right to identity, culture, religion, public and private use of language and alphabet and own education; the right to organize their own informative and publishing activities, the right to establish cultural and other societies in order to protect national and cultural identity. Articles 14 to 17 of this Constitutional Law work out in detail the education of members of minorities, Articles 18 to 20 the proportional participation in representational and other bodies of minorities' representatives, while Articles 21 to 57 define the districts (regions) with special self-governing (autonomous) status where the Serbian minority stands for the majority of population. Thus by indirect defining of minority rights, the Constitutional Law also defines the term "minority".

C)   Until the gaining of independence the following minorities (ethnic groups) were recognized in the Republic of Croatia : Italians, Hungarians, Czechs, Slovaks, Ruthenians and Ukrainians. The Constitution of the Republic of Croatia additionally guarantees minority status to the following ethnic communities : Slovenes, Serbians, Moslems, Montenegrins, Macedonians, Germans, Austrians, Romany and Jews.

D)   The Constitutional Law establishes two districts with a special status in which the Serbian minority represents more than 50 % of the population, according to the 1981 census. In these districts the Serbian minority is guaranteed cultural autonomy but also territorial autonomy (this privilege is not given to other minorities living in the Republic of Croatia). See also 11A.

Article 6 Paragraph e) of the Constitutional Law of the Republic of Croatia guarantees the members of all national or ethnic communities "the right to decide to which ethnic and national community or minority a citizen wishes to belong, and to exercise all the rights related to this choice, either individually or in association with other persons."

E)   The problems associated with minorities are viewed by the Republic of Croatia both in collective and individual term (as persons belonging to minorities).

F)   No, it cannot. Article 6 Paragraph d) of the Constitutional Law of the Republic of Croatia guarantees the members of all national or ethnic minorities "the protection of equality in participating in public affairs, e.g. the right to political and economic freedoms in social sphere, access to media, and in educational and cultural matters in general."

3. A)   In the Republic of Croatia the following multilateral international instruments relating to the protection of minorities are applied: the United Nations Charter; the Universal Declaration of Human

Rights; the International Covenant on Economic, Social and Cultural Rights; the International Covenant on Civil and Political Rights; the Final Act of the Conference on Security and Co-operation in Europe; the Charter of Paris for a New Europe and other CSCE documents (especially the Document of the Copenhagen CSCE Meeting on the Human Dimension, the Document of the Moscow CSCE Meeting on Human Dimension), the Principles of the Council of Europe Convention on the Protection of Human Rights and Basic Freedoms and its Protocols; the International Convention on the Elimination of All Forms of Racial Discrimination; the Convention on the Prevention and Punishment of the Crime of Genocide; the Convention on the Rights of the Child.

They are either incorporated in the domestic legislation or can be directly applied by the courts (and in that case have priority over national laws).

B)   Yes. By recognizing these international instruments the Constitutional Court of the Republic of Croatia has made a decision by which it guarantees the Serbian minority the proportional representation in the Parliament and Government.

4. A)   In compliance with Article 14 of the Constitution of the Republic of Croatia, the Constitutional principle of equality does not refer only to non-discrimination on the grounds of membership of a minority, since it states that all are equal before the law and all enjoy all rights regardless of national or social origin, property, education or other characteristics. According to the data gathered by the Croatian National Statistics Bureau and Public Attorney's Office, so far there have been no court decisions regarding cases of discrimination on the grounds of membership of a minority.

B)   In compliance with Article 4 Paragraph 1 of the Constitutional Law, the Republic of Croatia assists in the development of relations between ethnic and national communities or minorities with the nationality of their parent country in order to promote their national, cultural and language development.

In compliance with Article 13, the districts where the members of ethnic and national communities or minorities represent the majority of the population have a special status and will adopt their status in compliance with this Law.

Pursuant to Article 15 Paragraph 4 of the Constitutional Law, in towns and populated areas outside the territories of special-status districts in order to protect collective rights of indigenous ethnic and national communities or minorities, steps for special protection for taking part in public affairs shall be taken, as well as in education, culture, spiritual and religious life and in access to public media regardless of their share in total population.

In compliance with Article 43 Paragraph 2 of the Constitutional Law, in special- status districts, a special police administration shall be established and it will perform all the duties regarding the protection of public order an peace and the territory of special-status districts; the duties regarding the security of traffic, keeping of the republic records as well as issuing certificates and transcripts from these records and other internal affairs assigned to it by law.

C) In compliance with Article 14 of the Constitution of the Republic of Croatia, every citizen enjoys all rights and freedoms, regardless of race, colour, sex, language, religion, political or other opinion, national or social origin, property, birth, education, social status or other characteristics all are equal before the law.

Pursuant to Article 39 of the Constitution, any call for or incitement to war, or resort to violence, national, racial or religious hatred, or any form of intolerance shall be prohibited and punishable.

In accordance with Article 2 Paragraph j) of the Constitutional Law, the Republic of Croatia recognizes and protects all rights provided by the international instruments from Article 1 of this Law, depending only on the exceptions and restrictions enumerated in those instruments, without any discrimination based on race, colour, language, religion, political and other beliefs, national and social background, cultivating links with a national minority, property, status, achieved by birth or otherwise (Articles 14 and 17, Paragraph 3 of the Constitution).

5. A) In compliance with Article 41 of the Constitution, religious communities are free, in conformity with law, to publicly perform religious services, open their own schools, teaching establishments and other institutions.

Religious communities in Croatia run 50 kindergartens, eight publicly recognized and one unrecognized high school, two Universities and six other schools. So far religious communities have not opened primary schools, although there are legal possibilities for that. The largest religious schools are: Archiepiscopal Grammar School in Zagreb; Archiepiscopal Grammar Schools in Split and Zadar; Franciscan Grammar School at Sinj; Roman Catholic Theological Faculty in Zagreb; Theological College in Split; Theological College at Makarska; Evangelical High School in Osijek.

B) There are no decisions by national or international courts illustrating the difficulties encountered by religious or any other groups holding minority beliefs.

6. A) The Constitutional Law in Articles 14 through 17 contains provisions which protect minorities'rights in educational fields.

In compliance with Article 14 of the Constitutional Law, members of ethnic and national communities or minorities living in the Republic of Croatia are educated in kindergartens and schools in their own language and alphabet, with programs adequately presenting their history, culture and science if such a wish is expressed.

In accordance with Article 15 Paragraph 1 of the same Law, in towns and other areas outside the special-status districts (Article 21) where national and ethnic communities represent a relative majority of the population, and if the number of students allows it, separate educational institutions or school departments will be established with classes held in the language and alphabet of their particular national or ethnic community or minority, if such a wish is expressed.

Pursuant to Article 16 of the Constitutional Law, the Republic of Croatia provides adequate funding for the realization of the programmes enumerated in Article 14 of this Law.

In compliance with Article 17 of the same Law, members of national or ethnic communities may run private kindergartens, schools and other educational institutions.

B)C) Pursuant to Article 7 of the Law on Elementary Education of the Republic of Croatia, elementary education of members of minorities is provided in compliance with this Law and its provisions until a new law be adopted.

In accordance with Article 5 of the Law on Secondary Education (1992), secondary education of members of ethnic and national communities or minorities is provided in compliance with the provisions of the Constitutional Law on Human Rights and Freedoms and the Rights of National and Ethnic Communities or Minorities in the Republic of Croatia, as well as in compliance with the provisions of this Law and other laws and regulations providing for their rights.

In accordance with the existing legal provisions, there are no legal impediments for members of the minorities in Croatia to be educated in their mother tongue from primary school to the University.

Some minorities, e.g. Ruthenians, Ukrainians and Slovaks have organized education in their mother tongues only at primary school level, while Czechs and Hungarians have organized kindergartens, primary and high schools in their mother tongues. The Italian minority has kindergartens in its mother tongue and all school subjects are taught in their mother tongue, from kindergarten to the University.

In the special-status districts where Serbs are in majority, (the Constitutional Law gives such a status to the towns of Glina and Knin), in compliance with Article 11 of the same Law the members of the Serbian minority are educated, if such a wish is expressed, in kindergartens and schools in their language and alphabet with programmes adequately presenting their history, culture and science.

D) The above mentioned provisions have not given rise to any decisions by national or international courts.

7. A) The Constitutional Law of the Republic of Croatia contains provisions relating to the protection of minority languages. In compliance with Article 7, members of all ethnic or national communities or minorities are entitled to the free use of their language and alphabet, both publicly and privately.

In accordance with Article 12 Paragraph 2 of the Constitution of the Republic of Croatia, in individual local units another language and the Cyrillic or some other script may, along with the Croatian language ant the Latin script, be introduced under the conditions stipulated by law.

B) In compliance with the Constitution and the Constitutional Law on Human Rights and Freedoms and the Rights of National and Ethnic Communities or Minorities in the Republic of Croatia there is no difference between official and private use of the minority languages in the broad sense.

C) The mentioned provisions have not given rise to any decisions by national or international courts.

8. In compliance with Article 4 Paragraph 2 of the Constitutional Law, ethnic and national communities or minorities have the right to self-organization and association in order to realize their national or other rights in compliance with the Constitution and this Law.

In accordance with Article 10 of the Constitutional Law, members of national or ethnic communities are free to organize informative and publishing activities in their native language and alphabet. In accordance with Article 11 of same Law they are free to found cultural and other societies aimed at preserving their national and cultural identity. In compliance with Article 11 of the Constitutional Law, members of national and ethnic communities are free to found cultural and other societies aimed at preserving their national and cultural identity. These societies are autonomous and the Republic of Croatia and local self-governing bodies give financial support in accordance with their financial resources.

In compliance with Article 43 of the Constitution of the Republic of Croatia, citizens are guaranteed the right to free association for the purposes of protection of their interests or promotion of social, economic, political, national, cultural and other convictions and objectives.

9.   With the exception mentioned under 2D, neither the Constitution nor the Constitutional Law require the application of any specific legal rules to certain minorities.

10. A) The right of association of persons belonging to minorities extends beyond national borders and is not limited in any way.

   B) Organization and activities of political parties in the Republic of Croatia are provided for in the Law on Political Organizations (1990).

11. A) The presence of minorities has had repercussions on the provisions of the Constitutional Law on Human Rights and Freedoms and the Rights of National and Ethnic Communities or Minorities in the Republic of Croatia as well as on the Electoral Law.

   Article 18 of the Constitutional Law in Chapter IV. Proportional Participation in Representational and Other Bodies states: "Members of national and ethnic communities or minorities representing more than 8 % of the population of the Republic of Croatia are entitled to be proportionally represented in the Croatian Parliament and its Government as well as in the supreme judicial bodies.

   Members of national and ethnic communities or minorities whose share in the population of the Republic of Croatia is below 8 % are entitled to elect a total of five representatives to the House of Representatives of the Croatian Parliament."

   B) The provisions of the Constitutional Law on Human Rights and Freedoms and the Rights of National and Ethnic Communities or Minorities in the Republic of Croatia as well as the Electoral Law apply to Serbs as the largest minority but also to all other minorities in the Republic of Croatia. The provisions of the mentioned laws apply to the minorities on the entire territory of the Republic of Croatia.

C) The presence of the Serbian minority in the Republic of Croatia has had an effect on establishing districts (regions) with special self-governing (autonomous) status in which the members of this minority make relative or absolute majority according to the 1981 census. The establishment of the autonomous districts of Knin and Glina favours the autonomy of this minority in the Republic of Croatia.

12. A) By adopting the Constitutional Law on Human Rights and Freedoms and the Rights of National and Ethnic Communities or Minorities in the Republic of Croatia special measures have been taken for the integration of minorities in political life.

Article 18 of the same Law states that "members of national and ethnic communities or minorities representing more than 8 % of the population of the Republic of Croatia are entitled to being proportionally represented in the Croatian Parliament and its Government as well as in the supreme judicial bodies."

In accordance with the same Article of the Constitutional Law "representation of national and ethnic communities or minorities from Paragraph 1 of this Article in other government bodies of the Republic of Croatia is stipulated by the law on the organization of state authorities."

Article 19 of the Constitutional Law proclaims that: "members of national and ethnic communities or minorities are entitled to be represented in the bodies of local self-government in proportion to their share in the total population of a particular local self-governing unit.

Special measures for the integration of minorities into political life are also provided in Article 20 of the Constitutional Law: "In order to apply the provisions of this Law on the rights of ethnic and national communities or minorities regarding culture, education, access to media and to realize their proportional representation in public agencies and other institutions in these areas, the Government of the Republic of Croatia has its Office for Inter-Ethnic Relations."

B)   In compliance with Article 10 of the Law on Election of Representatives in the Croatian Parliament (Sabor), members of the Serbian minority representing more than 8 % of the population of the Republic of Croatia are entitled to be represented in the Parliament according to what proportion of the overall population they constitute (proportionally to their participation in the overall population). Members of other minorities who make up less than 8% of the population of the Republic of Croatia ("whose participation in the population of the Republic of Croatia is below 8 %) are entitled to elect at least five representatives in the House of Representatives of the Croatian Parliament, and one of them has to be elected by the members of each minority: Hungarian, Italian, Czech and Slovakian, as well as Ruthenian, Ukrainian, German and Austrian."

Article 26 of the same Law provides another special measure for the participation of minorities in political life: "If the representation of ethnic and national communities, as required under Article 10 hereof, is not reached in the elections for the representatives in the House of Representatives, the number of representatives in the House of Representatives shall be increased up to the number which is needed for the required representation to be attained, and the members of a certain community or minority, who have been put on state list but have not been elected, shall be considered as elected representatives in the order corresponding to the proportional success of each individual list in the elections."

According to the statutes of the ex-municipalities in compliance with the Constitution of the former SFR Yugoslavia which are still applied until new statutes are adopted, minorities in the Republic of Croatia, especially Italians in Istria, enjoy political minorities' rights.

13. A)   The law does not impose a special duty of loyalty on persons belonging to minorities.

14. A)   The Constitution and the Constitutional Law of the Republic of Croatia do not provide for the protection of "sub-minorities".

15.   In compliance with Article 58 of the Constitutional Law, the Republic of Croatia shall conclude an international agreement for the supervision of the implementation of the provisions of this Law on special-status districts. An international body, established on the basis of the agreement from Paragraph 1 of this Article shall supervise the implementation of the provisions about the special-status districts.

Pursuant to Article 60 of the same Law, every citizen of the Republic of Croatia can appeal to the Court for Human Rights, after having used all available internal legal remedies for cases in the field of human rights and freedoms and the rights and status of ethnic and national communities or minorities, which are guaranteed by the Constitution of the Republic of Croatia, this Law and other laws which are in force in the Republic of Croatia.

Until the establishment of the Court of Human Rights by the convention between all the states created on the territory of the former SFR Yugoslavia, the Provisional Court of Human Rights is established.

CYPRUS

1. A)   The Cyprus Constitution is based on the concept of bi-communality and only two Communities (the Greek and the Turkish) are recognised; all other citizens have to opt to belong to one of these two Communities. The relevant Article of the Constitution (Article 2) is worded as follows:

"For the purposes of this Constitution -

(1)   the Greek Community comprises all citizens of the Republic who are of Greek origin and whose mother tongue is Greek or who share the Greek cultural traditions or who are members of the Greek-Orthodox Church;

(2)   the Turkish Community comprises all citizens of the Republic who are of Turkish origin and whose mother tongue is Turkish or who share the Turkish cultural traditions or who are Moslems;

(3)   citizens of the Republic who do not come within the provisions of paragraph (1) or (2) of this Article shall, within three months of the date of the coming into operation of this Constitution, opt to belong to either the Greek or the Turkish Community as individuals, but if they belong to a religious group, shall so opt as a religious group and upon such option they shall be deemed to be members of such Community:

Provided that any citizen of the Republic who belongs to such a religious group may choose not to abide by the option of such group and by a written and signed declaration submitted within one month of the date of such option to the appropriate officer of the Republic and to the Presidents of the Greek and the Turkish Communal Chambers opt to belong to the Community other than that to which such group shall be deemed to belong:

Provided further that if an option of such religious group is not accepted on the ground that its members are below the requisite number any member of such group may within one month of the date of the refusal of acceptance of such option opt in the aforesaid manner as an individual to which Community he would like to belong.

For the purposes of this paragraph a "religious group" means a group of persons ordinarily resident in Cyprus professing the same religion and either belonging to the same rite or being subject to the same jurisdiction thereof the number of whom, on the date of the coming into operation of this Constitution, exceeds one thousand out of which at least five hundred become on such date citizens of the Republic;

(4)   a person who becomes a citizen of the Republic at any time after three months of the date of the coming into operation of this Constitution shall exercise the option provided in paragraph (3) of this Article within three months of the date of his so becoming a citizen;

(5)   a Greek or a Turkish citizen of the Republic who comes within the provisions of paragraph (1) or (2) of this Article may cease to belong to the Community of which he is a member and belong to the other Community upon:

> (a)   a written and signed declaration by such citizen to the effect that he desires such change, submitted to the appropriate officer of the Republic and to the Presidents of the Greek and the Turkish Communal Chambers;

> (b)   the appoval of the Communal Chamber of such other Community;

(6)   any individual or any religious group deemed to belong to either the Greek or the Turkish Community under the provisions of paragraph (3) of this Article may cease to belong to such Community and be deemed to belong to the other Community upon:

(a) a written and signed declaration by such individual or religious group to the effect that such change is desired, submitted to the appropriate officer of the Republic and to the Presidents of the Greek and the Turkish Communal Chambers;

(b) the approval of the Communal Chamber of such other Community;

(7) (a) a married woman shall belong to the Community to which her husband belongs;

(b) a male or female child under the age of twenty-one who is not married shall belong to the Community to which is or her father belongs, or, if the father is unknown and he or she has not been adopted, to the Community to which is or her mother belongs."

B) Not applicable.

C) No.

2. A) The notion of bi-communality excludes in practice the notion of minority.

B) Not applicable.

C) Not applicable.

D) Not applicable.

E) Not applicable.

F) Not applicable.

3. A) All such international instruments, after being ratified by law, are of superior force to municipal legislation.

B) Not regarding minorities.

4. A)   There is no direct reference, but there is sufficient indirect reference since Article 28.2 of the Constitution excludes discrimination on the ground, *inter alia*, of community, race, religion, language, national descent and colour.

    B)   No.

    C)   No such direct legislative provisions exist.

5. A)   The relevant Article of the Constitution (Article 18) is worded as follows:

    "1.   Every person has the right to freedom of thought, conscience and religion.

    2.   All religions whose doctrines or rites are not secret are free.

    3.   All religions are equal before the law. Without prejudice to the competence of the Communal Chambers under this Constitution, no legislative, executive or administrative act of the Republic shall discriminate against any religious institution or religion.

    4.   Every person is free and has the right to profess his faith and to manifest his religion or belief, in worship, teaching, practice or observance, either individually or collectively, in private or in public, and to change his religion or belief.

    5.   The use of physical or moral compulsion for the purpose of making a person change or preventing him from changing his religion is prohibited.

    6.   Freedom to manifest one's religion or belief shall be subject only to such limitations as are prescribed by law and are necessary in the interests of the security of the Republic or the constitutional order or the public safety or the public order or the public health or the public morals or for the protection of the rights and liberties guaranteed by this Constitution to any person.

7.   Until a person attains the age of sixteen the decision as to the religion to be professed by him shall be taken by the person having the lawful guardianship of such person.

8.   No person shall be compelled to pay any tax or duty the proceeds of which are specially allocated in whole or in part for the purposes of a religion other than his own."

B)   The only instances relate to the military obligations and education of Jehova's Witnesses.

6. A)   None as such.

B)   Not applicable.

C)   Not applicable.

D)   Not applicable.

7. A)   The relevant Article of the Constitution (Article 3) is worded as follows:

"1.   The official languages of the Republic are Greek and Turkish.

2.   Legislative, executive and administrative acts and documents shall be drawn up in both official languages and shall, where under the express provisions of this Constitution promulgation is required, be promulgated by publication in the official Gazette of the Republic in both official languages.

3.   Administrative or other official documents addressed to a Greek or a Turk shall be drawn up in the Greek or the Turkish language respectively.

4.   Judicial proceedings shall be conducted or made and judgments shall be drawn up in the Greek language if the parties are Greek, in the Turkish language if the parties are Turkish, and in both the Greek and the Turkish languages if the parties are Greek and Turkish. The official language or languages to be used

for such purposes in all other cases shall be specified by the Rules of Court made by the High Court under Article 163.

5.   Any text in the official Gazette of the Republic shall be published in both official languages in the same issue.

6.   (1)   Any difference between the Greek and the Turkish texts of any legislative, executive or administrative act or document published in the official Gazette of the Republic, shall be resolved by a competent court.

(2)   The prevailing text of any law or decision of a Communal Chamber published in the official Gazette of the Republic shall be that of the language of the Communal Chamber concerned.

(3)   Where any difference arises between the Greek and the Turkish texts of an executive or administrative act or document which, though not published in the official Gazette of the Republic, has otherwise been published, a statement by the Minister or any other authority concerned as to which text should prevail or which should be the correct text shall be final and conclusive.

(4)   A competent court may grant such remedies as it may deem just in any case of a difference in the texts as aforesaid.

7.   The two official languages shall be used on coins, currency notes and stamps.

8.   Every person shall have the right to address himself to the authorities of the Republic in either of the official languages."

B)   See the above-mentioned Article 3 of the Constitution.

C)   In the recent case of Hassanein (Admiralty Case 369/83) the Supreme Court ruled on 20 April 1994 that a Cypriot citizen who happened to be a British expatriate and could not speak fluently either Greek or Turkish could not address the Court in English with simultaneous translation into Greek by a translator provided at his own expense.

8.   No.

9.   There is provision for Family Courts for members of the Greek Orthodox Church and of other religious groups (Maronites, Armenians and Latins) who have opted to join the Greek Community.

10. A)   No relevant provision exists.

    B)   No.

11. A)   One representative from each religious group (Maronites, Armenians and Latins) is elected to the House of Representatives with the right to be heard but without a vote.

    B)   The religious groups of Maronites, Armenians and Latins are scattered throughout Cyprus.

    C)   No.

12. A)   No, other than what is stated in answer to question 11A).

    B)   Not applicable.

    C)   No.

13. A)   Not in addition to their duties as citizens.

    B)   Not applicable.

14. A)   No.

    B)   Not applicable.

15.   No.

DENMARK

1. A)   No.

    B)   The State of Denmark is not organised on a federal basis. The fact that Denmark consists of a number of counties and municipalities is due to administrative and democratic reasons only.

    C)   No.

2. A)   a)   According to Article 87 of the Constitution, citizens of Iceland who enjoy equal rights with citizens of Denmark under the Danish-Icelandic Union (Abolition), etc. Act, shall continue to enjoy the rights attached to Danish citizenship under the provisions of the Constitution.

          b)   No. Act No. 137 of March 23 , 1948 on home rule for the Faroe Islands, and Act No. 577 November 29, 1978 on home rule for Greenland, has granted these parts of the Kingdom of Denmark a considerable independence in relation to the authorities of the Realm. According to Article 10, section 1, of the Faroe Islands home rule Act a "Faroe" is defined as a Danish citizen domiciled in the Faroe Islands. According to Article 10, section 2, of the Act, it is prohibited to make distinction between the Faroes and other Danish citizens in legislation or administration.

          Article 1 of the Greenland home rule Act recognizes Greenland as a distinct society within the Kingdom of Denmark. The Act uses the term, "permanent residents of Greenland" which would include all Danish citizens; Inuits and others, permanently residing in Greenland.

          c)   -

    B)   See A) a).

C)   See A) a).

D)   The Constitution does not require recognition of certain minorities (or all minorities) by the State. The Constitution does not explicitly permit recognition of certain minorities; however, the Constitution does not exclude such recognition by law, should the Parliament wish to do so.

E)   -

F)   No.

3. A)   Denmark has - among other international instruments on the protection of human rights - acceded to the Elimination of all forms of Racial Discrimination and to the European Convention on the Protection of Human Rights. In 1992, the Parliament passed the "European Convention on the Protection of Human Rights Act" (Act No. 285 of April 29, 1992). According to this Act, the Convention has the same status as a law.

    B)   See A)

4. A)   -

    B)   No.

    C)   Yes. Article 266 b of the Penal Code (copy enclosed), and Consolidation Act No. 626 of September 9, 1987 on the Prohibition against Racial Discrimination etc.

5. A)   The civil liberties of the Constitution include in Articles 67, 68 and 70 religious liberty. According to Article 67, the citizens shall be entitled to form, congregations for the worship of God in a manner consistent with their convictions, provided that nothing at variance with good morals or public order shall be taught or done. According to Article 68, no one shall be liable to make personal contributions to any denomination other than the one to which he adheres. According to Article 70, no person shall for reasons of his creed or descent be deprived of access to complement enjoyment of his civic and political rights, nor shall he for such reasons evade compliance with any common civic duty.

B)   -

6. A)   According to Article 76 of the Constitution, all children of school age shall be entitled to free instruction in the elementary schools. Parents or guardians who themselves arrange for their children or wards receiving instruction equal to the elementary school standard, shall not be obliged to have their children or wards taught in elementary school. This provision applies for all children in Denmark, including children belonging to an ethnic or religious minority. The law furthermore contains provisions of importance to minorities, for example Article 5 of the Elementary School Act, according to which a child on request by his parents shall be excused from taking part in the school's teaching in Christianity.

   B)   -

   C)   Order No. 583 of November 20, 1984 on the elementary school's teaching of pupils of a foreign language, provides for the study of the minority language. The law does not explicitly provide for schooling in the minority language; but as mentioned under A), parents are free to arrange for their children's instruction themselves, provided that the elementary school standard is met.

   D)   No.

7. A)   According to the Faroe Islands Home Rule Act and the Greenland Home Rule Act, mentioned in re 2. A) b) above, the languages of the Faroe Islands and Greenland are recognized as the main languages.

   B)   -

   C)   No.

8.   No.

9.   No.

10. A)   According to Article 78 of the Constitution the citizens shall be entitled without previous permission to form associations for any

lawful purpose. This right also applies to persons belonging to minorities.

B) No.

11. A) The Parliament consists of one assembly of 179 members, of whom, 2 members are elected on the Faroe Islands, and 2 members in Greenland (Article 28 of the Constitution). Any Danish citizen, including those belonging to a minority, whose permanent residence is in the Realm, and who has the age qualification (18 years or more), has the right to vote at Parliament elections, provided that he or she has not been declared incapable of conducting his or her own affairs (Article 29 of the Constitution). Any person who has the right to vote at Parliament elections shall be eligible for membership at the Parliament, unless the person in question has been convicted of an act which in the eyes of the public makes him, or her unworthy of being a member of Parliament. A person who is not a Danish citizen can vote and be elected at local elections, provided that he or she has been a permanent resident in the country for more than two years.

B) See A).

C) No.

12. A) The right of non-danish citizens to vote and be elected at local elections is mentioned under A).

B) -

C) No.

13. A) No.

B) -

14. A) No.

B) -

15. No.

FINLAND

1. A)   No

   B)   Sec. 51, para. 3 of the Constitution Act of Finland: "In any rearrangement of the boundaries of administrative districts, care shall be taken that, where circumstances permit, the districts are monolingual, either Finnish-speaking or Swedish-speaking, or that their linguistic minorities are as small as possible."

   The self-Government of the Province of Åland (Aaland Islands) is based on the predominantly Swedish language and distinct culture of the population.

   C)   No.

2. A)   a)   The term "minority" is only used in sec. 51, referred to above (2B). Sec. 14 of the Constitution Act uses the expression "Finnish-speaking and Swedish-speaking populations" (the Finnish-speaking being in majority and the Swedish-speaking in minority in the Country).

   The Parliament Act (which is also a constitutional enactment) grants the Sámi a right to be heard in the parliamentary procedure in a matter of special consequence to them.

   b)   The Language Act uses the terms "language of the majority" and "language of the minority", referring to the Finnish-speaking or Swedish-speaking majority and minority, as the case may be, in the administrative district or municipality in question. The Act also uses the term "of the other language", referring to the minority language in the municipality. Chapter 13 (On crimes against humanity) of the Penal Code uses the expression "racial group, group of a national or ethnic origin, or religious group". The anti-discrimination provisions in the Employment Contracts Act and in the Civil Service Act mention, i.a., race and origin as prohibited grounds of discrimination.

The Act on the Use of the Sámi Language at the Authorities, 1991 uses the Finnish and Swedish equivalents of the term "Sámi" (denoting a Sámi person, a Lapp). The Act on the Improvement of the Housing Conditions of the Gypsy Population, 1975 uses the Finnish and Swedish equivalents (now out of use) of the term "Gypsy" (denoting a person belonging to the Roman population). (The 1975 Act is no more in force, but some of its provisions are still applied to housing projects effected under it.).

c)   Case law has not been studied to answer this question.

B)   The Sámi are defined in sec. 2 of the Act on the Use of the Sámi Language at the Authorities as follows: A Sámi is any person who considers himself to be a Sámi, provided that either he himself or any of his parents or grandparents learned the Sámi language as his first language. The definition implies neither Finnish citizenship nor a lasting presence in Finland or any part of it. The Gypsies were defined in sec. 1 of the Act on the Improvement of the Housing Conditions of the Gypsy Population as follows: A Gypsy is a person who considers himself to be a Gypsy, except when it is evident that he is not a Gypsy, as well as the spouse of such a person and his children living in the same household. This definition did not imply Finnish citizenship; but benefits under the Act could only be granted to resident persons.

The autonomous province of Åland has its own "citizens", i.e. Finnish citizens possessing the home region right of the province. The home region right was originally acquired by any Finnish citizen who was a resident of Åland on 1 January 1952 and either had been such a resident continuously for at least five years or could complete the five years' requirement afterwards. Besides such original possessors of the home region right and children of persons possessing the home region right, the home region right can only be acquired by "naturalization" in the province: it can be granted to Finnish citizens by the provincial authorities, in general only to persons who have resided in the province for at least five years and who have a fair command of the Swedish language.

C)   The constitutional provisions as well as the provisions of the Language Act refer to the two "constitutional" language groups of Finland: the Finnish-speaking population (in majority in the country as a whole, but in minority in some regions) and the Swedish-speaking population (in minority in the country, but in majority in some regions). The Sámi are a linguistic and ethnic minority. The Roman (Gypsies) are a distinct ethnic minority, whose own language is no more much in use. The predominantly Swedish-speaking population of the province of Åland forms itself a minority within the entire Swedish-speaking population (minority) of Finland, from which it is distinguished on the basis of the (insular) region where it lives (and on the basis of the home region right already referred to). As to the minorities protected by the anti-discrimination provisions of the Penal Code, the Employment Contracts Act and the Civil Service Act, see point 2 A b, supra.

D) There is no recognition procedure for minorities (except for the granting of the home region right in the Province of Åland, already mentioned). As to the Sámi and Roman, see above. The mother tongue of any person is entered to the Population Register according to his own (or his guardian's) notice. Membership of a minority cannot be imposed on any one.

E) The minorities are also viewed in collective terms. The Sámi population has an elected official representative body, and the Swedish-speaking population has an elected semi-official and state-subsidized representative body.

F) In cases where the acquisition of Finnish nationality depends on discretion, knowledge of the Finnish or Swedish language or Finnish or Swedish related ethnic origin may be considered. Membership of a minority can have no effect on the loss of Finnish nationality. Nor can the membership of a minority have any effect on the use of political rights, except at the elections to the bodies representing the minorities, such as the provincial legislature of Åland (where the home region right is a prerequisite) and the Sámi delegation.

3. A) The contents of any treaty binding, or intended to bind, Finland internationally are incorporated in Finnish domestic law by means of a specific statute to that effect. In so far as the treaty provisions to be incorporated are self-executing, the incorporating statute quite often only consists of a simple reference to the treaty itself.

If the statute incorporating any treaty provisions in domestic legislation has been expressly adopted (with a majority of two thirds of votes cast) as an exception to the Constitution, its takes precedence over the Constitution. All treaty provisions incorporated with an Act of Parliament have the same standing as other parliamentary legislation, prevailing over earlier statutes but liable to be affected by later Acts of Parliament.

B)   The self-government of the Province of Åland, based originally on a internal Finnish enactment of 1920, was enlarged with an enactment of 1922, based on an international instrument concluded under the auspices of the League of Nations.

4. A)   According to sec. 5 of the Constitution Act; all Finnish citizens shall be equal before the law. No specific reference to minorities is included in this provision. However, according to sec. 14, para. 3, the cultural and economic needs of the Finnish-speaking and the Swedish-speaking populations shall be met by the State on the same basis.

B)   The position of the Swedish language in the province of Åland as well as the specific rights of the population of the province (e.g. to own land) are protected by the Act on the Self-Government of Åland, with a Constitutional standing.

According to a specific enactment, Jehovah's Witnesses are in general exempted from compulsory military service as well as from the civilian service required of other conscientious objectors.

C)   According to chapter 13 (On crimes against humanity) of the Penal Code, already mentioned, genocide and incitement to hatred, directed against any "racial group, group of a national or ethnic origin, or religious group" shall be punished. Likewise, discrimination in shops and restaurants, at public authorities, etc., directed against any customer belonging to such a group shall be punished.

5. A)   According to sec. 8 of the Constitution Act, a Finnish citizen shall have the right, provided that the law or good custom are not infringed, to practice a religion in public or in private, and also the freedom to renounce the religious community to which he belongs

and to join another religious community. According to sec. 9, the rights and obligations of a Finnish citizen shall not depend on which religious community he belongs or wether he belongs to any such community.

B)   No.

6. A)   As to equal provision, according to the Constitution, for the cultural needs of the Finnish-speaking and the Swedish-speaking populations, see 4 A, supra. According to the Act on the Self-Government of Åland, all schools in the province, financed totally or partially by public funds shall have Swedish as the language of instruction, except as far as otherwise provided for by the provincial legislature.
According to the Elementary and Secondary School Acts, there shall be (outside the Province of Åland) Finnish and Swedish schools according to the needs of the population. In case a pupil is capable to participate in instruction in any of the two languages, his custodian has the right to choose the language of instruction. In the Sámi region, instruction is provided in Finnish and at least partially in Sámi, and the custodian of a pupil who is capable to participate in instruction in Finnish and in Sámi has the right to choose the language of instruction.

B)   In addition to these legal requirements, some instruction is for the members of the minorities in question provided of the Roman (Gypsy) language and of the maternal languages-dozens of them-of refugees and other immigrants.

C)   See A) and B), just above. In addition, there are some schools, private but partially subsidized, where the language of instruction is an international language, such as English, French, German or Russian.

D)   No.

7. A)   According to sec. 14 of the Constitution Act, the official languages of the Republic shall be Finnish and Swedish; and the right of a Finnish citizen to use his native language, whether Finnish or Swedish, as a party in proceedings before a court of law or an administrative agency, and to obtain from them documents in that

language, shall be guaranteed by law with care being taken to provide for the rights of the Finnish-speaking and Swedish-speaking populations of the country on the same basis. The official use of the two languages is regulated more in detail in the Language Act.

According to the Act on the Use of the Sámi Language at the Authorities, a Sámi language at the local and regional authorities and courts whose jurisdiction comprises the Sámi region or part of it as well as at the National courts and at several central authorities. A Sámi who is a party in a matter before the said courts and authorities has also the right to have an official Sámi translation appended to all documents which are not originally written in the Sámi language. - The Act on the Procedure at Administrative Authorities, 1982, provides for oral translation from any language to the official language of the matter, and vice versa, especially when the matter has been initiated ex officio. Similar provisions in the Language Decree govern translations in criminal proceedings initiated by an official prosecutor. The Aliens Act, 1991 contains additional provisions as to translations, especially as regards persons seeking asylum.

B) Informative labels on the sales packages of consumption goods shall be in Finnish and in Swedish, except as far as the information is given by means of symbols; however, for goods sold only within unilingual municipalities, information in the language in question is sufficient.

C) There are some Supreme Administrative Court precedents on the use of the National languages (Finnish and Swedish) in relations between administrative authorities and private parties.

8. There are no such particular rules. Broadcasting, also by way of cable networks, is by license only. In the governing body of the National broadcasting company, different social and language groups shall be represented. There is some radio broadcasting in Sámi, and theatre activities, with schooling, for the Roma.

9. According to the Names Act, a forename which otherwise would be illegal can be adopted on the basis of religious custom; and an otherwise illegal forename or surname can be adopted if it

corresponds to the usage in a foreign country to which the person in questions has family, nationality, or other special connections.

10. A) Yes, there are no limitations. Every one, even a foreigner, is entitled to join an association, domestic or foreign. The chairman and at least one half of the board members of a Finnish association must be domiciled in Finland. Exemptions may be granted by the Ministry of Justice; but all board members of a political association must be domiciled in Finland. In order to register an association as a political party, it must have at least, 5,000 supporters who are entitled to vote at general elections.

B) No.

11. A) Even though the parliamentary elections are proportional, with electoral districts electing seven to thirty representatives each, the autonomous Province of Åland forms an electoral district of its own, electing but one representative.

C) The Sámi region, already mentioned, comprises three municipalities and part of a fourth municipality. The Sámi are in majority in only one of the municipalities. (See also point 1 B, supra.)

12. A) The use in Parliament of the two National languages, Finnish and Swedish, translations from one of the languages to the other, etc., are minutiously regulated in the Parliament Act and in the Standing Orders of the Parliament. See also point 2 A as to the right of the Sámi to be heard in the parliamentary procedure.

In the provincial legislature of Åland, all debates are in Swedish.

In the municipal councils and boards of unilingual municipalities, the language of the municipality (Finnish or Swedish) must be used. In bilingual municipalities, any of the two languages may be used, and translated as far as i needed. In the four municipalities in the Sámi region, the same rule applies to the Finnish and Sámi languages.

B) See point 2. E), supra, as to the elected representative bodies of the Sámi population and the Swedish-speaking population. There is also an Advisory committee on Sámi matters, composed of representatives of administrative authorities and the Sámi population, and a corresponding Advisory committee for Roman matters. The Åland Delegation, consisting of the Governor of the Province of Åland as chairman as well as of two members appointed by the National Government and two members elected by the Provincial Legislature, handles and even decides certain matters concerning relations between the National Government and the self-governing Province.

C)   No.

13. A)   No.

14. A)   In order to protect the identity of the Province of Åland against a possible influx of Finnish-speaking immigrants, the rights of the Finnish-speaking minority in the province are restricted, e.g; as to the language of instruction in public schools (see point 6 A, supra). However, in relations with courts of law and State authorities in the province, Finnish language may be used by any Finnish citizen in his own matter, and the court or authority shall furnish such a party with a Finnish translation of any document in the matter (originally drafted in Swedish).

B)   Outside the Province of Åland, the Finnish-speaking population in any municipality with a Swedish-speaking majority is treated like the Swedish-speaking population in any municipality with a Finnish-speaking majority. In the Sámi region, the position of the non-Sámi population is not differentiated according to whether the Sámi are in a particular municipality in majority or not.

15.   No. The CSCE High Commissioner as well as the human rights organs of the Council of Europe and the United Nations are of course available.

GERMANY

1. A) The Basic Law, which is the constitution of the Federal Republic of Germany, does not include any reference to the ethnic, religious or linguistic composition or nature of the people.

It only uses the term "German People" in some provisions (i.e. in the preamble and in art. 1, 20 and 146 referring to the federal state structure, constitutional power and political rights), and defines the status of being a German in art. 116. A special privilege to attain German citizenship is granted to some people belonging to the German people (refugees, expellees of German ethnic origin, their spouses and descendants), a privilege which is due to the specific German post-war situation.

   B) The structure and organisation of Germany as a federation of individual states does not rely on ethnic, religious or linguistic differences of its constituent states, but on the historical diversity of regions as well as on the territorial division of the allied post-war zones of occupation.

   C) There is no article in the constitution providing for the protection of own minorities outside the national territory by the federal state.

2. A) a) The term "minority" is not used in the Basic Law, but is used or previewed in constitutions of some constituent states as residence states of minorities, like in art. 5 of the new constitution of Schleswig-Holstein of 1990 (using the terms "minorities and ethnic groups"), in art. 25 of the constitution of Brandenburg of 1992 (using the term "Sorbish people" to describe an ethnic minority) and in art. 6 of the constitution of Sachsen of 1992, using the term "national minorities".

Art. 40 of the constitution of the former German Democratic Republic of 1974 (repealed in 1990 in the course of the German reunification) used the term "Sorbish nationality".

Proposed articles for the Federal Basic Law as outlined by the constituent states Sachsen, Brandenburg and Niedersachsen for the protection of minorities use the terms "national and ethnic" (Sachsen), "ethnic, cultural, religious or linguistic" (Brandenburg) respectively "cultural minorities" (Niedersachsen).

b)   Federal and state law happen to use the term "minority" or equivalent terms, e.g. sec. 6 of the Federal Electoral Law ("national minorities") and sec. 3 of the Electoral Law of Schleswig-Holstein ("minority"), sec. 58 and 60 Schools Act of Schleswig-Holstein ("minority") and furthermore draft laws in matters of public concern like election, school, media and culture.

N° 14 of the Protocol to art. 35 of the German-German Unification Treaty of 1990 refers to "Sorbish nationality ... culture ... tradition ... people". The Unification Treaty itself uses the term "Sorbes" and "Sorbish population" in Appendix I, which is a constituent part of the treaty. The treaty is part of the German law.

c)   The term "minority" and equivalent terms are used in the constitutional as well as in the other jurisdictional branches. For the Federal Constitutional Court see e.g. below 10.B concerning the representation of minorities by political parties.

B)   Neither the federal or state constitution nor the statutes define the term "minority" or the equivalent terms used in the above mentioned texts.

But the texts imply both German citizenship (expressly stipulated in the proposed article of Sachsen for the Basic Law in view of the protection of minorities) and a lasting presence on the national territory, because the texts were outlined in consideration of the minorities already existing on the German territory, i.e. the Danish, Frisian and Sorbish minorities.

Only the article proposed by Brandenburg as an amendment to the Basic Law does not imply neither citizenship nor a lasting presence, because this proposal intends the protection also of aliens settling on German territory.

C)   The Danish (ca. 50.000 inhabitants), Frisian (ca. 10.000) and
Sorbish (ca. 70.000) minorities represent ethnic, cultural and
linguistic minorities. Only the Danish group forms a national
minority in the sense of an existing patronage state, the Kingdom
of Denmark. These minorities are covered by the texts.

Apart from those there are descendants of Polish industrial workers
immigrating after 1885 as well as some post-war repatriated and
displaced persons (ca. 75.000-200.000 inhabitants). Because of their
far-reaching ethnic, cultural and linguistic integration and
assimilation, and because they do not show intention to maintain
their specific national characteristics, they can be said to have lost
their specific characteristics.

Nevertheless, the German-Polish Treaty of 1991 on good
neighbourhood and peaceful cooperation grants in art. 20 to
German citizens of Polish origin avowing to Polish language,
culture or tradition the same rights as were guaranteed vice versa
to the German minority in Poland, i.e. the right to enjoy
individually or collectively their ethnic, cultural, linguistic and
religious identity, to belong to the minority as a matter of free
choice and not to be subdued to assimilation by public authorities.

Jews as a religious (or cultural) minority (ca. 30.000 inhabitants),
in general, do not appear to consider themselves or to be
considered as a minority, practising their religion or other
conviction in the scope of the fundamental right of freedom of
religion, ideological conviction, confession and worship, art. 4 of
the Basic Law (s. below 5.A), like all other Germans.

Special protection is being claimed by the committee of the
German Sinti and Roma (ca 50.000 inhabitants) concerning ethnic,
cultural, religious and especially linguistic rights. Specific
protection as a minority has not been provided so far by the
German state.

D)   The national law does not require any recognition of minorities by
public authorities.

Belonging to a minority exclusively depends on the individual's
free choice and can never be disposed nor imposed by public

authorities, s. art. 1, 2 Basic Law: guarantee of individual self-determination as part of the human dignity; s. also art. 5 of the constitution of Schleswig-Holstein, sec. 2, n° 1 of the governmental Declarations of Bonn and Copenhagen of 1955 stipulating that individual confession and membership of a minority is not to be denied nor verified. Pursuant to n° 14 of the Protocol to art. 35 of the Unification Treaty belonging to the Sorbish minority is a matter of free choice.

E) The problems associated with minorities and subject to a constitutional or legal (drafted) provision are always viewed in collective terms relating to specific minorities (state constitutions and state law) or to minorities in general (federal laws and the proposed article for the Basic Law relating to minorities).

F) Art. 3 Basic Law prohibits discrimination by public authorities for the reason of belonging to a minority, so that membership must not have any legal effect on the acquisition or loss of nationality.

The right to exercise political rights requires the status of a German, for the right to vote art. 38, 116 Basic Law and dec. 12 Federal Electoral Law. Citizens of member States of the European Community may acquire electoral rights at the level of communities and districts (municipalities) according to European Community Law and art. 28, sec. 1, cl. 3 Basic Law.

3. A) The Federal Republic of Germany is member of the European Convention on Human Rights. Art. 14 ECHR prohibits discrimination for the reason of being part of a minority. The Convention ranks as a federal statute; it has been incorporated into the national law.

The Federal Constitutional Court held that both the convention and the case law of the European Court of Human Rights also have to be regarded as aiding means of interpretation when determining the contents and meaning of national fundamental rights (BVerfGe 74, 358 seqq., 370).

Germany is also member of the International Convention for the prevention and punishment of genocide, which has also been adopted by the national legal system as statute law. Sec 220a of the Federal Criminal Code renders liable for committing genocide.

Appendix I of the bilateral Unification Treaty, which is part of the German law, stipulates for the Sorbish minority an exception from the general procedural rule of German to be the official language. Those exceptions are also drafted for procedural laws of the constituent states.

N° 14 of the Protocol to art. 35 of the Unification Treaty of 1990 guarantees to the Sorbish minority the individual and collective right to avow to the Sorbish tradition and culture and to use the Sorbish language also in public affairs.

The UN Covenant on Civil and Political Rights (CCPR) as well as the Optional Protocol have been accepted by Germany and were incorporated into German national law. Like the ECHR the CCPR ranks as statute law. Art. 27 CCPR refers to the protection of minorities and art. 1 seq. of the Optional Protocol to an appellate procedure in favour of individuals to enforce their rights stipulated in the CCPR.

The governmental Declarations of Bonn and Copenhagen of 1955 regard the protection of the Danish minority in Germany and the German minority in Denmark.

B) State law of Schleswig-Holstein in the domain of church, schools and media implemented the governmental Declarations of Bonn and Copenhagen of 1955.

The above (3. A) mentioned international legal instruments are incorporated into domestic law pursuant to art. 59, sec. 2 of the Basic Law by acts of consent. They possess an equal rank with federal statutes, but not as such with the Federal Constitution.

4. A) Art. 3, sec. 3, Basic Law provides that "no one may be disadvantaged or favoured because of his sex, his parentage, his race, his language, his homeland and origin, his faith or his religious or political opinions".

There has been an abundant constitutional and administrative case law enforcing the civil right of non-discrimination, though, case law specifically relating to minorities cannot be found so far.

B)   The principle of affirmative action promoting minorities by public authorities is not expressly provided for in the Basic Law, but is recognised by the proposed articles for the Basic Law (s. above 2. A) and by the constitutions of Schleswig-Holstein (art. 5), Brandenburg (art. 25) and Sachsen (art. 6). Theses provisions tend to improve the legal status of minorities and prescribe an explicit public obligation to promote them in the fields of language, religion and cultural identity and tradition.

School laws specify the recognition of independent schools teaching in minority languages and provide public allowances especially for them, s. secc. 58, 60 Schools Act Schleswig-Holstein, sec. 2 Schools Act of Sachsen and the draft Schools Act of Brandenburg.

C)   Minorities are protected by federal penal legislation. The Criminal Code restrains incitement to violence against parts of the population, sec. 130, incitement to cruelties, xenophobia and racial hatred and violence, sec. 131, genocide with regard to homicide of national, ethnic or religious minorities, sec. 220a, and also provides punishment for the formation of terrorist associations aiming to commit genocide, sec. 129a.

The provisions mentioned above are designed not only to protect individuals belonging to a minority, but also to protect the minority as a whole, the public peace and the peaceful development of the commonwealth of nations.

5. A)   Art. 4 Basic Law guarantees the freedom of belief, conscience and religious and ideological confession, including the right to conscientious objection. The freedom of religion protects individuals as well as religious communities.

As to the latter, art. 4 implies the collective right to form religious associations, guaranteed by art. 137 of the former Weimar constitution of 1919, as incorporated by art. 140 Basic Law; to that extent it is a special law to the general freedom of association as provided by art. 9 (s. below 10. A).

Art. 4 protects both formation and existence of an inner non-manifested conviction and its manifestation by statement and action.

It also covers the negative rights not to believe and not to confess, fully according to the mentioned positive rights.

Art. 4 contains a fundamental right which can be invoked by persons belonging to a religious minority as well as by the religious community itself. It can be invoked, in the final end, by means of constitutional complaint to the Federal Constitutional Court.

B) The freedom of religion, ideology and confession, as guaranteed by art. 4, ,is an unconditional and unreserved fundamental right. Restrictions can arise only from colliding constitutional rights and institutions; such restriction must result from balancing the both respective constitutional interests. Accordingly, statute law as such cannot put any restriction to art. 4, s. BVerfGE 28, 243 seqq., 260.

Objects of constitutional rank have been e.g. compulsory school attendance (BVerfGE 41, 29 seqq., 48) or the governmental obligation to protect life and physical integrity of individuals against interference from other persons, even when only practising their religion, s. art. 2 Basic Law as a colliding constitutional right (BverfGE 46, 160 seqq., 164).

Although, in general, nobody is obliged to disclose his conviction, he must do so, if he wishes to be dispensed from legal obligations contrary to his conviction like military service or state imposed church tax (BVerfGE 52, 223 seqq., 246).

The right to refuse military service for conscientious objections does not dispense from a non-military service which cannot be refused for conscientious objections, even not with regard to the fact that some medical services might serve as an indirect supply to the armed forces in case of war, s. BVerfGE 19, 135 seqq., 138 and 23, 127 seqq., 132.

Partial, timed, limited or conditioned objections to military service in view of certain arms, enemies, governments, periods of time or territories and other conditions will not be recognised.

Conscientious objections have to be declared unconditionally and unlimitedly, s BVerfGE 12, 45 seqq., 57.

A behaviour which is motivated by religion or conviction, but is contrary to the national legal system, can be penalised in accordance with art. 4 (freedom of religion), if the conviction concerned does not ultimately prescribe this conduct, but leaves a choice of behaving legally, (e.g. religiously inspired polygamy can be a criminal offence according to sec. 171 Criminal Code, s. BVerfGE 32, 98 seqq., 106; 69, 1 seqq., 34).

The freedom of religion and confession is not restricted to religious cults and customs, but also comprises the right to arrange one's every-day life pursuant to one's convictions (BVerfGE 32, 98 seqq., 106), even if they are not conform with occidental perceptions, s. BVerfGE 41, 29 seqq., 50 (e.g. Islamic girls are entitled to be dispensed from physical school education for religious reasons).

6. A)B)   The Basic Law contains several provisions protecting minorities' rights in the field of education as art. 4 (s. above), art. 3 (ban on discrimination for ethnic, religious, linguistic, political or cultural reasons), art. 2 (general freedom of action in its positive and negative form) and art. 7:

It is up to parental power to decide whether or not the child participates in religious instructions, even in public schools; from the age of 14 years on young people decide on their own (Acts on religious instructions to the children).

The establishment of private schools is guaranteed, public authorization is to be granted, if the private school guarantees both an equivalent educational and scientific standard and a financial concept how to fund the teaching staff, art. 7, sec. 4 Basic Law.

The constitutions of the residence states guarantee both protection and promotion of their minorities. Education is regarded to be a component factor of the linguistic and cultural life of minorities, s. art. 5 of the constitution of Schleswig-Holstein, art. 6 of the constitution of Sachsen. Art. 25 of the constitution of Brandenburg refers expressly to an active promotion of private and public schools, which are an active promotion of private and public schools, which are to be promoted with regard to the minority language and culture.

State Schools Acts specify the requirements and extent of authorization and promotion by financial and substantive means, s. e.g; secc. 58, 60, 63 Schools Act of Schleswig-Holstein and sec. 2 Schools Act of Sachsen.

The right to establish a private school (art. 7) also comprises an enforceable right to gain financial support by the state, if the school has been authorized. Nevertheless, public allowances can be claimed only if the private schools in the whole are threatened, not in case of financial needs of individual schools, s. BVerfGE 75, 40 seqq. This jurisdiction will, of course, not apply to special provisions on financial support.

Even the proposed articles to the Basic Law for the amelioration of the legal status of minorities (s. above 2. A) prescribe an explicit public obligation to promote them in the fields of language, religion and cultural identity and tradition.

Private primary schools will be admitted only for religious or confessional purposes, art. 7, sec. 5 Basic Law.

Art. 7 provides no reservation, restrictions could only be derived from conflicting constitutional rights.

Except for a limited federal power concerning framework legislation on tertiary education, art. 75 n° 1a Basic Law, legislative and executive powers over the school law lies with the constituent states pursuant to arts. 70, 30 Basic Law. It has been elaborated by laws of the constituent states including the licence procedure, s. art. 7.

In the Eastern states of Germany three years after reunification most of the laws are just drafted or still in the legislative procedure.

C)   The above mentioned constitutions and existing and drafted Schools Acts provide both for the study of and for the education in the languages of the Danish, Sorbish or Frisian minorities, not only in private schools, but also in public schools in the areas of settlement of the minorities (s. sec. 2 of the Schools Act of Sachsen).

D)   Case Law in the field of education with regard to minorities cannot be found.

7.   The Basic Law does not contain any reference to an official language.

Art. 25 of the constitution of Brandenburg provides for the right of the Sorbish people to use their language in public affairs. This right relates to the protocol referring to art. 35 of the Unification Treaty.

Federal and state law prescribe German as exclusive official language in public affairs, i.e. sec. 184 of the Federal Constitution of Courts Act, sec. 23 of the Federal and Uniform Administrative Procedure Acts and sec. 87 of the Federal Tax Code.

The restriction of German to be the official language is based on a general legal reservation pursuant to art. 2, sec. 1 Basic Law, which refers to the legal system as being in accordance with the constitutional order, s. BVerfGE 6, 32 seqq., 38).

Appendix I to Unification Treaty, which ranks as a federal statute, provides for the right to use the Sorbish minority language in public affairs and therefore constitutes an exception to sec. 184 of the Federal Constitution of Courts Act in favour of the Sorbish minority. This exception, which relates to the language in court only, resulted from the process of unification, which has taken into account that the "Sorbish privilege", set by art. 40 of the former east-German constitution, should be continued.

Art. 25 of the constitution of Brandenburg prescribes bilingual topographical information in the settlement area of the Sorbish minority.

The private use of minority languages is guaranteed as a fundamental right (freedom of language) in art. 1 (right of self-determination as expression of human dignity) and in art. 2 together with art. 1 (the right of personality contains the right to use or not to use a language. S. also art. 3 (ban on discrimination by public authorities for linguistic reasons), art. 5 (freedom of expression and liberty of the press), art. 6 (protection of marriage and family) and art. 7 (right to establish private schools).

8.   State constitutions refer to an active promotion of minorities by affirmative action in cultural matters, which has to be implemented by the public authorities in the administrative process.

9.   Such specific rules cannot be found, neither in federal nor in state law.

10. A)   Art. 9 Basic Law fully recognises the fundamental right of association without specific regard to minorities. This right can be restricted by law according to what is necessary in a democratic society.

The exercise of this right is not limited to the national territory, but covers extensions beyond.

10. B)   Sec. 6 Federal Electoral Law, sec. 3 Electoral Law of Schleswig-Holstein and sec. 7 cl. 6 Electoral Law of Sachsen provide obligatory exceptions from the 5 % - blocking clauses to parliament in favour of minorities. It only facilitates eligibility without guaranteeing a minimum membership in the respective legislative body.

The following case law of the Federal Constitutional Court concerns the status of political parties representing the interests of minorities:

BVerfGE 1 208 seqq., 239: There does not exist a general rule of international public law granting privileges to minorities in view of electoral law. Art. 25 Basic Law, which declares those general rules a constituent part of the federal law, can therefore not be claimed.

BVerfGe 4, 31 seqq., 42: The Basic Law does not engage the federal power to establish general privileges to political parties representing minorities.

BVerfGE 5, 77 seqq., 83: Statutory exceptions to the 5 % - blocking clauses to parliament in favour of political parties representing minorities are conform to the constitution.

BVerfGE 6, 84 seqq., 97: Preferential treatment of those political parties mentioned with regard to popular parties does not violate the principle of equality set by art. 3 and 21 Basic Law.

Furthermore there are no specific rules applying to political parties representing the interests of minorities.

All political parties can be banned only by the Federal Constitutional Court in case of pursuing unconstitutional aims according to art. 21, sec. 2 Basic Law, secs. 32 seqq. Political Parties Act and 43 seqq. Federal Constitutional Court Act.

11. A)   See above 10. on the rules of electoral law.

    B)   The mentioned legal privileges in the domain of federal electoral law are not restricted to certain minorities, but in fact only the Danish minority has succeeded to realise these rights. The above-mentioned rules of the constituent states apply to all members of the Danish minority in Schleswig-Holstein respectively, the Sorbish minority in Sachsen living within the constituent states.

The Danish, Sorbish and Frisian minorities are each factually confined to particular areas of settlement in the states Schleswig-Holstein, Niedersachsen, Brandenburg and Sachsen.

    C)   Electoral, administrative and juridical districts are not shaped with regard to the settlement areas of minorities.

12.   See above 10. and 11.

Art. 26 of the constitution of Brandenburg provides for an active participation of the Sorbish minority in the legislation process, as far as they are concerned.

Consulting and participation bodies in favour of minorities are part of the federal government as well as of the governments of those constituents states concerned:

At the federal level since 1965 a participation body was installed in favour of the Danish minority within the competencies of the Ministry of the Interior; at the state level a consulting body in favour of the Frisian minority and a state agent for minority affairs in Schleswig-Holstein; a body for participation even on legislative affairs is outlined in art. 26 of the constitution of Brandenburg.

c)   The Law does not provide for an official recognition of associations representing the interests of minorities, s.above 10.A.

13.   Members of minorities do not have any special duties.

14.   Sub-minorities in the settlement area of minorities don't have a minority status in the German legal system.

15.   Particular remedies do not exist; the legal remedies are administrative objection, protection in court, right of petition in art. 17 Basic Law an constitutional complaint pursuant to art. 93 Basic Law and secs. 13, 90 seqq. Federal Constitutional Court Act.

GRECE

1. A) Non, il n'existe pas une telle disposition dans la Constitution.

   B) La Grèce est un Etat unitaire.

   C) L'article 108 de la Constitution se rapproche de cette question. Il dispose que "l'Etat veille sur les conditions de vie des Hellènes de l'étranger et sur le maintien de leurs liens avec la mère-patrie. Il veille aussi sur l'instruction ainsi que la promotion sociale et professionnelle des ressortissants hellènes qui travaillent en dehors du territoire national".

2. A) Le terme de minorité ne se trouve pas dans la Constitution. On le trouve cependant dans le Décret-Loi 25/1923 qui a approuvé le Traité de Paix de Lausanne du 24 juillet 1923 (articles 27-45)[1] à propos de la minorité musulmane vivant en Thrace occidentale. D'autres lois particulières traitent également de cette minorité.

   B) Les textes ci-dessus mentionnés ne contiennent pas de définition précise du terme "minorité". Cependant la citoyenneté de l'Etat et la présence durable sur une portion du territoire national sont des éléments implicites de cette définition.

   C) Ces textes visent une minorité de caractère religieux: la minorité musulmane qui est composée de trois groupes distincts (personnes d'origine turque, pomaques, gitans).

   D) Il n'y a pas de telle disposition constitutionnelle ou législative sauf les lois précitées concernant la minorité musulmane. Une personne faisant, par ses traits distinctifs, partie d'une minorité dispose du libre choix d'appartenir ou non à cette minorité et l'autorité publique n'a pas à intervenir en l'occurrence.

---

[1] *Ces articles s'appliquent à la minorité grecque d'Istanbul et des îles Imbros et Tenedos - aujourd'hui malheureusement presque totalement disparue - ainsi qu'à la minorité musulmane de la Thrace occidentale.*

E)   La règle est l'approche individuelle. Cependant, la minorité musulmane jouit, en Grèce, de certains droits collectifs.

F)   Non, la qualité de minoritaire ne joue aucun rôle en ce qui concerne l'acquisition ou la perte de la nationalité. De même, les droits politiques sont les mêmes pour tous les citoyens, sans qu'il soit tenu compte de leur qualité de membre d'un groupe quel qu'il soit.

3. A) Oui, tous les traités approuvés législativement font partie intégrante du droit hellénique interne et ont une force supérieure aux lois internes tant antérieures que postérieures (art. 28 para. 1 de la Constitution).

    B) Oui, il existe des textes législatifs concernant la minorité musulmane, ainsi que des décisions afférentes des tribunaux grecs.

4. A) Non expressément, mais implicitement, l'article 4 de la Constitution consacrant l'égalité pour tous les citoyens sans aucune distinction (voir aussi article 5, para. 2).

    B) Oui, en faveur de la minorité musulmane, par la loi précitée qui a approuvé le Traité de Paix de Lausanne.

    C) Oui, la Loi 927/1979 dispose dans son article 1 para. 1er que: "Quiconque intentionnellement et en public incite verbalement ou par la voie de la presse ... ou par écrit ... la discrimination, la haine ou la violence contre des personnes ou un groupe des personnes, du seul fait de leur origine raciale ou ethnique, est passible d'emprisonnement jusqu'à deux ans ou d'une peine pécunière ..."

5. A) L'article 13 de la Constitution dispose dans ses paragraphes 1 et 2 ce qui suit:

        "1.   La liberté de la conscience religieuse est inviolable. La jouissance des droits individuels et civiques ne dépend pas des convictions religieuses de chacun.

        2.   Toute religion connue est libre; les pratiques de son culte s'exercent sans entrave sous la protection des lois. L'exercice du

culte ne peut pas porter atteinte à l'ordre public ou aux bonnes moeurs. Le prosélytisme est interdit".

Les dispositions ci-dessus n'affectent point le droit de la minorité musulmane à exercer librement sa religion. Par ailleurs, ces dispositions, garantissent la liberté de l'incroyance.

B)   L'article 13 para. 1 de la Constitution dispose que "Nul ne peut être dispensé de l'accomplissement de ses devoirs envers l'Etat ou refuser de se conformer aux lois, en raison de ses convictions religieuses".

Mais en ce qui concerne le service militaire, la loi permet aux objecteurs de conscience de l'effectuer sans armes dans les services administratifs et techniques de l'Armée. Il n'existe pas à notre connaisance de jurisprudence relative à des difficultés éventuelles rencontrées par "des minorités religieuses ou philosophiques".

6. A)   Oui, le Traité de Lausanne, ainsi que d'autres lois protègent les droits de la minorité musulmane en matière d'enseignement.

B)   L'enseignement est dispensé à la minorité musulmane par l'Etat tant au niveau primaire que secondaire.

C)   Oui, l'enseignement dispensé à la minorité précitée couvre aussi bien celui de la langue que celui dans la langue et ceci aux deux niveaux, primaire et secondaire.

D)   Non, il n'existe pas à notre connaissance de jurisprudence.

7. A)   Non. Cependant le droit de l'emploi des langues est inclus dans l'article 14 de la Constitution relatif à la liberté d'expression. Le paragraphe 1er dispose que "Chacun peut exprimer et diffuser ses pensées par la parole, par écrit et par la voie de la presse, en observant les lois de l'Etat".

B)   Il s'agit d'un usage privé.

C)   Non.

8. Oui, en particulier pour la presse, la radio, la TV et autres médias (dispositions législatives).

9. Oui, la loi y relative permet, pour ce qui est du statut personnel en particulier, l'application du droit islamique, pourvu qu'il ne soit pas contraire à l'ordre public.

10. A) Oui, par l'article 12 de la Constitution qui s'applique à <u>tous</u> les citoyens grecs, y compris bien entendu les membres de la minorité musulmane. Le paragraphe 1er de cet article dispose que: "Les Hellènes ont le droit de constituer des unions de personnes, associations à but non-lucratif en observant les lois de l'Etat, qui ne peuvent, en aucun cas, soumettre l'exercice de ce droit, à une autorisation préalable".

    B) Non. Cependant la minorité de Thrace a toujours des représentants au Parlement depuis 1927. En 1990 deux députés musulmans ont été élus à l'Assemblée Nationale comme indépendants.

11. A) Non.

    B) -

    C) Non.

12. A) Non. Cependant, en matière d'administration locale dans les villes et villages de Thrace à majorité musulmane, le maire est généralement musulman, alors que dans les communes à majorité chrétienne, plusieurs membres de la minorité musulmane font partie des conseils communaux. les membres de la minorité participent également à d'autres assemblées: chambres de commerce, etc.

    B) Voir réponse précitée.

    C) Non.

13. A) Pas de devoir spécial. Cependant ce dernier découle implicitement aussi bien de la Constitution que de la législation.

    B) La perte de la nationalité hellénique par exemple (voir article 20 para.1, al. c du Code hellénique de nationalité).

14. A)   Non.

    B)   -

15. A)   Non.

HONGRIE

1. A) La Constitution ne comporte pas de mention spéciale sur le caractère de la population dans ce sens. Elle dispose seulement à ce sujet (dans son article 68) que:

   "1) Les minorités nationales et ethniques vivant dans la République de Hongrie font partie du pouvoir du peuple ; elles sont des facteurs constitutifs de l'Etat.

   2) La République de Hongrie protège les minorités nationales et ethniques. Elle assure leur participation collective dans la vie publique, le développement de leur propre culture, le droit de l'utilisation de leur langue maternelle, l'enseignement dans la langue maternelle, le droit de l'utilisation de leur nom dans leur propre langue.

   3) Les lois de la République de Hongrie garantissent la représentation des minorités nationales et ethniques vivant sur le territoire du pays.

   4) Les minorités nationales et ethniques peuvent créer des organes d'autogestion locaux et nationaux.

   5) L'adoption de la loi sur les minorités nationales et ethniques requiert la majorité de deux tiers des voix des députés présents."

   B) La forme de l'Etat hongrois est unitaire.

   C) La Constitution ne contient pas d'obligation explicite, mais plutôt une simple déclaration : "La République de Hongrie se considère responsable du sort des Hongrois vivant en dehors de ses frontières et favorise le maintien de leurs relations avec la Hongrie." [Article 6, paragraphe 3].

Le contenu de cette déclaration au niveau de la Constitution se concrétise dans les dispositions prévues par les paragraphes (1er) et (2) de la loi n° LXXVII de l'an 1993 sur les minorités nationales et ethniques : "La République de Hongrie prohibe toute politique qui :

-    vise ou ait pour résultat l'assimilation de la minorité à la nation majoritaire ;
-    vise la modification au préjudice de la minorité respective des rapports nationaux ou ethniques sur les territoires habités par cette dernière ;
-    pourchasse une minorité nationale ou ethnique ou une personne appartenant à une telle minorité à cause de son appartenance, rend plus difficiles les circonstances d'existence pour elle ou l'entrave à l'exercice de ses droits ;
-    vise l'expulsion ou le transfert par contrainte d'une minorité nationale ou ethnique.

(2)   La République de Hongrie s'oppose dans ses relations internationales à toute aspiration politique qui aurait comme conséquences celles énumérées au paragraphe 1er. Pour assurer la protection contre une telle politique, elle fait des efforts par le biais des instruments du droit international et aussi par la conclusion de conventions internationales."

2. A)   a) "minorités nationales et ethniques"
           b) "minorités nationales et ethniques"
           c) à notre connaissance, il n'y a pas encore de décision   en la matière.

    B)   a) la citoyenneté ? : oui

          b) oui.

Les dispositions générales de la loi N° LXXVII de 1993 sur les droits des minorités nationales et ethniques prévoient, entre autres, ainsi le champ d'application de ladite loi:

"Article 1er

1) La présente loi sera appliquée à toutes les personnes ayant la citoyenneté hongroise vivant sur le territoire de la République de Hongrie qui se considèrent comme appartenant à une minorité nationale ou ethnique, ainsi qu'aux communautés formées par ces personnes.

2) Aux fins de la présente loi, une minorité nationale et ethnique (minorité par la suite) est tout un groupe de peuples habitant sur le territoire de la République de Hongrie, depuis au moins une décennie, qui constitue une minorité numérique dans la population de l'Etat, les membres duquel ont la citoyenneté/nationalité hongroise et qui diffèrent du reste de la population par leur langue maternelle, culture et traditions et qui manifestent en même temps une conscience de solidarité inhérente, qui vise à la protection de ces valeurs et à l'expression et à la protection des intérêts de leurs communautés développées historiquement.

3) La présente loi ne s'applique pas aux réfugiés, immigrés et personnes ayant la nationalité d'un Etat étranger mais résidant durablement en Hongrie ni aux apatrides."

C)   Les textes cités ci-dessus visent les minorités ethniques et nationales en général. Parmi les dispositions finales de la loi sur les droits des minorités, l'article 61 donne l'interprétation suivante :

"1) Au sens de la présente loi, sont qualifiés comme groupes de peuples habitant sur le territoire de la Hongrie, ceux des Bulgares, des Tziganes, des Grecs, des Croates, des Polonais, des Allemands, des Arméniens, des Roumains, des Routhènes, des Serbes, des Slovaques, des Slovènes et des Ukrainiens.

2) Au cas où une minorité ultérieure, en plus de celles qui ont été énumérées au paragraphe 1 ci-dessus, voudrait témoigner qu'elle remplirait les critères prévus par la loi, un nombre de 1.000 citoyens au moins, se déclarant comme appartenant à la minorité respective, pourra soumette son initiative populaire y relative au Président du Parlement. Lors de la procédure, les dispositions respectives de la loi N° XVII de 1989 sur le référendum et l'initiative populaire seront appliquées".

Concernant les spécificités de l'utilisation de la langue maternelle comme facteur composant des droits spécifiques communs des minorités, le Chapitre VII de la loi N° LXXVII de 1993 prévoit :

"Article 51

1) Dans la République de Hongrie, toute personne a le droit d'utiliser librement sa langue maternelle à tout moment et en tout lieu. Les préconditions pour l'utilisation de la langue maternelle des minorités - dans les cas prévus par une loi spéciale - seront assurées par l'Etat.

2) L'utilisation de la langue maternelle dans les procédures civiles et pénales, ainsi que dans les procédures devant les organes des autorités publiques, sera assurée par les lois sur les procédures respectives.

Article 52

1) Un député parlementaire, appartenant à une minorité, a le droit d'utiliser sa langue maternelle dans le Parlement.

2) Un député appartenant à une minorité a le droit d'utiliser sa langue maternelle dans l'organe représentatif de l'autogouvernement local. Au cas où sa contribution a lieu dans la langue de l'une des minorités, son texte en Hongrois ou l'extrait de son contenu sera annexé au procès-verbal de la réunion..."

La loi N° III de 1952 sur la procédure civile prévoit dans son article 8 - parmi les principes fondamentaux de la procédure - que:

1) La langue utilisée dans la procédure judiciaire est le Hongrois. La non-connaissance de la langue hongroise ne pourra porter préjudice au détriment de personne.

2) Dans la procédure judiciaire, tout le monde a le droit d'utiliser sa propre langue maternelle."

La loi N° I de 1973 sur la procédure pénale contient presque la même disposition :

"Article 8

1) La langue utilisée dans la procédure pénale est le Hongrois. La non-connaissance de la langue hongroise ne pourra porter préjudice au détriment de personne.

2) Dans la procédure pénale, tout le monde peut utiliser sa langue maternelle soit en écrit, soit oralement."

Dans la loi N° IV de 1957 sur les règles générales de la procédure des organes de l'administration publique, le paragraphe 5 de l'article 2 dispose que dans la procédure devant l'organe de l'administration publique, soit en écrit, soit oralement, tout le monde peut utiliser sa propre langue maternelle. La non-connaissance de la langue hongroise ne peut pas porter préjudice au détriment de personne."

D)   La Constitution et la loi sur les droits des minorités nationales et ethniques ne comportent pas d'énumération limitative des différentes minorités reconnues. Ce n'est que le paragraphe 2 de l'article premier de la loi qui contient la notion générale de minorité. Ceux qui remplissent les critères y spécifiés, bénéficient des droits spécifiques assurés aux minorités, en plus des droits prévus pour les citoyens composant la majorité numérique de la population. Il y a une énumération des groupes de peuples qui sont considérés comme habitant sur le territoire de la Hongrie [par. 1er de l'article 61] et certaines dispositions accordent des privilèges à ces grands groupes de minorités : par exemple, le paragraphe 4 de l'article 63 (l'allocation unique de fonds pour assurer les frais de fonctionnement des organes nationaux de l'autogouvernement des minorités - avec l'énumération des 13 minorités nationales et ethniques différentes) et l'annexe N° 3 de la loi, relative à l'article 65 (la détermination du nombre de personnes appartenant à une certaine minorité lors des élections des députés aux organes représentatifs des autogouvernements locaux - avec la même énumération de 13 nationalités).

La déclaration/confession et la manifestation de l'appartenance de l'individu à un certain groupe ou une minorité nationale ou ethnique sont le droit exclusif et inaliénable de l'individu. Personne ne sera obligé de déclarer son appartenance à un groupe de minorité, mais au sens d'un récent arrêt de la Cour constitutionnelle, tout le monde a le droit de le déclarer ou de le confesser.

Le droit de l'individu appartenant à une minorité de confesser son appartenance à une minorité s'exerce en secret et anonymement lors des recensements nationaux de la population (Articles 7-8 de la loi N° XLXXVII de l'an 1993).

E) Elle est envisagée, en général, en termes collectifs.

F) L'exercice de certains droits spécifiques des minorités est préconditionné par l'existence de la citoyenneté/nationalité hongroise (Voir la disposition légale sur la vigueur de la loi LXXVII de 1993), et l'exercice des droits politiques est en général lié à la possession de la citoyenneté/nationalité hongroise. La loi N° LV de 1993 sur la nationalité hongroise ne contient aucune disposition concernant les minorités vivant sur le territoire de la Hongrie.

3. A) Lors de l'élaboration du projet de modification en date du 23 octobre 1990 de la Constitution, les législateurs se sont fondés largement sur les instruments du droit international (p.e. la Charte de l'ONU, la Déclaration universelle des droits de l'homme, le Pacte international relatif aux droits civil et politique, la Convention européenne des droits de l'homme, la Convention de l'ONU sur la prohibition de toute forme de la discrimination, la Charte européenne des langues régionales ou minoritaires, etc...) et lors de la rédaction des lois respectives concrétisant le contenu des différents droits fondamentaux, on a abondamment puisé dans les textes du droit international. La Hongrie n'a que peu de traités bilatéraux sur la protection des minorités et ils sont récents (p.e. avec la Slovénie). L'article 7 de la Constitution prévoit que : "L'ordre légal de la République de Hongrie accepte les règles généralement reconnues du droit international et garantit l'harmonie entre ses engagements contractés dans le domaine du droit international et le droit interne." Au sens du décret-loi N° 27 de 1982 - encore en vigueur actuellement mais déjà bien dépassé - les instruments du droit international contractés partagent le sort de la norme juridique par laquelle ils ont été promulgués. Au sens de ce décret-loi, les traités internationaux qui établissent directement et avec effet général des droits et des obligations pour les personnes

physiques et morales seront promulgués sous forme d'une loi, d'un décret du Gouvernement ou d'un ministre.

B)   Les instruments du droit international sont intégrés à la législation interne par le biais des normes juridiques les promulguant, mais ils sont aussi confirmés par exemple par les dispositions de la Constitution ou des lois.

A notre connaissance, il n'y a pas encore de jurisprudence d'instance nationale ou internationale en la matière.

4. A)   L'article 70/A de la Constitution prévoit que :

"1) La République de Hongrie assure à toute personne séjournant sur son territoire les droits de l'homme et les droits civiques, sans discrimination aucune fondée sur la race, la couleur, le sexe, la langue, la religion, l'opinion politique ou autre, l'origine nationale ou fortune, la naissance ou toute autre situation.

2) La loi punit gravement toute discrimination préjudiciable selon l'alinéa 1 ci-dessus.

3) La République de Hongrie favorise la réalisation de l'égalité en droit par des mesures visant la suppression d'inégalité de chances."

A notre connaissance, il n'y a pas encore d'instance judiciaire en la matière.

B)   En plus du paragraphe 3 de l'article 70/A de la Constitution, c'est le Chapitre V de la Constitution qui dispose - entre autres - de l'institution du commissaire parlementaire des droits des minorités nationales et ethniques :

"Article 32/B ...

2) La tâche du commissaire parlementaire des droits des minorités nationales et ethniques est d'examiner ou de faire examiner les abus relatifs aux droits des minorités nationales et ethniques et parvenus à sa connaissance ainsi que de prendre l'initiative des mesures générales ou individuelles pour y remédier.
(...)

4) Le commissaire parlementaire des droits civiques et le commissaire parlementaire des droits des minorités nationales et ethniques sont élus sur la proposition du Président de la République par le Parlement, à la majorité de deux tiers des voix des députés. ..."

Le Chapitre V de la loi N° LXXVII de 1993 sur les droits des minorités nationales et ethniques prévoit l'institution du commissaire parlementaire des droits de minorités nationales et ethniques qui procédera dans les affaires incombant sous l'empire de la loi suscitée, et dispose aussi sur l'institution du porte-paroles local des minorités. Les intérêts de minorités nationales et ethniques sont médiatisés par la Haute Autorité des minorités nationales et ethniques (Nemzetiés Etnikai Kisebbségek Hivatala), subordonné directement à l'Office du Gouvernement ayant le statut d'organe gouvernemental, étant formée d'experts d'origine minoritaire.

C) La modification faite par la loi N° XXV de 1989 sur la modification de la loi N°IV de 1978 portant Code pénal, avait prévu la disposition suivante :

"Outrage à la communauté - Article 269 -

1) Celui qui, en présence d'un grand nombre de personnes, aura commis un acte de nature à inciter la haine contre :
   a) la nation hongroise ou une nationalité,
   b) une nation, religion ou race, ainsi que certains groupes de la population, sera puni d'une peine privative de liberté allant jusqu'à trois ans.

2) L'auteur de l'infraction encourra à cause d'un délit une peine privative de liberté allant jusqu'à un an, un travail rééducatif, ou une amende lorsqu'il aura utilisé devant d'autres personnes une expression injurieuse ou humiliante à l'encontre de la nation hongroise, à une autre nation ou nationalité, peuple, religion ou race ou aura commis un acte de ce genre. Néanmoins, tout en mettant l'accent sur le fait que les expériences graves tirées de l'histoire montrent combien les vues propageant une infériorité ou une supériorité du point de vue de la race, de l'ethnie, de la nationalité, de la religion, la prolifération des idées , de la haine, du mépris, de l'élimination menacent les valeurs de la civilisation de

l'humanité, a jugé que le texte du paragraphe 2 de l'article cité était en contradiction avec le droit fondamental à la libre expression, c'est pourquoi l'a annulé [arrêt N° 30 de l'an 1992 de la Cour constitutionnelle].

5. A)   L'article 8 de la Constitution prévoit que :

"1) La République de Hongrie reconnaît les droits fondamentaux, inviolables et inaliénables de l'homme ; leur respect et leur protection sont une obligation primordiale de l'Etat.

2) Dans la République de Hongrie, les règles relatives aux droits et obligations fondamentaux sont fixées par la loi qui, cependant, ne peut pas restreindre le contenu substantiel d'un droit fondamental."

L'article 60 prévoit que :

1) Dans la République de Hongrie, toute personne a droit à la liberté de pensée, de conscience et de religion.

2) Ce droit implique la liberté d'avoir ou d'adopter une religion ou une conviction de son choix, ainsi que la liberté de manifester ou de ne pas manifester sa religion ou sa conviction individuellement ou en commun, tant en public qu'en privé . En République de Hongrie, l'Eglise et l'Etat sont séparés.

4) L'adoption de la loi sur la liberté de conscience et de religion requiert la majorité de deux tiers des voix des députés présents ..."

Le contenu de cette disposition est développé par la loi N° IV de 1990 sur la liberté de la conscience et de la religion, ainsi que des Eglises. Cette loi déclare dans son article premier : "La liberté de conscience et de religion est une liberté fondamentale incombant à toute personne, l'exercice paisible de laquelle est assuré par la République de Hongrie." Son article 2 répète littéralement le texte de l'article 60 de la Constitution.

La Constitution et cette loi ne parlent pas d'incroyance ou de minorités religieuses, mais du libre choix de la conviction (religieuse ou autre). La loi spécifie les préconditions pour la constitution d'une Eglise, notamment :

"Article 8

1) les personnes, suivant les mêmes principes de foi, aux fins de l'exercice de leur culte, peuvent constituer des communautés religieuses, des confessions, des Eglises (Eglise par la suite).

2) Une Eglise peut être constituée pour l'accomplissement de toute activité religieuse qui n'est pas contraire à la Constitution et ne heurte pas à la loi. Pour qu'une Eglise soit enregistrée à la Cour (départementale ou municipale), la loi exige qu'elle soit constituée par cent personnes physiques au moins; que ses Statuts soient adoptés ; ses organes d'administration et de représentation soient élus ; et une déclaration faite par les fondateurs affirmant que l'organisation constituée par eux remplit les critères prévus à l'article 8 ci-dessus.

Aucune donnée relative à la religion ou la conviction de l'individu ne peut être inscrite sur les registres de l'Etat (des autorités publiques).

B) A notre connaissance, il n'y a plus de restriction dans ce domaine. Auparavant, le service militaire armé était obligatoire pour tous les jeunes hommes remplissant les critères de santé prévus, nonobstant leurs convictions. Maintenant, par suite d'une modification faite par la loi N° XXII de 1989, la loi (N° I de 1976) sur la défense prévoit aussi un service militaire non armé. Dans ce sens, la personne astreinte au service militaire peut accomplir un service civil en raison de ses convictions, sur la base d'une autorisation y relative. Le service civil n'est pas autorisé pour les personnes qui ont une autorisation de port d'arme. Auparavant, il y avait des procès pénaux en cas de refus du service militaire armé.

6. A) L'article 16 de la Constitution énonce "l'attention particulière" que la République de Hongrie manifeste à la qualité de la vie de la jeunesse, à son enseignement et à son éducation, ainsi qu'elle protège les intérêts de la jeunesse, et [par. 2 de l'article 67] que les parents ont le droit de choisir l'éducation à donner à leurs enfants. Les articles relatifs aux droits des minorités nationales et ethniques déjà cités ci-dessus, prévoient l'enseignement dans leur langue maternelle [art. 68 (2)]. Au sens de l'alinéa a) et b) de l'article 13 de la loi N° LXXVII, l'individu appartenant à une minorité a le

droit de connaître, cultiver, enrichir et transmettre sa langue maternelle, son histoire, sa culture et ses traditions ainsi que de participer à l'enseignement et à la formation culturelle dans sa langue maternelle.

B)   Le Chapitre VI de la loi N° LXXVII de 1993 traite en détails des droits des minorités nationales et ethniques à l'autogestion dans le domaine de la culture et de l'enseignement. Dans ce sens, l'Etat reconnaît les langues maternelles des minorités habitant en Hongrie comme facteur de cohésion de la communauté; il favorise leur enseignement - si elles le demandent - dans les institutions de l'enseignement public qui n'appartiennent pas aux organes locaux d'autogestion des minorités. Par conséquent, la loi parle du type d'enseignement officiel.

C)   L'enfant appartenant à une minorité, conformément à la décision des ses parents ou de son tuteur, participe ou peut participer à l'enseignement dans ou de sa langue maternelle (dans sa langue maternelle et dans la langue hongroise) ou à l'enseignement dans la langue hongroise. L'enseignement des minorités dans ou de leur langue maternelle, conformément aux possibilités et aux demandes se manifestant au niveau local, peut s'effectuer dans une école maternelle, une école primaire, une classe ou un groupe. En cas demande des parents ou des tuteurs de huit élèves appartenant à la même minorité nationale ou ethnique, la mise en place ou le fonctionnement d'une classe ou d'un groupe d'élèves est obligatoire. Les frais supplémentaires résultant de l'enseignement dans la langue maternelle ou de la langue maternelle des minorités sont à la charge de l'Etat ou de la municipalité locale. L'Etat a le devoir d'assurer la formation des pédagogues enseignant dans les ou des langues des minorités. L'Etat s'acquitte de cette tâche notamment par l'intermédiaire de la signature d'accords internationaux pour promouvoir la formation professionnelle et scientifique. Les diplômes acquis à l'étranger seront, compte tenu des lois et des conventions internationales, considérés comme équivalents à ceux obtenus en Hongrie. Les lois sur l'enseignement public (N° LXXIX de 1993) et sur l'éducation supérieure (N° LXXX de 1993) ne contiennent pas de disposition spécifique à ce sujet.

D)   A notre connaissance, non.

7. A)   Il n'y a pas de disposition dans la Constitution relative à sur l'emploi officiel des langues, sauf peut-être celle du paragraphe 2 de l'article 68 de la Constitution, qui reconnaît le droit de l'utilisation de la langue maternelle par des minorités nationales et ethniques. On a déjà mentionné les règles respectives des codes de la procédure civile, pénale et celles devant les organes de l'administration publique, ainsi que de la loi sur les droits des minorités (Voir 2/C).

B)   En plus des dispositions constitutionnelles et légales mentionnées ci-dessus ce sont les règles de la loi N° LXXVII sur les droits des minorités nationales et ethniques qui prévoient une réglementation détaillée en la matière. La municipalité est tenue d'assurer conformément à la demande de l'organe d'autogestion local du territoire sur lequel elle est compétente :

    a)   la promulgation des décrets, la publication des annonces - en plus du Hongrois - dans la langue de la minorité concernée;

    b)   que les formulaires utilisés dans la procédure des organes de l'administration publique soient disponibles aussi dans la langue de la minorité concernée;

    c)   que les inscriptions des plaques, indiquant les noms de la localité et des rues, ainsi que la dénomination des autorités publiques et des organismes, fournissant des services d'intérêt public ou les annonces relatives au fonctionnement de ceux-ci soient indiqués - en plus du texte et de la façon d'écrire en hongrois, avec le même contenu et sous la même forme - aussi dans la langue de la minorité concernée.

    Dans les localités habitées par une population appartenant à une minorité, lors du recrutement des fonctionnaires de l'Etat et des employés dans l'administration publique - tout en observant les exigences professionnelles générales - il faudra s'assurer que des personnes employées à ces postes, connaissent la langue maternelle de la minorité concernée (Article 53 et 54).

C)   Les cas de jurisprudence sont rarissimes dans ce domaine.
    Nous pourrions peut-être citer dans ce contexte la prise de position No 412 de la Cour Suprême, dans laquelle la haute juridiction a constaté que, dans le procès pénal, ne prêtera son concours en tant qu'interprète que la personne, commise par l'autorité publique (le

tribunal), pour laquelle les règles relatives aux experts judiciaires seraient applicables; l'utilisation par le tribunal de la personne invitée à l'accomplissement de ce devoir par le prévenu/justiciable porte atteinte aux règles de procédure (paragraphe premier de l'article 69 et le paragraphe (3) de l'article 80 du Code de la procédure pénale).

Compte tenu du fait que la Hongrie n'a adhéré au Protocole facultatif se rapportant au Pacte international relatif aux droits civils et politiques que le 7 septembre 1988 et n'a ratifié la Convention européenne des droits de l'homme que le 5 novembre 1992, en s'engageant à se soumettre à la juridiction de la Cour européenne des droits de l'homme, le temps est relativement court pour "être jugée" par des instances internationales.

8. A)   La Constitution ne contient pas de dispositions sur les mass-média. Le projet de nouvelle loi sur la presse est débattu au Parlement depuis plus de trois ans, mais étant donné l'importance et le caractère délicat du sujet qu'il couvre, et aussi que, conformément à la Constitution, une majorité de deux-tiers des voix des députés présents à la session est requise pour son adoption, la loi n'a pas été encore votée. L'article 18 de la loi No LXXVII sur les droits des minorités prévoit cependant comme droit commun que la radio et la télévision de service public - conformément aux dispositions de la loi particulière - assure la rédaction et la diffusion régulière pour les minorités nationales ou ethniques. Dans les territoires du pays habités par les minorités - l'Etat - également par le biais des traités internationaux - favorisera la réception des programmes diffusés par les radios et les télévisions des pays-mères. Enfin l'alinéa b) du paragraphe (2) de l'article 50 de cette loi, dispose que l'Etat soutient, entre autres, l'édition des livres et des périodiques des minorités. Les organes d'autogestion locaux ont le droit de fonder et de faire fonctionner -dans le cadre des sources financières étant à leur disposition - entre autres, la presse écrite et électronique locale [art. 27, par. (3) al. b)]. L'organe national d'autogestion des minorités -dans le cadre des lois - décide de façon autonome, notamment sur les principes d'utilisation et des moyens des chaînes de radio et de télévision dont il dispose, les principes et les moyens d'utilisation du temps de diffusion étant à sa disposition de la Radio et de la Télévision de service public, sur la publication des communiqués de presse [alinéas g), h) et i) de

l'article 37 de la loi suscitée]. Concernant les élections, la loi prévoit aussi que le dernier jour de la campagne électorale, la Radio et la Télévision hongroise et aussi les studios locaux assureront, en plus des résumés électoraux, un temps de programme spécial pour les candidats des minorités nationales et ethniques (paragraphe (3) de l'article 48 de la loi modifiée No LXIV de 1990 sur les élections des députés locaux des collectivités locales et des Maires).

9. Non, les dispositions légales sont les mêmes pour tous les citoyens, sans égard à leur appartenance minoritaire.

10. A) L'article 3 de la loi modifiée No II de 1989 sur le droit de l'association donne la définition générale de l'association comme telle selon ce qui suit:

"1) L'association sociale est une organisation, ayant une autogestion et qui est constituée volontairement et formée pour accomplir le but déterminé dans ses statuts, qui a des membres enregistrés et qui organise l'activité de ses membres pour atteindre son objectif.

2) Dans ses activités revêtant un caractère de mouvement de masse pourront participer aussi des membres non-enregistrés.

3) Les membres d'un parti ou d'un syndicat ne pourront être que des personnes physiques.

4) Il est requis pour la fondation d'une organisation sociale qu'au moins dix fondateurs déclarent la création de l'organisation, établissent ses statuts et élisent les organes de l'administration et de la représentation". Dans ce sens, l'existence d'un siège en Hongrie n'est pas requise, mais toutes les associations doivent être enregistrées à la Cour départementale ou municipale respective.

B) Le préambule de loi No XXXIII de 1989 sur le fonctionnement et l'économie des partis politiques détermine la destination générale suivante des partis politiques:

"La destination sociale des partis politiques est qu'il assurent les cadres organisationnels de la formation et de la manifestation des voeux du peuple, ainsi que de la mise en valeur du droit à la libre association, des droits politiques des citoyens, et promouvoir la manifestation démocratique et la mise en jeu des différents intérêts et valeurs, qui sont présents dans la société adopte la loi..." (sur les partis politiques). Le texte législatif ne contient pas de règle pour l'action positive en faveur des minorités. La loi No LXXVII de 1993 prévoit une seule déclaration à ce sujet dans son article 10: "La participation à la vie publique des personnes appartenant à une minorité ne sera pas restreinte. Pour la manifestation et la protection de leurs intérêts, elles peuvent - conformément à la réglementation constitutionnelle - constituer des associations, partis politiques ou d'autres associations sociales".

11. A) Par l'adoption de la loi sur les minorités nationales et ethniques, tout le Chapitre XI de la loi No LXIV sur les élections des députés locaux des collectivités locales/municipalités et des Maires a été renouvelé par l'insertion d'une réglementation détaillée en la matière, dont les dispositions seront applicables à partir des élections municipales générales des municipalités de 1994. On envisage aussi la modification de la loi No XXXIV de 1989 sur l'élection des députés parlementaires eu égard à l'existence des minorités, vu que l'article de la nouvelle loi déclare que les minorités ont droit - d'une manière prévue par une loi spéciale - à une représentation au Parlement [article 20, par. (1er)].

B) En raison d'évènements historiques - notamment de l'énorme sacrifice de vies humaines durant l'occupation turque et de la guerre d'indépendance et de libération -les anciens rois et reines ont donné leur assentiment à l'idée de l'invitation massive de main d'oeuvre d'autres nations, qui sont restées ensemble. C'est pourquoi les minorités vivent, en grande partie, concentrées aussi de nos jours.

C) L'article 36 de la loi No XXXIV de 1989 sur l'élection des députés parlementaires prévoit que les circonscriptions électorales doivent être formées au moins 10 jours avant le jour prévu des élections, et que le nombre et les limites géographiques d'une circonscription sont fixés par le corps des députés locaux de telle manière qu'une circonscription soit créée pour un nombre de 600-1000 citoyens-électeurs, mais que chacune des communes ait au moins une circonscription. Au niveau des élections locales, la loi No LXIV de 1990 sur les élections des députés locaux des collectivités locales et des Maires dispose que lors du découpage des circonscriptions électorales, il faudra aussi tenir compte des particularités locales ethniques. Le découpage des départements (administratifs) suit les traditions historiques (le système des comitats royaux) et les limites territoriales administratives et judiciaires sont identiques.

12. A)B)   La création de l'organe national d'autogestion minoritaire, la constitution des organes d'autogestion locaux ainsi que le financement et la subvention par le biais de la Fondation pour les minorités nationales et ethniques pourraient être mentionnés comme mesures spéciales pour la stimulation des minorités à la participation à la vie politique. Ces organes font partie du pouvoir exécutif, soit au niveau national (organe national d'autogestion des minorités) soit au niveau local (les organes locaux).

    C)   A titre d'exemple, on pourrait citer peut-être la disposition prévoyant qu'au cas ou l'une des minorités couverte par la loi sur les droits des minorités ne formerait pas d'organe d'autogestion au niveau national, le représentant de cette minorité au Conseil d'administration de la Fondation pour les minorités nationales et ethniques sera désigné en commun par les associations et organes de cette minorité, existant le jour de la promulgation de la loi disposant de cette fondation.

13. A)B)   Non.

14. A)B)   Non.

15. On pourrait y mentionner l'institution du commissaire parlementaire des droits des minorités nationales et ethniques [articles 32/B./2/ de la Constitution] et celle du porte-parole local des minorités [articles 40-41 de la loi No LXXVII de 1993 sur les droits des minorités].

ITALY

1. A)   According to art. 5 Const. the Italian Republic, which is the legal shape of Italy, is an unitary and indivisible State, but art. 6 provide for the protection of the linguistic minorities requiring the adoption of proper rules.

   B)   The State is organised on a regional basis, but this choice was adopted independently of the ethnic, linguistic or religious characters of the people. Only two Regions (Trentino-Alto Adige and Valle d'Aosta) were given a special autonomy because of the presence of the German-speaking minority and the French-speaking minority respectively, and in the frame of the Trentino-Alto Adige a special autonomy is granted to the Province of Bolzano where the German-speaking minority lives. The creation of the Trentino-Alto Adige is connected with the implementation of the De Gasperi - Gruber Agreement between Italy and Austria (September 5th, 1946).

   C)

2. A)   The term linguistic minority is used in the Constitution, in the laws aimed at the implementation of the Constitution and in the case-law of the Constitutional Court (a/c).

   B)   There is no precise definition of the linguistic minority, but the protection of the minorities is normally restricted to the territorial areas where the minorities are present and to people who are italian citizens.

   C)   The minorities which are protected, are the German-speaking minority in Trentino-Alto Adige, the French-speaking minority in Valle d'Aosta, and the Slovenian-speaking minority in the provinces of Trieste and Gorizia.

   D)   The constitutional protection of the minorities requires their recognition, but the effects of the recognition depends on the choices of the laws aimed at the implementation of the Constitution. At present the protection is restricted to the recognized minorities. The individual's membership of a minority always depends on the free decision of the people concerned.

E)   The connection between the special regional autonomy of Trentino-Alto Adige and of Valle d'Aosta and the protection of the German-speaking and the French-speaking minorities implies that the problems concerning the minorities are viewed in collective terms. For instance the s.c. Statuto (the constitutional law concerning the autonomy) of Trentino-Alto Adige allows the majority of the members of a linguistic group in the regional council or in the provincial council of Bolzano to make a complaint before the Constitutional Court against a law encroaching upon the rights of the relative minority (or against the decision rejecting their request for a vote on the basis of the linguistic groups). Also the regional council and the provincial councils of Trento and Bolzano can make complaints before the Constitutional Court when a national or regional (or provincial) law is supposed to encroach on the protection of a minority. Obviously these rules can also be applied when the rights of the Italian-speaking group in Trentino-Alto Adige or in the province of Bolzano are encroached.

F)   The membership of a minority does not have any effect on the acquisition or loss of nationality (citizenship) and the exercise of political rights.

3. A)   Two international bilateral instruments concern the protection of minorities in Italy: the mentioned De Gasperi-Gruber Agreement on the protection of the German-speaking minority and the s.c. Osimo Treaty between Italy and the former Yugoslavia (November 10th, 1975) on the protection of the Yugoslavian minority. The implementation of both the instruments depends on internal national acts, notwithstanding that the Osimo Treaty was approved by the Parliament with the law March 14th, 1977, n° 73.

B)   The De Gasperi-Gruber Agreement was implemented by the Statuto of Trentino-Alto Adige (the national constitutional law January 26th, 1948, n° 5), which was largely amended by the Constitutional law November 10th, 1971, n° 1, according the s.c. Pacchetto, a document agreed by the Italian Government and the representatives of the German-speaking minority and aimed at improving the protection of this minority. The implementation of the s.c. Osimo Treaty is supposed to largely depend on the previous laws already adopted in observance of the Memorandum agreed between Italy, United States of America, United Kingdom and the former Yugoslavia in London (October 5th, 1954): therefore its art. 8 is read as a confirmation of the protection in force.

4. A)   On the basis of art. 3 Const. all the citizens have the same social dignity and are equal before the law without any distinction of sex, race, language, religion, political ideas, personal and social conditions. This principle is confirmed in art. 2 of the Statuto of Trentino-Alto Adige, which provides for the equality of rights for all the citizens in the Region, whatever their linguistic group. Also in art. 3 of the Statuto of Friuli-Venezia Giulia (the national constitutional law which gives the Region special autonomy, January 31st, 1963, n° 1) equality of rights and treatment is recognized to all the citizens in the Region, whatever their linguistic group. This last provision, in its connection with art. 3 and 6 Const., is at the basis of two decisions of the Constitutional Court (n° 28/1982 and 62/1982) which recognized the right of the Slovenian-speaking minority in the province of Trieste to use their language and to be answered in the same language - if necessary with the help of interpreters - in criminal trials and other special judicial proceedings. The jurisprudence of the Constitutional Court was taken into account by the legislator in adopting the new criminal procedure code, whose art. 109 introduces the right to be examined in their language and for members of the minorities to use it in the territories where they live. Also the written acts directed to them have to be translated. But this provision does not regard the German-speaking minority which is protected by special rules.

    B)   There is no special constitutional provision on positive discrimination in favour of minorities. But the implementation of the rules on proportional distribution of the holding of public offices between the linguistic groups in the Province of Bolzano has required that positive discrimination be adopted to balance the presence of German-speaking officials with that of the Italian-speaking officials. Also the equalization purposes of the financial autonomy of Trentino-Alto Adige and of Valle d'Aosta and those of the additional national grants given to these Regions can imply a positive discrimination with regard to the other Regions.

C)   The prohibition of the extradition of citizens and foreigners for political reasons (art. 10 and 26 Const.) does not concern the crimes of genocide (national constitutional law June 21st, 1967, n° 1). The national law October 9th, 1967, n° 962, introduced the prohibition of genocide and of incitement to it.

5. A)B)   Art. 19 and 20 Const. provide for the freedom of religion and worship; it is a generally accepted that this provision regards not only religious minorities but also unbelievers (Constitutional Court 117/1979). The religious characters of an association or of an institution cannot justify special legal limitations or special tax burdens. The Constitutional Court (239/1984) decided that the legislator is not allowed to introduce the obligatory membership of the institutions of a religious minority for the members of the minority itself. Conscientious objectors are exempt from military obligations but are subject to alternative duties. The members of the religious minority or the unbelievers are allowed to swear adding to the wording of the oath the mention of the different values which are articles of their faith. The relations between the State and the religious minorities are governed by the law according to the terms agreed to by the State's bodies and the representatives of the minorities concerned.

6. A)   Art. 19 of the Statuto of Trentino-Alto Adige provides for the teaching of the German language and in the German language in State schools of the Province of Bolzano where students of the minority group are concerned. A similar provision is in art. 39 of the Statuto of Valle d'Aosta. For the Slovenian-speaking minority the same protection is provided for by the national law July 19th, 1961, n° 1012.

B)   The mentioned provisions interest every level of education, with the exception of the University.

C)   All the schooling is provided for in the minority language by mother tongue teachers. But in all the schools of Valle d'Aosta the pupils of the Italian-speaking-group and of the French-speaking group are taught together and the schooling time is equally divided among teaching in Italian language and teaching in French.

D) The jurisprudence of the Constitutional Court has specially interested the problems of the organization of the schools for the German-speaking minority with regard to the distribution of the administrative functions between the State and the province of Bolzano.

7. A) In the Regione Trentino-Alto Adige the German language has an equal legal status to the Italian language which is the official language of the State. In the province of Bolzano the German-speaking citizens have the right to use their language in relations with the judicial and administrative offices, in the meetings of the assemblies of the Region, of the Province and of the local government, and when they are dealing with the public services. Also the place-names have to be presented in the minority language (art. 99-101 Statuto of Trentino-Alto Adige).

Also the French language in Valle d'Aosta has equal status with the official language. All the public acts have to be written in Italian or French, with the exception of the judicial acts which require the official language (art. 38 Statuto of Valle d'Aosta).

In the Provinces of Trieste and Gorizia there are provisions for a service of interpreters in favour of the members of the Slovenian minority when they are dealing with public administrations, but they are allowed to use their language in the assemblies of the local government in the villages of the countryside only. With regard to the relations with the judicial authorities look at 4 A).

B) In the Province of Bolzano and in Valle d'Aosta the texts of the laws and the regulations are officially provided for in the language of the minorities. For the Slovenian minority there is an unofficial service only.

8. On the basis of an agreement with the State and according to specific legal provisions the State owned corporation, which runs the public radio and television service, supplies in Trentino-Alto Adige and in Valle d'Aosta special, regular and continuous radio and television broadcastings for the German speaking and French speaking minorities using their relative language. Also in Friuli-

Venezia-Giulia that corporation provides for Slovenian, regular radio broadcastings.
Public financial aid grants are given to the minorities institutions for the press and the theatres.

9.   In Trentino-Alto Adige the Statuto entrusts the Region and the Provincia of Bolzano with legislative competence in some fields where traditional local legal rules are present: e.g. the land registers, which are arranged according to the Austrian model; the s.c. "maso chiuso" (closed farm), whose purpose is ensuring the unity of a family agricultural enterprise in its management and through successive hereditary successions; and the s.c. "regole dell'arco alpino" (alpine rules), collective properties of pieces of land, which can be exploited for timber, pasture or plantation.

10. A) There are no specific or restrictive rules concerning the associations of the persons belonging to the linguistic minorities.

    B) The freedom to organise political parties representing the interests of linguistic minorities is not limited, and there are no specific rules concerning the exercise of this freedom.

11. A)B) Only the law concerning the elections of the Italian representatives in the European Parliament has special provisions concerning the linguistic minorities. They concern the Regions where linguistic minorities are present. Every list of candidates which is an expression of political parties of the minorities is allowed to join another list of candidates of the same constituency with the purpose of sharing the distribution of the seats assigned to this second list. When one of the candidates of the minority's list gains 50,000 individual votes he has the right to obtain one of the seats assigned to the second list.

    C) The territories of Trentino-Alto Adige, of the Province of Bolzano and of Valle d'Aosta are explicitly guaranteed by the respective Statuto. According to the London Memorandum (art. 7) Italy engaged not to change the administrative districts of the Province of Trieste where the Slovenian speaking minority is present.
    General, constitutional rules provide for the consultation of the population concerned when the regional and local government districts are changed (art. 132-133).

12. A)B)   According to art. 61 of the Trentino-Alto Adige Statuto the linguistic groups are given a proportional representation in the local government organs in the Province of Bolzano. This provision has to extend to the executive bodies of the Region, of the Province of Bolzano and also of the local government (when a linguistic group has at least two councillors in the local assembly).

In the Province of Bolzano the public offices are proportionally assigned to citizens who are members of the linguistic groups on the basis of the censuses (art. 89 Statuto of Trentino-Alto Adige).

In Valle d'Aosta, the public administration's officials have to know the French language or to be born in the valley (art. 38 Statuto of Valle d'Aosta).

C)   The law does not provide for the entrusting of recognized minorities' associations with special public prerogatives.

13. A)B)   The duty of fidelity regards all Italian citizens without any distinction of language, religion or personal and social conditions (art. 54 Const.).

14. A)B)   The provisions concerning sub-minorities regard the Italian-speaking group (which is a minority) in the Province of Bolzano, and in the same area the Ladin-speaking group.

In the Province of Bolzano the Italian-speaking group is treated in the same way as the German-speaking group.

The Ladin-speaking group is given the same treatment as the other linguistic groups in the Province of Bolzano with regard to the assignment of the public offices and the representation in the governing bodies of the local government according to proportional criteria. The electoral laws of the regional council of Trentino-Alto Adige, of the provincial council of Bolzano and of the minor council of the local government have to guarantee the presence of representatives of the Ladin-speaking group in those bodies. In the areas where the Ladin-speaking group live, the Ladin language is taught in the primary schools, and is used in the nursery schools. It can be used as a teaching language in all the other schools of the same areas. The Ladin place names have to be respected.

15.   See 2 E).

KYRGYZSTAN

The status of minorities is not regulated by the legislation and the law system is not based on case law, therefore we found it impossible to answer a number of these questions.

In this connection, we did not answer the questions for points 2. A), C), 6. D), 9. A) and other questions relating to case law.

1. A)   The Constitution of the Kyrgyz Republic speaks about multinational, multilinguistic and polyreligious character of the population of the republic.
    The draft Constitution of the Kyrgyz Republic submitted to the consideration of the Supreme Soviet also mentions the multinational, multilinguistic and polireligious character of the population.

   B)   The Republic of Kyrgyzstan is a unitary state. Administrative territorial division of the republic in accordance with the Constitution (and the draft Constitution) is not based on ethnic, linguistic or religious differences of the population.

   C)   The Constitution of Kyrgyzstan (and the draft Constitution) does not determine the legal status of any minority and it does not guarantee the protection of minorities outside the territory of the republic.

2. A)B)C) The term "minority" is not used in the Constitution (and draft Constitution) of the Kyrgyz Republic. However, this term is used in by-laws and international treaties of Kyrgyzstan concerning national minorities. Among the first was the Presidential decree of 29 January 1992 "On the organisation of German cultural districts and national commercial structures in the Republic of Kyrgyzstan" concerning citizens of the Republic of Kyrgyzstan of German origin. The second was the Agreement between CIS-countries of 9 October 1992 "On the matters regarding the rehabilitation of the

rights of deported persons, national minorities and peoples" concerning citizens of CIS.

D)   Both the Constitution of the Republic of Kyrgyzstan and the Draft of the new Constitution neither put the State under obligation to recognize national minorities nor prohibit the State to do so. This provision is applicable to all other laws of the Republic of Kyrgyzstan.

The belonging to this or that nationality depends on the free choice of an individual but within his or her mother's or father's nationality. The choice of nationality takes place when issuing a passport of a citizen; further change is prohibited.

E)   -

F)   The choice of one's nationality is limited by his/her mother's or father's nationality and can be made only once. The acquisition of one's mother's or father's nationality cannot limit political and other rights of a citizen of the republic.

3. A)B)   At the present time the Republic of Kyrgyzstan is a participant of CIS countries' Agreement of 9 October 1992 "On the matters regarding the rehabilitation of the rights of deported persons, national minorities and peoples". The Republic of Kyrgyzstan did not take any special decision in the process of drafting this Agreement.

In accordance with point 3 of Article 12 of the draft Constitution of the Kyrgyz Republic, international treaties and other norms of International Law" shall be a component and directly applicable part of legislation and have the force of a law.

4. A)B)C)   The Constitutional principle of equality is applied to all citizens of the Republic of Kyrgyzstan irrespective of their origin, social or property position, sex, language, education, religion and other circumstances (Article 32 of the Constitution and Article 15 of the draft Constitution).

Para. 3 of Article 34 of the Constitution and Article 15 of the draft Constitution prohibit the restriction of the rights, establishment of direct or indirect privileges on the grounds of race or nationality as well as any kind of propaganda of race superiority, violence and xenophobia. Criminal punishment is envisaged for the violation of racial and national equality (Article 68 of the Criminal Code of the Republic of Kyrgyzstan).

5. A) Article 50 of the Constitution guarantees to citizens of the Republic of Kyrgyzstan the freedom of belief and worship or the propaganda of atheism. The encouragement of hostility and hatred on religious grounds is prohibited.

This provision was embodied in the Law of the Republic of Kyrgyzstan "On the freedom of belief and religious organisations". Article 4 of this law establishes equality of citizens irrespective of their attitude to religion as well as envisaging punishment for any kind of restrictions of the rights or establishment of any kind of privileges for citizens on religious grounds and encouragement of hostility and hatred or insult of citizens' feelings, destruction of objects of worship.

Article 17 of the draft Constitution of the Kyrgyz Republic guarantees freedom of belief and worship, spirit and cults.

B) To avoid the problems connected with religious beliefs of citizens called to service in the Armed Forces of the Republic, the Law of the Republic of Kyrgyzstan of 16 December 1992 "On alternative (out of Army) service" states that a citizen who is a member of a registered religious organisation has the rights to alternative (out of Army) service if his religion prohibits him from joining the Army.

6. A)B) Everyone enjoys equal rights in the educational field. The rights of minorities are protected in the linguistic field.

C) In accordance with Article 25 of the Law of the Republic of Kyrgyzstan "On the official language of the Republic of Kyrgyzstan" the schooling, broadcasting is held in the minority languages in the regions of the compact dwelling of national and ethnic groups (the Uzbec, Tadgic, German, Ulgur and others).

In accordance with Article 21 of this law, the teaching in vocational and higher educational institutions is held in the Russian language or other languages along with the studying of the official language (the Kyrgyz language).

D)   -

7. A)   In accordance with Article 71 of the Constitution of the Republic of Kyrgyzstan the official language is the Kyrgyz language.

The draft Constitution of the Kyrgyz Republic establishes in Article 5 the Kyrgyz language as the official one. Point 2 of that Article contains the following provision: "The Kyrgyz Republic shall guarantee the preservation, equal and free functioning of the Russian language and other languages which are used by the population of the republic".

The law of the Republic of Kyrgyzstan "On the official language of the Kyrgyz Republic", in addition to this Constitutional provisions, guarantees the freedom to choose the language for education (Article 21), the freedom to choose the language for scientific research (Article 23) and freedom to choose the language of communication (Article 6)

B)   The official language is the working language of bodies of state power and administration. The acts of bodies of state power and administration are submitted in the official language and published in the official and the Russian language (Article 11 and 12).

Local bodies of state power and administration in the territory of compact dwelling of national groups have the right either to use the minority languages or to provide the translation (Article 16). Court actions are held in the official language or in the language of the majority of the population residing in that locality with interpretation provided (Article 26).

8.   According to the Constitution all citizens of the Republic are equal before Law and Court and have the right to enjoy cultural benefits (Article 44 of the Constitution and point 3 of Article 37 of the draft Constitution of the Kyrgyz Republic).

9. A)   -

10. A)   Citizens of the Republic of Kyrgyzstan have the right of association according to their interests (Article 49 of the Constitution of the year 1978 and part 2 Article 17 of the draft Constitution of the Kyrgyz Republic).

The Law of the Republic of Kyrgyzstan "On public associations" allows the organisation of international associations in the Republic of Kyrgyzstan (part 2 of Article 6).

B)   The law "On public associations" does not establish any specific rules or limitations to political parties representing the interests of minorities.

11. A)B)C)   The presence of minorities has no repercussions on the provisions of the election law of the Republic of Kyrgyzstan and the territorial division of the country to electoral, administrative territorial and judicial districts.

The places of compact dwelling of minorities are often located within one or several administrative territorial units therefore there is a tendency to promote the autonomy;

12. A)B)   No special measures have been taken as regards the participation of minorities in political life because the political activity of all groups of the population is rather high.

C)   The Law provides for the recognition of minorities' associations giving them opportunities on equal grounds with other civic associations.

13. A)B)   Citizens of the Republic of Kyrgyzstan have equal rights and perform equal duties. The Constitution and other normative acts do not establish any special duties to any group of the population of the Republic.

14. A)B)   The Constitution of the Republic of Kyrgyzstan other laws, the draft Constitution of the Kyrgyz Republic do not mention minorities or "sub-minorities".

15.   The legislation of the Republic of Kyrgyzstan does not provide for certain particular remedies to persons belonging to a minority.

LIECHTENSTEIN

1. A)   La Principauté de Liechtenstein forme, par l'union de ses deux pays Vaduz et Schellenberg, un tout indivisible et inaliénable (Art. 1 de la Constitution). Les communes jouissent de l'autonomie locale (reconnue, en jurisprudence, dans son noyau comme un droit fondamental corporatif).

   B)   -

   C)   Non.

2. A)   Non (à l'exception du § 283 du Code pénal, voir infra 4. C).

   B)   -

   C)   -

   D)   -

   E)   -

   F)   -

3. A)   Convention européenne DH (Art. 14), qui s'applique directement dans l'ordre interne. Rang dans la hiérarchie interne des normes: rang de norme constitutionnelle ou supralégale (question non-décise).

   B)   Amendement de l'art. 23 de la loi concernant la Court d'état (Staatsgerichtshofgesetz) assurant la protection des droits et libertés de la CEDH devant cette Court (constitutionnelle).

4. A)   La garantie de l'égalité devant la loi (Art. 31 de la Constitution) s'applique (en principe) à tout individu (jurisprudence StGH 1980/4 LES 1981, 185).

B) -

C) Le § 283 du Code pénal (StGB) réprime l'incitation à la violence ou à la haine ou l'insulte contre une église ou une association religieuse et réprime également expressément l'incitation à la violence ou à la haine contre des groupes ethniques et l'insulte envers ceux-ci.

5. A) Selon l'art. 37 de la Constitution, la liberté religieuse et de conscience est garantie à chacun. L'exercice de la religion et la célébration du culte sont garanties à toute confession, dans les limites des bonnes moeurs et de l'ordre public (L'église caholique romaine et l'Eglise nationale et jouit à ce titre de l'entière protection de l'Etat).

Selon l'art. 38 de la Cosntitution sont garantis la propriété et tous les autres droits patrimoniaux des sociétés culturelles et des associations religieuses.

L'art. 9 de la CEDH (en combinaison avec l'art. 14 de la CEDH) complète la protection de la liberté de religion et de conscience.

B) Non.

6. A) Non.

B) -

C) Non.

D) -

7. A) La langue allemande est la langue nationale et officielle (Art. 6 de la Constitution).

B) -

C) -

8. Non.

9.   Non.

10. A)   Le droit de réunion et d'association est autorisé (dans les limites de la loi) sans discrimination (Art. 41 de la Constitution).

    B)   Non.

11. A)   Non, en l'absence de minorités ethniques, religieuses etc. dans l'électorat.

    B)   -

    C)   Non.

12. A)   Non.

    B)   -

    C)   Non.

13. A)   Non.

    B)   -

14. A)   Non.

    B)   -

15.   Non.

LUXEMBOURG

1. A) La Constitution luxembourgeoise ne comprend pas de mention relative au caractère de sa population.

   Il se dégage seulement de l'article 32 de la Constitution que la puissance souveraine réside dans la Nation. Ce n'est ainsi qu'indirectement que le législateur constitutionnel consacre le caractère unitaire de la population luxembourgeoise.

   B) Le Grand-Duché de Luxembourg est un Etat unitaire. Cette forme de l'Etat est consacrée par l'article 1er de la Constitution qui dispose que le "Grand-Duché de Luxembourg forme un Etat libre, indépendant et indivisible".

   C) La Constitution luxembourgeoise ne prévoit pas cette obligation.

2. A) Ni la constitution, ni la loi, ni la jurisprudence n'emploient le terme de "minorité" ou un terme équivalent.

   B) Aucune définition précise du terme de minorité ou d'un terme équivalent n'est donnée. La philosophie du législateur luxembourgeois est de garantir les droits des minorités moyennant la protection accordée aux droits et aux libertés individuelles.

   C) Par l'intermédiaire de la protection accordée aux droits et libertés individuelles, ce sont tant les droits des minorités religieuses, qu'ethniques et linguistiques qui sont garanties.

   D) Les termes de la Constitution obligent également l'Etat qui doit veiller à la garantie des droits et libertés individuelles accordées aux citoyens. Implicitement la constitution impose donc à l'Etat la reconnaissance des droits de certaines minorités. L'appartenance d'un individu à une minorité ne dépend que de son libre choix.

   E) La problématique des minorités est envisagée en termes strictement individuels.

F)   L'appartenance à une minorité ethnique peut avoir une incidence sur l'exercice des droits politiques alors que ceux-ci sont pour l'instant uniquement réservés aux Luxembourgeois.

3. A)   En l'absence de dispositions constitutionnelles, le droit de la protection des minorités provient surtout des instruments internationaux.(art 27 du pacte ONU sur les droits civils et politiques, convention sur la prévention et la répression du crime de génocide)

Ces instruments trouvent à s'appliquer en Droit interne luxembourgeois. La tendance majoritaire de la doctrine luxembourgeoise va dans le sens de reconnaître aux instruments internationaux la prééminence par rapport à la Constitution.

B)   Ces instruments ont été transcrits en droit interne suivant la procédure normale prévue pour l'approbation des traités internationaux.

4. A)   L'article 11 al. 2 de la Constitution dispose que les "Luxembourgeois sont égaux devant la loi".

Le droit constitutionnel luxembourgeois ne fait donc pas référence à la non-discrimination en fonction de l'appartenance à une minorité. La Constitution luxembourgeoise ne garantit *stricto sensu* l'égalité devant la loi qu'aux seuls Luxembourgeois. Il n'en demeure pas moins que les termes de la disposition précitée sont interprétés largement de sorte qu'en pratique l'égalité devant la loi est reconnue tant aux Luxembourgeois qu'aux étrangers.

B)   Le législateur luxembourgeois n'a pas encore édicté de règles écrites relatives à ce sujet. Les dispositions de droit international ainsi que les principes généraux de droit en la matière sont cependant reconnus en droit luxembourgeois.

C)   Hormis les traités internationaux (notamment *conv.* contre le crime de génocide), il n'existe pas de législation à ce sujet au Grand-Duché.

5. A)   Le principe de la liberté de conscience est garanti au Luxembourg. Ainsi l'article 19 de la Constitution dispose que la liberté des cultes, celle de leur exercice public, ainsi que la liberté de manifester ses opinions religieuses, sont garanties, sauf la répression des délits commis à l'occasion de l'usage de ces libertés. Cet article de base garantissant la liberté des cultes, trouve un corollaire à l'article 20 de la Constitution lequel dispose: "Nul ne peut être contraint de concourir d'une manière quelconque aux actes et aux cérémonies d'un culte, ni d'en observer les jours de repos".

   B)   La Constitution luxembourgeoise règle aussi les rapports entre l'Eglise et l'Etat. Il n'existe au Luxembourg pas de séparation rigide entre l'Eglise et l'Etat. Au Luxembourg, en vertu de l'article 106 de la Constitution, l'Etat rémunère les ministres des cultes. Cependant les cultes ne sont pas expressément énumérés. En fait, les trois grandes corporations religieuses ayant existé au Luxembourg au moment de l'entrée en vigueur du texte constitutionnel, à savoir les religions catholique , juive et protestante, jouissent de cette disposition. Cela ne signifie pas que les religions minoritaire ne se trouvent lésées alors même que des religions interdites dans d'autres régions du monde peuvent être librement pratiquées au Luxembourg et même obtenir des subventions de l'Etat pour leurs ministres des cultes.

6. A)   La Constitution luxembourgeoise ne proclame pas la liberté de l'enseignement. La charte fondamentale luxembourgeoise confie à l'Etat le soin d'organiser, de réglementer et de surveiller l'enseignement.

   D'après l'article 23 de la Constitution, tout ce qui est relatif à l'enseignement peut être réglé par la loi.

   La Constitution luxembourgeoise n'accorde donc pas expressément a chacun le droit d'ouvrir une école et d'enseigner ou de recevoir l'enseignement qu'il préfère, à l'école de son choix. La Constitution met toutefois à charge de l'Etat de veiller à ce que tout Luxembourgeois reçoive l'instruction primaire, qui sera obligatoire et gratuite.

Alors même que la Constitution ne parle que des seuls Luxembourgeois, les droits et devoirs des citoyens du Grand-Duché en matière d'enseignement sont garanties indistinctement de tout critère de nationalité ou de religion.

B)   -

C)   Il existe au Luxembourg diverses disposition légales qui organisent des cours dans la langue de l'une ou l'autre minorité étrangère sans qu'une obligation n'en soit toutefois faite à charge de l'Etat.

D)   -

7. A)   L'article 29 de la Constitution dispose que "la loi réglera l'emploi des langues en matière administrative et judiciaire".

Avant la révision constitutionnelle de 1948, l'emploi des langues française ou allemande était facultatif. La Constitution interdisait aux pouvoirs publics de restreindre cette liberté.

Ce principe de la liberté d'utilisation de la langue française ou allemande a été vidé en 1940 par l'occupant nazi qui avait interdit l'emploi de la langue française sur tout le territoire du Grand-Duché.

A noter que depuis 1984, le Luxembourgeois est reconnu comme langue officielle du pays, ce qui fait que depuis lors chacun a le droit de s'adresser en Luxembourgeois à une administration ou à un service public.

B)   En pratique les administrations publiques emploient de préférence le français dans leurs rapports entre elles, et , selon le cas, le français ou l'allemand dans leurs rapports avec les particuliers.

La langue employée par les Cours et Tribunaux est le français.

C)   -

8.   Selon l'article 24 de la Constitution, la liberté de la presse est garantie, sauf la répression des délits commis à l'occasion de l'exercice de ces libertés.

La Constitution luxembourgeoise garantit ainsi la liberté de la presse sans en accorder cependant une protection spécifique en faveur des minorités.

En matière de radiodiffusion, une loi vient de déterminer des critères d'attribution des fréquences. L'application pratique de ces critères fait que certaines minorités ethniques se voient réservées des programmes spécifiques.

Tout comme les autres libertés constitutionnelles, la liberté de la presse est limitée par l'intérêt supérieur de la société et par le respect des droits d'autrui. La loi détermine les cas où cette liberté devient abusive et partant punissable.

9.   La Constitution ne parle pas de la «famille» en tant que telle. La protection en est assurée par la protection individuelle des membres qui la compose. Les lois sur la police des étrangers prévoient cependant des dispositions favorisant le regroupement sur le territoire luxembourgeois des familles étrangères.

10. A) La liberté d'association est consacrée par l'article 26 de la Constitution: Les Luxembourgeois ont le droit de s'associer. Ce droit ne peut être soumis à aucune autorisation préalable.

L'article 26 de la Constitution ne parle que des Luxembourgeois. En fait, tout comme le droit de réunion, le droit d'association existe également pour les étrangers, sans préjudice de la faculté que garde le législateur de restreindre éventuellement ce droit en ce qui les concerne.

La liberté d'association n'est pas absolue. Si les pouvoirs publics n'ont pas le droit de soumettre la création d'une association à une autorisation préalable, ils peuvent cependant prendre des mesures réglementaires et répressives pour éviter que l'exercice du droit d'association ne porte atteinte à l'ordre public.

Par ailleurs, l'article 26 al. 2 de la Constitution fait une exception à la liberté d'association en prescrivant que l'établissement de toute corporation religieuse doit être autorisé par la loi.

B)   Ni la Constitution ni la loi ne mentionnent l'existence de partis politiques. Seul le règlement de la Chambre des Députés reconnaît l'existence de groupes politiques ou sein du Parlement, et la loi du 21 avril 1928 sur les associations sans but lucratif permet aux partis politiques de se constituer en associations revêtues de la personnalité juridique, comme toute association de ce type.

11. A) Le système électoral en vigueur pour les élections législatives est celui de la représentation proportionnelle .

Le pays est divisé en quatre circonscriptions électorales.

Ce système permet une certaine représentativité des minorités politiques au sein du parlement alors qu'aucun pourcentage minimum de voix n'est requis pour pouvoir entrer au parlement.

Il n'existe cependant pas de mandats réservés à certaines minorités.

Le Luxembourg est en train d'élaborer une nouvelle législation mettant les dispositions du droit luxembourgeois en harmonisation avec la législation communautaire sur le droit de vote des étrangers.

B) -

C) -

12. A) De telles mesures spéciales existent à différents niveaux, tant pour des minorités ethniques que pour des minorités religieuses. Ces minorités participent indirectement à la vie politique par le biais de différents organes consultatifs (ex. Commission des étrangers dans les communes) où elles sont représentées.

B) En attendant la mise en oeuvre des nouvelles dispositions communautaires, il n'existe pour l'instant pas encore d'organe du pouvoir exécutif, législatif ou judiciaire où des minorités ethniques (en l'occurrence des étrangers) soient représentées.

C) -

13. A) La Constitution et la loi ne prévoient pas expressément un devoir spécial de loyauté ou de fidélité aux personnes appartenant à des minorités.

Toujours est-il que la protection des minorités est indirectement assurée par la consécration dans la Constitution des libertés individuelles généralement reconnues dans les démocraties modernes.

B)   -

14. A)   Le droit luxembourgeois ne connaît pas de dispositions assurant une protection à des "sous-minorités".

B)   -

15.   En droit luxembourgeois les voies de recours administratifs ou juridictionnels de droit commun sont ouvertes à toute personne intéressée, indistinctement de considérations de nationalité ou autres.

Il n'existe au contraire pas de voies de recours spécifiquement réservées à des personnes appartenant à des minorités.

MALTA

1. A)   The Maltese Constitution does not contain any provision which specifically characterizes the nature of its population with regard to ethnicity, language or religion. Such is an essential consequence due to the homogeneous nature of the local population.

   B)   Malta is not organized on a federal basis.

   C)   The Maltese Constitution contains no provision which provides for the protection of own minorities outside the national territory.

2. A)   The term minority in the sense of ethnic, religious or linguistic minority is not used in the local Constitution. Furthermore, there is no general legislation which has as its main objective the protection of minorities. Furthermore, one may ascertain that Maltese law does not regulate directly the treatment of minorities within the territory. Without hesitation Malta may be considered fortunate, especially in view of its geographical position and its size, in not having any significant minority problem.

       However, it is interesting to note that Chapter IV of the Constitution contains an extensive and enforceable bill of rights and opens with a provision in the nature of a preamble which refers, in the first instance in general terms, to the entitlement of every person in Malta to the fundamental rights and freedoms of the individual, irrespective of his race, place of origin, political opinions, colour, creed or sex, but subject to respect for the rights and freedoms of others and for the public interest (Article 32).

   B)   -

   C)   -

   D)   The Constitution does not regulate the issue concerning the recognition of minorities.

E)   -

F)   No.

3. A)   Malta has signed, with an accompanying declaration, the International Convention on the Elimination of all Forms of Racial Discrimination. Furthermore, Malta has signed and ratified the European Convention on Human Rights. On the 19th August, 1987, the European Convention Act (Act No. XIV of 1987), passed by the House of Representatives on the 12th August, 1987, came into force, whereby the substantive provisions of the Convention and its first Protocol were incorporated into domestic law.

    B)   Subsequent to the enactment of the European Convention Act, Article 14 of the Convention - which refers to national minorities - forms part of domestic law.

4. A)   Protection from discrimination is specifically dealt with in Article 45 of the Constitution, which proclaims the principle that no law may make any provision that is discriminatory either of itself or in its effect and that no person may be treated in a discriminatory manner by any person acting by virtue of any written law or in the performance of the functions of any public office or any public authority. The expression 'discriminatory' is defined as affording different treatment to different persons attributable wholly or mainly to their respective descriptions by race, place of origin, political opinions, colour or creed whereby persons of one such description are subjected to disabilities or restrictions to which persons of another such description are not made subject or are accorded privileges or advantages which are not accorded to persons of another such description. This provision then introduces a number of permissible exceptions, including one concerning provisions made by law in respect of non Maltese citizens.

    B)   -

    C)   Within this context, reference is made to the Seditious Propaganda (Prohibition) Ordinance, enacted in 1932 and which, apart from empowering the Head of State to do various things in relation to seditious matter, provides (Section 6) that any person who prints, publishes, imports, sells or offers for sale, distributes, exhibits or exposes, or without lawful excuse has in his possession any seditious matter, commits an offence under the Ordinance punishable with a term of imprisonment. Such is deemed to include such matter as promotes feelings of ill-will and hostility between different classes or race.

5. A)   Article 2 of the Constitution stipulates that the religion of Malta is the Roman Apostolic Religion and that the teaching of the Roman Apostolic Faith shall be provided in all State schools as part of compulsory education. However, no person under the age of sixteen is required to receive instruction in religion, if objection to such requirement is made by the person exercising according to law authority over such minor.

On the other hand, Article 40 of the Constitution guarantees to all persons in Malta the full freedom of conscience and the enjoyment of the free exercise of their respective mode of religious worship. Exceptions are applicable to the extent that any law contrary to the above principle is 'reasonably required' in the interests of public safety, public order, public morality or decency. Accordingly, the rights and obligations of a Maltese citizen do not depend on which religious community he belongs to or whether he belongs to any such community.

    B)   -

6. A)   According to Article 10 of the Constitution primary education is compulsory. Education in State schools and the University shall be free to all and sundry without any distinction (Education Act - Act XXIV of 1988).

    B)   -

    C)   -

    D)   -

7. A)   Article 5 of the Constitution provides that the Maltese language is the national language. As to the official languages these are the Maltese and the English language, and such other language as may

be prescribed by the House of Representatives (by a law passed by not less than 2/3 of all members).

B)   -

C)   -

8.   No such particular rules exist, and broadcasting is by licence, and plurality is ensured by law.

9.   No.

10. A)   Article 42 of the Constitution provides that <u>no person</u> (therefore even a foreigner) is to be hindered in the enjoyment of his freedom of peaceful assembly and association, and in particular to form or belong to trade or other unions or associations for the protection of his interests. Therefore, once again no specific regard is had to minorities.

             Limitations in the exercise of this right may be imposed in the interests of defence, public safety, public order, and public morality.

B)   No.

11. A)   No.

B)   -

C)   No.

12. A)   No.

B)   -

C)   No.

13. A)   No.

B)   -

14. A)   No.

    B)   -

15.   All persons have the same administrative and judicial remedies without any distinction.

THE NETHERLANDS

Preliminary remark: Since the questionnaire did not refer specifically to national or non-national minorities the answers given apply to both categories.

1. A) The Constitution does not mention of the unitary or homogeneous nature of the population nor does it explicitly indicate it's multi-ethnic, multilingual or multi-religious nature. In the first chapter, The Dutch Constitution does however contain provisions (fundamental rights) in which the protection of minorities vis à vis the government is safeguarded. These rights enable minorities to practice their religion or life-convictions, to express their opinions, to have their own organisations, to hold meetings and so on.

   B) The regional organisation of the State (provinces and municipalities) is not based on the heterogeneity of the population.

   C) No.

2. A)B)C) The term "minority" is not used in the Constitution and does not appear in the law or in the case-law of the Dutch judiciary.

   D) Neither the Constitution nor other legal instruments require or permit State recognition of minorities. In policy documents, however, the government has identified target groups which are the main beneficiaries of minority policies. There are no legal consequences attached to target group status. The membership of a minority in principle depends on the free choice of the individual concerned, unless of course belonging to such a minority is the result of objective criteria like colour etc.

   E) The minority policies are applicable to groups as well as individuals.

   F) Membership of a minority has no effect whatsoever on the acquisition or loss of nationality or the exercise of political rights.

3. A)   According to Dutch constitutional law, self-executing provisions of international treaties are directly applicable in the domestic legal order and may be invoked by individuals in judicial proceedings. If the court finds that statutory regulations in force within the Kingdom contravene a self-executing treaty provision, it will apply international law, leaving aside the relevant national law (articles 93-94 of the Constitution). The only directly applicable article concerning minorities in the Dutch legal order is article 27 of the ICCPR.

    B)   The implementation of this article has not resulted in the enactment of national law provisions. The Human Rights Committee has not adopted views under article 27 concerning the Netherlands. However, the courts have referred to article 27 in one or two cases.

4. A)   Article 1 of the Constitution contains the principle of equality and the prohibition against discrimination on the grounds of religion, life-conviction, political opinion, race, gender, or other status. There has not been much case-law on the basis of this article because under Article 120 of the Constitution judges are not involved in deciding on the constitutionality of Acts of Parliament. Other (lower) legislative instruments may however be tested against constitutional provisions.

    B)   The principle of positive discrimination is recognized in the Equal Treatment of Men and Women Act of 1980. This Act has led to a considerable amount of case-law regarding this subject. Recently a General Bill on Equal Treatment has been enacted which also recognises the principle of positive discrimination.

    C)   Yes, there are several provisions in the penal code which protect minorities from different expressions of racial violence etc. Furthermore the recent General Act on Equal Treatment provides a new instrument for enforcement of equal treatment and non-discrimination in civil suits.

5. A)   Article 6 of the Constitution enshrines the right of religious freedom and life-conviction. This provision applies equally to all religious minorities. The provision distinguishes between the exercise of this right inside buildings and enclosed places on the

one hand and outside buildings and enclosed places on the other. Only the legislator is competent to impose limitations upon the former. In the second situation the legislator is empowered to delegate in order to protect certain interests. The Act on Public Demonstration regulates, among other matters, the right to exercise this fundamental right outside buildings and enclosed places. This Act grants specific powers of limitation to town councils and mayors.

B)   Yes, there is case-law regarding these issues.

6. A)B)   Article 23 of the Constitution guarantees the freedom to provide education. This freedom is subject to legal limitations. The government has the right to supervise the provision of education in accordance with the rules laid down by or pursuant to an Act of Parliament and to set standards of competence and moral integrity for teachers according to the type of education indicated by Act of Parliament. A special feature of Article 23 is that it assumes as a matter of principle that State and denominational (mostly religious-based) education will be financed by the government on an equal footing. The latter have to apply the same quality standards as State schools. Requirements regarding educational standards are regulated by Act of Parliament, having due regard to the freedom of religious orientation. Thus, in setting standards for denominational schools the legislator must not interfere with their religious character.

C)   According to Dutch law in the educational field part of the curriculum may be taught in Frisian. Furthermore, the study of Frisian is optional in schools in the province called Friesland.

D)   No case-law has resulted from these provisions.

7. A)   Cf. 6C.

B)   The law on Frisian Language only applies to official use and to use in the educational field.

8.   No.

9.   Dutch law does not contain any such permission or requirement. Nonetheless, several policy documents have stressed that the Netherlands has become a multicultural society, respecting values and rules of foreign origin. The Dutch judiciary tends to take such rules and values into account whenever they are invoked by the parties concerned..

10. A)   The right of association is fully recognised in Article 9 of the Constitution. This right is however subject to limitations deemed desirable by the formal legislator.

    B)   No.

11. A)B)   Only in so far that the right to vote and to stand for election for the municipal council has also been granted to non-nationals.

    C)   No.

12. A)B)C) In addition to the measures in the electoral field already mentioned above, central government has established a national consultation council in which all ethnic minority groups are represented. The council discusses all major policy initiatives and can make recommendations with regard to them.

13. A)B)   No.

14. A)B)   No.

15.   At the moment no such special remedies exist.

NORWAY

1. A)   The Norwegian Constitution has a specific provision, protecting the cultural identity of the Sami population (Article 110 a).

   B)   No relevance.

   C)   No.

2. A)   The Sami minority is referred to - both in the Constitution and in the legislation - as the "Sami population".

   B)   No, the texts does not define the Sami population in an exact way. The right to vote in the elections to the Sami Parliament is, however, carefully described in the respective law. In principle, non-citizens, who meet the other requirements in the legislation, are entitled to vote in these elections.

   C)   The Sami population is both an ethnic, linguistic and partly religious minority.

   D)   A formal recognition is not necessary. Membership depends totally on a person's free choice.

   E)   I think it is fair to say both on an individual, as well as on a collective basis.

   F)   No.

3. A)B)   For the time being, the principle of "dualism" is governing the legal thinking, although the courts to a high degree make efforts to interpret the domestic legislation in conformity with the international commitments. When the new provision in the Constitution was elaborated, the international human rights law played an important role.
   In some years time, Norway will probably apply a more "monistic" system.

4. A) The Norwegian Constitution does not explicitly recognise a principle of equality (although this principle is most certainly implied in the main principles on which the Constitution is based).

B) Article 110 a is in itself a provision constituting a commitment to exercise positive discrimination vis-à-vis the Sami population.

C) Yes.

5. A) The Constitution (Article 2) recognises the principle of freedom of religion. This covers all kind of minorities, irrespective of their beliefs.

B) In principle yes, although they are of little practical importance.

6. A) No.

B) The Sami population has the right to study the minority language, as well as to be taught in their own language (at the primary and secondary level).
As for other minorities, the situation is different and more complicated to describe. Some of the minority groups are being taught in their mother tongue, the main part of the education is, however, carried out in Norwegian.

C) Not to my knowledge.

7. A) Not explicitly, although Article 110 a refers to the right to secure and develop i. a. the language.

B)C) Not of relevance.

8. No.

9. No.

10. No, not in the Constitution.

11. A)B)C) Not in the general elections. The elections to the Sami Parliament is organised according to specific legislation.

12. A)B)   Special efforts have been taken to make sure that the Sami
           Parliament is an active instrument for the Sami population.

    C)   No.

13. A)B)   No.

14.   No.

15.   No.

POLAND

1. A) The Constitution[1] does not refer explicitly to the question of the unitary/multiethnic nature of the population.

   B) The State is not organised on a federal or regional basis. The current discussions on the territorial structure of the State refer predominantly to economic and organisational aspects and not to "the heterogeneousness of the population", as mentioned in the second question.

   C) The Constitution does not explicitly put the State under an obligation to protect Polish minorities outside the territory of Poland. Art. 89 of Chapter Eight of the Constitution (a similar provision is contained in the draft Charter) reads: "Polish citizens staying abroad shall enjoy the protection of the Republic of Poland". Taking into account the definition of minorities (citizens of States they live in), one cannot apply this provision to their protection.

2. A) The term "minority" is not used in the Constitution yet. However, the draft Constitutions contain, as a rule, special provisions relating to the protection of minorities. This notion appears sporadically in

---

[1] *Poland is still in the process of elaborating a new Constitution. With regard to individual rights and freedoms, Chapter Eight of the 1952 with amendments remains in force. This part of the autumn constitutional law is felt by politicians and specialists to be outdated. In the fall of 1992, the President of the State submitted a draft Charter on Rights and Freedoms to the Parliament which, when adopted, should have constitutional rank and replace the above-mentioned chapter eight. Simultaneously, seven draft constitutions have been submitted to the Constitutional Committee of the National Assembly (both chambers of Parliament). These drafts also contain chapters devoted to individual rights and freedoms. Considering that the constitutional law in this respect might be expected to be changed soon, by adopting either the mentioned Charter or the new Constitution, answers to the questionnaire shall refer not only to the binding Constitution but also to the expected solutions. In particular, the draft of the Charter is to be taken into account, which after the discussion so far seems to have a good chance of being adopted.*

the underconstitutional sources of law laws (e.g. 1991 and 1993 Electoral Laws - the last one: Journal of Laws 1993, No 45, Pos. 205; 1992 Ordonnance of the Ministry of Education concerning the organisation of education for maintaining the national, ethnic and linguistic identity of pupils who belong to national minorities - Journal of Laws 1992, No 34, Pos. 150).

B) Neither the Constitution nor the laws contain a definition of minorities.

C) The draft Constitutions relate to national, ethnic, linguistic and religious minorities. The previously above-mentioned Electoral Laws refer exclusively to national minorities. Similarly, the mentioned Ordonnance which speaks about the national, ethnic and linguistic identity only of pupils who belong to national minorities.

D) Neither the Constitution nor the laws require or permit recognition of any minorities by the State. An individual's identification with a minority depends exclusively on his free choice.

E) The binding Constitution and the draft Charter refer to the question of minorities only by laying down the principle of equality formulated "in individual terms". Some of the draft Constitutions speak, however, about the protection of minorities understood in the collective sense as well. Also the Electoral Law indicates a collective meaning of the term "national minority".

F) The membership of a minority cannot have an effect on the acquisition or loss of nationality nor on the exercise of political rights.

3. A) Poland is a party to most of the international human rights treaties as well as to the European Convention on Human Rights. According to prevailing opinion, treaties which were ratified without the consent of Parliament (under the 1952 Constitution prior to its amendment in 1989) are binding in the domestic legal order *ex proprio vigore*. To this extent, international treaties may be applied within the domestic legal order but it remains controversial which rank they should possess. This category embraces the majority of international human rights treaties, including both International Covenants. Treaties ratified with the

consent of the Parliament, expressed by a statute, could be (according to prevailing opinion and the interpretation by the Supreme Court) applied directly in the Polish legal order with the rank of a statute. For example, the European Convention on Human Rights enjoys this status. The majority of the draft Constitutions lay down the principle of the superiority over statutes of international treaties ratified with parliamentary consent.

Poland has also concluded with its neighbours a number of bilateral treaties on a friendly neighbourhood[2], which contain *inter alia* exhaustive provisions relating to the protection of minorities. These provisions follow the concept of the minorities protection adopted in the CSCE Documents, particularly in the Copenhagen Document. The bilateral treaties were ratified with the consent of Parliament.

B) The need for the implementation of the treaties mentioned under "A" influenced both State's policy and law-making.

C) The bilateral treaties (see: point "A") lay down that one of the principles of the good neighbourhood is recognition of minorities as a natural bridge between societies and their valuable contribution to the life of the community. Parties to the treaties condemn totalitarinism, national and ethnic hatred, antisemitism, xenophobia, discrimination, as well as persecution for religious or political reasons. They commit themselves to respect the right of members of minorities, individually or collectively, to free expression, maintenance and development of their ethnic, cultural, linguistic and religious identity without any attempt at forced assimilation, and the right to a full and effective enjoyment of human rights and fundamental freedoms without any discrimination and in full equality before law. The State-Parties also commit themselves, in their bilateral relations, to protect the ethnic, cultural, linguistic and religious identity of the national minorities of the other Party and to establish conditions supporting such an identity. The bilateral treaties also specify the fundamental rights of minorities.

---

[2] *See inter alia: the Treaty with the Federal Republic of Germany - Journal of Laws 1992, No 14, Pos. 56; the Treaty with the Czech and Slovak Federal Republic - Journal of Laws 1992, No 59, Pos. 296; the Treaty with the Republic of Hungary - Journal of Laws 1992, No 59, Pos. 298.*

4. A) Art. 67 of the binding Constitution (and art. 4 § 2 of the Charter) prohibits discrimination based *inter alia* on nationality, race or religion. Art. 81 provides for:

"1. Citizens of the Republic of Poland, irrespective of nationality, race or religion, shall enjoy equal rights in all fields of public, political, economic, social and cultural life. Infringement of this principle by any direct or indirect privileges or restrictions of rights by reference to nationality, race or religion shall be punishable.

2. The spreading of hatred or contempt, the provocation of discord, or humiliation of man on account of national, racial or religious differences, shall be prohibited."

Art. 272 of the Penal Code reads:
Whoever publicly incites to discord on the basis of national, ethnic, racial or religious differences or publicly extols such discords, shall be punished with a term of imprisonment of between 6 months and 5 years.

Art. 273 of the Penal Code reads:
§ 1. Whoever commits an act specified in article [...] 272 by using the press or other mass media shall be punished with a term of imprisonment of between 1 and 10 years.
§ 2. Whoever, for the purpose of their dissemination, produces, stores, transports, transfers, or dispatches written, printed or other subjects containing issues specified in art. [...] 272, shall be punished with a term of imprisonment of of between 6 months and 5 years.

Art. 274 of the Penal Code reads:
§ 1. Whoever publicly insults, scoffs at or degrades a group of people or an individual person by reason of their or his/her national, ethnic or racial origin, shall be punished with a term of imprisonment not exceeding 3 years.
§ 2. Whoever commits an act of assault against a human being for a reason specified in § 1, shall be punished with a term of imprisonment of between 6 months and 5 years".

By virtue of the quoted art. 274 eight persons have been convicted in the years: 1986-1990.

§ 2. Whoever commits an act of assault against a human being for a reason specified in § 1, shall be punished with a term of imprisonment of between 6 months and 5 years".

By virtue of the quoted art. 274 eight persons have been convicted in the years: 1986-1990.

B)   The binding Constitution does not refer explicitly to positive discrimination (affirmative action). However, some of the draft Constitutions do. Positive discrimination as a concept relating to the protection of minorities is supported by prevailing opinion. The Ordonnance quoted under 2. A) is an example of a legal regulation establishing the obligation of the State to take affirmative action with regard to education in mother tongue.

C)   See point "A". The victims can also base their claims in the horizontal dimension on the provisions of Civil Code.

5. A)   Article 82 of the binding Constitution reads:

1. The Republic of Poland shall guarantee freedom of conscience and religion to its citizens. The Church and other religious organisations shall freely exercise their religious functions. Citizens shall not be prevented from taking part in religious activities and rites. No one may be compelled to participate in religious activities or rites.

2.   The Church shall be separate from the State. The principles of the relationship between the State and Church, and the legal and property rights of religious organisations shall be defined by laws.

Article 8 of the draft Charter reads:

§ 1. Every one has the right to freedom of conscience and to a free choice of religion.

§ 2. Every one has the right to the freedom of exercising, both in public and in private, individually and collectively, his/her religious belief practices. The religious practices in public may be constrained by statute.

Freedom of religion is guaranteed by a number of statutes. The Statute on the guarantees of freedom of conscience and belief of 19.05.1989 (Journal of Laws 1989, No 29, Pos. 155) is the most important. According to its article 2 both Polish citizens (without any distinction) and foreigners may:

- establish churches and religious communities, be members of them and leave them,
- participate in religious activities and rites,
- manifest their religion and beliefs,
- bring up children according to their convictions,
- keep private matters related to their religion and belief,
- maintain contacts with other members of the religious community, including participation in the activities of international religious organisations,
- take advantage of the sources of information regarding religion,
- produce and purchase objects needed for religious practices,
- choose the status of priest or member of an order,
- create and become members of lay-organisations in order to fulfil obligations stemming from their religion.
- refrain from any religious activities and other forms of manifestation of one's beliefs.

The mentioned provisions protect members of the Catholic Church, the strongest among religious communities in Poland (which according to accepted evaluations accounts for about 90 % of the population), members of other religious communities and non-believers as well. Despite this Statute, Parliament adopted statutes on the relationship of the State with all the major religious communities in Poland. They contained also relevant provisions from the point of view of the freedom of religion and belief as well as of the principle of non-discrimination whatever one's religion or belief. For instance, the Statute on the relationship of the State to the Polish Orthodox Church, adopted in 1991 (Journal of Laws 1991, No 66, Pos. 287), lays down that the Church in its internal activities uses the orthodox-slavic language and the languages of its members.

B)   The Constitutional Court considered in the nineties a question raised by the Commissioner for Citizens Rights as to whether the conscripts based their claims for alternative service on their membership of religious communities. The courts refused to accept this motif in regard to the members of Catholic Church, stating that the Roman-Catholic religion does not prevent anyone from performing their military service.

6. A)B) C)D) The Constitution does not contain any provisions specifically relating to the education for minorities. The Ordonnance referred to in point 2 A) establishes the framework for teaching in and of the language of minorities. Such teaching can take place in kindergartens and in schools of all levels and types. Provided there is a proper number of pupils who so wish wishing that (in primary schools -up to the eighth class - a minimum of 7 pupils in the class; in the secondary schools, a minimum of 14 pupils in the class), teaching takes place in the class, otherwise in interclass groups. If the number of interested pupils in the school is too small, interschool groups for the teaching of minorities' languages can be organised. The Ordonnance has been applied in practice but there is no case-law related thereto.

It is to be pointed out that pursuant to the binding law members of minorities, equally with other citizens, may run private schools.

7. A)B)C) Neither the Constitution, nor the statutes contain provisions relating to the official use of minorities' languages. But, the bilateral treaties with neighbours do (see: point 3 A)). For instance, they establish the right of the respective minorities to the free use of their mother language in public and private life, the right to have access to information in their mother language, and to disseminate and exchange such information. They also grant the right of persons belonging to minorities to use their names in the mother tongue. There is no case-law in this respect.

8. There are no particular legal rules relating to minorities as far as the press, theatre, cinema, radio, television or other media are concerned. Respective legal regulations are, however, liberal, and minorities take advantage of this.

9. The binding law does not contain any specific rules regarding to certain minorities only.

10. A)   The right of association of persons belonging to minorities is based on general constitutional and statutory provisions relating to the right of association which are interpreted as a part of personal freedom. On the basis of these rules, the right extends across national borders.

    B)   Political parties can be established exclusively by Polish citizens. They cannot receive any financial support from abroad. The Statute on political parties does not refer specifically to the situation of minorities or persons belonging to them.

11. A)   The desire to provide minorities with equal chances in general elections was the motivation behing the following special provisions:

-    to register a country list, the electoral committee of a minority has to register 5 district lists instead of registering half of the districts, which is required from other electoral committees,

-    the electoral committee of a minority can declare before the elections that it wishes to be relieved of one of the generally binding limits imposed on the electoral committees: the committee of a minority can be relieved of the threshold of votes which is required if an electoral committee should get mandates from the district lists (5 percent of votes country-wide) or of the threshold of votes which is required if an electoral committee should get mandates from the country list (7 percent of votes country-wide).[3]

    B)   These privileged conditions have been created for the national minorities. The fact that a minority is confined to a particular area or scattered throughout the country is irrelevant.

    C)   -

12. A)B)C)   In spite of the solutions adopted in the Electoral Law (see: point 11) Polish law does not establish any special rules relating to minorities' participation in political life. There is also no procedure

---

[3]   *A lowering of electoral criteria (they differed to a certain extend from the current solution) helped the German minority to gain 7 mandates in the Parliament of the last term.*

B)   These privileged conditions have been created for the national minorities. The fact that a minority is confined to a particular area or scattered throughout the country is irrelevant.

C)   -

12. A)B)C) In spite of the solutions adopted in the Electoral Law (see: point 11) Polish law does not establish any special rules relating to minorities' participation in political life. There is also no procedure concerning an official recognition of minorities' associations giving them public prerogatives.

The bilateral treaties (see point 3 A)) speak about the right of minorities to establish their own organisations and associations and to participate in international non-governmental organisations.

13. A)B)   Neither the Constitution nor the statutes impose a special duty of loyalty or fidelity on persons belonging to minorities.

14. A)B)   The situation of the so called sub-minorities is not dealt with by Polish law separately. It seems that general rules are to be applied in such a case.

15.   In order to support the work of State administration with regard to minorities' protection, a Commission on National Minorities was established as a consultative body of the Council of Ministers. Its main tasks are:

-       the elaboration of the governmental programme in favour of national and ethnic minorities,
-       the formulation of assessments and proposals concerning the implementation of rights and claims of national and ethnic minorities,
-       the formulation of assessments and motions concerning the efficiency of measures preventing violations of rights of national and ethnic minorities and initiation of measures aiming at combating such violations,
-       the popularisation of minorities' related issues and minorities' culture.

Both chambers of the Parliament have established committees dealing with minorities' matters. They cooperate with minorities. Members of minorities and their organisations can also contact members of Parliament, in particular the mentioned committees, and submit complaints and proposals to them in the framework of legally established contacts between voters and members of Parliament.

Minorities and their members can also submit complaints to the Commissioner for Civic Rights who takes care of the implementation of civic rights and freedoms.

PORTUGAL

1. A) La Constitution portugaise dispose que "sont citoyens portugais tous ceux qui sont considérés comme tels par la loi ou par une convention internationale" (article 4). La loi de la nationalité (Loi 37/81, du 3 octobre), où se trouvent établis les critères pour la détermination de la citoyenneté portugaise, ne contient à son tour aucune mention d'éléments de nature ethnique, religieuse ou linguistique qui puissent être à la base de cette même détermination.

Il faudra en outre mentionner que l'article 26 de la Constitution reconnaît à tous, sans distinction aucune, le **droit à la citoyenneté**, autrement dit, le droit d'acquérir la qualité de citoyen portugais pourvu que soient remplies les conditions requises par la loi.

Par ailleurs, d'après l'article 13, qui établit le principe essentiel de l'égalité de tous les citoyens devant la loi, *"nul ne peut être privilégié, avantagé, défavorisé, privé d'un droit ou exempté d'un devoir en raison de son ascendance, de son sexe, de sa race, de sa langue, de son lieu d'origine, de sa religion, de ses convictions politiques ou idéologiques, de son instruction, de sa situation économique ou de sa condition sociale".*

B) Dans son article 6, la Constitution définit l'Etat portugais comme un Etat **unitaire** - cette caractéristique doit néanmoins se conjuguer avec les principes tant de l'autonomie locale et régionale que de la décentralisation démocratique de l'administration publique.

Le principe de l'autonomie régionale a entraîné la consécration, par la Constitution, des régions autonomes (les archipels des Açores et Madère), douées d'organes législatifs et exécutifs qui leur sont propres.

La raison d'être de l'autonomie reconnue à ces deux parties du territoire portugais se trouve essentiellement dans leur séparation géographique du reste du territoire national et non pas dans une quelconque rupture de l'homogénéité de la population portugaise en général, du point de vue linguistique, ethnique ou religieux.

C) L'article 14 de la Constitution énonce un principe général ayant trait à la protection des citoyens portugais séjournant ou résidant à l'étranger. Ce principe est développé par la législation interne ainsi que par d'autres principes constitutionnels, notamment celui qui assure aux enfants des émigrants portugais l'apprentissage de la langue portugaise et l'accès à la culture portugaise (article 74, paragraphe 3, alinéa h).

2. A)B)C) Le terme "**minorité**", au sens de minorité ethnique, religieuse ou linguistique, n'est employédans aucun des 298 articles de la Constitution portugaise. De plus, outre l'absence de législation d'ordre général ayant pour objectif principal protection des minorités, il existe peu de dispositions législatives d'origine interne qui contiennent ce terme. Mais nous pouvons mentionner quelques exceptions :

- La Résolution 38/93 du Conseil des Ministres du 8 avril, par laquelle furent approuvées des mesures en faveur des émigrants et des **minorités ethniques** ;

- La Loi 87/88 du 30 juillet, relative à l'exercice de l'activité de radiodiffusion, selon laquelle le but spécifique du service public de radiodiffusion est de promouvoir la création de programmes pédagogiques d'information et de formation en faveur des **minorités culturelles;** la loi qui réglemente le régime de l'activité de télévision (Loi 58/90 du 7 septembre) contient une disposition à tous égards analogue.

- La Résolution du Conseil des Ministres qui créa le "Programme Enseignement pour Tous" (Résolution 29/91 du 16 mai) en vue d'assurer la scolarité obligatoire et de rendre l'enseignement secondaire accessible à tous , énonce comme l'un de ses objectifs celui de promouvoir l'adoption de mesures d'intervention orientées vers la réussite scolaire des élèves qui ont des besoins particuliers en matière d'enseignement, notamment ceux qui appartiennent à des **minorités ethniques et linguistiques** ;

- L'Arrêté ministériel 63/91 du 13 mars, portant création du Secrétariat coordinateur des programmes d'éducation multiculturelle, auquel sont assignées les tâches de coordonner, d'encourager et de promouvoir, dans le domaine du système éducatif, les programmes et les actions qui visent l'éducation pour les valeurs de l'amitié, de la tolérance, du dialogue et de la solidarité entre **différents peuples, ethnies et cultures.**

Aucun des textes précités ne contient une définition des **minorités.**

En ce qui concerne la jurisprudence soit du Tribunal constitutionnel soit des tribunaux communs, parmi leurs décisions connues ayant trait à des aspects se rapportant à la discrimination en raison de la race, de la langue ou confession religieuse, aucune n'utilise ce concept ni n'en donne définition.

D) Non.

E) Dans tous les textes mentionnés au point 2. A., on trouve une approche des minorités comme des groupes qui méritent, en tant que tels, des actions positives tenant compte de leur dimension collective. Ceci, évidemment, sans préjudice de la protection dont bénéficie, sur le plan individuel, chacun des membres de ces minorités, eu égard à l'application concrète du principe fondamental de l'égalité devant la loi, tel qu'il est énoncé à l'article 13 de la Constitution.

F) Non. Les critères qui déterminent l'acquisition ou la perte de la nationalité, ainsi que l'exercice des droits politiques, sont objectifs et ne tiennent pas compte de la qualité de membre d'un groupe quel qu'il soit.

3. A) Oui. Le Portugal a ratifié le Pacte international relatif aux droits civils et politiques, la Convention concernant la lutte contre la discrimination dans le domaine de l'enseignement, la Convention internationale sur l'élimination de toutes les formes de discrimination raciale et la Convention relative aux droits de l'enfant.

En ce qui concerne le rang de ces conventions dans la hiérarchie des sources de droit applicables au niveau national, voir la réponse du Portugal au questionnaire sur les apports entre le droit interne et le droit international (CDL (92)35 Addendum II). Rappelons donc, quoique d'une façon succincte, ce qui fut dit au sujet des rapports entre le droit interne et les normes figurant dans des traités ou accords internationaux:

"à la lumière de la Constitution, les traités et accords internationaux auront une valeur supralégale, ne pouvant pas être mis en cause par une loi postérieure, mais ils auront toujours, en toute circonstance, une valeur infraconstitutionnelle".

B)   La mise en oeuvre de ces conventions n'a jusqu'à présent débouché sur aucun cas de jurisprudence ayant directement trait aux questions touchant la protection des minorités.

4. A)   Le principe constitutionnel de l'égalité de tous les citoyens devant la loi (article 13 de la Constitution) détermine expressément que nul ne peut être privilégié, avantagé, défavorisé, privé d'un droit ou exempté d'un devoir en raison notamment de sa race, de sa langue ou de sa religion.

Un arrêt du Tribunal constitutionnel illustrant cette interdiction de toute forme de discrimination, a déclaré inconstitutionnelle une norme qui figurait au Règlement de la "Guarda Nacional Republicana" (un corps spécial de troupes ayant spécialement pour but la sûreté, le maintien de l'ordre public, la protection et la défense des populations) et se rapportait indirectement aux populations gitanes, du fait que cette norme là permettait *"les perquisitions pendant la nuit et sans mandat délivré par l'autorité judiciaire compétente dans les chariots, roulottes ou tentes des nomades"*. Le Tribunal a estimé que ces lieux sont assimilés à la notion de domicile consacrée par la loi et, que dès lors, le Règlement mis en cause portait atteinte à l'article 34 de la Constitution qui consacre le principe de l'inviolabilité du domicile et interdit l'entrée au domicile des citoyens contre leur volonté, sans un mandat délivré par l'autorité judiciaire compétente, ou pendant la nuit. Le Tribunal a également reconnu qu'en établissant des normes portant sur un régime policier spécial orienté vers des individus appartenant à l'ethnie gitane, on enfreignait le principe constitutionnel d'égalité.

B)   Bien que certins de ses articles prévoient des mesures compensatrices de la situation d'inégalité de certaines catégories de personnes (les orphelins et les enfants abandonnés, art. 69, par. 2 ; les jeunes travailleurs, art. 70, par. 1er ; les travailleurs féminins, art. 68, par. 3), la Constitution n'établit aucune forme de discrimination positive au profit de minorités ethniques, religieuses ou linguistiques.

Toutefois, les dispositions législatives citées au point 2 révèlent le souci des autorités publiques d'assurer une protection particulière qu'il faudra accorder à des personnes appartenant à l'une des minorités y mentionnées.

C)   L'article 189 du Code Pénal punit *"la diffusion d'idées incitant à la discrimination raciale ou à l'encouragement à toute activité de nature raciste, soit par la défense de ces idées, soit par la participation à des organisations qui les défendent, soit par l'appui assuré à toute activité de nature raciste, y compris leur financement"*.

Etant donné l'importance de cette norme dans le contexte de la protection de groupes minoritaires, il convient de reproduire son libellé :

Article 189
(Génocide et discrimination raciale)

1.   Celui qui, dans le but d'anéantir, en tout ou en partie, une communauté ou un groupe national, ethnique, racial, religieux ou social, commet un ou plusieurs des actes suivants :

    a)   homicide des membres de la communauté ou du groupe ;

    b)   atteinte grave à l'intégrité physique ou psychique des membres de la communauté ou du groupe ;

    c)   soumission de la communauté ou du groupe à des conditions de vie ou à des traitements inhumains, qui soient de nature à provoquer l'anéantissement de la communauté ou du groupe ;

d)   transfèrement violent d'enfants vers une autre communauté ou un autre groupe ;

sera puni d'une peine privative de liberté de dix à vingt-cinq ans.

2.   Est puni d'une peine privative de liberté d'un à cinq ans celui qui, dans une réunion publique, par diffusion d'écrits ou par tout moyen de communication de masse :

a)   diffame ou injurie une personne ou un groupe de personnes ou les expose au mépris public en raison de leur race, de leur couleur ou origine ethnique ;

b)   provoque des actes de violence contre une personne ou groupe de personnes d'une autre race, d'une autre couleur ou origine ethnique.

3.   Est puni d'une peine privative de liberté de deux à huit ans celui qui :

a)   fonde ou constitue des organisations ou même des activités de propagande organisée incitant à la discrimination, à la haine ou à la violence raciales ou les encouragent ;

b)   participe aux organisations ou activités visées par l'alinéa précédent ou donne assistance à des activités racistes, y compris leur financement.

5. A)   La Constitution établit, dans son article 41, le principe de l'inviolabilité de la liberté de conscience, de religion et de culte.

De même, la Constitution garantit, en tant que corollaire de ce principe, non seulement l'interdiction, sous quelque forme que ce soit, de toute persécution ou discrimination fondée sur des considérations religieuses, mais aussi le droit de chacun à la protection de ses convictions religieuses.

Elle énonce en outre le principe fondamental de la séparation des églises et de l'Etat, assure la liberté d'enseignement de toute religion ainsi que l'accès aux mass média pour la divulgation de croyances.

Ce principe constitutionnel est développé dans de nombreuses législations particulières. En effet, il convient à cet égard de signaler l'existence d'une réglementation spécifique concrétisant le principe de la liberté de religion et de culte, notamment au sein des forces armées (Décret-loi 93/91 du 26 février), des établissements tutélaires de mineurs (Décret-loi 345/85 du 23 août), dans le domaine de l'éducation (Arrêté ministériel n° 104/89 du 16 novembre) et des moyens d'information appartenant au secteur public (Loi 58/90 portant sur le régime de l'activité de télévision).

B)   Au Portugal, les médias ont rapporté des initiatives, organisées par des membres de confessions religieuses minoritaires, visant à attirer l'attention sur le maintien de privilèges octroyés par la loi ou pratique administrative à une (des) confession(s) religieuse(s) déterminée(s), ce qui violerait le principe constitutionnel de non-discrimination en fonction de la religion. On ne connaît toutefois aucune jurisprudence qui se soit prononcée au sujet des difficultés rencontrées par une minorité quelle qu'elle soit.

6. A)B)C) Aux termes de la Constitution, tous ont droit à l'enseignement, lequel doit contribuer à surmonter les inégalités économiques, sociales et culturelles, permettre aux citoyens de participer démocratiquement à une société libre, ainsi que promouvoir la compréhension mutuelle, la tolérance et l'esprit de solidarité (article 74). Ce principe constitutionnel d'égalité au trait de l'accès à l'enseignement est à son tour développé par la Loi de Bases du Système Educatif (Loi 46/86 du 14 octobre).

Les trois textes légaux mentionnés au point 2 - Résolution 38/93 du Conseil des Ministres sur les mesures d'appui aux émigrants et aux minorités ethniques, Résolution 29/91 du Conseil des Ministres créant le Programme Enseignement pour tous et Arrêté ministériel 63/91 portant création du Secrétariat Coordinateur des Programmes d'Education Multiculturelle - contiennent des références directes à des actions positives qui ont pour but l'éducation d'enfants ou d'élèves appartenant à des communautés ethniques ou linguistiques minoritaires.

D)   Il n'existe aucune jurisprudence nationale en matière de protection des minorités dans le domaine de l'enseignement.

7.   L'uniformité linguistique que l'on vérifie dans l'ensemble du territoire portugais ne connaît qu'une exception : l'utilisation du "mirandês", un dialecte du nord-est du pays - région de Miranda do Douro - qui n'est aujourd'hui parlé, parallèlement au Portugais, que par quelques centaines de personnes. C'est pourquoi, il n'a pas paru nécessaire d'inscrire dans la Constitution l'utilisation du Portugais comme langue officielle unique. Quoiqu'il en soit, l'alinéa f) de l'article 9 de la Constitution établit comme l'une des tâches primordiales de l'Etat celle d'*"assurer l'enseignement et la valorisation permanente, défendre l'usage de la langue portugaise et promouvoir sa diffusion internationale"*.

A Macao, territoire encore sous administration portugaise, l'emploi de la langue chinoise est officiellement reconnu. En fait, par le biais du Décret-loi 455/91 du 31 décembre, le chinois jouit à Macao d'un statut officiel, lui étant accordée la même valeur juridique que celle qui est reconnue à la langue portugaise.

8.   Oui. Voir réponse à la question 2 : il existe deux textes législatifs, en matière des médias appartenant au secteur public (télévision et radiodiffusion), qui contiennent des dispositions visant à promouvoir la création de programmes adressés à des groupes minoritaires en particulier.

9.   Non.

10.   La liberté d'association, telle qu'elle se trouve reconnue dans la Constitution et développée par la loi, concerne tous les citoyens sans aucune distinction, rien n'étant stipulé quant à l'association de personnes appartenant à des minorités. Il faudra, à cet égard, ajouter que la loi 4/71 du 21 août, qui promulgue les bases relatives à la liberté religieuse, dispose que les confessions religieuses peuvent obtenir une reconnaissance qui entraîne l'attribution de personnalité juridique à l'organisation rassemblant l'ensemble des croyants de cette confession.

Il n'existe, d'autre part, aucune règle spécifique ayant trait à la constitution de partis représentatifs de groupes minoritaires.

Il importe toutefois de noter qu'aux termes de la Constitution "*les partis politiques ne peuvent, sans préjudice de la philosophie ou de l'idéologie qui inspire leur programme, user d'une appellation contenant des expressions qui évoquent directement une religion ou une église, ni d'emblèmes pouvant être confondus avec des symboles nationaux ou religieux*" (article 51, par. 3).

11. Non.

12. Non.

13. Non.

14. Non.

15. Non.

ROUMANIE

Précision

Dans le titre du Questionnaire, ainsi que dans le texte de certaines questions, on utilise l'expression "droits des minorités" qui n'est pas consacrée dans le droit international.

Par la suite, la réponse roumaine au Questionnaire se réfère en exclusivité aux droits des personnes appartenant à des minorités, en tant que droits strictement individuels.

1. A)   Constitution, art. 1, par. 1: "La Roumanie est un Etat national, souverain et indépendant, unitaire et indivisible".

   B)   -

   C)   Non.
        Constitution, art. 7: "L'Etat soutient le resserrement des liaisons avec les roumains vivant au-delà des frontières du pays et agit pour préserver, développer et exprimer leur identité ethnique, culturelle, linguistique et religieuse, avec le respect de la législation de l'Etat dont ils sont les citoyens."

2. A)   Le terme "minorité" (ou un terme équivalent) en tant que tel (minorité = entité) n'est pas utilisé dans la Constitution ou dans la loi.

        a) La Constitution utilise l'expression "personnes appartenant aux minorités nationales" (art. 6, art. 32 par. 3) ou "citoyens appartenant aux minorités nationales" (art. 59 par. 2, art. 127 par. 2).

        b) La Loi de l'administration publique locale - Loi n° 69 du 26 novembre 1991 (art. 30 alinéa 3, art. 54 alinéa 2) ainsi que la Loi pour l'élection de la Chambre des Députés et du Sénat - Loi n° 68 du 15 juillet 1992 (art. 4 alinéa 1-4) utilisent l'expression "citoyens appartenant aux minorités nationales").

B) -

C) Sont visées les personnes appartenant à des minorités nationales en liaison avec l'identité ethnique, culturelle, linguistique et religieuse de ces personnes.

La Constitution ne permet pas la reconnaissance par l'Etat de minorités en tant que telles, c'est à dire en tant qu'entités.

D) Conformément à la Constitution, l'Etat reconnaît et garantit aux personnes appartenant aux minorités nationales le droit de conserver, de développer et d'exprimer leur identité ethnique, culturelle, linguistique et religieuse" (art. 6 par. 1). De cette manière est prévue la reconnaissance par l'Etat de l'existence sur son territoire des personnes appartenant à des minorités (toutes les minorités).

L'appartenance ou la non-appartenance d'un individu à une minorité dépend toujours de son libre choix.

E) La problématique des minorités est envisagée en termes strictement individuels (personnes appartenant à des minorités).

F) Non.

3. A) Constitution, art. 11, par. 2): "Les traités ratifiés par le Parlement, conformément à la loi, font partie du droit interne".

Etant donné que la ratification est faite par une loi, les instruments internationaux ont le même rang dans la hiérarchie des normes que les lois.

Constitution, art. 20, par. 1 et 2: "Les dispositions constitutionnelles portant sur les droits et les libertés des citoyens seront interprétées et appliquées en concordance avec la Déclaration Universelle des Droits de l'Homme, avec les pactes et les autres traités auxquels la Roumanie est partie.

"S'il y a des non-concordances entre les pactes et les traités portant sur les droits fondamentaux de l'homme, auxquels la Roumanie est partie, et les lois internes, les réglementations internationales ont la primauté".

B)   Non.

4. A)   Constitution, art. 4, par. 2: "La Roumanie est la patrie commune et indivisible de tous ses citoyens, sans distinction de race, (...), d'origine ethnique, de langue, de religion," (...).

Constitution, art. 16, par.1er: "Les citoyens sont égaux devant la loi et les autorités publiques, sans privilèges et sans discriminations."

B)   Non.

C)   Constitution, art. 30, par. 7: "Sont interdites par la loi la diffamation du pays et de la nation, l'exhortation (...) à la haine nationale, raciale (...) ou religieuse, l'incitation à la discrimination, au séparatisme territorial ou à la violence publique" (...).

5. A)   Constitution, art. 29: "La liberté de pensée et d'opinion, ainsi que la liberté de religion ne peuvent être limitées aucunement. Nul ne peut être contraint à adopter une opinion ou à adhérer à une religion qui soient contraires à ses convictions.

"La liberté de conscience est garantie; elle doit se manifester dans un esprit de tolérance et de respect réciproque.

"Les cultes religieux sont libres et ils s'organisent conformément à leurs propres statuts, dans les conditions de la loi.

"Dans les relations entre les cultes sont interdites toutes formes, tous moyens, actes ou actions de discorde religieuse.

"Les cultes religieux sont autonomes par rapport à l'Etat et jouissent de son soutien, y inclus par les facilités créées pour donner assistance religieuse dans l'armée, dans les hôpitaux, dans les établissements pénitentiaires, dans les asiles et dans les orphelinats.

"Les parents ou les tuteurs ont le droit d'assurer, en accord avec leurs propres convictions, l'éducation des enfants mineurs dont la responsabilité leur incombe."

B)   -

6.   A)   Constitution, art. 32, par. 3, 4 et 7: "Le droit des personnes appartenant aux minorités nationales d'apprendre leur langue maternelle et le droit de pouvoir être instruites dans cette langue sont garantis: les modalités de l'exercice de ces droits sont déterminées par la loi.

"L'enseignement public est gratuit, conformément à la loi.

"L'Etat assure la liberté de l'enseignement religieux, d'accord avec les nécessités spécifiques de chaque culte. Dans les école publiques, l'enseignement religieux est organisé et garanti par la loi."

B)C)   Les personnes appartenant à des minorités nationales ont le droit d'étudier et de s'instruire dans leur langue maternelle pour toutes les formes d'enseignement.

Dans les localités où habitent également des personnes appartenant à des minorités nationales peuvent fonctionner des jardins d'enfants, des écoles primaires, des gymnases, des lycées, des écoles normales, des sections, des classes ou des groupes où l'enseignement est dispensé dans la langue maternelle de ces personnes.

L'établissement de ces institutions scolaires, sections, classes ou groupes est effectué par les inspectorats scolaires en fonction de sollicitations et du poids de la population scolaire minoritaire en zone.

L'histoire et la géographie de la Roumanie seront enseignées en roumain.

Dans l'enseignement supérieur seront organisées des groupes, des années ou des sections où l'enseignement sera dispensé dans la langue maternelle des personnes appartenant à des minorités pour former le personnel nécessaire dans l'activité didactique, culturelle et artistique.

Les jeunes appartenant à des minorités nationales, doivent connaître la langue roumaine, les conditions nécessaires étant assurées.

La langue et la littérature roumaines sont une épreuve obligatoire pour le concours d'admission dans l'enseignement lycée et à l'examen de baccalauréat.

Pour les jeunes provenant des minorités nationales qui ont opté de fréquenter des classes où l'enseignement est dispensé en roumain, sont assurées, sur leur demande, les conditions pour apprendre et étudier leur langue maternelle.

Aux concours d'admission dans l'enseignement dans tous les degrés d'enseignement, les candidats provenant des minorités nationales peuvent soutenir les épreuves dans leur langue maternelle aux disciplines qu'ils ont étudié en cette langue.
(Décision du Gouvernement n° 283 du 21 juin 1993 sur certaines mesures concernant le déroulement de l'enseignement dans l'année scolaire (universitaire) 1993/1994, art. 59 - 63).

D)   -

7. A)   Constitution, art. 13: "En Roumanie, la langue officielle est la langue roumaine."

B)   La procédure judiciaire se déroule en langue roumaine.

Constitution, art. 127, par. 1 et 2: "Les citoyens appartenant aux minorités nationales ainsi que les personnes ne comprenant pas ou ne parlant pas la langue roumaine ont le droit de prendre connaissance de tous les actes et les documents du dossier, de parler en instance et de déposer des conclusions, par l'intermédiaire d'un interprète; dans les causes pénales ce droit est assuré gratuitement."

C)   -

8.   -

9.   Non.

10. A)   Le droit fondamental d'association, pleinement reconnu par la loi fondamentale, s'applique également aux personnes appartenant à des minorités.

Constitution, art. 37, par. 1 et 2: "Les citoyens peuvent s'associer librement en partis politiques, en syndicats et en d'autres formes d'association.

"Les partis ou les organisations qui, par leurs objectifs ou par leur activité, militent contre le pluralisme politique, les principes de l'Etat de droit ou la souveraineté, l'intégrité ou l'indépendance de la Roumanie sont inconstitutionnels."

B)   Non.

11. A)B)   Constitution, art. 59 par. 2: "Les organisations des citoyens appartenant aux minorités nationales, lesquelles ne réunissent pas aux élections le nombre de votes nécessaires pour être représentées au Parlement, ont droit à un siège de député chacune, dans les conditions de la loi électorale. Les citoyens d'une minorité nationale peuvent être représentés uniquement par une seule organisation."

Loi n° 68 du 15 juillet 1992 pour l'élection de la Chambre des Députés et du Sénat, art. 4:

1) "Les organisations des citoyens appartenant à une minorité nationale, légalement constituées, lesquelles n'ont pas obtenu aux élections au moins un siège de député ou de sénateur, ont le droit toutes ensemble, conformément à l'article 59, alinéa (2) de la Constitution, à un siège de député, si elles ont obtenu, dans le pays entier, un nombre de suffrages égal au moins à 5 p. 100 du nombre moyen de suffrages valablement exprimés dans le pays entier pour l'élection d'un député.

2) "Les organisations des citoyens appartenant aux minorités nationales participant aux élections sont assimilées, du point de vue juridique, aux partis politiques, pour ce qui est des opérations électorales.

3) "Bénéficient également des dispositions de l'alinéa (1er) les organisations des citoyens appartenant aux minorités nationales qui ont participé aux élections sur la liste commune de ces organisations; dans ce cas, si aucun des candidats inscrits sur la liste commune n'a été élu, on attribuera à toutes les organisations ayant proposé la liste un siège de député, en observant dispositions de l'alinéa (1er).

4) "Les dispositions de l'alinéa (3) ne seront pas appliquées à l'organisation des citoyens appartenant aux minorités nationales ayant participé aux élections sur liste commune avec un parti politique ou une autre formation politique ou sur des listes communes, conformément à l'alinéa (3), aussi bien que sur leurs propres listes.

5) "Le siège de député réparti conformément à l'alinéa (1er) ou (3) sera attribué en outre du nombre total de députés résulté de la norme de représentation."

C)   Non.

12. A)B)   Voir supra 11. A) et B)

La création du Conseil pour les minorités nationales, organisme consultatif du Gouvernement de la Roumanie.
(Décision du Gouvernement n° 137 du 6 avril 1993 concernant l'organisation et le fonctionnement du Conseil pour les minorités nationales).

C)   -

13. A)B)   Non. Constitution, art. 50, par. 1: Tous les citoyens roumains, y compris ceux appartenant à des minorités nationales, ont le même devoir de fidélité sacrée envers la Roumanie.

14. A)B)   Voir supra 4. A) ainsi que:

Constitution, art. 54: "Les citoyens roumains, les citoyens étrangers et les apatrides doivent exercer leurs droits et leurs libertés constitutionnels de bonne foi, sans violer les droits et les libertés d'autrui."

Constitution, art. 6, par. 2: "Les mesures de protection prises par l'Etat pour la conservation, le développement et l'expression de l'identité (ethnique, culturelle, linguistique ou religieuse) des personnes appartenant aux minorités nationales, doivent être conformes aux principes d'égalité et de non-discrimination par rapport aux autres citoyens roumains."

15.   Non.

RUSSIE

1. A)   La Constitution de la Fédération de Russie ne comporte pas une mention du caractère "unitaire" et "homogène" tant de la population que de l'Etat national. Elle contient les mentions "le peuple", "les peuples", "le peuple multinational", "le peuple national" (aux articles 3, 5, 9, 19, 26, 29, 69, 71 (alinéa c), 72 (alinéa b), 82, 135) qui mettent en lumière la composition ethnique, multi-ethnique, multilingue et multinationale de la population de la Fédération de Russie.

   B)   La Russie est un Etat fédéral ayant une structure régionale reflétant la composition multinationale de sa population du point de vue ethnique, linguistique et religieux. Au cours des dernières années, on a adopté des lois sur l'élévation du statut étatique et juridique des formations autonomes. L'article 5 de la Constitution de la Fédération de Russie établit l'égalité en droits de tous les sujets de la Fédération de Russie.

   Une partie des sujets de la Fédération de Russie sont des formations nationales étatiques (les républiques) et nationales territoriales (la région autonome, les arrondissements autonomes). Conformément à l'article 65 de la Constitution de la Fédération de Russie, cette dernière compte actuellement 89 sujets : 21 républiques, 6 territoires, 49 régions, une région autonome, 10 arrondissements autonomes et deux villes d'importance fédérale. La population qui habite dans les formations nationales étatiques, nationales territoriales et administratives territoriales possède sa confession, se sert librement de sa langue maternelle et de la langue de la communication entre nationalités.

   Les lois des républiques de Bouriatie et de Carélie prévoient la possibilité de la création, dans les lieux d'habitation compacte des petits peuples, des régions nationales, des bourgs et des colonies ruraux nationaux. Dans le message du Président de la Fédération de Russie à l'Assemblée Fédérale "Sur le renforcement de l'Etat de Russie" du 24 février 1994, la tâche a été fixée d'élaborer un projet de loi fédérale sur le statut des conseils nationaux, des régions, des arrondissements et des colonies et sur l'autonomie nationale culturelle.

C)   Cette question comporte deux aspects :

a) la protection des intérêts des minorités sur le territoire de l'Etat quel que soit le lieu d'habitation ou de séjour ;

b) la protection des intérêts des citoyens de l'Etat à l'extérieur de son territoire.

Le chapitre 2 de la Constitution de la fédération de Russie établit un système de droits et de libertés de l'homme et du citoyen de la Fédération de Russie dont jouissent tous ses citoyens quelles que soit leurs nationalité, origine raciale et lieu d'habitation. Selon l'article 2 de la Loi "Sur la citoyenneté de la Fédération de Russie", la citoyenneté est égale indépendamment des motifs de son acquisition. Le paragraphe 2 de l'article 61 de la Constitution de la Fédération de Russie stipule : "la Fédération de Russie garantit à ses citoyens la défense et la protection hors de ses frontières".

Par conséquent, la Constitution de la Fédération de Russie et la Loi sur la citoyenneté chargent l'Etat de la défense des intérêts de chaque citoyen sur l'ensemble du territoire de la Fédération de Russie ainsi que hors de ses frontières.

2. A)   Dans la Constitution de la Fédération de Russie, on emploie les termes : "les peuples autochtones peu nombreux" (art. 69), "les minorités nationales" (art. 71, alinéa c, art. 72, alinéa b ; "les communautés ethniques peu nombreuses" (art. 72, alinéa 1). Une série de lois de la Fédération de Russie emploient aussi les termes "les groupes ethniques", "les peuples peu nombreux du Nord".

B)   La Constitution de la Fédération de Russie ne contient pas leur définition précise. Cependant, dans le contexte des articles correspondants de la Constitution de la Fédération de Russie les termes "les peuples peu nombreux", "les minorités nationales", "les communautés ethniques" impliquent aussi bien la citoyenneté de l'Etat donné qu'une présence durable de la population sur le territoire national.

C)   Pour les minorités nationales ou les peuples peu nombreux, les particularités (les différences) ethniques, linguistiques et religieuses sont caractéristiques. La plupart d'entre eux n'appartient pas à une religion quelconque mais garde des rites du culte religieux.

D)   Dans la Fédération de Russie, on reconnaît sur le plan constitutionnel et législatif toutes les minorités nationales. Leur établissement dans telle ou telle région est une condition indispensable d'une telle reconnaissance. L'appartenance de l'individu à une minorité nationale est déterminée par les autorités conformément à son appartenance ethnique et linguistique. En outre, l'article 26 de la Constitution de la Fédération de Russie dispose : "Chacun a le droit de déterminer et de mentionner son appartenance nationale. Personne ne peut être contraint de déterminer et de mentionner son appartenance nationale". De cette disposition découle la possibilité d'une solution libre et indépendante par l'individu de la question de son appartenance à une minorité nationale quelconque.

E)   La problématique des minorités est généralement traitée dans la Constitution et les lois de la Fédération de Russie dans son ensemble. On adopte également des lois sur certains groupes de minorités, notamment sur les peuples du Nord.

F)   Selon la Constitution de la Fédération de Russie et la Loi "Sur la citoyenneté de la Fédération de Russie" du 28 novembre 1991, l'appartenance à une minorité n'a pas une incidence sur l'acquisition ou la perte de la nationalité et l'exercice des droits politiques. Le premier alinéa de l'article 6 de la Constitution de la Fédération de Russie et le premier paragraphe de l'article 1 de la loi sus-mentionnée fixent le droit de chaque personne à la citoyenneté dans la Fédération de Russie, qui est unique et égale indépendamment des motifs de son acquisition. Le deuxième alinéa de l'article 6 de la Constitution stipule : "Chaque citoyen de la Fédération de Russie possède sur son territoire tous les droits et libertés et est tenu par des obligations égales, prévues par la Constitution de la Fédération de Russie".

3. A)   La Fédération de Russie a conclu plusieurs traités, surtout avec les anciennes républiques de l'URSS qui font partie actuellement de la

- 246 -

Communauté des Etats Indépendants, contenant des clauses sur la protection des droits des minorités.

Le rang des normes des traités internationaux et du droit interne, prévoyant la protection des droits des minorités, est établi à l'article 69 de la Constitution de la Fédération de Russie : "La Fédération de Russie garantit les droits des peuples autochtones peu nombreux, conformément aux principes et normes universellement reconnus du droit international et aux traités internationaux de la Fédération de Russie". Cet article est dérivé des dispositions générales de la Constitution de la Fédération de Russie selon lesquelles les principes et normes universellement reconnus du droit international et les traités internationaux de la Fédération de Russie font partie intégrante de son système juridique (alinéa 4 de l'article 15, alinéa 1 de l'article 17).

B)   Par exemple, l'article 14 du Traité d'amitié, de coopération et d'entraide mutuelle entre la Russie et le Kazakhstan du 25 mai 1992 prévoit l'engagement des parties de contribuer au développement et d'assurer la protection de l'originalité ethnique, culturelle, linguistique et religieuse des minorités nationales sur leur territoire et de créer des conditions pour l'encouragement de cette originalité.

Les engagements de ce genre sont exposés de façon plus détaillée à l'article 7 du Traité sur les fondements des rapports entre Etats, l'amitié et la coopération entre la Russie et l'Ouzbékistan du 30 mai 1992, dans l'introduction duquel les parties confirment que "le respect des droits des personnes appartenant aux minorités nationales en tant que partie des droits de l'homme universellement reconnus, est un facteur important de la paix, de la justice, de la stabilité et de la démocratie" dans les deux Etats.

En outre, les engagements pris par l'Etat prédécesseur dans le cadre du processus pan-européen ont passé à la Russie en qualité de successeur en droits.

4.   A)   Le principe constitutionnel de l'égalité des droits et des libertés de l'homme et du citoyen indépendamment de sa race, de sa nationalité, de sa langue, de son origine sociale, de sa situation patrimoniale et professionnelle, du lieu de sa résidence, de son

attitude à l'égard de la religion, de ses convictions, de son appartenance à des associations publiques, ainsi que d'autres considérations, est consacré aux articles 6 et 19 de la Constitution de la Fédération de Russie. En outre, la régulation et la protection des droits des minorités nationales relèvent de la compétence de la Fédération de Russie (alinéa c de l'article 71 de la Constitution de la Fédération de Russie) ; mais "la protection des droits et libertés de l'homme et du citoyen", "la protection des droits des minorités nationales", "la protection du milieu d'habitation habituel et du milieu de vie traditionnel des communautés ethniques peu nombreuses" (alinéas b et l de l'article 72) relèvent de la compétence commune de la Fédération de Russie et de ses sujets. Ces dispositions de la Constitution de la Fédération de Russie se rapportent directement à la non- discrimination envers les personnes appartenant aux minorités. Nous n'avons pas de renseignements sur les décisions des instances judiciaires nationales ou internationales au sujet de la discrimination à l'égard des minorités nationales. On a adopté la Loi de la Fédération de Russie "Sur la réhabilitation des peuples réprimés" du 26 avril 1991, parmi lesquels il y avait certaines minorités nationales.

B)   La Constitution de la Fédération de Russie, comme la jurisprudence, n'établit pas directement le principe de mesures positives en faveur des minorités. On adopte des lois en vue de rendre avantageuses les conditions matérielles, sociales et de vie et d'autres conditions de l'activité vitale des minorités. Ainsi, par exemple, le Décret du Président de la Fédération de Russie du 22 avril 1992 "Sur les mesures urgentes à prendre pour défendre les lieux de résidence et de l'activité économique des peuples peu nombreux du Nord" a chargé "les Conseils des ministres des républiques dans le cadre de la Fédération de Russie, les organes du pouvoir exécutif des territoires, régions et arrondissements autonomes où habitent les peuples peu nombreux du Nord :

-   de déterminer dans les lieux de résidence et d'activité économique des peuples peu nombreux du Nord les territoires de l'usage traditionnel des ressources naturelles qui sont le bien inaliénable de ces peuples et ne peuvent pas être aliénées sans leur accord aux fins d'utilisation industrielle et de toute autre utilisation qui n'est pas liée à la gestion économique traditionnelle;

-    de transmettre gratuitement les pâturages de rennes, les
     domaines de chasse, de pêche et autres domaines en vue de
     leur utilisation complexe (élevage du renne, chasse, pêche,
     chasse du fauve marin, cueillette des baies, champignons,
     noisettes, plantes médicinales et autres) aux communautés
     clanales et aux familles des peuples peu nombreux du Nord
     liés aux industries et aux métiers traditionnels, à la
     possession héritée à vie ou à bail, et aux kolkhozes et
     sovkhozes - en jouissance permanente (sans terme) ou à bail;

-    d'accorder le droit prioritaire de conclusion des contrats et de
     réception des licences sur l'utilisation des ressources
     naturelles récupérables aux communes clanales, aux familles,
     à certains représentants des peuples peu nombreux du Nord
     dans les lieux de leur usage traditionnel des ressources
     naturelles..."

Ces dernières années, le parlement et le gouvernement ont adopté
des décisions sur le soutien social aux peuples peu nombreux de la
République Sakha (Iakoutie), de la région d'Irkoutsk, du district de
Touroukhansk, du territoire de Krasnoïarsk, de la région de Tchita,
de l'arrondissement autonome Nénetskiy et de plusieurs autres
régions.

La liste des régions de résidence des peuples peu nombreux du
Nord a été arrêtée par la décision du Gouvernement de la
Fédération de Russie du 11 janvier 1993, n° 22.

Le Code foncier prévoit un régime spécial des terres dans les lieux
de résidence et d'activité économique des peuples peu nombreux :
l'octroi à la jouissance provisoire jusqu'à 25 ans des lots de terre
pour l'élevage du renne du Nord et pour l'élevage d'été du bétail,
la possibilité d'utiliser les terrains destinés à la protection de la
nature, les bois et les forêts pour faire paître les rennes, faire la
chasse et réaliser d'autres besoins, l'exemption des rentes foncières
des entreprises des citoyens pratiquant les métiers traditionnels, la
prise en compte de leurs avis lors de l'affectation des lots de terre
aux fins qui ne sont pas liées aux activités économiques des
peuples en question (articles 4, 14, 28, 51, 89, 90, 94).

Les fondements de la législation forestière autorisent les peuples peu nombreux et les groupes ethniques à jouir du régime de la sylviculture, de l'exploitation et de la jouissance des forêts sur le territoire de leur résidence, qui assurent le maintien et le soutien des conditions de vie nécessaires et la pratique de l'activité économique traditionnelle de ces peuples (articles 4, 51); la Loi sur le sous-sol stipule que lors de la jouissance du sous-sol dans les régions de résidence des peuples peu nombreux et des groupes ethniques, une partie des taxes revenant au budget des républiques dans le cadre de la Fédération de Russie, des territoires, des régions, des formations autonomes est utilisée pour le développement social et économique de ces peuples et groupes (article 42) ; la Loi sur la privatisation des entreprises d'Etat et municipales consacre le droit prioritaire des peuples autochtones à l'acquisition de la propriété, contre versement de la valeur des entreprises, des exploitations traditionnelles et des métiers (article 20) ; le Programme interrépublicain de privatisation des entreprises d'Etat et municipales dans les régions du Grand Nord et dans les zones assimilées, approuvé par le Décret du Président de la Fédération de Russie du 24 décembre 1993, prévoit en plus la création des fonds d'investissement spécialisés de chèques accumulant les chèques de privatisation de ces peuples, et la formation, sur la base des sommes financières obtenues grâce à la privatisation, du fonds du développement économique et culturel des peuples peu nombreux du Grand Nord ; les Principes fondamentaux de la législation de la Fédération de Russie sur la culture garantissent la protection de l'Etat à l'égard des cultures des communautés ethniques peu nombreuses (article 22) ; la Loi sur l'impôt sur les revenus perçus par les personnes physiques prévoit que, lors de l'imposition, le revenu global ne comprend pas les revenus (sauf le salaire) obtenus par les membres des communautés tribales nomades des peuples peu nombreux du Nord, si de telles communautés ont été enregistrées au Soviet local (alinéa ia[2] de l'article 3). La loi de la Fédération de Russie sur l'enseignement, assurant les droits des minorités, suppose l'établissement des standards étatiques d'enseignement comprenant les composantes fédérale et nationale-régionale, la possibilité d'acquérir l'instruction générale de base dans sa langue maternelle (article 5, 7).

La nouvelle Constitution de la République Sakha (Iakoutie) charge l'Etat de créer, dans le cadre du budget républicain, les fonds de protection et de développement des peuples peu nombreux du Nord, de sauvegarder leur milieu d'habitation d'origine et leur mode de vie traditionnel (article 38); elle garantit les droits des peuples peu nombreux à la possession et à la jouissance des terres et des ressources dans les domaines tribaux agricoles, de chasse et de pêche, à la protection contre toute forme d'assimilation, d'atteinte à leur originalité ethnique, aux lieux historiques et sacrés, aux monuments de la culture spirituelle et matérielle (article 42) ; elle reconnaît la possibilité de la création de formations administratives et territoriales nationales fonctionnant sur la base des principes de l'autoadministration locale (article 43), dans les régions de résidence compacte des peuples du Nord, proclame officielles leurs langues, autorise la formation des Soviets nomades (des communautés tribales) et des circonscriptions électorales avec un nombre moins élevé d'électeurs (articles 46, 85, 112).

C)   La Constitution de la Fédération de Russie prévoit, au deuxième alinéa de l'article 19, l'inadmissibilité de toute forme de limitation des droits du citoyen selon des critères d'appartenance sociale, raciale, nationale, linguistique ou religieuse. Dans le deuxième alinéa de l'article 29, il est dit à ce sujet : "Est interdite la propagande ou l'agitation incitant à l'hostilité et à la haine sociale, raciale, nationale ou religieuse. Est interdite la propagande relative à la supériorité sociale, raciale, nationale, religieuse ou linguistique".

5. A)   L'article 14 de la Constitution de la Fédération de Russie prescrit:

"1.   La Fédération de Russie est un Etat laïc. Aucune religion ne peut s'instaurer en qualité de religion d'Etat ou obligatoire.

2.   Les associations religieuses sont séparées de l'Etat et égales devant la loi". Ces dispositions sont développées dans l'article 28 qui prescrit : "A chacun est garantie la liberté de conscience, la liberté de croyance, y compris le droit de professer individuellement ou avec d'autres toute religion ou de n'en professer aucune, de choisir librement, d'avoir et de propager des convictions religieuses et autres et d'agir conformément à celles-ci".

B)   Il n'existe pas de jurisprudence internationale illustrant les difficultés éventuelles rencontrées par les minorités religieuses de la Fédération de Russie. En ce qui concerne la jurisprudence nationale à ce sujet, les renseignements sur la question sont absents.

6. A)   Dans la Constitution et les lois de la Fédération de Russie, il n'y a pas de prescriptions limitant les droits des minorités en matière d'enseignement. La Loi de la Fédération de Russie "Sur l'enseignement" adoptée le 10 juin 1992 prescrit : "On garantit aux citoyens de la Fédération de Russie sur son territoire la possibilité d'acquérir l'instruction indépendamment de la race, de la nationalité, de la langue, du sexe, de l'âge, de l'état de santé, de la condition sociale, matrimoniale et professionnelle, de l'origine sociale, du lieu de résidence, de l'attitude envers la religion, des convictions, de l'appartenance au parti, de la condamnation judiciaire" (alinéa 1 de l'article 5). La possibilité de l'extension des droits des minorités en matière d'enseignement est prévue aux articles 9 et 10 de la loi.

    B)   L'article 43 de la Constitution de la Fédération de Russie et l'alinéa 3 de l'article 5 de la Loi de la Fédération de Russie "Sur l'enseignement" prévoient le droit de tous les citoyens d'avoir l'accès général à l'enseignement gratuit dans le cadre du standard étatique d'enseignement général ainsi que, sur la base d'un concours, de suivre gratuitement l'enseignement supérieur dans les établissements d'enseignement d'Etat. La Loi de la Fédération de Russie "Sur l'enseignement" prévoit "La protection par le système d'enseignement des cultures nationales et des traditions culturelles régionales dans les conditions de l'Etat multinational" (alinéa b de l'article 2). Conformément à cette loi, la législation de la Fédération de Russie comprend "aussi les lois et autres textes juridiques des sujets de la fédération en matière d'enseignement" (alinéa 1 de l'article 3).

    La disposition de la Loi sur la réception de "l'enseignement général de base en langue maternelle ainsi que sur le choix de la langue d'enseignement dans le cadre des possibilités offertes par le système d'enseignement, sur la création des établissements d'enseignement, des classes, des groupes et d'autres conditions nécessaires pour leur fonctionnement (alinéa 2 de l'article 6), ainsi que sur la formation des spécialistes pour réaliser le processus d'enseignement en langues des peuples de la Fédération de Russie n'ayant pas de structure étatique" (alinéa 7 de l'article 6) est une garantie importante de la réalisation des droits des minorités en matière d'enseignement.

La loi de la Fédération de Russie "Sur l'enseignement" soumet la solution de la question sur l'introduction de nouveaux avantages, types et normes fédéraux de l'équipement matériel des élèves et étudiants à la compétence des républiques dans le cadre de la Fédération de Russie, des territoires, des régions, des villes de Moscou et de Saint-Petersbourg, de la région autonome et des arrondissements autonomes (alinéa n) de l'article 29). Dans le cadre de cette disposition peuvent être résolues les questions de l'octroi aux diverses minorités nationales du droit d'acquérir une instruction gratuite ou partiellement subventionnée.

C) L'alinéa 2 de l'article 26 de la Constitution de la Fédération de Russie prévoit le droit de chacun des citoyens de la Fédération de Russie "d'utiliser sa langue maternelle, de choisir librement la langue de communication, d'éducation, d'étude et de création".

L'alinéa 3 de l'article 68 stipule que la Fédération de Russie "garantit à tous ses peuples le droit de conserver leur langue maternelle et la création de conditions permettant son étude et son développement.

Les questions générales de la politique linguistique en matière d'enseignement sont réglementées par la Loi de la Fédération de Russie "Sur les langues des peuples de la Fédération de Russie" et par la Loi de la Fédération de Russie "Sur l'enseignement". "La liberté et le pluralisme en matière d'enseignement" (alinéa e) de l'article 2 de la Loi "Sur l'enseignement" sont deux principes fondamentaux de la politique linguistique étatique en matière d'enseignement. Ainsi, la législation prévoit la possibilité d'une libre solution, par les citoyens de la majorité de la population des collectivités nationales étatiques et nationales territoriales, de la question de l'étude de la langue de la minorité.

La définition des niveaux éventuels d'enseignement dans la langue de la minorité est réglementée par l'article 6 de la Loi "Sur l'enseignement", qui stipule "Les citoyens de la Fédération de Russie ont le droit de recevoir une instruction générale de base dans leur langue maternelle ainsi que de choisir la langue de l'instruction dans le cadre des possibilités offertes par le système d'enseignement" (alinéa 2). "La langue (les langues) de l'enseignement et de l'éducation dans l'établissement d'enseignement général sont déterminées par l'établissement et (ou) par les Statuts de l'établissement d'enseignement général" (alinéa 3). La conception et la réalisation des programmes républicains et régionaux de développement de l'enseignement, y compris les programmes internationaux, compte tenu des particularités nationales, ainsi que sociales et économiques, écologiques, culturelles, démographiques et des autres particularités républicaines, et la fixation des composantes nationales et régionales des standards d'Etat en matière d'enseignement compte tenu de la composition nationale de la population, relèvent de la compétence des sujets de la Fédération de Russie (alinéas 2 c et f de l'article 29 de la loi). Ainsi, par exemple, la Loi de la République de Bouriatie "Sur les langues des peuples de la République de Bouriatie" stipule : "compte tenu des intérêts des Evenques et d'autres nationalités en résidence compacte dans les régions de la république, on assure la création d'établissements préscolaires et scolaires secondaires, de groupes, classes et autres formes d'enseignement et d'éducation dans leur langue maternelle" (alinéa 3 de l'article 21).

Par conséquent, le niveau de l'enseignement pouvant être atteint dans la langue maternelle est déterminé en fonction de la grandeur numérique d'une minorité donnée, de la concentration de sa résidence et de plusieurs autres facteurs concrets.

Dans le but d'une réalisation pratique des droits de toutes les minorités à l'instruction dans leur langue maternelle, la Loi établit que l'Etat doit offrir "son concours à la formation des spécialistes pour utiliser le processus d'enseignement dans leur langue des peuples de la Fédération de Russie n'ayant pas leur propre Etat" (alinéa 7 de l'article 6).

7. A)   La Constitution de la Fédération de Russie consacre le droit de chaque citoyen "d'utiliser sa langue maternelle, de choisir librement la langue de communication, d'éducation, d'étude et de création" (alinéa 2 de l'article 26). Dans l'introduction de la Loi "Sur les langues des peuples de la Fédération de Russie", il est dit : "Les langues des peuples de la Fédération de Russie sont le patrimoine

national de l'Etat de Russie. Elles sont l'héritage culturel et se trouvent sous la protection de l'Etat... Le bilinguisme et le multilinguisme sont une norme traditionnelle de l'existence linguistique sur le territoire de la Fédération de Russie ayant une composition multinationale... L'Etat, sur tout le territoire de la Fédération de Russie, contribue au développement des langues nationales, du bilinguisme et du multilinguisme".

La Loi ne prescrit pas de normes juridiques sur l'emploi des langues des peuples de la Fédération de Russie dans les rapports personnels non officiels ainsi que dans l'activité des associations et organisations sociales et religieuses (alinéa 1 de l'article 2).

La Loi prévoit une garantie d'Etat de la souveraineté linguistique de chaque peuple indépendamment de son nombre et de son statut juridique, et la souveraineté linguistique de l'individu quelle que soit son origine, sa situation sociale et patrimoniale, son appartenance raciale et nationale, son sexe, son instruction, son attitude à l'égard de la religion et son lieu de résidence (alinéa 2 de l'article 2).

La souveraineté linguistique des peuples et de l'individu est protégée par la loi. Personne n'est en droit d'imposer à l'individu l'emploi de telle ou telle langue contre sa volonté sauf dans les cas prévus par la législation de la Fédération de Russie. Les normes fixées par ladite loi sont valables pour les citoyens de la Fédération de Russie ainsi que pour les apatrides se trouvant en résidence permanente sur le territoire de la Fédération de Russie (alinéa 3 de l'article 2).

B)   Sur l'ensemble du territoire de la Fédération de Russie, le russe, ayant le statut de langue officielle, est la langue de communication entre nations du fait des traditions historiques et culturelles existantes (alinéa 1 de l'article 68 de la Constitution de la Fédération de Russie, alinéa 2 de l'article 2 de la loi sur les langues des peuples de la Fédération de Russie). En même temps, l'alinéa 2 de l'article 68 de la Constitution de la Fédération de Russie prévoit la compétence des républiques dans le cadre de la Fédération de Russie d'établir de leur propre chef leurs langues officielles, et la Loi sur les langues des peuples de la Fédération de Russie prévoit le droit des républiques de prendre des décisions sur le statut des langues des peuples résidant sur leur territoire. Dans les régions de résidence compacte d'une population n'ayant pas sa propre collectivité nationale-étatique et nationale-territoriale ou résidant hors d'une telle collectivité, la langue de la population de cette région peut être employée simultanément avec la langue russe et la langue officielle des républiques dans les domaines officiels (alinéa 4 de l'article 3).

La Loi fait obligation aux organismes du pouvoir législatif, exécutif et judiciaire de la Fédération de Russie de garantir et d'assurer la protection sociale, économique et juridique de toutes les langues des peuples de la Fédération de Russie.

La protection sociale des langues prévoit une politique linguistique scientifiquement justifiée visant à sauvegarder, développer et étudier toutes les langues des peuples de la Fédération de Russie sur son territoire.

La protection économique des langues suppose l'allocation orientée des ressources budgétaires et financières des programmes étatiques et scientifiques de sauvegarde et de développement des langues des peuples de la Fédération de Russie et la réalisation d'une politique fiscale avantageuse pour atteindre ces objectifs.

La protection juridique des langues suppose la garantie de la responsabilité des personnes morales et physiques pour la violation de la législation de la Fédération de Russie sur les langues des peuples de la Fédération de Russie (alinéas 1, 2, 3, 4 de l'article 4).

En outre, la Loi stipule que l'Etat garantit aux citoyens de la Fédération de Russie l'exercice des droits politiques, économiques, sociaux et culturels fondamentaux quelle que soit leur connaissance d'une langue quelconque.

La connaissance ou la méconnaissance de la langue ne peut pas servir de raison pour limiter les droits linguistiques des citoyens de la Fédération de Russie. La violation des droits linguistiques des peuples et de l'individu a pour conséquence la responsabilité en vertu de la Loi (alinéas 1 et 2 de l'article 5).

Conformément à ces dispositions, la Loi fixe les modalités de l'emploi des langues des peuples de la Fédération de Russie dans le domaine de la législation, de l'administration et de la procédure judiciaire.

Dans les organismes législatifs supérieurs de la Fédération de Russie, les travaux sont accomplis dans la langue officielle de la Fédération de Russie. Il est aussi permis de s'exprimer dans la langue officielle des républiques dans le cadre de la Fédération de Russie. Les mêmes modalités sont observées lors de la discussion des projets de loi et d'autres textes normatifs (article 11).

Dans l'activité des organismes, organisations, entreprises et établissements d'Etat de la Fédération de Russie, on utilise la langue officielle de la Fédération de Russie, les langues officielles des républiques dans le cadre de la Fédération, et les autres langues des peuples de la Fédération de Russie (article 15). Ce principe est à la base de l'activité de la Cour Constitutionnelle de la Fédération de Russie, de la Cour Suprême et de la Cour Supérieure d'Arbitrage de la Fédération de Russie, des autres organes chargés de la protection des lois de la Fédération de Russie ainsi que des organes chargés de la protection des lois correspondantes des républiques dans le cadre de la Fédération de Russie (article 18).

Ainsi, la question de l'emploi officiel de la langue officielle de la Fédération de Russie, des langues de tous les peuples de la Fédération de Russie dans les organes du pouvoir d'Etat, les organes de l'autoadministration locale, y compris l'administration de la justice, est réglementée par la Constitution et la législation de la Fédération de Russie.

8. A) La disposition constitutionnelle sur le droit des citoyens de la Fédération de Russie à un libre emploi de la langue maternelle, y compris l'enseignement et l'éducation dans la langue maternelle, est mise en oeuvre par le principe du fonctionnement de la langue officielle de la Fédération de Russie, des langues officielles des républiques dans le cadre de la Fédération et des autres langues des peuples qui résident sur leur territoire. Ce principe, selon l'article 20 de la Loi "Sur les langues des peuples de la Fédération de Russie" est appliqué dans le domaine des mass média (dans la publication des journaux et revues, dans la traduction et le doublage

des films et des oeuvres video), dans la création des théâtres nationaux etc. Développant cette disposition, l'alinéa 2 de l'article 7 de la Loi dispose : les programmes d'Etat de maintien et de développement des langues prévoient les directions telles que le concours à la publication des oeuvres littéraires dans toutes les langues des peuples de la Fédération de Russie, le financement de leurs recherches scientifiques, la création des conditions de l'emploi de différentes langues dans les mass média.

Dans le projet de la loi de la Fédération de Russie sur "Les principes fondamentaux de la législation de la Fédération de Russie sur le statut juridique des peuples autochtones peu nombreux", on envisage de charger les organes du pouvoir d'Etat et de l'autoadministration locale d'apporter une aide financière, matérielle, technique et autre aux publications imprimées dans les langues des peuples autochtones peu nombreux et d'organiser des émissions de télévision et de radio dans les langues de ces peuples (article 32).

9.   La Constitution et les lois de la Fédération de Russie ne prévoient pas et n'interdisent pas l'application de règles de droit spécifiques à l'égard des minorités, y compris dans le droit de la famille.

10. A)   La Constitution de la Fédération de Russie consacre le droit d'association de chaque citoyen, y compris le citoyen appartenant à une minorité nationale. L'article 30 stipule :

"1. Chacun a le droit d'association, y compris le droit de créer des syndicats pour la défense de ses intérêts. La liberté de fonctionnement des associations est garantie.

2. Personne ne peut être contraint d'adhérer à une association quelconque ou d'y demeurer."

Le droit d'association des citoyens est réglementé plus concrètement par la Loi de l'URSS "Sur les associations sociales" qui est actuellement en vigueur sur le territoire de la Fédération de Russie. Conformément à l'article 1 de cette loi, sont reconnues comme associations sociales, outre les partis politiques, les mouvements de masse, les organisations syndicales et autres, "les amicales, les fonds et les autres associations" dans lesquels peuvent s'unir les individus appartenant à des minorités nationales. En vertu des articles 23 et 24 de cette loi, le droit d'association des citoyens de la Fédération de Russie, y compris les citoyens appartenant à des minorités nationales, va au-delà des frontières de l'Etat, si leur activité n'est pas contraire à la Constitution et aux lois de l'Etat ainsi qu'aux Statuts de cette association.

Actuellement, le Ministère de la justice de la Fédération de Russie a enregistré 12 associations sociales des peuples autochtones peu nombreux du Nord, de la Sibérie et de l'Extrême-Orient de la Russie.

B)   Dans la Constitution et les lois de la Fédération de Russie, il n'y a pas de normes spécifiques relatives aux partis politiques représentatifs des intérêts des minorités nationales. La Constitution de la Fédération de Russie prévoit la protection des intérêts de tous les citoyens de l'Etat, y compris des minorités nationales, contre l'activité des partis, organisations et mouvements qui ont pour objectif l'incitation à la haine sociale, raciale, nationale et religieuse (article 13, alinéa 5).

11. A)   Les droits fondamentaux des citoyens de la Fédération de Russie d'élire et d'être élus dans les organes du pouvoir d'Etat sont déterminés aux articles 32 (alinéas 2 et 3) et 97 (alinéas 1 et 2) de la Constitution de la Fédération de Russie.

La présence des minorités est reflétée dans la législation électorale des sujets de la Fédération de Russie. L'article 112 de la Constitution de la République Sakha (Iakoutie) stipule que, "dans les lieux de résidence compacte des peuples peu nombreux du Nord, on peut créer des circonscriptions électorales avec un nombre moindre d'électeurs". La Constitution de la République de Bouriatie garantit l'élection des députés au Khoural populaire de la République de Bouriatie "compte tenu de la représentation territoriale et nationale" (article 80).

Actuellement, la législation électorale fédérale ne contient pas de règles spécifiques sur les minorités, leurs droits sont garantis dans le cadre des droits et libertés constitutionnels généraux de l'homme et du citoyen.

Le projet de Loi de la Fédération de Russie sur "Les Principes fondamentaux de la législation de la Fédération de Russie sur le statut juridique des peuples autochtones peu nombreux" actuellement débattu à la Douma d'Etat, détermine que la représentation des peuples autochtones peu nombreux n'ayant pas de collectivités nationales territoriales, aura des quotas de mandats de députés dans les organes représentatifs locaux du pouvoir d'Etat (article 15).

B)   Il s'agit surtout de minorités ayant une résidence compacte sur les territoires des sujets de la Fédération de Russie.

L'incidence de l'existence de minorités sur le découpage des circonscriptions électorales, administratives ou judiciaires est conditionnée par leur résidence compacte et leur nombre.

12. A)   La participation des minorités à la vie politique est assurée essentiellement par les prescriptions constitutionnelles dans le cadre général des droits et libertés égaux de l'homme et du citoyen dans tous les domaines de l'activité étatique et sociale. Comme cela a été mentionné, on a prévu des mesures spéciales pour les minorités en matière d'enseignement des langues et dans d'autres règles de droit.

B)   La question des organes du pouvoir et des niveaux de direction a été déterminée dans les chapitres suivants de la Constitution de la Fédération de Russie : sur l'organisation fédérale (chapitre 3), sur le Président de la Fédération de Russie (chapitre 4), sur l'Assemblée fédérale (chapitre 5), sur le Gouvernement de la Fédération de Russie (chapitre 6), sur le pouvoir judiciaire (chapitre 7), sur l'autoadministration locale (chapitre 8).

C)   Cette question fait écho à la question du point 10.A). Ici on ajoute seulement que la Loi de l'URSS "Sur les associations sociales" prévoit aussi la création non seulement des associations sociales centrales mais aussi des associations sociales locales (alinéa 1 de l'article 6), qui peuvent être créées à l'initiative d'au moins dix citoyens (alinéa 1 de l'article 8). Ces dispositions de la Loi permettent de créer des associations sociales de toutes les minorités.

Conformément à l'article 11 de ladite Loi, la reconnaissance officielle des associations des minorités nationales, en leur conférant certains pouvoirs de droit public, comme aux autres associations, est assurée sur le plan législatif par l'enregistrement de ces associations suivant les modalités fixées par la Loi (article 11 de la Loi).

13.   La Constitution et les lois de la Fédération de Russie n'imposent pas un devoir spécial aux personnes appartenant à des minorités qui serait différent du devoir constitutionnel des autres citoyens de l'Etat.

14. A)   La Constitution et les lois de la Fédération de Russie ne prévoient pas les formes complémentaires de la protection des sous-minorités.

B)   Au niveau de l'Etat elles ne sont pas traitées comme une minorité.

15.   A côté des recours constitutionnels, administratifs ou juridictionnels on adopte, pour assurer une protection complémentaire des intérêts des minorités, comme cela a été indiqué plus haut, des lois, arrêtés et règlements des organes du pouvoir et des organes administratifs de la Fédération de Russie pour améliorer leurs conditions de vie, le développement des formes traditionnelles de production et de culture, la protection du milieu écologique etc.

SLOVAKIA

1. A)   The Constitution of the Slovak Republic (No. 460/1992, Coll. of Acts) in its preamble upholds the rights of nations to their self-determination, in compliance with the existence of national minorities living in the territory of the Slovak Republic, following the civic principle.
"We the Slovak nation... stemming from the natural right of every nation to self-determination, together with the members of national minorities and ethnic groups living in the territory of the Slovak Republic,... thus, we, the citizens of the Slovak Republic, decide upon this Constitution through our representatives".
The character of inhabitation in the state is thus identified by the Constitution as a national and at the same time a more ethnic one, cumulated in citizenship.

   B)   In the context of the Constitution, the Slovak Republic is a unified, unitary state with a united and indivisible territory (Article 3, paragraph 1).

   C)   The duty of the state to protect its own minorities living outside the territory of the Slovak Republic is not contained either in the Constitution or in the law.

2. A)   Yes, the Constitution of the Slovak Republic, in compliance with minorities protection, uses the expression "national minority or ethic group" (second chapter, fourth part - Articles 33 and 34, Constitution of the Slovak Republic).
The Document of Basic Rights and Freedoms, Constitutional Act No. 23/1991, Coll. of Acts, which in the context of Article 152, Constitution of the Slovak Republic, is also in force throughout the territory of the Slovak Republic, uses the expression "national and ethnic minority" (Articles 24 and 25 of the Document). The expression "national minority" is also used in the SNC Act No. 428/1990, Coll. of Acts, about official languages (§ 6, paragraph 2).

B)   The Constitution of the Slovak Republic and the law in force in the Slovak Republic do not contain an exact definition of a minority, but the subjects of the minority rights are defined as citizens (state citizens of the Slovak Republic) belonging to national minorities or to ethnic groups (Articles 33 and 34, Constitution of the Slovak Republic).
Note: The Constitution does not define criteria for the determination of persons belonging to a minority.

C)   The Constitution of the Slovak Republic, recognising the rights of minorities, covers groups different from the rest of population on an ethnic basis. For their determination, as mentioned above, it uses, however, two expressions - "national minority" and "ethnic group", but this fact does not contain a classifying or evaluating aspect, neither does it implicate the way of a legislative approach. In the Constitution, the provision of the various rights does not depend on whether a national or an ethnic group is concerned. The text stated under A) and B) does not cover explicitly religious minorities.

D)   The Constitution and the law do not require and naturally do not determine any procedure of recognition of a minority by the state through some formal - legal - act. In the context of the Constitution of the Slovak Republic (Article 12, paragraph 3), individual membership of a minority always depends on the free decision of every physical person. At the same time, the Constitution prohibits any influence upon this decision and all forms of pressure directed towards a loss of nationality as well. This means that any compulsion (including by state bodies) to become a member of some minority is prohibited by the Constitution.

E)   More on an individual level, but an unambiguous assessment of this question is complicated. Up till now, the question of individual and collective rights has not been clarified either in international documents or in the legislation of the states. The rights of minority members, recognised as individual ones, can be understood as collective ones and vice versa at the same time (see, e.g. the Document of the Committee of Experts for the Protection of National Minorities DH-MIN, Strasbourg, January-March 1993). Does any more exact border exist between them? Does any right exist (excluding the right of self-determination) which cannot be understood as an individual right in any case? If we accept that "collective rights" will be considered as rights which (were obtained by an individual through his membership of a certain group), and which create some positive demands upon a citizen towards the state, then, following the formulation of Article 34 of the Constitution, which talks about "citizens forming national minorities or ethnic groups", it may be concluded that these rights are conferred upon individuals or parts of bigger units (minorities), whose existence is assumed for the recognition of the rights as stated in the Constitution. Thus, the sense and condition of protecting these rights of an individual is conditioned by the existence of a unit, and the Constitutions by stating "especially the right together with other members of minority", supposes that these rights will be implemented together (collectively).

F)	Membership of a minority, in compliance with the legal order in force in the Slovak Republic, does not have any effect upon state citizenship of the Slovak Republic nor upon the practical performance of political rights.

According to Article 12, paragraph 4, of the Constitution of the Slovak Republic "No person must suffer a loss of rights because they exercise their basic rights and freedoms". Article 33 of the Constitution emphasises that "Membership of a national minority or ethnic group must not harm anyone". The Constitution, when recognising political rights, makes no difference according to membership of an ethnic group. It provides them for "everyone", to the "citizens".

Act No. 40/1993, Coll. of Acts about state citizenship, in provisions about the obtaining and loss of state citizenship, does not see any relation between membership of an ethnic group, or, as the case may be, a nationality, and citizenship generally. (Theoretically, it is possible to mention only one such case, if a citizen of the Slovak Republic, a member of a national minority, upon his own application, lost his state citizenship, then he would not be a subject of minority rights in the context of the Constitution).

3.	A)	The legal conditions of national minorities are standardised also by international conventions.

According to Article 11 of the Constitution of the Slovak Republic "International agreements on human rights and basic freedoms, ratified by the Slovak Republic and proclaimed in accordance with approved law, take precedence over constitutional Acts, if they guarantee greater constitutional rights and freedoms". § 2, Document on basic rights and freedoms also has a similar wording. From the point of view of national minorities rights, a special place is occupied by the agreement between the leading powers, united and associated, and Czechoslovakia, concluded in Saint-Germain-en-Laye on September 10, 1919 (published in Coll. of Acts and regulation No. 508/1921). This agreement became a legal guarantee of the minimum existence of minorities who, without their own guilt, remained within the borders of the Czechoslovak state. Signing this agreement, Czechoslovakia accepted an international obligation to undertake a certain protection of minorities within its internal state legal order. In the context of Article 1 of this agreement, "Czechoslovakia is obliged to recognise the provisions contained in Articles 2 - 8 of this chapter as basic laws and no law, provision or official act which is contrary to them will have any power". Articles 2 - 8 of the agreement mentioned concern especially the principles of equality regardless of language, race or religion, equality before the law, religious freedom and free use of language. The provisions mentioned are minimum, if not more extensively applied in the effective order of the Slovak Republic. Apart from that, from the wording of § 2, introductory act to the Document on basic rights and freedoms, and in compliance with Article 153, Constitution of the Slovak Republic, it follows that the relevant provisions of this agreement which concern minorities are also obligatory in the Slovak Republic, and take precedence over the acts.

B) We have no knowledge about the existence of decisions made by international or national bodies.

4. A) The constitutional principle of equality, contained in Articles 12 and 33 of the Constitution, prohibits discrimination as well. In the territory of the Slovak Republic, basic rights and freedoms are guaranteed to all, regardless of... race, colour of skin, language, beliefs and religion,... nationality or ethnic group. No one may be harmed, advantaged or disadvantaged for these reasons. Membership of any minority must not be detrimental to anybody.

B) Explicitly, the principle of "positive discrimination" is not formulated either in the Constitution or in the law. The

Constitution, in Article 34, guarantees the specific rights of minorities in the areas of language, culture, associations and education.

C) Minorities in the Slovak Republic are protected by the standards of criminal law in the context mentioned (Criminal law No. 140/1961, Coll. of Acts in the full wording No. 392/1992, Coll. of Acts). Concretely, the Criminal Law states that both the slandering of a nation, its language, race or conviction (§ 198) and the initiating of national or racial hatred (§ 198a) are criminal acts. Genocide toward any national, ethnic, racial or religious group is also a criminal act (§259).

The Constitution of the Slovak Republic formulates this freedom broadly. In the context of Article 24, paragraph 1, the Constitution guarantees freedom of opinion, conscience and religion, and includes them into a group of basic human rights and freedoms. This right includes also the possibility of changing religion or beliefs. Everyone has the right not to have religious beliefs and equally everyone has the right to express publicly his opinions. In the context of the Constitution, everybody has the right to express his religion or beliefs, either alone or together with others, privately or publicly, in the form of mass, religious services or by rites, and to take part in religious teaching (Article 24, paragraph 2 of the Constitution).

The Constitution of the Slovak Republic confers this right on an individual basis. At the same time, it is drawn up as a law which can be performed together with other people. Naturally, there is also a criminal-legal protection of this right as an individual one (§ 236 CL about limitation of the confession freedom) and also as a collective one (§ 198 CL about slandering of nation, race and beliefs). According to the provision quoted "Whoever publicly slanders...a group of inhabitants because of their political conviction, confession or because they are without confession, will be punished...".

B) We have no knowledge about a similar national or international decisions.

6. A)   The Constitution of the Slovak Republic guarantees minority members, under the conditions given by law, and excepting the right to acquire the state language, the right to education in their mother tongue (Article 34, paragraph 2 of the Constitution), as well the right to establish and maintain educational institutions (Article 34, paragraph 1 of the Constitution). It is a specification of the right to education, recognised otherwise to everybody, contained in Article 42 of the Constitution.

This right is also confirmed by § 3, paragraph 1, Act No. 29/1984, Coll. of Acts, in the wording of amendments and additions on basic and secondary schools, in the context of which the right to education in their own language is guaranteed to citizens who are minority members in the range, relevant to the interest of developing their national language.

B)   The right is guaranteed to all national minorities and ethnic groups equally. The legal starting points are equal and guaranteed by the state at the level of basic and secondary schools. Naturally, the Constitution also enables schools other than state (i.e. private or church) schools to be established in compliance with the legislation of the state, but the state does not determine the teaching language in such schools (see, e.g. regulation of Ministry of Education, No. 11/1991, Coll. of Acts on private schools).

In the Slovak Republic, the right to education of minorities members is fully guaranteed. As an illustration, let us mention statistical data about the number of schools established for Hungarian minority in the school year 1991/92:

Kindergartens: 229 schools with Hungarian as the teaching language.

105 schools in which parallel to Slovak classes, classes with Hungarian as the teaching language were established.

Altogether in these schools, 13.182 children of Hungarian minority are educated.

Basic schools: 264 schools with Hungarian as the teaching language.

28 schools in which classes with Hungarian as the teaching language were established.

Altogether in these schools, 47.882 pupils of Hungarian minority are educated.

Grammar schools: 8 schools of mixed type.

Altogether at grammar schools with Hungarian as the teaching language, 4.054 students of Hungarian minority are studying.
<u>Other secondary schools</u>: 5 schools with Hungarian as the teaching language.
18 schools in which Hungarian classes are established.

C) No act contains unambiguous provision about study of a minority language, neither about study in a minority language, nor of a certain minority. In the context of the Act on universities (No. 172/1990, Coll of Acts), the establishment of pedagogic and scientific working places, as well the determination of the content of their activities, is a decision for the universities, or possibly the faculties. Up till now, an independent university for a certain minority has not been established, but the establishment of the Faculty of minority and ethnic cultures is being prepared in Nitra. For studies of minority languages, there is the Department of Hungarian language and literature at the Faculty of Philosophy, Comenius University in Bratislava, the Hungarian section of the Pedagogic University in Nitra and the Department of Ukrainian language and literature at the Pedagogic Faculty, University of Pavel Josef Šafarik in Prešov.

D) We are not aware of the existence of internal state or international legal decisions in this area.

7. A) The Constitution of the Slovak Republic, in Article 34, paragraph 2b, guarantees citizens belonging to minorities, under conditions given by law, the right to use their own language in official communication. This constitutional issue is contained in Act No. 428/1990, Coll. of Acts on official languages in the Slovak Republic which in § 6, paragraph 2 admits the right to use the mother tongue in official communication in communities in which the minority members represent at least 20 percent.

B) The Act on official languages, when admitting the right to use minority languages in official communication, does not distinguish between individual bodies and does not touch the language rights of minorities which follow special regulations. These are mainly provisions in § 12, paragraph 4, Criminal order and § 18 Civil court order, according to which everybody, including a participant of a proceeding, has the right to use his mother tongue before bodies in criminal proceedings as well as in civil legal proceedings. The right to use one's own language before the courts is not limited by the law only to mixed ethnic regions.

The possibility of using a minority language in private life, i.e. outside the legal and state sphere, can be partially concluded from Article 34, paragraph 1 of the Constitution, in the context of which citizens forming national minorities and ethnic groups are guaranteed... namely the right, together with other members of minorities or ethnic groups, to develop their own culture, to distribute and obtain information in their mother tongue. Here we can appeal to Article 7 of the Saint-Germain Agreement, in compliance with which no limitation will be imposed upon state citizens as far as the free usage of any language is concerned in private or commercial contacts, in matters concerning religion, the press or in public expressions at public meetings.

Protection of language against slandering is contained in a general form in § 198, Criminal law.

C) We have no knowledge of the existence of a concrete legal decision, caused by the provisions quoted.

8. The Constitution of the Slovak Republic, in Article 34, paragraph 1, guarantees the right of minorities to distribute and to obtain information in their mother tongue. It follows from the Act No. 36/1978, Coll. of Acts, in the wording of Act No. 115/1989, Coll. of Acts, on theatre activity, that the Ministry of Culture must take care of the interests of national minorities and ethnic groups in the sphere of theatre culture and create conditions for the satisfaction of these interests.

Practice: in the Slovak Republic, three permanent theatres have been established which perform in the minority language. In Košice and Komárno there are Hungarian theatres and in Prešov, there is an Ukrainian-Ruthenian theatre.

Act No. 255/1991, Coll. of Acts, in the wording of Act No. 483/1992, Coll. of Acts, on Slovak radio (§ 5, paragraph 2) states that Slovak radio must ensure by means of radio transmission in the mother tongue the implementation of interests of national minorities and ethnic groups living in the Slovak Republic. By its radio transmissions, Slovak radio must contribute to the development... of the culture of national minorities (§ 6d of the act quoted).

Practice: regular radio transmissions in the Hungarian and Ukrainian languages.
The same provisions are contained in Act No. 254/1991, Coll. of Acts, in the wording of Act No. 482/1992, Coll. of Acts, on TV transmissions in relation to minorities (§ 3, paragraph 3 and § 6c of the act quoted).
Practice: a regular TV transmission in the Hungarian language.

9.   Neither the Constitution, nor the law requires a practical application of specific legal rules exclusively in relation to minorities.

10. A) The right of association of persons belonging to minorities is fully respected. Generally, it is guaranteed in Article 29, paragraph 1 of the Constitution, according to which everyone (and thus also minority members) has the right, together with other persons, to form associations, societies or other groups. This right of minority members to associate in national associations is especially guaranteed by Article 34, paragraph 1 of the Constitution. In the context of Act No. 83/1990, Coll. of Acts, on the association of citizens, this right is defined generally in the sense that associations "whose objective is to deny or to limit personal, political or other rights of citizens because of their nationality..., race..., religious confession, to initiate hatred and intolerance based upon these reasons, to support violence or to break the Constitution and law in another way", are not permitted.
The right of citizens (as well as minority members) to establish political parties and movements and to associate in them follows from Article 29, paragraph 2 of the Constitution and from Act No. 424/1991, Coll. of Acts on political parties. Concerning the respect of this right in the Slovak Republic, the best proof is given in practice - the existence of four (4) political parties of Hungarian minorities.

B)   A special legal regulation, relating especially to political parties representing minorities in the Slovak Republic, does not exist.

11. A) No. In the Slovak Republic, in compliance with the legal regulation in force, a proportional election system is used for elections to the parliament, and for conmmunal elections, a majority system with a relative majority is used, without any exceptions for particular groups of the population.

B)   -

C)   The presence of minorities has no influence upon the creation of electoral or court districts and up to now, not upon the administration division of the state. In the context of the Constitution (Article 64, paragraphs 1 and 2) and Act No. 517/1990, Coll. of Acts, on territorial and administrative division of the Slovak Republic, this division has two levels - communities and regions. Legislative amendment of a new administrative-territorial division of the Slovak Republic is in the preparatory phase.

12. A) The participation of minority members in political life is amended by regulations, effective for all citizens, in the context of Article 30 of the Constitution, according to which citizens have the right to take part in the management of public matters directly or through free elections of their representatives, as well as to equal conditions of access to elected or other public functions. In relation to minority members, this right is specified in Article 34, paragraph 2c, guaranteeing them the right to take part in the resolution of matters relating to national minorities and ethnic groups. No special measures were accepted for the participation of minorities in political life.

B)   In the Slovak Republic, up to now, this right has been implemented through advisory bodies of minorities, at the level of central bodies of executive power. Their legal regulation is insufficient.

C)   There are no special provisions relating to the right of association of minorities in the Slovak Republic. Associations, as well as political parties, established by minorities have to be registered in the context of the law in force, the same as with other associations or political parties.

13. A) The Constitution of the Slovak Republic, Article 34, paragraph 3 states that "the assertion of rights of citizens belonging to minorities, guaranteed in this Constitution, must not threaten the sovereignty and territorial integrity of the Slovak Republic nor discriminate against the rest of its population".

B)   This provision has a more general character and in no case does it reflect in any legal or external legal limitation of the rights of minority members.

14. A)   Neither the Constitution nor the law provide any protection for "sub-minorities".

   B)   -

15.   Minority members have at their disposal the same administrative or judicial means as the rest of the citizens. There are no special, extraordinary means in the legal order of the Slovak Republic which are provided exclusively for minorities.

SLOVENIA

1. A)   The Constitution of the Republic of Slovenia does not contain provisions specifically characterising the nature of its population with regard to ethnicity, language or religion. Slovenia is defined as a state of all its citizens based on the permanent and inalienable right of the Slovenian people to self-determination (Article 3).

   B)   In the Constitution Slovenia is defined as a territorially indivisible state (Article 4). Neveertheless, pursuant to the provisions on local self-government it is possible for municipalities to joint other municipalities in establishing wider self-governing local communities or regional communities (Article 143). This also enables the regional joining of ethnically mixed municipalities, for example in the coastal area (Italians) and in the northeastern area (Hungarians).

   C)   Article 5 of the Constitution determines, among other tasks of the state, the obligation to attend to the welfare of (but not to protect) the autochtonous Slovenian ethnic minorities in neighbouring countries and of Slovenian emigrants and migrant workers abroad, as well as to promote their contacts with the homeland. It also determines that Slovenians not holding Slovenian citizenship shall enjoy special rights and privileges in Slovenia (for example, in the acquisition of citizenship, residence permit etc.).

2. A)   Article 64 of the Constitution regulates the special rights of Italians and Hungarians who are autochthonous inhabitants of Slovenia and designates them as ethnic communities; Article 65 determines that the special status and rights of the Gypsy community will be determined by law. it recognises a special status for them since they have lived on the territory of this country for many centuries. Italian and Hungarian ethnic communities are treated as ethnic minorities, but the Constutition does not define the status of the Gypsies. However, we may conclude that they are an ethnic community with some elements of ethnic minority.

B)C)D) The Constitution does not regulate the issue of recognising certain minorities, however, for certain autochthonous peoples or ethnic minorities and their members, it guarantees special rights in addition to the special rights guaranteed to all members of ethnic linguistic or cultural minorities (the right to freely express one's ethnic identily, to foster and express one's culture, to use one's language and script in dealings with state bodies). With these provisions the Constitution exlicitly emphasises that being a member of a minority depends solely upon an individual's free will.

E)F) The Constitution guarantees the rights of communities as well as of individual members of minorities. Being a member of a minority has no influence on the acquisition or loss of an individual's citizenship but it is important for the exercise of those special rights guaranteed by the Constitution and legislation.

3. A) The majority of international acts referring to the protection of minorities were concluded in the former Yugoslavia. They are binding upon the Republic of Slovenia in accordance with the Enabling Statute for the Implementation of the Basic Constitutional Charter on Independence and Sovereignty of the Republic of Slovenia of 25 June 1991 and in compliance with the new Constitution of the Republic of Slovenia. These are primarily bilateral agreements between the former Yugoslavia and particulary the Italian Republic and the Republic of Hungary, which partly also refer to the status of ethnic minorities in all three countries. Among the universal international acts one should mention the International Convention on the Abolition of All Forms of Racial Discrimination and also the conventions of specialised agencies particularly the International Labour Organisation convention on discrimination in the field of employment and the UNESCO convention on discrimination in the field of education. All these acts have influenced the content of domestic law (federal, republic and local) which was and is adopted predominantly on the basis of the former or new constitutional system which guaranteed and guarantees minorities and their members a high level of protection.

Until the adoption of the new Constitution of the Republic of Slovenia, ratified international agreements had the status of laws or government regulations in the hierarchy of legal acts. Pursuant to the Constitution, they now have a higher status in the legal hierarchy than laws since the Constitution stipulates that laws and other regulations must comply with the generally accepted principles of international law and international agreements binding upon Slovenia (Article 8).

B)   -

4. A)   The constitutional provision on the principle of equality explicitly applies to the members of minorities since it determines that in Slovenia each individual is guaranteed equal human rights irrespective of national origin, race, sex, language, religion, political or other beliefs (Article 14), and that all persons are equal beforre the law.

   B)C)   The Constitution determines special rights ("positive discrimination") in order to protect minorities and their members and also forms the basis for laws and other regulations. The Constitution especially and explicitly determines that any kind of incitement to ethnic, racial, religious or other inequality or any call to ethnic, racial, religious or other hatred or intolerance is unconstitutional.

5. A)   Article 41 of the Constitution determines the freedo of religion and belief in the following manner:

   The profession of religious and other beliefs of any person in private and in public life shall be free.

   No person shall be compelled to admit his religious or other beliefs.

   Parents shall be entitled to give their children a moral and religious upbringing which accords with the beliefs of the parents. The religious and moral upbringing given to a child shall be such as is appropriate to his age and to his level of maturity as well as being in accordance with the child's free conscience and religious and other beliefs or convictions.

   B)   -

6. A)B)C) The Constitution guarantees to the Italian and Hungarian ethnic minorities and their members the constitutional right to education and schooling in their own language as well as the right to plan and develop this education and schooling. In the ethnically mixed territory of northeastern Slovenia, in accordance with the wishes of this community, compulsory bilingual primary schooling was introduced by law, wherein lessons are carried out in both languages, Slovenian and Hungarian. In addition to Slovenian public primary and secondary schools, there are in Slovenia such schools providing lessons in Italian as well as bilingual schools providing lessons in Slovenian and Hungarian. The Constitution and the legislation permit private schools with lessons in a language other than Slovenian to be established.

    D) -

7. A)B) As has already been mentioned, the Constitution guarantees each person the right to use his own language and script privately or in dealings with the state bodies in which he gives effect to his rights. Although the official language is Slovenian, in the areas where Italians and Hungarians reside the official language is also Italian or Hungarian (Article 11).

    C) -

8. The Constitution guarantees each member of an ethnic minority the right to foster and express his culture. It especially guarantees the Italian and Hungarian ethnic minorities and their members the right to preserve their national identity and to establish organisations as well as to develop cultural and scientific research activities and activities in the field of mess media and publishing; the Constitution also binds the state to support financially and morally the exercising of these rights.

9. With the exception of bilingual primary schooling in areas where members of the Hungarian ethnic minority reside, the Constitution does not determine special arrangements for individual minorities; nevertheless it does not prohibit such arrangements if they are in the interest of preserving and developing the identity of an individual minority. The Constitution also explicitly determines that the self-governing organisations of Italians and Hungarians may be

- 276 -

authorised by the state to perform as public authorities specific tasks which are within the jurisdiction of the state, i.e. at least partly in a different manner if so demanded by the conditions and interests of individual minorities.

10. A)   The Constitution guarantees each person, including members of all kinds of minorities, the right to freely associate and it permits lawful restrictions due to general reasons, in circumstances involving national security, public safety and protection of the public against the spread of infectious diseases (Article 42). It even determines an obligation for the Italian and Hungarian ethnic communities to join into self-governing ethnic communities in order to exercise public authorisations and in order that they may be directly represented in the National Assembly (parliament) -to which they elect one deputy each- and in the representative bodies of the local communities.

The Constitution does not prevent association between members of minorities across the state border; it even guarantees members of the Hungarian and Italian minorities the right to foster contacts with their native peoples and their countries. Therefore the right to associate can only be restricted by law for the general reasons listed above.

B)   There are no special provisions on political parties which represent the interests of minorities.

11. A)B)   As mentioned, the Constitution guarantees direct representation of the Italian
and Hungarian ethnic communities in the National Assembly and in the representative bodies of local communities in the areas inhabited autochthonously by members of both minorities (the Italians on the Adriatic coast, in the municipalities of Koper, Izola and Piran, the Hungarians in the extreme northeastern part of the country along the border with Hungary, in the municipalities of Murska Sobota and Lendava).

C)   The new Constitution envisages a new way of forming municipalities as local self-governing communities and the possibility of forming regions, but the legislation is still being prepared. We expect the existence and interests of both ethnic minorities to have an impact on this legislation.

12. The Constitution especially determines that laws, regulations and other legislative measures (on the national, regional, and local levels), concerning the exercising of constitutional rights and the status of the Italian and Hungarian ethnic minorities, may not be adopted without the consent of the representatives of the ethnic communities. The Constitution also explicitly enables the transfer of public authorizations to the organisation of ethnic communities. These two provisions enable the further development of political and other rights as well as facilitating the development of ethnic minorities.

13. A) The Constitution does not explicitly require members of ethnic minorities to be faithful or loyal to the state.

   B) -

14. A) Members of minorities in the Republic of Slovenia do not constitute the majority of its population, nor even in the municipalities where they are autochthonous inhabitants.

   B) -

15. There are no special legal means for members of minorities in the present system.

APPENDIX
to Slovenia's replies

An overview of some decrees of the Slovenian Constitutional and Supreme Courts referring to the rights of minorities with a computer designation of their contents

A. Constitutional Court

1) Name of Submitter
    The people of Lendava

    Act
    The law on schools with lessons in the Italian or Hungarian language and on bilingual schools in the Socialist Republic of Slovenia (Official Gazette of SRS, N° 7-44/65), individual provisions

    Problem
    Defining special conditions for the introduction of bilingual lessons in schools.
    Separate opinions by judges of the constitutional court.

    Finding
    The law on schools with lessons in the Italian or Hungarian language and on bilingual schools in the Socialist Republic of Slovenia (Official Gazette of SRS, N° 7-44/65) does not violate the Constitution of the Socialist Republic of Slovenia, therefore the proceeding to evaluate its conformity with the Constitution of the Socialist Republic of Slovenia is stopped.

    Text
    In order to guarantee the constitutional principles of equality and solidarity, the law may, in the areas inhabited by people of Slovenian nationality and members of ethnic minorities, introduce, under certain special conditions, compulsory bilingual schooling.

2) Name of Submitter
   Rihard Silič, Lendava

   Act
   The decree of the Municipal Assembly of Lendava on the flag of the people
   of Hungarian nationality as a national symbol of the Hungarian nationality
   in the municipality of Lendava (Official publications, N° 18/79).

   Problem
   Determination of the national symbol (flag).

   Finding
   The initiative to evaluate the constitutionality of the contested decree is not
   adopted.

   Text
   The decree of the Municipal Assembly of Lendava on the flag as a national
   symbol does not violate the Constitution since the rights of the Hungarian
   nationality to use national symbols are guaranteed by the Constitution.

3) Name of Submitter
   Jože Campa, Loke pri Kisovcu

   Act
   The decree of the Municipal Assembly of Zagorje ob savi on funeral
   ceremonies in the area of the municipality of Zagorje ob Savi (Official
   Journal of Zasavje, Nos. 1/90 and 5/90) - the second and third paragraphs
   of Article 8.

   Problem
   The municipal decree oversteps the legal authorisation. The performing of
   funeral ceremonies and the prohibition on the funeral procession from going
   into and out of the church.
   Obliging a religious community to perform a specific religious ceremony in
   a determined location.

   Finding
   The provisions of the contested decree are null and void.

Text
The provisions of the municipal decree prohibiting funeral processions with a coffin or an urn containing the remains of the deceased from going into or out of the church and which oblige a religious community to say funeral mass in a determined location do not conform with the Constitution or republic law and violate federal law.

4) Name of submitter
Jožef Gjuran, Lendava

Act
Law on identity cards (Official Gazette of SRS, N° 16/74 and 29/79) Article 4a.

Problem
Issuing of identity cards on bilingual forms (in Slovenian and Italian/Hungarian).

Finding
The initiative to evaluate the constitutionality of the contested article is not adopted.

Text
The legal provision according to which, in the areas inhabited by members of the Italian or Hungarian ethnic minorities in addition to people of Slovenian nationality, an identity card is issued on a bilingual form, does not violate the Constitution.

5) Name of submitter
Association for the Preservation of Equality Among Citizens, Ljubljana
Dragiša Marojević, Ljubljana

Act
Law on elections and recall of the president and members of the presidency of the SR Slovenia (Official Gazette of SRS, N°42/89), the second paragraph of Article 2 and the third paragraph of Article 8.

Problem
Citizenship of the republic as a condition for being elected president or a member of the presidency of the republic.

Equality among citizens on the territory of the republic due to their citizenship or the fact that they are members of other Yugoslav peoples or nationalities.
Sociopolitical organisation (party) as a submitter before the constitutional court.

Finding
The legal provisions contested do not violate the Constitution.

Text
Legal provisions according to which only a citizen of the SR Slovenia has the right to be elected president or member of the presidency of the SR Slovenia or according to which a submitted nomination must be accompanied by a certificate proving that a candidate is a citizen of the SR Slovenia do not violate the Constitution.

6) Name of submitter
Coastal self-governing community of members of the Italian nationality, Koper

Act
The decree by the board of directors of Spar-Mercator, Ltd. Ljubljana, on the required profile for the operations director of 24/1/1991 and 7/3/1991.

Problem
It is not within the jurisdiction of the constitutional court to give an evaluation of a job advertisement as an implemental act of a decree of the board of directors of a joint-stock company (individual act - specific act). Nationality of the candidate as a condition for the performance of duties and functions (director).

Finding
The initiative for the evaluation of the constitutionality and lawfulness of the contested decree is not adopted.

Text
The job advertisement is the implemental act of the general act on required conditions for a specific job and its evaluation is not within the jurisdiction of the constitutional court.
The constitutional court did not adopt the initiative and has not begun proceedings to evaluate the lawfulness of the general act on required

conditions for a specific job since, with the initiative, the contested act was in the meantime changed to comply with the Constitution and therefore unconstitutional and unlawful consequences did not occur.

B. The Supreme Court

Fundamental violation of provisions of the law on legal proceedings - language of the nationality

Text

If, in ethnically mixed territory where members of the Italian (or Hungarian) nationality reside, a party in a legal proceeding is a member of this nationality, the proceeding is always conducted and the provisions issued in the language of the minority, unless the party explicitly declines this right. A violation of this principle is a fundamental violation of the provisions of the first paragraph of Article 343 of the law on Legal Proceedings.

ESPAGNE

1. A)   La Constitution espagnole de 1978 ne contient pas formellement de
          déclaration claire sur le "caractère unitaire national ou homogène"
          de la population. Cependant, l'article 2 de la Constitution reconnaît
          un contenu très étendu au droit à l'autonomie
          ("autogouvernement"), en faveur des nationalités et régions, bien
          que le texte constitutionnel ne contienne pas de définition concrète
          de ce que sont les nationalités et régions; en tout cas, on peut
          penser que l'article 143, réglant la procédure d'exercice du droit
          cité, concrétise ces notions en donnant la possibilité
          d'autogouvernement aux provinces limitrophes ayant des
          caractéristiques historiques, culturelles et économiques communes.
          De même, l'article 3 constate et rend officiel le pluralisme
          linguistique, selon les termes indiqués plus loin, en mettant en
          relief le caractère positif de ce fait, le qualifiant comme "patrimoine
          culturel qui sera l'objet d'un respect particulier et sera protégé"
          (voir point 7).

   B)   D'après ce qui vient d'être indiqué, la structure territoriale de
          l'organisation étatique (que matérialise le droit à l'autonomie cité)
          se fonde sur les identités historiques et culturelles spécifiques des
          régions, parmi lesquelles peuvent être signalées, entre autres, les
          particularités linguistiques de certaines régions.

   C)   Non. La Constitution contient deux allusions aux Espagnols qui se
          trouvent à l'étranger, l'une pour proclamer comme un principe
          d'orientation de l'action des pouvoirs publics "la sauvegarde des
          droits économiques et sociaux des travailleurs espagnols à
          l'étranger" (article 42) et l'autre qui constitue un mandat au
          législateur pour qu'il facilite "l'exercice du droit de suffrage des
          Espagnols hors du territoire de l'Espagne" (article 68.5): ni l'une
          ni l'autre ne font référence aux minorités qui pourraient exister
          dans la société espagnole.

2. A)B)C) Le terme "minorité" n'est pas utilisé par le texte constitutionnel
          espagnol et il n'apparaît pas non plus dans la législation, plus

étendue, de caractère constitutionnel. Il est possible que cette expression soit utilisée sous une forme très précise dans des normes de rang inférieur. La jurisprudence constitutionnelle n'a pas discuté non plus ce concept précis du point de vue signalé ici (il apparaît néanmoins par exemple dans une perspective strictement politique où on l'oppose à la majorité parlementaire), Il ne faut pas pour autant oublier quelques allusions indirectes dans certains arrêts (l'arrêt du Tribunal constitutionnel qui s'est référé plus explicitement aux "groupes ethniques" sera repris plus loin).

D) Comme cela vient d'être dit, le droit espagnol n'a pas examiné spécifiquement la question des "minorités". Cependant, il contient des énoncés qui peuvent être considérés comme le résultat d'une combinaison de la reconnaissance du principe d'égalité et de la protection des droits ethniques, linguistiques ou religieuses existant à l'intérieur de la société espagnole. A ce sujet, on peut qualifier de révélateur l'article 9 de la Constitution qui allant plus loin que l'article 14 qui consacre le principe libéral traditionnel de l'égalité devant la loi, impose aux pouvoirs publics la tâche de promouvoir les conditions pour que la liberté et l'égalité de tout individu et des groupes auxquels il appartient soient réelles et effectives.

Ce mandat constitutionnel a été développé par plusieurs textes législatifs qui, d'une façon ou d'une autre, sont orientés vers le constat et la protection de la liberté et de l'égalité des différents groupes présents dans la société espagnole et, au-delà, vers la défense de la situation des minorités. Ainsi, l'Etat espagnol a souscrit des conventions avec plusieurs confessions religieuses afin de garantir le plein exercice du droit à la liberté religieuse (Accords de Coopération avec la Fédération des Entités Religieuses Evangéliques d'Espagne, avec la Fédération des Communautés Israélites d'Espagne et avec la Commission Islamique de l'Espagne, tous du 10 novembre 1992). Des normes de nature et de rang très différents ont également développé le principe de pluralisme linguistique consacré par l'article 3 de la Constitution.

D'autre part, la jurisprudence constitutionnelle se faisant l'écho de ce type de principes a reconnu le droit d'ester en justice d'une citoyenne espagnole juive afin de défendre les intérêts du groupe racial auquel elle appartenait (Arrêt 214/1991, Affaire Violeta Friedman: "compte tenu du fait que les groupes ethniques, sociaux et même religieux sont, en général, des entités sans personnalité juridique et manquent d'organes de représentation à qui l'ordre juridique pourrait attribuer l'exercice d'actions civiles et pénales, pour la défense de leur honneur collectif, le fait de ne pas reconnaître le droit d'agir des membres de ce groupe, résidant dans notre pays, pour réagir par voie judiciaire face aux atteintes à l'honneur du groupe aboutirait à laisser non seulement intactes les violations de ce droit fondamental que subiraient à part égale tous et chacun de ses membres, mais aussi à ce que l'Etat espagnol de droit permettrait le surgissement de campagnes discriminatoires, racistes ou de caractère xénophobe...").

E)   Comme il a été précédemment dit, l'ordre constitutionnel espagnol ne contient pas de références formelles et précises au problème des minorités. Néanmoins, lorsque le droit espagnol s'est occupé matériellement de la question des minorités, il les a considérées aussi bien en termes collectifs que d'un point de vue strictement individuel.

F)   Non.

3.   A)B)   A partir de l'entrée en vigueur de la Constitution espagnole du 29 décembre 1978, les conventions et traités internationaux ont en droit espagnol validité immédiate et priment le droit interne.

D'une part, le mandat précis de l'article 96 de la Constitution prévoit que les traités internationaux validement conclus, une fois officiellement publiés en Espagne et quelle que soit leur matière, sont partie intégrante de l'ordre juridique.

La doctrine espagnole a amplement débattu sur la place de ces normes conventionnelles dans l'ordre juridique interne. Pour certains auteurs, la disposition constitutionnelle citée, dans la mesure où elle dispose que les dispositions d'un traité "ne pourront être abrogées que dans la forme prévue par les traités eux-mêmes ou conformément aux règles générales du droit international", constitue la reconnaissance d'une certaine supériorité hiérarchique des traités (la loi ordinaire ne peut modifier une norme conventionnelle antérieure). D'autres secteurs doctrinaux, au contraire, considèrent préférable d'expliquer la norme constitutionnelle en question sur la base du principe de compétence

- 286 -

(les dispositions d'un traité ne sont pas supérieures dans la hiérarchie par rapport à la loi parlementaire, mais elles se bornent à délimiter le cadre matériel en leur faveur,qui ne peut être envahi par le législateur ordinaire).

D'autre part, l'article 10 de la Constitution, particulièrement pertinent pour question qui nous occupe, indique "que les normes relatives aux droits fondamentaux que la Constitution reconnaît seront interprétées conformément à la Déclaration universelle des Droits de l'Homme et aux traités et conventions internationaux portant sur les mêmes matières, ratifiés par l'Espagne". Cette disposition situe ces traités à un niveau quasiment constitutionnel, dans la mesure où ils projettent leur force d'interprétation sur les dispositions constitutionnelles et jouissent en conséquence d'une force réfléchie des normes constitutionnelles sur lesquelles ils opèrent (à noter que selon le texte de l'article 10.2 déjà cité, comme la doctrine l'a signalé à plusieurs reprises, ce sont les normes constitutionnelles qui sont interprétées à la lumière des traités).

4. A)   Oui. L'article 14 de la Constitution, qui consacre le principe d'égalité devant la loi, contient de manière claire une interdiction de la discrimination "pour cause de naissance, de race, de sexe, de religion, d'opinion ou de toute autre condition ou circonstance personnelle ou sociale". Dès le début, la jurisprudence constitutionnelle a déclaré à plusieurs reprises que l'énumération de l'article 14 n'a pas un caractère fermé, de sorte que toute autre différence de traitement dépourvue de fondement rationnel doit être considérée comme comprise parmi les interdictions de l'article 14 sus-mentionné.

La jurisprudence nationale a eu l'occasion de se prononcer sur la question à différentes occasions. Voir, par exemple, l'arrêt du 10 novembre 1981, STC 19/1981 du 5 mai.

B)   Voir réponses 2.D).

C)   Pour le moment non. Mais l'avant-projet de loi organique du Code pénal, présenté le 20 mai 1994, énumère comme délits certains actes qui entraînent une discrimination ou provoquent la violence en raison de la race, de l'origine nationale, de la religion, etc.

5. A) La Constitution espagnole considère la liberté d'opinion, religieuse et de culte comme appartenant à la catégorie la plus élevée de règles, étant donné que, consacrée à l'article 16 de la Constitution, elle bénéficie d'une protection au plus haut niveau: la réforme constitutionnelle de cette disposition (tout comme celle des autres droits de l'homme fondamentaux) exige une procédure particulièrement complexe; son développement législatif doit être mis en oeuvre par loi organique (adoptée par la majorité absolue au Congrès des Députés) est assuré non seulement par la juridiction ordinaire mais aussi par la juridiction constitutionnelle par le biais du recours d'amparo.

Cette disposition constitutionnelle a été consacrée par les accords conclus avec les différentes confessions religieuses citées précédemment (voir réponse 2.D)), ainsi que par la Loi organique 7/1985 du 5 juillet sur la liberté religieuse. Son article 2 déclare concrètement que "la liberté religieuse et de culte comprend tant l'interdiction de toute contrainte que le droit de toute personne de professer les croyances religieuses librement choisies par elle ou de n'en professer aucune.

B) Il existe une abondante jurisprudence, provenant aussi bien du Tribunal Constitutionnel que du Tribunal Suprême, qui s'étend sur les aspects les plus divers du droit à la liberté religieuse, surtout si l'on tient compte des conséquences que la qualification de l'Etat comme non confessionnel entraîne pour l'unité juridictionnelle et pour le régime du mariage. Parmi la jurisprudence du Tribunal Constitutionnel interprétant l'article 16 de la Constitution, il convient de citer, du fait de leur importance, les arrêts 101/1983 du 18 novembre (le devoir de prêter serment ou promesse de respecter la Constitution nécessaire pour remplir des fonctions publiques n'enfreint pas la liberté de croyance), 19/1985 du 13 février (qui n'accorde pas l'amparo à un travailleur licencié à cause de son refus de travailler le samedi pour des raisons religieuses), et 47/1985 du 27 mars (qui déclare que le licenciement d'une enseignante pour des raisons idéologiques dans une école privée enfreint le droit à la liberté religieuse).

6. A) La Constitution espagnole contient une référence précise à la liberté d'enseignement à son article 27. Cette disposition consacre textuellement le droit, à l'éducation et à la liberté d'enseignement,

ainsi que le droit pour les parents, de décider que leurs enfants reçoivent la formation religieuse et morale conforme à leurs propres convictions. Les lois organiques 8/1985 du 3 juillet, réglant le droit à l'éducation, et 1/1990 du 3 octobre, d'aménagement général du système de l'éducation, ont mis en oeuvre ce droit constitutionnel. Ces deux textes de loi contiennent l'un et l'autre des allusions indirectes à la question qui nous occupe. L'article 4 de la première des lois citées indique que "les parents ou tuteurs ont droit à ce que leurs enfants ou pupilles reçoivent la formation religieuse et morale adaptée à leurs propres convictions". L'article 6 de la Loi organique 1/1990 proclame le principe de "l'égalité effective de droits entre les sexes et du rejet de toute sorte de discrimination ainsi que le respect de toutes les cultures."

B)   Il n'existe pas de disposition légale à ce sujet dans l'ordre juridique espagnol.

C)D)   L'article 1, alinéa 1 (d) de la Loi organique 1/1990 établit que le système éducatif espagnol sera orienté vers "la formation dans le respect à la pluralité linguistique et culturelle de l'Espagne". En tout cas, ce sont les lois des Communautés Autonomes ayant des particularités linguistiques qui, sur la base de la compétence conférée par l'article 148.1.17 (les Communautés Autonomes pourront assumer des compétences dans l'aide à la culture, la recherche, et, le cas échéant, l'enseignement de la langue de la Communauté Autonome), ont le plus développé les voies pour l'enseignement des langues autonomes, provoquant plusieurs conflits de compétences dont la résolution par le Tribunal Constitutionnel demeure en suspens. En tout cas, cet organe juridictionnel a déjà déclaré que le droit à l'éducation que consacre l'article 27 de la Constitution ne renferme pas dans son contenu l'option linguistique (arrêt 19/1992 du 12 février).

7. A)B)C) L'article 3 de la Constitution espagnole, en développant un principe proclamé dans le Préambule ("La Nation espagnole proclame sa volonté de... protéger tous les Espagnols et peuples de l'Espagne dans l'exercice des droits de l'homme, de leurs cultures et traditions, langues et institutions") aborde cette question en déclarant l'espagnol langue officielle. Il en découle le droit de l'utiliser et le devoir de le connaître, et de plus, la coofficialité de

toutes les autres langues espagnoles au sein des Communautés autonomes respectives conformément à leurs statuts. Finalement, le troisième alinéa de la disposition souligne la richesse culturelle que représente le pluralisme linguistique et, en conséquence, le devoir implicite de respect et de protection de la part des pouvoirs publics.

Cet article n'est pas le seul à proclamer le pluralisme linguistique de la société espagnole dans la Constitution; l'article 20.3 consacré au régime des mass-médias dépendant de l'Etat, et l'article 148.1.17, qui fixe le cadre des compétences des Communautés autonomes, s'occupent aussi de la question. Mais en tout cas, le premier des articles cités est celui qui, en réalité, établit le régime général et de base du plurilinguisme dans la constitution. Par conséquent, il mérite un commentaire.

Premièrement, il faut constater que le caractère officiel de l'espagnol, son utilisation générale comme moyen de communication entre les citoyens et les pouvoirs publics et son implantation sociale dans tout l'Espagne qui en font le moyen linguistique commun de communication entre tous les Espagnols, impliquent l'obligation de connaître cette langue. D'un autre côté, les "autres langues espagnoles" bénéficient d'un caractère officiel, qui est défini par les divers statuts d'autonomie et limité aux territoires déterminés par l'étendue territoriale de la communauté autonome correspondante. En tout cas, la déclaration de coofficialité implique le droit de tout citoyen de s'exprimer dans n'importe laquelle des langues officielles de la Communauté autonome (espagnol ou langue régionale) dans ses relations avec des pouvoirs publics ayant des compétences définies dans le cadre de la Communauté autonome en question.

Plusieurs Statuts d'autonomie, conformément à l'article 3 de la Constitution, ont proclamé la coofficialité linguistique dans leurs Communautés autonomes respectives (Catalogne, Pays Basque, Galice, Valence et Iles Baléares en particulier), et plusieurs normes ayant force de loi issues aussi bien de l'Etat que des Communautés autonomes basque, catalane, galicienne, valencienne ou baléare ont développé des mécanismes précis pour donner un sens à la défense et à la promotion de la valeur culturelle que représente le pluralisme linguistique.

- 290 -

L'activité normative de l'Etat a été orientée principalement vers la réglementation de la communication linguistique entre le citoyen et les pouvoirs publics, ce qui correspond en principe à l'idée de l'officialité de l'espagnol et de la coofficialité des langues régionales; on peut souligner à ce propos l'article 36 de la loi 30/1992 du Régime juridique des Administrations publiques concernant les relations citoyen/administration[1] et les articles 231 de la loi organique 6/85 du Pouvoir judiciaire[2] et 540 de la loi de procédure criminelle pour ce qui est des relations du citoyen avec l'Administration de la justice.

Dans le cadre de la législation autonome, les normes édictées amplifient le rôle de moyen de communication des langues autonomes en utilisant l'argument implicite de la nécessité de protection et de promotion de leur usage, compte tenu du caractère prépondérant et dominant de l'espagnol au sein du corps social des communautés autonomes. Cette hégémonie et cette domination sont d'ailleurs très souvent plus rhétoriques que réelles. Sous l'euphémisme de "Loi de normalisation linguistique", des lois réglementant la question ont été édictées au Pays Basque (loi du Parlement basque 10/82 du 24 novembre, de base pour la normalisation de l'usage de l'euskera), en Catalogne (loi du Parlement catalan 7/83 du 18 avril, de normalisation linguistique), en Galice (loi du Parlement de Galice 3/83, du 15 juin, de normalisation linguistique), aux Baléares (loi du Parlement baléare 3/86, du 29 avril, de normalisation linguistique des Iles). Ces lois qui, à un certain moment, ont fait l'objet de recours auprès du

---

[1] *"La langue des procédures de l'Administration centrale sera l'espagnol. Nonobstant cette affirmation, les personnes intéressées qui s'adresseront aux organes de l'Administration centrale siégeant sur le territoire d'une Communauté autonome pourront aussi utiliser la langue "coofficielle". Dans ce cas, la procédure se déroulera dans la langue choisie par la personne intéressée..."*

[2] *"Dans toutes les procédures judiciaires, les juges, magistrats et autres fonctionnaires des cours et tribunaux utiliseront l'espagnol, langue officielle de l'Etat... Ils pourront utiliser de même la langue officielle originaire de la Communauté autonome, sauf opposition de l'une des parties, invoquant une méconnaissance qui pourrait gêner sa défense. Les Parties au litige, leurs représentants et ceux qui les dirigent, de même que les témoins et les experts pourront utiliser la langue officielle sur le territoire des Communautés autonomes où les procédures ont lieu..."*

Tribunal constitutionnel, ont ultérieurement été déclarées conformes à la Constitution (Arrêts 82/86, 83/86, du 26 juin et 123/88, du 23 juin, respectivement).

8. Non.

9. Non.

10. A) Oui. Il est pleinement reconnu sans obstacle.

    B) Non.

11. A)B) Non.

    C) Non.

12. A)B)C) Non.

13. A)B) Les règlements des chambres parlementaires, (Congrès des députés et Sénat), ainsi que de quelques Assemblées législatives autonomes (par exemple, le Parlement de Galice), ont établi de manière générale l'exigence de prêter serment ou promesse de respecter la Constitution comme une condition du plein accès au statut de parlementaire. Le Tribunal constitutionnel a considéré cette condition conforme à la Constitution, puisqu'elle ne viole pas le droit égal de participation politique comme le prétendaient les requérants (voir entre autres, les arrêts 101/1983 du 18 novembre et 122/1983 du 16 décembre). En revanche, l'arrêt 119/1990 du 21 juin a considéré contraire aux énoncés constitutionnels, en tant qu'elle limitait le droit de participation politique sans aucune justification objective et raisonnable, la règle imposant le serment ou la promesse cité se fasse suivant une formule rituelle et non pas à travers l'expression employée par certains parlementaires.

14. A)B) La Constitution espagnole manque de dispositions claires à ce sujet.

15. Non. Pas de manière explicite. Cependant, à travers l'arrêt du Tribunal constitutionnel 214/1991 du 11 novembre déjà cité (Affaire Violeta Friedman), le haut organe juridictionnel a considéré Mme Friedman comme la personne légitimement à même de présenter un recours contentieux afin de défendre son droit à

l'honneur, par présomption de vulnérabilité à cause des déclarations injurieuses pour la race juive d'un ancien nazi dans la presse (voir les phrases les plus significatives de cet arrêt au point 2. in fine).

SWEDEN

1. A)   No

   B)   The State is not organised on a federal basis.

   C)   No

2. A)   Yes. According to Chapter 2, Article 15 of the Instrument of Government (IG), which is the central part of the Swedish Constitution, "no Act of law or other statutory instrument may entail the discrimination of any citizen because he belongs to a minority on grounds of race, skin colour, or ethnic origin". Positive discrimination in favour of minorities is also recognised by the Constitution where it is laid down that "opportunities should be promoted for ethnic, linguistic and religious minorities to minorities to preserve and develop a cultural and social life of their own" (chapter 1, article 2 of the IG).

   B)   The ban on discrimination of "citizens" formally refers to Swedish citizens but according to Chapter 2, article 20 of the IG a foreigner within the Realm shall be equated with Swedish citizens in this respect.

   C)   All kinds of minorities.

   D)   No

   E)   The minorities are also viewed in collective terms. It is, for example, a crime to agitate against ethnic groups (Chapter 16, Article 8 of the Penal Code).

   F)   No

3.   Sweden has, for example, acceded to the UN Convention on the Elimination of all forms of Racial Discrimination and to the European Convention on Human Rights. To be applied in domestic

law treaty provisions must first be incorporated in Swedish law by means of legislation or other regulation. Concerning the first of the two conventions mentioned, this has been done by legislation referred to under 4C) below. The European Convention on Human Rights is supposed to be incorporated in its entirety from 1 January 1995.

4. A)   -

   B)   Yes. See 2 A) about Chapter 1, Article 2 of the IG. It could be mentioned that, according to the law, the Sami population has exclusive right to use soil and water to support themselves and their reindeer.

   C)   Yes. In Chapter 16, Article 8 of the Penal Code it is laid down that if a person in a statement or other communication which is spread threatens or expresses contempt for an ethnic group or other such group of persons with allusion to race, skin-colour, national or ethnic origin or religious creed, he shall be sentenced for agitation against ethnic group. According to Chapter 16, Article 9 of the same Code a businessman shall be sentenced if he in the conduct of his business discriminates against someone on the ground of his race, skin colour, national or ethnic origin or religious creed by refusing to deal with him on the same conditions the businessman applies to other in the conduct of his business; likewise, an organiser of a public assembly or entertainment may be sentenced for unlawful discrimination if he discriminates against someone on the ground of his race etc. by refusing to allow him to enter the assembly or entertainment on the same conditions as apply to others. In 1986 a special act was passed prohibiting discrimination on ethnic grounds. Under the provisions of the Act the Government has appointed an Ombudsman against discrimination who is charged with ensuring that the act is complied with.

5.   The freedom of worship, defined as the freedom to practise one's own religion either alone or in company with others, is guaranteed in Chapter 2, Article 1 of the IG, and according to Article 2 of the same chapter all citizens (including foreigners living in Sweden) shall be protected against all coercion to belong to any religious congregation.

6. A)   Provided that the prescribed standard is met, it is possible to found subsidised private schools; this option is open also to minority groups. Children belonging to the Sami community are educated in a special school, funded by the State. The board of this school is elected by the representative assembly of the Sami population (see 12 C).

    B)   -

    C)   The regulation concerning the elementary school provides for the study of the minority language. If a minority group wants to establish an elementary school (see above) the education can, of course, be given in the minority language.

    D)   No

7. A)   See 2A) about Chapter 1, article 2 of the IG (on positive discrimination).

    B)   The laws on procedure generally guarantee the right of persons belonging to minorities to use their own language in their contacts with the authorities. These regulations are aimed not only at verbal interpretation during negotiations, hearings etc., but also at written translation, when documents in a foreign language are submitted to the authorities or where these authorities are to communicate with someone who does not understand Swedish.

    C)   No

8.   There are no such rules laid down in the Constitution. Ordinary acts of law concerning radio and television provides for broadcasting in a lot of languages, and it is also possible for minority groups to produce programmes of their own in local radio. Economic support is provided through state funds for the publishing, also by minority groups, of newspapers and magazines.

9. No

10. A)   There are no limits on the right of association of persons belonging to minorities.

B) No

11. A)   A person who is not a Swedish citizen can vote and be elected at local elections (the municipal councils and the county councils), provided that he or she has been a permanent resident in the country for at least three years.

    B)   -

    C)   No

12. A)   See 11A).

    B)   -

    C)   The elected representative body of the Sami population is recognised as a Swedish authority with limited decision-making power concerning, among other things, the allocation of state funds.

13. No

14. No

15. No

SUISSE

1. A) Voir le préambule de la Constitution fédérale de 1874 :

> "La Confédération suisse, voulant affermir l'alliance des confédérés, maintenir et accroître l'unité, la force et l'honneur de la nation suisse, a adopté la constitution fédérale suivante."

Ce préambule exprime deux idées fondamentales :

1) l'idée fédérative - la Suisse est un Etat fédéral composé de cantons.

2) l'idée nationale - malgré leurs différences de langues, de cultures, de confessions et d'intérêts, les cantons suisses ont, à travers l'alliance confédérale, un destin commun.

- D'autres dispositions constitutionnelles expriment encore le caractère fédéral de la Suisse (voir, par exemple, les articles 1, 2, 5 et 6 Const. féd.).

B) La "Confédération suisse" est bien, malgré le libellé de la Constitution, un **Etat fédéral** et non une confédération d'Etats. Cet Etat fédéral s'est constitué en 1848 à partir d'une confédération d'Etats indépendants - les cantons suisses - liés conventionnellement (avant 1798 et entre 1815 et 1848).

L'article 1 Const. féd. (*voir Annexe n° 1*) énumère les cantons suisses qui représentent l'élément de base de la structure fédérative de la Suisse.

La forme fédérale de la Suisse résulte donc directement de la préexistence de cantons "indépendants" et de la volonté d'intégrer les diversités culturelles, confessionnelles et linguistiques que représentaient ces derniers en vue d'un destin commun.

C)   Non.

2. A)   a)   Il n'y a pas d'utilisation spécifique de ce terme dans la Constitution. Pour une utilisation résiduelle, voir l'article 34 ter al. 2 Const. féd. (*voir Annexe n° 2*). L'article 27 al. 3 Const. féd. (*voir Annexe n° 9*) fait **implicitement** référence aux minorités religieuses.

b)   Il n'y a pas d'utilisation spécifique de ce terme dans la législation. Certaines dispositions législatives font cependant **indirectement** référence aux minorités (voir, par exemple, *la loi fédérale sur les subventions aux cantons des Grisons et du Tessin pour la sauvegarde de leur culture et de leurs langues - Annexe n° 12*).

c)   Il n'y a pas d'utilisation spécifique de ce terme dans la jurisprudence fédérale (selon le *Répertoire général du Recueil officiel des Arrêts du Tribunal fédéral suisse*). Certains arrêts du Tribunal fédéral suisse font cependant **indirectement** référence aux minorités (concernant les minorités religieuses voir, par exemple, l'*ATF 119 Ia 1978 A et M* ainsi que l'*ATF 113 Ia 304 Nehal Ahmed Syed*).

B)   Il n'y a pas dans la Constitution, la législation ou la jurisprudence fédérale de définition précise de ce terme.

C)   La Constitution, la législation et la jurisprudence fédérale visent parfois implicitement les minorités religieuses et linguistiques (voir supra question 2 A).

D)   La Constitution et la législation n'envisagent pas expressément la problématique de la reconnaissance des minorités. La reconnaissance n'est pas imposée, elle est implicitement admise. Dans les faits, les minorités sont indirectement reconnues (voir, par exemple, les articles 27 al. 3 et 116 Const. féd.).

L'appartenance d'un individu à une minorité ne peut résulter unilatéralement d'une décision de l'autorité publique.

E)   La Constitution, la législation et la jurisprudence n'envisagent pas la question des minorités de manière spécifique. Cette question est englobée et abordée dans le cadre du traitement d'autres

problématiques : voir, par exemple, le principe général de l'égalité -
art. 4 Const.féd. -, la liberté de croyance et de culte - art. 49 et 50
Const. féd. -, la liberté de la langue - droit constitutionnel non écrit
- ... Dans ces autres contextes, la problématique des minorités est
abordée en termes plutôt individuels (*voir infra les autres
questions*). Voir cependant le **principe de la territorialité** - *infra
question 7 B* - qui est appliqué dans le domaine de la liberté de la
langue.

F)   Non.

3. A)   Voir le *Pacte international relatif aux droits civils et politiques* (ou
Pacte - Nations Unies, 1966) et plus particulièrement son art. 27.

Voir la *Convention de sauvegarde des droits de l'homme et des
libertés fondamentales* (ou CEDH - Conseil de l'Europe, 1950) et
plus particulièrement son art. 14 - le principe de non discrimination
- ainsi que l'interprétation jurisprudentielle strasbourgeoise de
certaines dispositions de la CEDH - art. 9, 10 CEDH et art. 2
Protocole additionnel.

Le rang des traités dans la hiérarchie des actes normatifs en Suisse
est une question complexe ayant donné lieu à des controverses
doctrinales. On peut cependant poser de façon schématique que :

i) La **Constitution** l'emporte sur des **traités antérieurs** : une
modification constitutionnelle, résultant d'un vote positif
d'une majorité du peuple suisse et des cantons, peut
soustraire la Suisse à une obligation découlant d'un traité
international **"de peu d'importance"**.

Mais, lorsqu'un traité contient des règles de *jus cogens* - par
exemple un traité sur les droits de l'homme -, une bonne
partie de la doctrine estime qu'une révision de la
Constitution qui irait à l'encontre d'un tel traité devrait être
considérée comme dépourvue d'effet.

Concernant les **traités postérieurs**, l'art. 113 al. 3 Const.
féd. (*voir Annexe n° 3*) empêche les tribunaux d'en contrôler
la constitutionnalité, de sorte qu'ils peuvent théoriquement
déroger à la Constitution.

ii) La doctrine majoritaire et la jurisprudence récente confirment le principe de la supériorité des traités sur les **lois fédérales antérieures ou postérieures.**

Une évolution jurisprudentielle récente tendrait à admettre que le législateur fédéral peut exceptionnellement, en pleine connaissance de cause, édicter une règle contraire au droit international lorsqu'il s'agit de sauvegarder des intérêts très importants.

iii) Il ne fait aucun doute que les traités internationaux l'emportent sur l'ensemble des **actes normatifs infralégaux** et sur l'ensemble du **droit cantonal et intercantonal.**

B)   La CEDH et le Pacte ont été ratifiés et sont entrés en vigueur respectivement le 28.11.1974 et le 18.9.1992.

La mise en oeuvre de ces instruments n'a pas, concernant les articles afférents aux minorités, débouché sur des *dispositions législatives.*

Concernant l'art. 27 du Pacte : il n'y a pas encore de cas de *jurisprudence* impliquant la Suisse à signaler.

Concernant l'art. 14 CEDH : Le Tribunal fédéral suisse ainsi que la Commission européenne des droits de l'homme de Strasbourg ont eu à traiter plusieurs cas concernant la Suisse. Dans toutes ces affaires, les problèmes de discrimination ne concernaient pas la problématique des minorités au sens strict du terme, mais touchaient à des questions "périphériques" - femmes, mineurs, détenus ...

4. A)   Voir l'article 4 al. 1 Const. féd. (*voir Annexe n° 4*). Il n'y a pas de référence explicite à la non discrimination en fonction de l'appartenance à une minorité. A noter que l'article 14 CEDH, applicable en Suisse, y fait expressément référence.

L'article 4 al. 1 Const. féd. pose le principe de l'égalité **dans** la loi - des discriminations légales fondées sur la race, la confession, le sexe, la langue ... d'une personne ne sont admissibles que lorsqu'elles se justifient par des raisons pertinentes et sérieuses découlant des faits à réglementer - et le principe de l'égalité **devant la loi** - interdictions, entre autres, de l'inégalité de traitement et de l'arbitraire.

Contrairement à la lettre de cette disposition, les titulaires de ce droit constitutionnel sont non seulement les Suisses, mais aussi les étrangers. Les exemples jurisprudentiels n'ont pas trait à la problématique des minorités au sens strict du terme, mais ils concernent des problèmes "périphériques" comme des distinctions fondées sur le sexe, la profession ...

B)   Non, il n'y a pas de reconnaissance d'un tel principe en faveur des minorités.

C)   *De lege lata* : il n'existe pas en Suisse de législation spécifique réprimant l'incitation à la haine et la violence raciale et la xénophobie. Certaines dispositions du Code pénal suisse (CPS) peuvent cependant s'appliquer - voir par exemple l'art. 177 CPS concernant le délit d'injure ...

De lege ferenda : l'Assemblée fédérale suisse a adopté récemment un nouvel article du CPS (art. 261 bis CPS) réprimant la discrimination raciale (*voir Annexe n° 5*). Cet ajout législatif a fait l'objet d'une demande de référendum de la part du peuple suisse.

5. A)   Réponse incluse infra dans le point B.

B)   En Suisse, la **liberté religieuse** comporte un double aspect, individuel (**i**) et institutionnel (**ii**).

i) La liberté religieuse confère à chacun un droit subjectif de croire et de pratiquer la religion selon le choix que lui dicte sa conscience - voir la **liberté de conscience et de croyance** (art. 49 Const. féd. et art. 9 CEDH) et la **liberté de culte** (art. 50 Const. féd.).

La **liberté de conscience et de croyance** est consacrée à l'**art. 49 al. 1 Const. féd.** (*voir Annexe n° 6*). Elle confère à tout individu le droit d'avoir (ou de ne pas avoir) et de pratiquer une croyance ou une conviction religieuse. Elle lie également l'Etat qui ne peut forcer quiconque à faire usage de sa liberté, c'est-à-dire contraindre une personne à adhérer à une confession déterminée ou à accomplir un acte religieux. Cette liberté appartient à toutes les personnes physiques sans distinction d'origine, d'âge ou de nationalité.

Aux termes de l'**art. 49 al. 2 Const. féd.**, l'Etat ne peut empêcher qui que ce soit d'entrer ou de sortir d'une communauté religieuse et ne peut forcer quiconque à suivre un enseignement religieux.

Selon l'**art. 49 al. 6 Const. féd.**, l'Etat ne peut contraindre personne à s'acquitter d'un impôt ecclésiastique qui profite à une communauté religieuse à laquelle elle n'appartient pas. C'est sur ce point que porte pour l'essentiel la jurisprudence du Tribunal fédéral relative à l'art. 49 Const. féd.

L'**art. 50 Const. féd.** (*voir Annexe n° 7*) garantit le **libre exercice des cultes**. Alors que la liberté de conscience et de croyance protège l'aspect individuel de la liberté religieuse, la liberté de culte en protège plutôt l'aspect collectif. Cette liberté, qui a été relativement peu invoquée jusqu'à présente, risque de l'être de plus en plus du fait du fort brassage actuel de la population résultant principalement de la migration Sud-Nord (voir l'*ATF 113 Ia 304 Nehal Ahmed Syed* où les détenus musulmans d'un pénitencier demandaient de pouvoir se réunir régulièrement pour une prière commune le vendredi).

ii) La liberté religieuse vise également à garantir la paix religieuse par l'intermédiaire notamment de la neutralité religieuse de l'Etat, la tolérance religieuse et l'égalité des religions. On vise ici les relations entre l'Etat et les différentes communautés religieuses. Dans notre Etat fédéral - répartition des compétences oblige - les rapports entre l'Etat et l'Eglise relèvent de la compétence des cantons, sous réserve de quelques règles fédérales impératives. Cette "décentralisation", qui a engendré des régimes aussi variés que compliqués, devait permettre "d'assurer la diversité des statuts publics de la religion et, à travers cette diversité, de garantir la protection des minorités religieuses".

L'**art. 49 al. 4 Const. féd.** consacre le principe de la neutralité religieuse de l'Etat. L'Etat ne doit donc pas s'identifier à une croyance, une confession ou à une conviction déterminée. Comme le relève notre Tribunal fédéral : "L'Etat doit dans les actes publics s'abstenir de toute considération confessionnelle susceptible de

compromettre la liberté des citoyens **dans une société pluraliste.**"
(nous soulignons) (*ATF 116 Ia 252, 260 Comune di Cadro*).

Remarque : l'ancien art. 25 bis Const. féd. interdisant l'abattage
israélite a trouvé confirmation au niveau législatif après son
abrogation au niveau constitutionnel *(voir Annexe n° 8)*. Cette
interdiction constitue une importante restriction à la liberté de culte
judaïque lequel défend à ses adeptes de manger de la viande
provenant d'animaux non saignés.

6. A)   Pas de manière directe, mais seulement implicitement.

Selon l'**art. 49 al. 2 Const. féd.**, l'Etat ne peut forcer quiconque à
suivre un enseignement religieux. L'enseignement religieux dans les
écoles publiques doit être **facultatif** *(voir JAAC 1983 N° 32)*.

L'**art. 27 al. 2 et al. 3 Const. féd.** *(voir Annexe n° 9)* consacre le
principe de la neutralité religieuse de l'Etat en matière scolaire -
interdiction des écoles publiques professionnelles. Les écoles
publiques doivent donc pouvoir être fréquentées par les adhérents
de toutes les confessions.

Concernant l'**art. 49 al. 5 Const. féd.** et les lois cantonales
imposant l'obligation de fréquenter l'école le *samedi* - avec refus
d'accorder une dispense générale de l'enseignement scolaire ledit
jour pour des motifs religieux -, le Tribunal fédéral exige que les
conditions de l'intérêt public et de la proportionnalité de pareilles
obligations soient scrupuleusement respectées *(voir ATF 117 Ia 311
E, ATF 114 Ia 129 MR)*. Concernant les dispenses de certains
enseignements pour des motifs religieux, voir l'ATF 119 Ia 178 A
et M où il s'agissait de la dispense, pour des enfants musulmans,
des cours de natation.

L'ordre constitutionnel suisse ne proscrit pas les écoles privées
confessionnelles pour autant qu'elles soient placées sous la
surveillance de l'Etat. Le Tribunal fédéral semble même déduire de
l'art. 49 Const. féd. un droit constitutionnel à un enseignement
primaire privé pour les adeptes de communautés religieuses qui
sont trop marginales pour que l'école publique puisse prendre en
considération leurs exigences culturelles *(voir ATF 114 Ia 129, 133
M R)*.

B)   - ...

C)   L'enseignement primaire et secondaire est de la compétence des cantons. Ceux-ci déterminent également l'usage officiel des langues par et devant les autorités cantonales. Les cantons sont donc compétents pour déterminer la ou les langues d'enseignement ainsi que la ou les langues à enseigner *(voir encore infra question 7 B)*.

Dans la pratique, on peut constater que dans les cantons bi ou trilingues, là où se trouvent des minorités linguistiques, l'enseignement est aussi donné dans leur langue. D'une manière générale, une deuxième langue nationale est toujours enseignée dans les écoles de notre pays.

D)   Réponse incluse supra point A et C.

7. A)   Réponse incluse infra dans le point B.

B)   Remarques initiales :

Malgré le fait que la Suisse soit un Etat *plurilingue*, il y a toujours régné, dans l'ensemble, la paix linguistique.

La population de nationalité suisse se composait en 1980 de **73,5** % de germanophones, 20 % de francophones, 4,5 % d'italophones et 1 % de romanches. On dénombrait également environ **un million** d'étrangers parlant une multitude de langues autres que les quatre langues nationales suisses.

La Suisse compte 26 cantons et demi-cantons. 14 sont de langue allemande, quatre de langue française - Vaud, Neuchâtel, Genève, Jura - un de langue italienne - Tessin -, trois bilingues -Berne, Fribourg, Valais - et un trilingue -Grisons.

La **liberté de la langue** n'est pas garantie expressément par la Constitution fédérale (voir cependant le projet du nouvel art. 116 Const. - *voir Annexe n° 10)*. C'est le Tribunal fédéral suisse qui l'a consacrée, en 1965, comme un droit constitutionnel non écrit *(ATF 91 Ia 480, 486 Association de l'école française)*. Cette liberté garantit de manière générale le droit de chacun de s'exprimer oralement ou par écrit dans la langue de son choix, mais surtout dans sa langue maternelle. Concernant la portée de cette liberté - surtout dans son aspect privé - certains auteurs tendent à démontrer qu'elle n'a pas, dans son application pratique, de spécificité propre, indépendante d'autres libertés spéciales - voir la liberté personnelle, la liberté de la presse, le principe général d'égalité ...

De manière générale, la doctrine distingue, concernant la liberté de la langue, deux domaines distincts d'application.

- Le **domaine privé** où **tous** les individus doivent pouvoir choisir librement, sans intervention étatique, la langue dans laquelle ils communiquent entre eux **à titre privé**.

- Le **domaine public** où l'autorité définit la ou les langues dans lesquelles elle entre en communication avec les individus et réciproquement. C'est la réglementation des **langues officielles** de l'Etat.

En Suisse, structure fédérale et répartition des compétences obligent, la réglementation de l'usage officiel des langues est une compétence parallèle de la Confédération et des cantons. A la première, la réglementation de l'usage officiel des langues par et devant les autorités fédérales **(a)**, aux seconds celle qui détermine cet usage par et devant les autorités cantonales et communales **(b)**. Ceci doit permettre de garantir la diversité culturelle et le pluralisme linguistique en Suisse.

a) L'article 116 Const. féd. *(voir Annexe n° 11)* énumère, en son alinéa premier, les **quatre langues nationales** que sont l'allemand, le français, l'italien et le romanche. On admet généralement que cet article peut servir de base à des **mesures d'encouragement** prises en faveur des langues minoritaires que sont le romanche et l'italien *(voir Annexe n° 12)*.

En son alinéa 2, l'art. 116 Const. féd. énonce les **trois langues officielles** de la Confédération : l'allemand, le français et l'italien. Celles-ci sont placées, concernant l'utilisation de la langue dans le secteur public, sur un pied de stricte égalité.

b) Chaque canton est libre d'instituer une réglementation propre en matière de langue officielle. Tous les cantons multilingues ont adopté des dispositions constitutionnelles sur leurs langues officielles *(voir Annexe n° 13)*. Dans les autres cantons, la détermination de la langue officielle est implicite.

L'autonomie cantonale en matière linguistique implique aussi la compétence, pour les cantons, de prendre des mesures pouvant prescrire l'emploi d'une langue déterminée dans les rapports entre les particuliers et l'Etat. Ces mesures, qui tendent en principe à favoriser l'homogénéité ou, au contraire, la diversité linguistique dans le canton concerné, se doivent de respecter le principe général d'égalité - art. 4 Const. féd. - ainsi que l'ensemble des autres libertés constitutionnelles (l'essentiel de la jurisprudence en ce domaine a trait à l'utilisation de la langue devant les tribunaux et dans l'enseignement : voir notamment, *ATF 109 V 224 Boggi, ATF 106 Ia 299 Brunner, ATF 100 IA 462 Derungs, ATF 91 Ia 480 Association de l'école française ...*). Pour le Tribunal fédéral suisse, cette faculté résulte plus précisément du **principe dit de la territorialité**. En effet, selon lui, l'art. 116 al. 1 Const. garantit "la répartition territoriale traditionnelle des langues en Suisse" et il résulte de ce fait qu'il "incombe aux cantons, dans les limites de leurs frontières, de veiller à la conservation de l'étendue et de l'homogénéité de leur territoire linguistique" *(voir ATF 91 Ia 480, 486 et ATF 100 Ia 462, 466 op.cit.)*. Ainsi les cantons seraient habilités à "prendre des mesures pour maintenir les limites traditionnelles des régions linguistiques et leur homogénéité, **même si la liberté du particulier à utiliser sa langue maternelle s'en trouve restreinte.**" (nous soulignons) (voir *ATF 106 Ia 299, 302 op.cit)*.

C)   Références incluses supra dans le point B.

8.   Sous l'expression "libertés de communication" on peut regrouper un ensemble de libertés qui ont pour but "de garantir la libre formation, la libre expression et la libre réception des opinions par la parole, l'écrit, l'image, le geste et le symbole". Concernant ces libertés, le droit suisse ne prévoit pas de règles spécifiques pour les minorités. Voir :

-      **La liberté de la presse** - art. 55 Const. féd.

- La **liberté d'expression et d'opinion** - droit constitutionnel non écrit depuis sa concrétisation en 1961 *(ATF 87 I 114, 117 Sphinx Films Sa).*

- La **liberté d'information** implique le droit de recevoir librement, sans contrôle de l'autorité, des nouvelles et des opinions et de se renseigner aux sources accessibles de manière générale - corollaire de la liberté de la presse et d'expression *(ATF 104 Ia88, 94 Schweizerische Journalisten-Union).*

- La **liberté de la radio-télévision** - art. 55 bis Const. féd. *(voir Annexe n° 14)* -appartient principalement aux auditeurs et aux téléspectateurs. En effet, selon l'alinéa 2 de l'art. 55 bis Const., le système de radiodiffusion et de télévision doit assurer leur **développement culturel**, la libre formation de leur opinion et leur divertissement. Mais surtout, cette même disposition stipule que les émissions de radio et de télévision doivent tenir compte **"des particularités du pays et des besoins des cantons"**, ceci devant permettre d'assurer le pluralisme culturel et linguistique au sein du système de radio-télévision. La conformité des émissions avec ces exigences constitutionnelles peut être examinée par une autorité de plainte au sens de l'alinéa 5 de l'art. 55 Const. féd.

9. A)   Non.

10. A)   La **liberté d'association** est expressément consacrée par l'art. 56 Const. féd. *(voir Annexe n° 15)* et l'art. 11 CEDH. Malgré le libellé de cette disposition constitutionnelle -"citoyens"-, la nationalité n'est plus considérée comme un critère pertinent pour définir la titularité de cette liberté. En principe, la liberté d'association appartient tant aux Suisses qu'aux étrangers et aux apatrides. Elle peut être invoquée par les personnes appartenant à des minorités. Peuvent faire partie d'associations ayant leur siège en Suisse également des personnes qui sont domiciliées à l'étranger. La liberté d'association est donc pleinement reconnue, même au-delà des frontières. Seules peuvent être interdites les associations qui mettent en danger l'ordre public.

B)   Il n'existe pas en Suisse de partis politiques qui représentent les intérêts des minorités ou qui ont été créés dans ce but là.

11. A)   Réponse incluse infra dans le point C.

B)   Réponse incluse infra dans le point C.

C)   On peut affirmer qu'au plan fédéral des critères linguistiques ont eu une certaine influence concernant le mode d'élection des principaux organes de la Confédération.

- L'élection selon le système proportionnel dans les circonscriptions formées par les cantons permet de garantir une représentation de toutes les langues nationales au **Conseil National** (Chambre basse de notre Parlement).

- Pour le **Conseil des Etats** (Chambre haute de notre Parlement), le règle de la représentation égalitaire de chaque canton - 2 sièges par canton - a pour effet que la voix des cantons à langue minoritaire y est représentée directement.

- La Loi fédérale sur les rapports entre les conseils exige, en son alinéa 2 de l'art. 8 quinquies, qu'il soit tenu compte des langues officielles dans la composition des commissions parlementaires.

- Selon une règle coutumière, doivent siéger au sein du **Conseil fédéral** (l'exécutif fédéral) au moins deux représentants des cantons latins.

- L'art. 107 Const. féd. *(voir Annexe n° 16)* stipule que les trois langues officielles doivent être représentées au Tribunal fédéral.

12. A)   Non, pas au plan fédéral.

B)   -

C)   Non.

13. A)   Non.

   B)   -

14. A)   Non.

   B)   -

15. A)   Il n'existe pas de recours spécifiques en faveur des personnes appartenant à une minorité.

ANNEXES
aux réponses de la Suisse

Annexe n° 1 : Préambule et Article 1 Constitution fédérale

Au nom de Dieu Tout-Puissant !

La Confédération suisse,
voulant affermir l'alliance des confédérés, maintenir et accroître l'unité, la force
et l'honneur de la nation suisse, a adopté la constitution fédérale suivante.

Chapitre premier : Dispositions générales

Article premier

Les peuples des vingt-trois cantons souverains de la Suisse, unis par la présente
alliance, savoir : Zurich, Berne, Lucerne, Uri, Schwyz, Unterwald (le Haut et le
Bas), Glaris, Zoug, Fribourg, Soleure, Bâle (Ville et Campagne), Schaffhouse,
Appenzell (les deux Rhodes), Saint-Gall, Grisons, Argovie, Thurgovie, Tessin,
Vaud, Valais, Neuchâtel, Genève et Jura, forment dans leur ensemble la
Confédération suisse.

Annexe n° 2 : Article 34 ter al. 2 Constitution fédérale

Article 34ter

1. La Confédération a le droit de légiférer :

    a.   Sur la protection des employés ou ouvriers ;

    b.   Sur les rapports entre employeurs et employés ou ouvriers,
notamment sur la réglementation en commun des questions
intéressant l'entreprise et la profession ;

    c.   Sur la force obligatoire générale de contrats collectifs de travail ou
d'autres accords entre associations d'employeurs et d'employés ou
ouvriers en vue de favoriser la paix du travail ;

d. Sur une compensation appropriée du salaire ou du gain perdu par suite de service militaire ;

e. Sur le service de placement ;

f. ...

g. Sur la formation professionnelle dans l'industrie, les arts et métiers, le commerce, l'agriculture et le service de maison.

2. La force obligatoire générale prévue sous lettre c ne pourra être statuée que dans des domaines touchant les rapports de travail entre employeurs et employés ou ouvriers, à condition toutefois que les dispositions considérées tiennent suffisamment compte des diversités régionales, des intérêts légitimes des minorités et respectent l'égalité devant la loi ainsi que la liberté d'association.

3. ...

4. Les dispositions de l'article 32 sont applicables par analogie.

Annexe n° 3 : Article 113 al. 3 Constitution fédérale

Article 113

1. Le Tribunal fédéral connaît, en outre :

    1) Des conflits de compétence entre les autorités fédérales, d'une part, et les autorités cantonales, d'autre part ;

    2) Des différends entre cantons, lorsque ces différends sont du domaine du droit public ;

    3) Des réclamations pour violation de droits constitutionnels des citoyens, ainsi que des réclamations de particuliers pour violation de concordats ou de traités.

2. Sont réservées les contestations administratives à déterminer par la législation fédérale.

3. Dans tous les cas prémentionnés, le Tribunal fédéral appliquera les lois votées par l'Assemblée fédérale et les arrêtés de cette assemblée qui ont une portée générale. Il se conformera également aux traités que l'Assemblée fédérale aura ratifiés.

Annexe n° 4 : Article 4 al. 1 Constitution fédérale

Article 4

1. Tous les Suisses sont égaux devant la loi. Il n'y a en Suisse ni sujets, ni privilèges de lieu, de naissance, de personnes ou de familles.

2. L'homme et la femme sont égaux en droits. La loi pourvoit à l'égalité, en particulier dans les domaines de la famille, de l'instruction et du travail. Les hommes et les femmes ont droit à un salaire égal pour un travail de valeur égale.

Annexe n° 5 : Article 261 bis CPS

Annexe n° 6 : Article 49 Constitution fédérale

Article 49

1. La liberté de conscience et de croyance est inviolable.

2. Nul ne peut être contraint de faire partie d'une association religieuse, de suivre un enseignement religieux, d'accomplir un acte religieux, ni encourir des peines, de quelque nature qu'elles soient, pour cause d'opinion religieuse.

3. La personne qui exerce l'autorité paternelle ou tutélaire a le droit de disposer, conformément aux principes ci-dessus, de l'éducation religieuse des enfants jusqu'à l'âge de 16 ans révolus.

4. L'exercice des droits civils ou politiques ne peut être restreint par des prescriptions ou des conditions de nature ecclésiastique ou religieuse, quelles qu'elles soient.

5. Nul ne peut, pour cause d'opinion religieuse, s'affranchir de l'accomplissement d'un devoir civique.

6. Nul n'est tenu de payer des impôts dont le produit est spécialement affecté aux frais proprement dits du culte d'une communauté religieuse à laquelle

il n'appartient pas. L'exécution ultérieure de ce principe reste réservée à la législation fédérale.

Annexe n° 7 : Article 50 Constitution fédérale

Article 50

1. Le libre exercice des cultes est garanti dans les limites compatibles avec l'ordre public et les bonnes moeurs.

2. Les cantons et la Confédération peuvent prendre les mesures nécessaires pour le maintien de l'ordre public et de la paix entre les membres des diverses communautés religieuses, ainsi que contre les empiétements des autorités ecclésiastiques sur les droits des citoyens et de l'Etat.

3. Les contestations de droit public ou de droit privé auxquelles donne lieu la création de communautés religieuses ou une scission de communautés religieuses existantes, peuvent être portées par voie de recours devant les autorités fédérales compétentes.

4. Il ne peut être érigé d'évêchés sur le territoire suisse sans l'approbation de la Confédération.

Annexe n° 8 : Loi fédérale sur la protection des animaux (RS 455)

Section 7 : Abattage d'animaux

Article 20 Etourdissement obligatoire

1. L'abattage de mammifères sans étourdissement précédant la saignée est interdit.

2. Le Conseil fédéral peut également prescrire, pour de grandes exploitations, l'étourdissement des volailles avant leur abattage.

Article 21 Méthodes d'étourdissement

1. L'étourdissement doit autant que possible agir sur-le-champ ; si son action se produit tardivement, il ne doit occasionner aucune douleur.

2. Le Conseil fédéral spécifie les méthodes d'étourdissement autorisées.

Annexe n° 9 : Article 27 al. 2 et al. 3 Constitution fédérale

Article 27

1. La Confédération a le droit de créer, outre l'école polytechnique existante, une université fédérale et d'autres établissements d'instruction supérieure ou de subventionner des établissements de ce genre.

2. Les cantons pourvoient à l'instruction primaire, qui doit être suffisante et placée exclusivement sous la direction de l'autorité civile. Elle est obligatoire et, dans les écoles publiques, gratuite.

3. Les écoles publiques doivent pouvoir être fréquentées par les adhérents de toutes les confessions, sans qu'ils aient à souffrir d'aucune façon dans leur liberté de conscience ou de croyance.

3bis.
    Pendant la période de la scolarité obligatoire, l'année scolaire débute entre la mi-août et la mi-septembre.

4. La Confédération prendra les mesures nécessaires contre les cantons qui ne satisferaient pas à ces obligations.

Annexe n° 10 :   Projet du nouvel article 116 Constitution fédérale (FF 1991 II p. 301)

Article 116

1. La liberté de la langue est garantie.

2. Les langues nationales de la Suisse sont l'allemand, le français, l'italien et le romanche.

3. La Confédération et les cantons veillent à sauvegarder et à promouvoir les quatre langues nationales dans leurs territoires de diffusion. Les cantons prennent des mesures particulières afin de protéger les langues nationales

qui sont menacées dans un territoire donné ; la Confédération leur accorde un soutien à cet effet.

4. La Confédération et les cantons encouragent la compréhension entre les communautés linguistiques et la présence des quatre langues nationales dans l'ensemble de la Suisse.

5. Les langues officielles de la Suisse sont l'allemand, le français et l'italien. Le romanche est langue officielle pour les rapports que la Confédération entretient avec les citoyennes et citoyens romanches et avec les institutions romanches. Les modalités sont réglées par la loi.

Annexe n° 11 : Article 116 Constitution fédérale

Article 116

1. L'allemand, le français, l'italien et le romanche sont les langues nationales de la Suisse.

2. Sont déclarés langues officielles de la Confédération : l'allemand, le français et l'italien.

Annexe n° 12 : Loi fédérale sur les subventions aux cantons des Grisons et du Tessin pour la sauvegarde de leur culture et de leurs langues (RS 441.3)

L'Assemblée fédérale de la Confédération suisse,

vu l'article 116 de la constitution fédérale,
vu le message du Conseil fédéral du 28 septembre 1981,

arrête :

Article premier Subvention au canton des Grisons

1. La Confédération alloue au canton des Grisons une subvention annuelle de 3 750 000 francs pour sauvegarder la culture et la langue rhéto-romanes ainsi que la culture et la langue des vallées italophones.

2. De ce montant, 1 875 000 francs au moins doivent être alloués à la Lia Rumantscha pour son activité en faveur de la culture et de la langue rhéto-romanes et 562 500 francs au moins à l'association Pro Grigioni Italiano pour son activité en faveur de la culture et de la langue des vallées italophones du canton des Grisons.

3. La subvention fédérale est subordonnée à la condition que le canton des Grisons alloue de son côté une subvention annuelle de 400 000 francs à la Lia Rumantscha et une autre de 100 000 francs à l'association Pro Grigioni Italiano.

Article 2   Subvention au canton du Tessin

La Confédération alloue au canton du Tessin une subvention annuelle de 2,5 millions de francs pour sauvegarder son identité culturelle et linguistique.

Article 3   Rapports

Les cantons des Grisons et du Tessin présentent au Département fédéral de l'intérieur un rapport annuel sur l'emploi qu'ils ont fait de leurs subventions. La Lia Rumantscha et l'association Pro Grigioni Italiano lui soumettent en outre chaque année, par l'entremise des autorités cantonales, un programme et un budget.

Article 4   Abrogation du droit en vigueur

Sont abrogés :

1. l'article 5 de la loi fédérale du 19 juin 1953 subventionnant l'école primaire publique ;

2. l'arrêté fédéral du 23 septembre 1974 allouant une aide financière à la Ligia Romontscha/Lia Rumantscha et à «Pro Grigioni Italiano» ;

3. la loi fédérale du 19 décembre 1980 allouant une aide financière au canton du Tessin pour la sauvegarde de sa culture et de sa langue.

Article 5   Référendum et entrée en vigueur

1. La présente loi est sujette au référendum facultatif.

2. Le Conseil fédéral fixe la date de l'entrée en vigueur.

Date de l'entrée en vigueur : 1ᵉʳ janvier 1984

Annexe n° 13 : extraits de constitutions cantonales

Berne (RS 131.212)

Article 6

1. Le français et l'allemand sont les langues nationales et officielles du canton de Berne.

2. Les langues officielles sont :

    a.   le français dans le Jura bernois,
    b.   le français et l'allemand dans le district de Bienne,
    c.   l'allemand dans les autres districts.

3. Le canton et les communes peuvent tenir compte de situations particulières résultant du caractère bilingue du canton.

4. Toute personne peut s'adresser dans la langue officielle de son choix aux autorités compétentes pour l'ensemble du canton.

Fribourg (RS 131.219)

Article 21

1. Le français et l'allemand sont les langues officielles. Leur utilisation est réglée dans le respect du principe de la territorialité.

2. L'Etat favorise la compréhension entre les deux communautés linguistiques.

Grisons (RS 131.226)

Article 46
Die drei Sprachen des Kantons sind als Landessprachen gewährleistet.

Valais (RS 131.232)

Article 12

1. La langue française et la langue allemande sont déclarées nationales.

2. L'égalité de traitement entre les deux langues doit être observée dans la législation et dans l'administration.

Jura (RS 131.235)

Article 3   Langue

Le français est la langue nationale et officielle de la République et Canton du Jura.

Annexes n° 14 : Article 55 et Article 55 bis Constitution fédérale

Article 55

1. La liberté de la presse est garantie.

2. et ...

Article 55 bis

1. La législation sur la radio et la télévision, ainsi que sur d'autres formes de diffusion publique de productions et d'informations au moyen des techniques de télécommunication est du domaine de la Confédération.

2. La radio et la télévision contribuent au développement culturel des auditeurs et téléspectateurs, à la libre formation de leur opinion et à leur divertissement. Elles tiennent compte des particularités du pays et des besoins des cantons. Elles présentent les événements fidèlement et reflètent équitablement la diversité des opinions.

3. L'indépendance de la radio et de la télévision ainsi que l'autonomie dans la conception des programmes sont garanties dans les limites fixées au 2e alinéa.

4. Il sera tenu compte de la tâche et de la situation des autres moyens de communication, en particulier de la presse.

5. La Confédération crée une autorité indépendante chargée de l'examen des plaintes.

Annexe n° 15 : Article 56 Constitution fédérale

Article 56

Les citoyens ont le droit de former des associations, pourvu qu'il n'y ait dans le but de ces associations ou dans les moyens qu'elles emploient rien d'illicite ou de dangereux pour l'Etat. Les lois cantonales statuent les mesures nécessaires à la répression des abus.

Annexe n° 16 : Article 107 Constitution fédérale

Article 107

1. Les membres et les suppléants du Tribunal fédéral sont nommés par l'Assemblée fédérale, qui aura égard à ce que les trois langues officielles de la Confédération y soient représentées.

2. La loi détermine l'organisation du Tribunal fédéral et de ses sections, le nombre de ses membres et des suppléants, la durée de leurs fonctions et leur traitement.

TURKEY

1. A)   Although the Constitution (1982) does not use the term "unitary" state, in Article 2 it states that the Turkish state is committed to the "nationalism of Atatürk". Article 3 states that "The Turkish state is an indivisible entity with its nation and territory". These provisions indicate that the Turkish state is perceived as both "unitary" and "national". There are no references to a "multiethnic", "multilingual" or "multireligious" nature.

   B)   See A above.

   C)   No.

2. A)   a)   No.

         b)   It is used, in a negative sense, in the Law on Political Parties (dated 22 April 1983). According to the provisions of this Law, political parties cannot pursue the aim of changing the unitary nature of the state (Art. 80). They cannot put forward the claim that there are minorities in the territory of the Turkish Republic, based on differences of national or religious culture, or of sect, race or language. They cannot pursue the aim of creating minorities in the territory of the Turkish Republic by protecting, developing or diffusing languages and cultures other than the Turkish language and culture. They cannot use any language other than Turkish in their official documents, congresses, meetings, and propaganda activities (Art. 81). They cannot engage in activities with the aim of promoting regionalism or racism (Art. 82). They cannot engage in activities against the principle of equality before law without any discrimination, regardless of language, race, color, sex, political opinion, philosophical belief, religion and sect, or any such consideration (Art. 83).

         c)   The Constitutional Court has banned several parties which were found to be in violation of the above restrictions.

B)   No.

C)   See 2 A, b above.

D)   No.

E)   In strictly individual terms.

F)   No.

3. A)   The only relevant international instrument is the Peace Treaty of Lausanne. Part II, Section III (Art. 37-45) of the Treaty carries the title "Protection of Minorities" and has as its aim to protect the "non-Moslem" minorities living in Turkey. It does not include Moslem minorities. The following rights of the non-Moslem minorities are recognized by the Treaty:

-       Non-discrimination;

-       Freedom of religion;

-       Freedom of travel and migration;

-       Freedom to enjoy the same civil and political rights as enjoyed by Moslem Turks;

-       Freedom to use the language of their choice in their commercial transactions, religious rites, mass media, and open meetings;

-       Non-Moslem minorities will enjoy the necessary facilities to use their own languages in the courts;

-       Freedom to establish all kinds of religious, charitable, and educational organisations, and to use their own language therein;

-       Churches, sinagogues, cemeteries and other religious institutions of non-Moslem minorities are under full protection;

-       Freedom not be forced to any kind of action inconsistent with their religious beliefs and ceremonies;

-       Freedom to use their own customory law in the fields of family law and personal status. However, after the adoption of the Turkish Civil Code in 1926 (based on the Swiss Civil Code), the Greek Orthodox, Armenian and Jewish communities renounced this privilege.

Under Article 37 of the Lausanne Treaty, no laws and regulations contrary to the Articles 38-44 of the Treaty (protection of minorities) can be adopted. In this sense, these Articles have constitutional status, and the rule of "lex posteriori" would not be applicable in this case.

B) Article 42 of the 1982 Constitution makes a reference to the Lausanne Treaty. Under this Article, "No language other than Turkish shall be taught as mother tongue to Turkish citizens at any institution of training or education... The provisions of international treaties are reserved."

4. A) Yes. The constitutional principle of equality (Art. 10) forbids discrimination on the basis of language, race, color, religion and sect, or any such consideration.

B) No.

C) Article 312 of the Turkish Criminal Code punishes incitement to hatred or animosity on the basis of differences of class, religion, sect, or region.

5. A) The Constitution provides for freedom of belief and worship for everybody. This includes the recognition of unbelief, particularly by the third paragraph of the Article which states that "no one shall be compelled to worship, or to participate in religious ceremonies and rites, to reveal religious beliefs and convictions, or be blamed or accused because of his religious beliefs and convictions."

B) No. However, Turkish laws do not recognise conscientious objection regarding military service.

6. A) See 3 A and B above.

B) Private for the relevant cases at primary and intermediate levels. Although the Lausanne Treaty seems to cover all levels of education, there is no minority university in practice.

C) Schooling in the minority language in relevant cases, although Turkish language and literature, Turkish history and geography are compulsory courses and have to be taught in Turkish.

7. A)   Under Article 3 of the Constitution, the language of the Turkish
          state is Turkish. There is no provision for the official use of other
          languages, the recognition and protection of minority languages,
          and the freedom of languages. The provisions of the Lausanne
          Treaty are reserved.

   B)   There are no restrictions on the private use of languages.

   C)   No.

8.   No.

9.   No. See, however, 3 A above.

10. A)   They have the same rights as others.

    B)   See 2 A, b, above.

11. A)   No.

    B)   -

    C)   No.

12. A)   No.

    B)   -

    C)   No.

13. A)   No.

14. A)   No.

    B)   -

15. No.

The protection of minorities
in federal and regional states

The protection of minorities in federal and regional states:
consolidated report based upon studies carried out in relation
to Austria, Belgium, Canada, Germany,
Italy, Spain and Switzerland

I. Introduction

The notion of a minority (whether it be linguistic, ethnic, religious, cultural or otherwise) can refer to very diverse situations. In particular, concentrated minorities, for which territorial solutions are possible, should be clearly distinguished from dispersed minorities, for which such solutions are evidently excluded. It is therefore understandable that national law, and consequently that national reports, should be concerned with a very extensive range of circumstances.

The purpose of this consolidated report is to attempt to define certain types of rules on the protection of minorities which are found to exist in federal or regional States. It is based on reports relating to Council of Europe member States with a federal or regional structure, as well as on a report relating to Canada. The following countries are considered: Austria, Belgium, Canada, Germany and Switzerland (federal States); and Spain and Italy (regional States).

Federal or regional States in other parts of the world, and the specific case of Russia in particular, are not dealt with in this report.

Two types of rules may form the basis for the protection of minorities in a federal or regional State: rules concerning fundamental rights, which are not distinctly characteristic of federal or regional States and which apply to concentrated minorities as well as to dispersed minorities, and rules specific to such States, relating to concentrated minorities. Each of these two categories of rules will be examined in turn.

II. Guarantees of fundamental rights, particularly linguistic freedoms

Fundamental rights are of course guaranteed to members of a minority, as to everybody, in federal and regional States as they are in any State[1]. The principle of equality, for example, stands opposed to any discrimination against members of a minority.

Certain rules set out to protect minorities, or a particular minority, more directly. Thus, the Canadian Constitution provides special protection for autochthonous peoples in paragraph 91(24) of the Constitutional Law of 1867, in Article 25 of the Canadian Charter of Rights and Freedoms and in Articles 35 and 35(1) of the Constitutional Law of 1982. In addition, electoral laws take account of the presence, throughout Canada, of autochthonous peoples. The electoral law of Canada allows for certain exceptions, notably in respect of the conduct of the count, in autochthonous reservations.

Certain features specific to federal and regional States must be emphasised in the context of confessional and linguistic rights. Thus, in Canada, the rights of Catholic and of Protestant groups are protected as such, notably in matters of teaching and of taxation. Thus, a right is recognised, subject to certain conditions, of access to confessional State-funded schools.

There is no need here to dwell on fundamental rights of an individual nature guaranteed to everyone. It may be recalled, first, that the principle of equality stands opposed to discrimination against the members of a minority, and that there are also relevant individual freedoms, such as religious freedom.

In Canada still, the right to have one's children educated in the minority language of a province is recognised fairly widely. However, the right to have such instruction financed from the public purse or to have children receive instruction in minority language educational facilities provided out of public funds is subject to the condition that there is a sufficient number of children of citizens enjoying the above-mentioned right.

At the parliamentary, legislative and judicial levels, the federal Constitution provides for equality between English and French as regards the federal system

---

[1] *For further information on the question of fundamental rights enjoyed by persons belonging to national minorities, see the Report on the Replies to the Questionnaire on the Rights of Minorities (CDL-MIN (94) 5 revised, point IV.C).*

of government and the provinces of Quebec, New Brunswick and Manitoba, but not the other provinces.

Swiss language rules are different in nature. The Federal Constitution implicitly recognises the principle of territoriality as a general rule. The individual right to linguistic freedom is therefore restricted in scope in relations with cantonal authorities. However, it also follows implicitly from the Constitution that it is possible to communicate with the political, administrative and judicial authorities at federal level in the three official languages, irrespective of their majority (German) or minority (French or Italian) status. In addition, a federal law of 24 June 1983 on subsidies for the cantons of Grisons and Tessin for the safeguarding of their culture and their languages aims to support the two least-spoken national languages, rheto-romanche and Italian.

Broader individual rights - including the choice of the language of communication with the authorities - are provided for in the bilingual and trilingual cantons (Fribourg, Valais, Bern and Graubünden).

The Belgian system is fairly similar as it is also based on the principle of territoriality. For example, education is organised only in the language of the region, except in certain fringe communes where nursery and primary education may be organised in the language of the minority, on certain conditions. The Brussels-capital region is bilingual.

The use of languages in administrative matters is subject to the rule of unilingualism in the three single-language regions and to the rule of bilingualism in the Brussels-capital region. Here again, the linguistic minorities of certain fringe communes are granted special status.

The situation in Italy is unusual: although Italian is the language of the immense majority of the population, the German-speaking minority represents the bulk of the inhabitants of Bolzano (a province in the region of Trentino-Alto Adige). The autonomous statute of this region provides for proportional representation of the linguistic communities within provincial bodies and minor local authorities, as well as for certain rights in the educational field; some of these rules are also applicable to the Ladinian-speaking minority.

As regards relations with the public authorities, German and Italian have the same constitutional status at regional level and in the province of Bolzano. It has to be observed, therefore, that what we see here are essentially organisational principles rather than individual rights. French, in the Valle d'Aosta, and Slovenian, in Friuli-Venezia Giulia, are protected by similar rights.

In the case of Spain, minority languages are widely spoken in five autonomous communities (Catalonia, the Basque country, Galicia, Valencia and the Balearic Islands). Under Article 3 of the Constitution (Castilian is the official language of the State and the other Spanish languages are also official in the respective autonomous Communities, in accordance with their statutes), the statutes of autonomy of those nationalities and regions enshrine the concept of equal official status of the languages. Autonomy statutes are of a dual nature since, although the peoples concerned participated directly in their preparation through their political representatives, the resulting legal text is in every case a rule having the status of State law and embodied in the legal order of the State. In effect, these texts provide that the regional language, along with Castilian, is the official language in the community and that any citizen is entitled to use either that language or Castilian in his relations with those public authorities whose jurisdiction is limited to the territory of the community concerned, whether they be regional or state bodies. This constitutional corpus has been elaborated upon in the various Autonomous Communities through laws prepared by their respective assemblies, in most cases for the purpose of promoting regional languages.

The situation in Germany and Austria is different, in as much as these countries have no minorities which constitute the bulk of the population in any particular region. In Austria, the Constitutional Court has recognised that the right to instruction in the Slovenian language for persons belonging to that minority in Carinthia is guaranteed by the Federal Constitution. Certain other rights are recognised at the legislative level.

In the case of Germany, the Unification Treaty provides for a rule in favour of the Sorbian minority, specifically in respect of language: the Sorbian language may be used before the district courts in regions of the land of Saxony where the Sorbian minority is present.

The other rules on behalf of minorities are enshrined in the legislation of the Länder and provide for certain entitlements for minorities to receive education in their own language, and also for measures of affirmative action.

It is also of interest to note that Articles 8 and 9 of the draft European Convention for the Protection of Minorities prepared by the European

Commission for Democracy through Law[2] deal with the question of linguistic rights in a manner fairly similar to some of the above-mentioned rules. It should be noted in particular that the right to communicate with the authorities or to receive public instruction in the language of the minority is subject to the condition that the number of members of the minority be sufficient.

III.   The rules proper to federal or regional states

Unlike the rules concerning fundamental rights (including language rights), which may also be found in a unitary State, certain rules for the protection of concentrated minorities are peculiar to federal or regional States. Indeed, they are bound up with the powers of federated (or regional) entities or their representation within central government. This carries the obvious implication that the minority, nationally speaking, should form a majority within certain federated States or regions, so that States like Germany or Austria cannot be concerned by such measures. If federated authorities or regions have extended legislative and executive competences, a minority can participate directly in political life.

This report does not aim at describing the powers of the entities comprising the State, which would require a study in itself, but at determining what these entities are. For most of the States studied, they are federated States or regions having a specified territorial area.

The situation in Belgium is different, however. There the Regions (territorial) are superimposed on the Communities (language). There are three Regions: the Flemish Region (monolingual), the Walloon Region, to which the

---

[2]   *Article 8: Whenever a minority reaches a substantial percentage of the population of a region or of the total population, its members shall have the right, as far as possible, to speak and write in their own language to the political, administrative and judicial authorities of this region or, where appropriate, of the State. These authorities shall have a corresponding obligation.*

Article 9: Whenever the conditions of Article 8 are fulfilled, in State schools, obligatory schooling shall include, for pupils belonging to the minority, study of their mother tongue. As far as possible, all or part of the schooling shall be given in the mother tongue of pupils belonging to the minority. However, should the State not be in a position to provide such schooling, it must permit children who so wish to attend private schools. In such a case, the State shall have the right to prescribe that the official language or languages also be taught in such schools.

French-speaking area and the small German-speaking area belong, and the Brussels-capital Region (bilingual). There are also three language Communities: Flemish, French and German. The powers of the Flemish-speaking and French-speaking Communities extend not only to the Flemish and Walloon regions respectively (apart from the small German-speaking region) but also the Brussels-capital Region. In the absence of Flemish or French-speaking sub-nationality, however, the principle of personality holds no more sway than that of territoriality, and the situation is of a mixed type where, in a certain portion of the territory, two political bodies have a relationship with the institutions which "represent" their culture or their language.

In Belgium still, the Council of Ministers must comprise an equal number of French-speaking and Dutch-speaking Ministers, if necessary without counting the Prime Minister: parity between language groups, and not between regions, is guaranteed. The two Federal Chambers (Chamber of Representatives and Senate) are divided into two language groups. Certain laws which are essential for the balance of the country or for the protection of minorities, known as special laws can be adopted only by a two-thirds' majority, and are subject to the presence of a quorum known as special laws, and of a majority in each language group in both federal assemblies. In addition, a language group may declare, by a three-quarters' majority, that a particular bill or draft law is of a nature to cause serious prejudice to relations between the communities. In this case, the procedure is suspended and the text submitted to the Council of Ministers, in which the languages have equal representation and which must take a decision.

Language parity applies to the judicial branch also (Arbitration Court, Court of Cassation and Council of State) as well as, in the political domain, to the Conciliation Committee, a body designed to prevent and, if possible, to settle conflicts of interest between State bodies.

In Switzerland, the House representing the cantons, the Council of States, of which almost all members are elected under the majority system, comprises two members for each canton and one for each half-canton. This means that the small cantons are as well represented as the large ones. In addition, in the bilingual cantons and the trilingual one, one of the Councillors to the States frequently represents the minority language of that canton.

The members of the House representing the people, the National Council, are also elected at cantonal level, under the proportional system: the same party will sometimes put forward separate linguistic lists within the same canton.

Minorities, especially linguistic minorities, are thus assured of adequate representation in both Houses.

The Federal Constitution provides that it is not possible for more than one member of the Federal Council (Government) to be chosen from the same canton. Moreover, there is an unwritten rule to the effect that two or sometimes three federal councillors out of seven should represent the Latin minorities, although the latter account for less than 25% of the population.

The Constitution also provides for the use of the three official languages of the Confederation in the Federal Court. In practice, they are represented on a proportional basis. This situation in no way calls into question the federal structure of the state.

In Canada, the system of representation according to population in the House of Commons, from constituencies in which first-past-the-post voting rules apply, guarantees a degree of representation for the French-speaking minority in Quebec. In addition, Quebec is assigned 24 senators out of a total of 104.

The representation of minorities in the central governmental organs of a regional State is more rarely governed by rules of positive law. In Spain, with few exceptions, the provinces are entitled to have four representatives elected directly to the Senate, whereas the legislative assemblies of the Autonomous Communities appoint a number of Senators varying in accordance with the population of the Community, the result being in practice that the number of Senators elected in the context of the province predominates over those strictly representing the Autonomous Community. Nonetheless, this composition of the Spanish Senate can be seen to give some guarantee of minimum representation for the regions where a minority has majority status.

There are also more direct means of participation in the State decision-making process by federated States or regions, especially those in which a national minority has majority status. For example, both the Swiss cantons and the Spanish Autonomous Communities enjoy the right to propose legislation or constitutional amendments. The Swiss cantons are also frequently consulted before decisions are taken at central government level, while the Spanish Autonomous Communities participate in the work of joint bodies which are involved in the process of taking decisions of a general nature.

Generally speaking, a federal or regional structure obviously enables a minority - in cases where it has majority status - to exercise important powers. However, the precise definition of such powers stands outside the scope of this report. Consideration should nevertheless be given to certain particular features of the Italian legal system. A special autonomous status is enjoyed by regions with recognised minorities, namely Valle d'Aosta, Trentino-Alto Adige and Friuli-Venezia Giulia. In addition, the province of Bolzano, which has a German-speaking majority, enjoys a special form of autonomy very similar to the autonomy of the regions. In the other Italian regions, the special competences of the regional legislature in the field of culture and local tradition allow the adoption of special measures in favour of the other minor linguistic groups.

In Spain, the Autonomous Communities of Catalonia, the Basque country and Galicia, where minority languages are most widely spoken, were set up, like the Autonomous Community of Andalusia, under a more complex procedure, and were called upon more quickly than the others to exercise responsibilities similar to those of the federated entities of a federal State. Today, however, these distinctions have been reduced due to an expansion of the powers of the other Autonomous Communities. Nevertheless, the special language situations of Catalonia, the Basque country and Galicia have continued to be used by nationalist factions within the Autonomous Communities with a view to obtaining wider powers (referred to as the "differential factor").

Federalism - or indeed regionalism - is undoubtedly a system which enables minorities to obtain a degree of autonomy within the framework of the existing State structure. The question of a territory's accession to federated or regional status, so as to enable a minority to form a territorial majority, is a problem of a different kind but one which can also provide the solution to a situation of conflict. This was the case with the establishment of the canton of Jura in Switzerland; the francophone Districts which wished to separate from the canton of Berne, were empowered, by means of an ad hoc constitutional provision at cantonal level and following a series of plebiscites, to form a distinct canton, and this did away in large measure with "the problem of Jura".

IV. Conclusion

The preceding pages have shown the difficulty of identifying common principal elements in national rules on the protection of minorities in federal and regional States. On the contrary, this is a field where each national situation is specific and has been dealt with in an original manner in a given historical context.

In general terms, however, the following may be noted in addition to the overall guarantee of conventional individual rights (such as freedom of association, freedom of thought, conscience and religion or linguistic freedoms):

1. Certain rules are specific to federal or even regional States, and these may be described as falling into two categories:

a) On the one hand, federated States and regions have extended competences and, in some cases, are organs of the central State (as in <u>Switzerland</u> in respect of cantons in the matter of constitutional referenda), or play a specific role in the establishment of the organs of the central State (notably the Swiss Council of States and the Spanish Senate). When a minority is itself in the majority in a federated State or region, it indirectly benefits from such competences and from such participation in central government.

b) On the other hand (more often in cases of concentrated minorities), the legislation of federated States can provide for certain minority rights in addition to those guaranteed by central government, for example by means of:

- a more precise regulation of linguistic questions at the federated State level than at the level of central government (in <u>Switzerland</u>, in <u>Canada</u>, as well as in <u>Germany</u> where, apart from the reference to the Sorabe minority in Article 35 of the Treaty of Unification, the protection of linguistic minorities falls exclusively within the laws of Länder);

- the granting of political rights in cantonal or communal matters, by two Swiss cantons, to certain foreigners;

- special electoral provisions for the election of organs of federated States (for example, in the Länder of Schleswig-Holstein and of Saxony the 5% quorum does not apply to minorities).

2. Some rules are more commonly encountered in a federal or regional State than in a unitary State and can apply equally to dispersed minorities as to concentrated minorities, such as:

-   the representation of linguistic minorities in the organs of central government, Switzerland and Belgium being examples of countries in which this principle is of general application;

-   rights specific to religious or linguistic minorities, in the field of education in particular (notably in Canada).

National reports:

Austria
Belgium
Canada
Germany
Italy
Spain
Switzerland

Austria

FEDERALISM AND PROTECTION OF MINORITIES

Constitutional aspects in Austria

by

Professor Franz MATSCHER,
Professor, University of Salzburg (Austria)
Judge at the European Court of Human Rights

MINORITIES IN THE FEDERAL STRUCTURE
OF THE AUSTRIAN STATE

According to Article 2 of the 1920 Constitution of the Republic of Austria, the latter is a federal state composed of nine regions (Länder).

The Constitution divides legislative and executive powers between the Federation (Bund) and the regions; nevertheless, the most important powers, especially those concerned with the protection of minorities, come under the jurisdiction of the Federation.

A number of persons in Carinthia and Styria belong to the Slovenian minority, others in the Burgenland belong to the Croat and Hungarian minorities. There are minority groups of Croats, Hungarians and Czechs in Vienna.

As explained above, the protection of minorities is chiefly dealt with in federal (national) legislation. It is therefore not surprising that the constitutions of the regions in question (Carinthia, Styria, the Burgenland and Vienna) do not contain any provisions on the protection of minorities.

It should be noted that the constitutions of Carinthia, Styria, the Burgenland and Lower Austria follow the example of Article 8 of the Federal Constitution by stipulating that the official language of the region is German, save as otherwise provided in national laws on the use of minority languages (cf in particular the Law on Ethnic Groups of 1976).

It should be pointed out that, under the Carinthian constitution, the whole region used to form a single electoral district. The Slovenian minority (dispersed throughout the region, but more heavily concentrated in the south-eastern districts) could therefore muster enough votes to elect a candidate of its own. Nevertheless, in 1978, the Constitutional Court decided that the constitution required the division of the regions into several electoral districts.

In 1979 the regional constitution of Carinthia was amended to comply with this decision, and the region was split up into four electoral districts. Since then it has been almost impossible for a minority list to pick up enough votes in one district to return a member to parliament.

It must, however, be added that when regional and national elections are held, the lists of the political parties generally include representatives of the Slovenian minority, and municipal councils and other bodies (chambers of commerce, agriculture or industry) contain representatives elected from the minorities' own lists.

It is easier for federal states like Austria than for centralised states to make appropriate arrangements to take account of the presence of minority groups in a region. For example, the regional government of Carinthia (Landesregierung) has set up a special office to deal with questions concerning minorities (Bureau für Volksgruppenfragen).

Belgium

FEDERALISM AND PROTECTION OF MINORITIES

by

Professor Jean-Claude SCHOLSEM
Professor at the Law Faculty, University of Liège (Belgium)

1.1 It is of course extremely difficult, shortly after the completion of a major overhaul of the Constitution[1], which has been elaborated upon in legislation, to give a precise description of the contribution of the "Belgian federal model" to the general problem area of protection for minorities.

However, the originality of the Belgian model can and must be emphasised. In our view, the solutions implemented in this country provide all sorts of lessons - both positive and negative - for other States confronted with the same problems and the same difficulties.

1.2 The main distinguishing feature of Belgian federalism - as distinct from that of, say, Switzerland or the United States - is that it is not an original form of federalism but one built on the foundations of a unitary State. Belgian federalism has been established gradually to meet the growing need for autonomy expressed by the two great "peoples", Flemish and Walloon, who comprise the State.

All federal structures are the fruit of historical circumstances and can be understood only in relation to their specific history; this is particularly true of the very special and atypical brand of federalism found in Belgium, one which is dissociative in as much as it has grown out of a unitary State. It was only after 140 years of this unitary State's existence (1830-1970) that federal-type structures were introduced gradually and in stages. This process was partial and fragmentary in every case, since it required four major revisions of the Constitution, in 1970, 1980, 1988 and most recently in 1993.

1.3 The historical catalyst for this transformation of a unitary State into a federal State was the desire of the Flemish population to have its language, Dutch, placed on an equal footing with French.

Indeed, when it first came into being and during the early decades of its existence, the Belgian State was dominated by a middle class whose vehicle of expression, in both the north and the south of the country, was the French language. French was the only official language. If a "linguistic frontier" existed, the origins of which are lost in the mists of time, that frontier was of hardly any importance since French was the language of the

---

[1] *Constitutional amendments of 5 May 1993, Moniteur belge, 8 May 1993.*

élites and the ruling classes throughout the country. In terms of theories applied to minorities, therefore, Belgium represents an interesting special case since the language of the majority of the population, in numerical terms, had the status of a minority language. In the 19th century, the linguistic divide was far more of a social cleavage than a geographical one. In the northern part of the country, various types of Flemish patois were spoken, while Walloon, Picardy and Lorrainese dialects were used in the south. The French language was the cement which bound together the élites and the Belgian State.

1.4 The gradual extension of the right to vote, definitively acquired by men after the first world war and by women after the second world war, was to pose a radical threat to the very balance of this unitary State bound together by linguistic and cultural unity. From the end of the 19th century, a whole series of laws tended to place Dutch on the same footing as French. From the end of the 19th century onwards, an entire set of "language" laws was drafted, in respect of the official use of languages. These laws were limited in scope, at least in theory, by the principle of linguistic freedom set out in Article 23 of the Constitution (Article 30 of the Co-ordinated Constitution)[2] which is amenable to regulation by law only in the case of acts by public authorities and in matters of a judicial nature. However, this constitutional provision has been interpreted very broadly in legislative texts.

At the same time, the Flemish movement placed increasingly distinct emphasis on the principle of territoriality, which was seen as a means of defending a less widely used language, although one spoken by a majority in the country, against a language of wider international prevalence. A distinct change took place in this connection. The language laws of the period between the two wars provided for flexible dividing lines between languages, in as much as individual communes were able, on basis of the linguistic censuses carried out periodically, to change their language rules or to obtain special "facilities" entitling them to provide for the official use of the language of the minority if the latter became large enough. This system usually worked to the advantage of French speakers, especially on the outskirts of Brussels. After the second world war, the Flemings succeeded in having the linguistic census abolished. Acts of 1961 and 1962

---

[2]   *The text of the Belgian Constitution, which became difficult to read after the numerous revisions it had undergone since 1970, was co-ordinated on 17 February 1994. In this document, reference is made to both the old and the new numeration (Co-ordinated Constitution).*

laid down a definitive linguistic frontier, with no further reference to subsequent population movements or the wishes of the inhabitants. The establishment of this "frontier" produced some points of friction, as in the case of the commune of Fourons which caused a number of political difficulties at the highest level. Finally in 1970, the Constitution finished off a long-term task by itself recognising the existence of four linguistic regions: the French-, Dutch- and German-speaking regions and the bilingual region of Brussels-capital (Article 3 bis; Article 4 of the Co-ordinated Constitution).

1.5 The historical developments outlined above would appear to justify the somewhat simplistic label of "linguistic quarrels" which is sometimes applied to the vicissitudes of Belgian political life.

As we shall attempt to show, there are many other aspects to the gradual federalisation of the country, which as a matter of fact began in 1970. However, it is important to bear in mind the "language battle" fought by the Flemish people, which resulted in the division of the territory into "linguistic regions" under the 1970 Constitution. The boundaries of those regions could henceforth no longer be modified except by so-called special legislation, ie laws adopted by a special majority (two-thirds of the votes in the two chambers, requisite quorum, and a majority of votes within each language group in each of the chambers). The regions thus served as a territorial base for the various regional and community institutions which were to be set up and developed from 1970 onwards. In other words, language frontiers paved the way for the development of political boundaries, and it was these boundaries (extremely difficult to alter in law and considered politically immutable by the Flemish political community) which provided the framework for the establishment of the regional and Community institutions proper to post-unitary Belgium.

2.1 It is not part of our intention to give a detailed description of present-day institutions in Belgium. At the level of both the federal State and the federated entities (Regions and Communities), these institutions are extremely complex and furthermore - as was mentioned above - they recently underwent a further overhaul, in May 1993, which will no doubt not be the last one. Nor is it possible to dwell on the development of these reforms which were carried out in four major stages (1970 - 1980 - 1988 - 1993).

The aim will be to show how federal techniques of a particular nature have been applied in a country facing what is doubtless one of the most difficult situations to handle, namely a division between two populations separated by differences of language, culture and sensibility. As has been mentioned, this division did not become apparent right away, but was the outcome of a slow process which came to fruition in the fullness of time. This explains the radical break in the history of Belgium, between a relatively long period (140 years) during which the State existed in a unitary form, and a period of intense upheavals (1970 to the present day).

2.2 Emphasis should therefore be placed on certain characteristics of Belgium's federal structure which are little or poorly understood abroad. It is also necessary to show how the special federal techniques applied in Belgium ensure the peaceful coexistence of majorities and minorities - albeit not without difficulty - at both national and local level.

As was pointed out above, Belgian federalism grew out of the transformation of a unitary State into a federal structure. This is an historically very rare case of federation by dissociation, and as such poses very different problems from those raised by a conventional - that is to say associative - type of federalism. In the case of Belgium, the regional and Community institutions were created from scratch, so to speak. Their autonomy, jurisdiction and organisational structure were fashioned by the central Government itself. Federalism was thus conceded, as it were, and this explains many of the features of the Belgian federal structure. After nearly twenty-five years of reorganisation, the State may still appear highly centralised to an observer familiar with genuine federalism. For example, the federated entities have no say in the process of revising the Constitution, residual jurisdiction lies with the federal State, the entire judicial system is also federal in structure and the level of taxation differs very little between federated entities. The latter have no Constitution of their own.[3] Moreover, the former territorial divisions of the unitary State, including the provinces in particular, have been kept intact. The situation of the local authorities is especially complex since they depend partly on the central Government (for their basic legislation, for example) and partly on the Regions (for finance and general supervision), as well as in some cases on the Communities. Under the most recent reform, in 1993, the province of Brabant - the last vestige of the Belgian unitary State since its territory

---

[3] *Although a certain amount of "constituent autonomy" was allowed under the reform of 5 May 1993.*

encroached on all three Regions - was divided into Flemish Brabant and Walloon Brabant, while the Brussels-capital region was no longer attached to any province.

This situation contrasts with the system of associative federalism, where the aim is to restrict existing sovereign or quasi-sovereign powers.

In the case of Belgium, the prevailing trend is centrifugal, while in most other federal States it is centripetal. In addition, the Belgian pattern of government comprises only a small number of units, and this obviously makes it more difficult to operate a federal system. Officially, the federal State is composed of three Regions and three Communities (Article 1 para. 1 of the Constitution; Article 1 of the Co-ordinated Constitution).

2.3 This is precisely one of the most puzzling aspects of the current structure of the Belgian State. Belgian federalism is a two-tier form of federalism. The federated entities comprise both communities and regions. There is some territorial overlapping between communities and regions. Moreover, the notion of a community is not entirely territorial and opens the way for a "personal" type of federalism.

Once again, only history can explain this particularly complex situation. To simplify matters, it can be said that community-style federalism corresponds to a Flemish aspiration, while institutions of a regional nature meet the wishes of the Walloons and, to a lesser extent, the French-speaking inhabitants of Brussels. There is therefore a debate in Belgium about the very nature of the entities which are to be federated. The very difficulty of settling this question leads to the emergence of a structure which, in a manner of speaking, combines and seeks to reconcile these two approaches in a fragile balance liable at all times to be called in question.

2.4 On the Flemish side, the language dispute and the need for cultural assertion, in a situation long perceived as deriving from a psychological minority, are naturally conducive to the espousal of the community concept. Indeed, since 1970, the Communities have been responsible for everything connected with the use of languages and culture. Their powers were broadened in 1980 to include various matters of a social nature (so-called "personalisable" matters) and since 1989 they have encompassed the entire field of education. Accordingly, Belgium is divided into three communities: a Flemish Community, a French Community and a German-speaking Community.

The latter is small in size and in fact reflects the wish to protect and guarantee the autonomy of a genuine minority. With a few exceptions (with regard to the use of languages, for example), German-speaking Belgians, of whom there are some 66 000, enjoy the benefit of the same Community institutions, the same areas of jurisdiction and the same degree of autonomy as the country's two major communities, namely the Flemings and the francophones. Consequently, despite its small numerical size, the German-speaking Community has full jurisdiction within the areas of culture, social ("personalisable") matters and education within the German linguistic region. In this respect, it is clearly a highly protected linguistic and cultural minority. However, it must immediately be added that, from the standpoint of the decision-making machinery at federal State level, Belgium's German speakers as such are almost totally excluded from the relevant mechanisms which are designed to ensure a balance between Flemings and French speakers. In other words, while German-speaking Belgians are protected as a linguistic and cultural minority, they are hardly or not at all involved, as such, in the workings of the federal State.

The essentially Flemish idea of a community-style federalism, ie with its focus on language, culture and education, entails a conception based to some extent on non-territorial principles. Indeed, while the German-speaking Community is in the straightforward position of having jurisdiction over a clearly defined territory, namely the German-language region, the situation is much more awkward for the French and Flemish Communities which are required, in a manner of speaking, to "share" Brussels, or more precisely speaking the bilingual region of Brussels-capital. In this region, both Communities have jurisdiction over the same territory. However, Belgian law makes no provision for sub-nationality: neither Flemings nor French speakers are recognised under the law. That being the case, in the bilingual region of Brussels-capital, decrees (which are the equivalent of laws at the Community level) cannot be made applicable to persons but only to cultural and social institutions which have a direct connection with the culture or the "community" in question. It is in this respect that the community aspect of Belgian federalism is not entirely based on territorial principles. Nor does it constitute what is known as a personalised form of federalism, since there is no personal link binding individuals to a community. The solution adopted is a composite one, whereby two political groupings have dealings with the institutions "representing" their culture or their language in a given part of the territory.

2.5 Among French speakers and more especially the Walloons, the federalisation of the country is primarily thought of in regional terms. From this point of view, Belgium comprises three regions: the Walloon Region, the Flemish Region and the Region of Brussels-capital.

The regions do not fully correspond to the Community "territories" described above. If the division of the country into linguistic regions is taken as the starting point, it is found that the Walloon Region comprises two linguistic regions, namely the French language region and the German language region. The German speaking Community, which has responsibility for cultural and social affairs within its territory, therefore forms part of the Walloon Region whose areas of responsibility are primarily economic. The Brussels-capital Region coincides with the bilingual linguistic region, that is to say the area where the Communities' responsibilities overlap. The Flemish Region corresponds to the monolingual, Dutch-speaking linguistic region.

Responsibilities are assigned to the Regions in the same way as to the Communities, while residual jurisdiction continues to lie with the central Government. These responsibilities mainly concern the economy, the environment, transport and subordinate powers. From the Walloon point of view, Belgium is divided into three distinct socio-economic units. Cultural or community-type claims are much less assertive among French-speaking Belgians who have never had to defend their language and their culture; on the contrary, the latter were for a long time predominant. The concept of regional federalism, that is to say a federal State with three component parts, one of them including the national capital (the Region of Brussels-capital), was for a long time vehemently opposed by the Flemings who feared that, since the central region of the country had over the years become home to a clear majority of French speakers, the division of the country into three component parts, including two (the Walloon Region and the Brussels Region) in which the majority were French speakers, would structurally place them in the position of a minority (two against one), despite their demographic ascendancy (roughly 60% of the population) and their growing economic dominance.

3.1 Federal Belgium is thus seen to have grown out of a unitary State split between two separatist tendencies, one being linguistic, cultural and essentially dualistic in nature (bearing in mind that, in this regard, the German-speaking Community is not a component part of the State but a protected minority), while the other is socio-economic, focusing on the existence of three regions.

Each of these conceptions is partially recognised in positive law, as a result of lengthy and laborious compromises worked out between Flemings and French speakers.

With regard to the actual organisation of the federal State, it is the dualistic approach which has certainly prevailed. As a result, the mechanisms for the protection of minorities incorporated in the Belgian Constitution are targeted not at the regions, but at the two great population groups characterised by their language. Since 1970, the Council of Ministers has had an equi-representative structure: with the possible exception of the Prime Minister, it must comprise an equal number of French- speaking and Dutch-speaking Ministers. This guarantee of parity representation at the highest level of government constitutes the most effective means of protection for the French-speaking population. In practice it is difficult, in a country applying the system of proportional representation, to set up a federal government which does not enjoy majority support or at least have an adequate base both north and south of the linguistic divide. Moreover, equal representation on the Council of Ministers is the extension of the linguistic parity introduced at the highest levels of central government.

Various other legal mechanisms highlight the fundamental duality of Belgium's central government institutions. For example, the two federal Chambers (House of Representatives and Senate) are divided into two language groups.

These groups exercise a major influence. Indeed, since 1970, the Constitution itself has laid down the requirement of a special majority for the adoption of a growing number of laws essential to the balance of the country or the protection of minorities. This requirement involves not only an overall majority of two-thirds but the presence of a quorum and of a majority in each language group, within both federal assemblies. For example, the "language frontier" could be altered only by a law of this type. Similarly, all essential aspects of the organisation of regional and Community institutions, as well as their powers and their financing, depend either on the constitution itself or, pursuant to the constitution, on laws of this kind known in Belgium as special laws.

It is through the requirement of such special laws, to a far greater extent than, for example, through the organisation and powers of the Senate, that the protection of the French-speaking minority is given practical effect in Belgium, subject to the restrictions imposed by the Constitution. In this regard, Belgium's system of federalism differs from the conventional type found in such countries as Switzerland and the United States, where the second chamber is the major instrument of participation by the federated states in the political life of the federal State. The Belgian Senate was recently subjected to far-reaching reforms, in 1993, but these reforms - which we cannot describe here in detail - have not made the Belgian Senate a federal chamber like the Swiss Council of States or the American senate.

The language groups in the House and the Senate are also entitled to make use of a special protective mechanism which is very rarely used in practice. This mechanism, known familiarly as the "alarm bell", enables a language group to declare, on the basis of a three-quarters majority, that a Government Bill or a private member's Bill is likely to cause serious prejudice to relations between the communities. In such cases, the procedure is suspended and the text is submitted to the Council of Ministers, in which the language groups have equal representation and which must take a decision. This mechanism has been used only once since it was introduced in 1970, but it is not beyond belief that its mere existence may have something of a preventive effect and, more specifically, a protective effect for the French-speaking minority

3.2 Apart from equal representation in the Council of Ministers and the requirement that laws be adopted by a special "linguistic" majority, other institutions reflect the dualistic nature of Belgium's federal system. For example, the Constitutional Court, which is known as the Arbitration Court, is composed of six French-speaking judges and six Dutch-speaking judges, on an equi-representative basis. An ingenious system is used to prevent deadlock in the pronouncement of judgments. This Court's original purpose was to monitor compliance with the apportionment of powers between the State, the Communities and the Regions, but it was subsequently given broader responsibilities. Through its task of reviewing compliance with the principle of equality, which was entrusted to it in 1989, it operates in many respects as a fully-fledged Constitutional Court. Language parity within this Court is therefore an essential element of balance in Belgium.

The same language parity is found in the highest ordinary and administrative courts (Court of Cassation and Council of State). Similarly, the membership of the Consultation Committee, a political body set up to prevent and, if possible, settle conflicts of interest between component units of central government, is linguistically equi-representative. The above are only a few of the almost unlimited instances of this phenomenon.

4.1 While it is clear that the federal structure of the Belgian State is essentially dualistic, the fact remains that it is composed of three Communities and three Regions.

This two-tier federal structure has already been described. It only remains to give an account of its practical workings and how it has developed. It is obviously quite difficult to ensure the harmonious operation of a federal structure of this type. Indeed, the federal State retains residuary jurisdiction, while different institutions (Regions and Communities) exercise a variety of exclusive powers with regard to territories which partially overlap. The difficulty is compounded by the fact that responsibilities are assigned almost entirely on the basis of the system of exclusive jurisdiction. Belgian law only rarely has recourse to the technique of concurrent jurisdiction, with its mandatory corollary, namely that federal rules should take precedence over rules adopted by federated entities. The use of this technique would appear in a way to contradict the centrifugal tendency characteristic of Belgian federalism. The system of exclusive jurisdiction is therefore bound up with the desire for autonomy of the newly established entities which have no wish to see the federal State "take back" what it has recently given them, by means of concurrent legislation. The fact remains, though, that the system of exclusive jurisdiction, which is practically the only one used in Belgium, makes the procedures for sharing responsibilities extremely rigid.

4.2 All this goes hand in hand with a federal structure comprising two tiers, the Communities on the one hand and the Regions on the other. However, this system is subject to major deviations in institutional practice. Since 1980, the Flemish have carried out a "merger" of regional and Community institutions. The decision-making bodies are the same in all cases: it is sufficient to exclude the Flemings of Brussels from their membership when regional Flemish issues are being considered. The small proportion (2 to 3%) of Brussels Flemings in relation to the total Flemish population enabled this solution to be adopted in the north of the country. It is a very effective one in policy-making and administrative terms, as well as with respect to budgetary matters, as it facilitates transfers from one budget to another (regional and Community budgets). At the same time, it enables the Flemings to confirm and consolidate the position of the Brussels Flemings -

who are substantially outnumbered by French speakers in Brussels - in the Flemish Community. Symbolically, the Flemings have chosen Brussels as the capital of their community.

The francophones have not taken the step of "amalgamating" their regional and Community institutions, a step which - it has to be admitted - would have had completely different political and financial implications from the one taken in the north of the country. The French speakers of Wallonia represent only about 32% of the population, or 3,200,000 people. The number of French speakers in Brussels is estimated at approximately 800,000. In other words, although the French speakers of Brussels constitute a minority within their Community, they nevertheless account for roughly one fifth of that Community's population. In addition, economic conditions and living standards are considerably different in Wallonia and Brussels. Lastly, as has already been mentioned, the idea of a Community does not have the same historical and symbolic appeal for the French speakers as it does for the Flemings. That is why French speakers and Walloons fought a fierce battle to obtain the establishment of a Region in Brussels, with success coming only in 1989. Flemish acceptance of the establishment of this Region, with its own autonomy, was made subject to several conditions.

The first condition is that the Region in question, in the institutional sense of the term, should correspond to the bilingual region of Brussels-capital. This is limited to 19 communes (including the city of Brussels proper). It does not coincide with the socio-economic region of Brussels which, like all major cities, is tending to broaden its economic hinterland extensively. However, this economic hinterland, especially in terms of housing, is located in the Flemish Region, a region which surrounds the Brussels Region on all sides. Some of the communes adjoining Brussels, which were originally Flemish, have absorbed a great deal of French influence and enjoy so-called "linguistic facilities". Other communes have been given no such facilities, even though they have substantial French-speaking or foreign minorities. This is because of the Flemish desire to check the particularly significant inroads made by French influence in the area of Flemish-Brabant around Brussels.

The second condition laid down by the Flemings for the establishment of the region of Brussels-capital was the adoption of a set of measures to protect the Flemish minority in Brussels. At the 1989 elections for the Council of the Region, roughly 15% of the votes were cast for Dutch-speaking lists. The regional institutions of Brussels thus provide for a whole range of guarantees on behalf of this minority. Broadly speaking, it may be said that the guarantees in question are modelled on those granted to French speakers within the federal State. For example, two of the five members of the Brussels regional government must be Flemings, and this corresponds, *mutatis mutandis*, to the level of parity representation in the federal Council of Ministers.

4.3 The establishment of the region of Brussels in 1989 enabled the francophones and the Walloons to envisage an institutional set-up based essentially on regional realities. For the demographic and economic reasons outlined above, they allowed the Community institutions and regional institutions to remain in coexistence, although this coexistence is very difficult to manage. Indeed, the French Community is isolated in institutional and budgetary terms, unlike the Flemish Community, which remains closely identified with its region. This Community has consequently been confronted with financial problems, especially since 1989, the first year in which the enormous education budget was transferred to it. Unlike the Flemish Community which receives regional grants on account of the merger of institutions, the French Community has to cope with its budgetary constraints unassisted. Moreover, the very special nature of its jurisdiction with regard to the territory of the bilingual region of Brussels-capital makes it awkward if not impossible for it to resort to taxation. The exercise of fiscal powers is hardly reconcilable with a brand of federalism that is not entirely based on territorial principles.

This problem area was central to the constitutional review carried out in the spring of 1993, a review which, on the basis of complex mechanisms, makes it possible for some of the powers of the French Community to be exercised at regional level in Wallonia and, what is more, to be exercised by institutions proper to the French speakers, institutions set up within the region of Brussels-capital.

The institutional map of Belgium will therefore once again be redrawn, since the two great Communities will no longer exercise the same powers. On the French-speaking side, certain responsibilities will be taken over either by the Walloon region or by the French-speaking representatives of the Brussels regional institutions.

The lack of symmetry between the two major component parts of the country is becoming even more marked than before. Although this complexity is perplexing to the foreign observer, it merely confirms the diagnosis above: the difficulty with Belgian federalism stems not only from its centrifugal nature or the small number of federated entities, but to an even greater extent from the <u>fundamental debate about the nature of those entities</u>. While the idea of a community is given clear priority by the Flemings, making their approach a more coherent one, preference is given to a regional philosophy in the south of the country. This is all the more true following the recent central government overhaul which provides for a radical re-organisation of the apportionment of responsibilities among French-speaking Community institutions and Walloon and Brussels regional institutions. The very idea of a French Community has been partially challenged. It is quite obvious that the process of Belgian federal construction has not yet been placed on a fully stable footing.

5.1 Certain problems relating to the protection of minorities also arise at the local level. The solutions applied to them have changed substantially over the years, as a result of the growing insistence by the Flemish movement on the principle of territoriality.

As was mentioned above, the language frontier had been definitively established by law in the early 1960s, and this led to difficulties, some of which had significant political repercussions (the problem of Fourons). After 1970, the language frontier could no longer be modified otherwise than by means of a law adopted by a special majority.

At the same time, the 1970 Constitution gave the Flemish and French Communities the task of regulating the use of languages in three areas: (i) administrative matters; (ii) education in institutions established, subsidised or recognised by the public authorities; (iii) social relations between employers and staff as well as the measures and documents required of firms by laws and regulations.

This Community jurisdiction in respect of the use of languages is broader than the powers previously (and still) exercised by the legislature under Article 23 of the original text of the Constitution (Article 30 of the Co-ordinated Constitution). Basically, this jurisdiction reflects an aspiration on the part of the Flemings to establish the maximum possible linguistic homogeneity (especially in social and economic matters) within their linguistic field of influence, that is to say in the Dutch-speaking region. It should be pointed out, however, that these areas of jurisdiction remain limited and that, what is more, the principle of <u>linguistic freedom</u> is regaining ascendancy. It should also be added that, out of a concern to protect minorities, certain exceptions to the Communities' jurisdiction in respect of languages has been provided for in the relevant legislation. The Communities never exercise such jurisdiction in the bilingual region of Brussels-capital, where the use of languages continues to be governed by national law. Similarly, the Flemish and French Communities have no authority over certain communes, although the latter are situated in a monolingual region: six communes on the outskirts of Brussels (situated in the Dutch-speaking region) and the so-called "language frontier commmunes" which have Flemish, French-speaking or German-speaking minorities, as the case may be. The linguistic status of these communes was regarded as so important that in 1988 it was decided by the constitution-making body that only a law adopted by a special majority could modify that status.

The territoriality rule is sometimes resented by French speakers as a sort of violation of "human rights". They conceive of language rights primarily as personal rights. It was precisely to counter this conception that the Flemish movement reacted, stressing the need to defend the linguistic homogeneity of Flemish territory against francophone "imperialism". In its famous judgment on the linguistic rules applicable to education in Belgium[4], the European Court of Human Rights recognised the overall legitimacy of the aim pursued by Belgian linguistic legislation, namely the maintenance of regional linguistic homogeneity.

5.2 Over and above the application of laws concerning the use of languages, the existence of local linguistic minorities also gives rise to a problem with regard to the drawing of constituency boundaries for national elections. In this connection, one particular constituency, that of Brussels-Hal-Vilvorde, plays a key role. This highly populated electoral district comprises both the bilingual region of Brussels-capital and the district of Hal-Vilvorde in the Flemish region. However, a large number of French speakers (approximately 100,000) are included in the population of this Flemish district, whether because they live in the six peripheral communes with special facilities or because they are resident in purely Flemish communes.

The amalgamation of these two administrative districts for the purpose of general elections thus enables a large number of French speakers living in Flanders to choose elected representatives who will take the oath in French

---

4. *Judgment of 23 July 1968, Series A No. 6.*

and form part of the French language group in the House and the Senate. During the most recent institutional negotiations in Belgium, which resulted in the revision of the Constitution in May 1993, the Flemings demanded the splitting up of the constituency of Brussels-Hal-Vilvorde on the basis of the strict application of the territoriality rule. However, the French speakers were able to keep the district intact, both for elections to the House and for the direct election of senators.

The situation is different with regard to the Community Councils. Prior to the 1993 revision of the Constitution, as is illustrated by the judgment of the European Court of Human Rights in the Clerfayt and Mathieu Mahin case[5], French speakers living in the Hal-Vilvorde district could appoint representatives to the Council of the French Community through their votes cast in general elections. However, this Community had no territorial jurisdiction over them and, furthermore, by casting the votes in question, French-speaking voters forfeited all rights to regional representation.

This situation is radically altered by the current reform which eliminates the "dual mandate" system and provides for direct elections. These elections will take place on a purely regional basis: it follows that the large French-speaking minority established in Flemish Brabant will henceforth be required to vote exclusively for Flemish regional and Community representatives.

---

[5]   *Judgment of 2 March 1987, Series A No. 113.*

Canada

THE CONSTITUTIONAL PROTECTION OF MINORITIES IN CANADA

by

Senator Gérald-A. BEAUDOIN,
Professor in the Faculty of Law,
University of Ottawa (Canada)

CONTENTS

INTRODUCTION

Canada is a constitutional monarchy and a parliamentary democracy. It became a federation in 1867. Its constitution is partly written and partly unwritten. A Charter of Rights and Freedoms has been part of the Constitution since 1982. The principle of the rule of law applies in Canada, where the judicial system is both powerful and independent.

The Constitution Act of 1867, our basic law, contains several provisions covering the protection of minorities. In 1982, a second Constitution Act took this protection system further by embodying, *inter alia*, a Charter of Rights and Freedoms in the Constitution.

This paper will answer the following questions: has the division of legislative powers been influenced by the presence of minorities? Are minorities protected in federal and provincial institutions? Does the Canadian Constitution protect religious rights? language rights? fundamental rights? the rights of the aboriginal peoples? What conclusions can be reached regarding this protection?

I. THE DIVISION OF LEGISLATIVE POWERS AND THE PROTECTION OF MINORITIES

The division of powers adopted in 1867 was intended, first and foremost, to be politically, economically and socially functional, but it also took account of the presence of minorities in Canada.

Canada's decision to opt for a federal structure in 1867, instead of the legislative union desired by the Upper Canadian (Ontario) leader, Sir John A. MacDonald, was taken partly because Sir Georges Etienne-Carter, leader of the then Lower Canada (now Quebec), wanted this as way of protecting French-speaking "Canadians", who were a minority in the country as a whole, although they formed the majority in Quebec. Legislative union would have been unacceptable to Quebec.

Since Canada was a heterogeneous federation with more than one language and more than one culture, the thirty-three Fathers of the Federation decided, in Section 93 of the 1867 Constitution, to make education the preserve of the provinces; Quebec was thus able to choose its own education system.

Cartier, one of the Fathers of the Federation and mainly responsible for the Constitution's federal character[1], was very careful to include, in Section 92, "property and civil rights" - a category which, as the courts have pointed out[2], comes straight from the Quebec Act of 1774. This allowed Quebec to keep its own private and civil law, which it had codified and which had come into force on 1 August 1866. Sections 94 and 98 of the Constitution Act of 1867 put the finishing touches to this guarantee. Not being mentioned in Section 94, Quebec escapes the possibility of private law's being harmonised. Section 98 provides that Quebec judges must be trained in civil law. The French-speaking minority in Canada - mainly (though not solely) concentrated in Quebec - is thus protected by the Constitution. The common law system applies in the other provinces.

Finally, Section 41 of the Constitution Act of 1982 states that the unanimous consent of the federal government and the ten provinces is required for any change in the constitutional laws relating to the Supreme Court. The scope of this provision is a source of some discussion, since the Supreme Court Act is not mentioned among the constitutional laws[3]. If it does in fact make the "6-3" composition a constitutional requirement, then Quebec enjoys special protection here. In my opinion, the term "composition" in Section 41 covers both the figure "nine" and the "6-3" distribution.

II. THE PROTECTION OF MINORITIES IN INSTITUTIONS

A. The central institutions

"Representation according to population", current in Canada before the advent of federalism, still applies in the House of Commons in Ottawa. There are no exceptions to this basic principle of our parliamentary democracy.

In the Senate, the Fathers of the Federation opted for representation by region. Quebec and Ontario are both regions, with 24 senators each out of a total of 104. In 1867, the three maritime provinces formed a single region, which was assigned 24 senators. This is still the case today. Newfoundland joined the

---

[1] See M. Wade, "Les Canadiens français de 1760 à nos jours", vol. I, Cercle du Livre de France, 1963, p 340.

[2] See the Parsons Judgment, (1881-1882) 7 A.C. 96.

[3] P.W. Hogg, "Canada Act 1982 Annotated", Toronto, Carswell, 1982.

Canadian Federation in 1949 and was given six senators. The West of Canada comprises four provinces with six senators each. The federal territories, the Yukon and North-West, have one senator each.

Several provinces, apart from Quebec and Ontario, have been calling for the past twenty years or so for a Senate that would be "equal by province", rather than "by region". This principle has not so far been incorporated in the Constitution.

The Senate's composition provides, I believe, some protection for Quebec, which has had almost a quarter of the seats since 1915, as has Ontario. In 1867, each of these two provinces had a third of the seats. Cartier had accepted representation according to population in the House of Commons on condition that Quebec was given a third of the Senate seats and maintained parity with Ontario, whose population was larger.

The principle of representation by region is partly intended to protect Quebec. This protection is relative, however. Under the Constitution, it could be withdrawn. A consensus of the federal authorities and seven provinces representing 50% of the population would be enough to do this. This is one of the principal gaps in the constitutional amendment procedure adopted in 1982. The right of withdrawal provided for in Section 38 (3) of the Constitution Act of 1982 cannot protect Quebec here; withdrawal from the Senate is not possible.

The Senate was deprived of its right to veto constitutional changes on 17 April 1982 by Section 47 of the Constitution Act. Its veto now applies only in cases provided for in Section 44, which states:

> Subject to Sections 41 and 42, Parliament may exclusively make laws amending the Constitution of Canada in relation to the executive government of Canada or the Senate and House of Commons.

The scope of this power is restricted. It replaces Section 91 (1) of the Constitution Act of 1867, which was repealed in 1982.

In the Supreme Court, the court of last instance, Quebec appoints three of the nine judges, or one-third of the total. This provides special protection for Quebec which, as stated above, is the only province with a civil law system.

B. The provincial institutions

The provinces have only one legislative chamber. The principle of representation according to population applies, as it does in the Canadian Parliament.

The "first-past-the-post" electoral system applies at both provincial and federal levels.

III. RELIGIOUS RIGHTS

Education was considered very important in 1867, as indeed it is today. A separate article, Section 93, was devoted to it in the section covering the division of legislative powers. In the opinion of Chief Justice Duff, one of our leading legal authorities, this was one of the main elements in the great compromise of 1867[4]. This legislative power is backed by constitutional guarantees to protect the rights of the Catholics and Protestants, who made up almost the whole population in 1867, as well as the right to dissent. A system of special and conditional appeal by religious groups to the federal political authorities was also devised, although this proved ineffective in the Manitoba Schools case between 1890 and 1896 and has since fallen into disuse[5].

In Quebec, religious rights include the right to denominational schools in Montreal and Quebec, and elsewhere the right to dissent; they also include the right to manage schools, recruit teachers, choose textbooks and levy taxes. This list is not intended to be restrictive[6].

The guarantees contained in Section 93 gave rise to a number of celebrated judgments from the federation's earliest years, particularly from the 1890s on,

---

[4] *"In Re Adoption Act of Ontario", (1938), S.C.R. 398, p. 402.*

[5] *G.-A. Beaudoin, "La loi 22: à propos du désaveu, du référé et de l'appel à l'exécutif fédéral", (1974) 5 R.G.D. 385. This protection still exists de jure, but has not been used for nearly a century. It is difficult to imagine the federal government's intervening in such a case.*

[6] *Professor Pierre Carignan has devoted a whole book to the question of religious rights: P. Carignan, "Les garanties confessionnelles à la lumière du Renvoi relatif aux écoles séparées de l'Ontario: Un cas de primauté d'un droit collectif sur le droit individuel à l'égalité", Montreal, Editions Thémis, 1992, P.268.*

with the Barrett judgment being one of the most significant[7]. The Catholic and Protestant communities then realised that these guarantees were relative, since they left Manitoba free, for example, to levy double taxes. It took some of the provinces many years to arrive at acceptable political compromises in this area.

The minorities also discovered, in 1917[8], that classroom languages were not protected by Section 93. This gap was not filled until 1982, when the Canadian Charter of Rights and Freedoms was adopted. In the meantime, it had done immense injustice to the French-speaking minorities outside Quebec, and had seriously shaken the Canadian federation.

Under Section 93, education is still exclusively a matter for the provinces. This article is subject to two constitutional guarantees: religious since 1867, and linguistic since 1982.

In its Greater Hull School Board judgment[9], the Supreme Court ruled that Sections 339, 346, 353, 362, 366, 375, 382, 495, 498, 499 and 500 of a Quebec local taxation act (Act No. 57) were invalid, since they failed to stipulate that grants must be distributed proportionally and since, if a referendum were held, the wishes of a school board might be outweighed by the wishes of voters other than those for whom the board was responsible[10].

[7]   *Ex parte Renaud (1872-73) 14 N.B.R. 273; City of Winnipeg v. Barrett (1892) A.C. 445; Brophy v. A.G.Manitoba (1895) A.C. 202; Roman Catholic Separate School Trustees for Tiny v. The King (1928) A.C. 363. The Court's attitude in this judgment was less legalistic than in the Barrett judgment. See a study by F.Chevrette, H. Marx and A.Tremblay, "Les problèmes constitutionnels posés par la restructuration scolaire de l'Ile de Montréal", Quebec, Editeur Officiel, 1971. See P.Carignan, "De la notion de droit collectif et de son application en matière scolaire au Québec", (1984) 18 R.J.T. 1-103.*

[8]   *Trustees of the Roman Catholic Separate Schools for Ottawa v. Mackell, (1917) A.C.62.*

[9]   *Greater Hull School Board and Lavigne v. P.G. du Quebec (1981) C.S.337; (1983) C.A. 370, (1984) 2 R.C.S. 575; 56 N.R. 93. On the question of the Catholic and Protestant communities' control over their schools, the decision of the Supreme Court of Canada in Caldwell v. Stuart (1984), 2 R.C.S. 603, is of interest.*

[10] *P.G.(Qué) v. Greater Hull School Board (1984), 2 R.C.S. 575, p.598.*

In this judgment, the Supreme Court in no way departed from the earlier Hirsch judgment[11], which remains of capital importance, since it clearly defined the scope of Section 93. In a sense, it served as the basis of the later judgment. In it, the Court had ruled that the right of Protestants and Roman Catholics to manage and control their own denominational schools had been legally recognised in 1867 and that, in the matter of finance, the law gave school governors and school boards the right to receive proportional subsidies and to levy taxes in their own municipal areas[12].

In their schools legislation, the provincial legislatures must respect the religious rights given Catholics and Protestants in 1867. The Hirsch judgment shows, however, that they may also establish a neutral sector - Jewish, Moslem or other.

Since 1982, denominational education has also been protected by Section 29 of the Canadian Charter of Rights and Freedoms. The religious guarantees of Section 93 of the Constitution Act of 1867 are still in force; the Charter makes no changes here.

When asked for a ruling on Ontario Act No. 30[13], which deals with the financing of Catholic secondary schools in Ontario, the Supreme Court concluded that it was valid under the introductory provision and sub-section 3 of Section 93 of the Constitution Act of 1867. Under the great political compromise concluded in 1867, the religious rights and privileges already granted at that time were to continue, and the legislatures might establish others as the necessity arose.

The protection provided by Section 93 (1) is not the same as that provided by Section 93 (3), since laws adopted under the second provision may be amended or repealed, while rights conferred under the first are inalienable. The Court ruled that the rights covered by Section 93 (1) were protected by the Charter, even without Section 29 of the latter. The rights covered by Section 93 (3) were protected by the Charter because of the absolute power of the provinces to enact these laws. In short, as the Court declared, the confederal compromise is to be

---

[11]   *Hirsch v. P.B.S.C.M. (1928) A.C. 200.*

[12]   *Supra, note 10.*

[13]   *"Re an Act to Amend the Education Act (Bill No. 30) (1987) 1 R.C.S. 1148.*

found in the whole of Section 93, and not in its constituent parts taken separately[14].

Judges Estey and Beetz took the view that provincial legislatures could legislate on educational matters with two restrictions: no law might violate the minimum constitutional guarantees set out in Section 93 (1), and the provinces' exercise of their powers could be limited by federal intervention under Section 93 (4).

In the Greater Montreal Protestant Schools Board case[15], the Supreme Court upheld two regulations issued by the Quebec Minister of Education, which introduced a common curriculum for all non-religious subjects in all Quebec schools.

According to the Court, Section 93 (1) of the Constitution Act of 1867 protects not only the religious aspects of denominational schools, but also the non-religious aspects which are needed to make the religious guarantees effective. The constitutional right of certain groups to denominational schools, financed by the state in a manner prescribed by law, must not be interpreted as an individual right or freedom guaranteed by Section 29 of the Charter, but rather as a right guaranteed by Section 93. The Court declared that the regulations in question did not have the effect of determining the content of moral or religious instruction in Protestant schools. The limited power to regulate the curriculum in denominational schools which school commissioners and governors had in 1867 is constitutionally guaranteed only insofar as it is needed to make the religious guarantees effective. The subsidiary argument that Section 93 (2) gave no constitutional force to rights and privileges conferred by the law existing in Ontario and Quebec in 1867 was rejected.

Chief Justice Dickson and Judge Wilson declared that, even if Section 93 (2) was intended to increase the constitutional protection of dissenting schools in Quebec in order to put them on an equal footing with the separate schools in Ontario, the Quebec legislature would still have authority to regulate the powers of the governors of dissenting schools concerning the curriculum, provided that such regulation was not prejudicial to the denominational character of those schools.

---

[14]   Ibid., p.1198.

[15]   Commission des écoles protestantes du Grand Montréal c. P.G. Québec (1989) 1 R.C.S. 377.

Finally, Judge Beetz, speaking for the majority, held that Section 93 of the Constitution Act of 1867 did not confer rights or freedoms of the kind provided for in the Canadian Charter but, rather, privileges and that it should, to this extent, be seen as an exception. He argued that, although it might have its roots in the concepts of tolerance and diversity, the exception stated in Section 93 did not constitute a general affirmation of freedom of religion or conscience. The constitutional right of certain groups of people in a province to have denominational schools, financed by the State in a manner prescribed by law, must not be interpreted as an individual right or freedom guaranteed by the Charter or, as Professor Peter Hogg had put it, as a small declaration of rights for the protection of religious minorities[16].

IV. LANGUAGE RIGHTS

A. In Schools

Section 23 of the Canadian Charter of Rights and Freedoms introduces a linguistic guarantee in the educational field. It applies to all ten provinces and provides that:

23. (1) Citizens of Canada

   (a) whose first language learned and still understood is that of the English or French linguistic minority population of the province in which they reside, or

   (b) who have received their primary school instruction in Canada in English or French and reside in a province where the language in which they received that instruction is the language of the English or French linguistic minority population ofthe province, have the right to have their children receive primary and secondary school instruction in that language in that province.

   (2) Citizens of Canada of whom any child has received or is receiving primary or secondary school instruction in English or French in Canada, have the right to have all their children receive primary and secondary school instruction in the same language.

---

[16]   *Ibid., p. 401 ;*

(3) The right of citizens of Canada under subsections (1) and (2) to have their children receive primary and secondary school instruction in the language of the English or French liguistic minority population of a province

(a) applies wherever in the province the number of children of citizens who have such a right is sufficient to warrant the provision to them out of public funds of minority language instruction; and

(b) includes, where the number of those children so warrants, the right to have them receive that instruction in minority language educational facilities provided out of public funds.

In the French Language Charter case of 1984[17], the Supreme Court unanimously decided that Sections 72 and 73 of the French Language Charter (Act No. 101), adopted by Quebec, were incompatible with Section 23 of the Canadian Charter and thus invalidated, to that extent, by Section 52 of the Constitution Act of 1982. The Court added that the restrictions imposed by Section 73 were not legitimate restrictions within the meaning of Section 1 of the Charter.

The Court said that Section 23 of the Charter had been regarded by the framers of the Act in 1981 as a perfect example of the kind of situation which required reform. Had Section 73 been adopted after the Charter's coming into force, the decision would have been the same.

Section 73 of the French Language Charter is clear, precise and specific. It derogates sharply from Section 23 of the Canadian Charter and has the effect of modifying it. This is its true effect. The restrictive clause in Section 1 of the Charter cannot amount to a derogation (as provided for by Section 33 of the Charter in certain sectors) or to an amendment of the Charter, the procedure for which is specified in Sections 38ff of the Constitution Act of 1982.
The Supreme Court noted that Section 23 of the Charter guaranteed certain rights to certain categories of person; these categories were clearly specified. No provincial legislature was entitled to redefine or alter them. It was bound by the Charter and could not disengage from it.

In the Supreme Court's view, Section 23 was so precise, the right guaranteed so specific and the categories so clearly defined that the restriction incorporated

---

[17]   O.A.P.S.B. c. P.G. Québec (1984) 2 R.C.S. 66.

in Section 73 could be regarded only as a straightforward derogation from it or a direct alteration of it. No real scope was left for Section 1 to come into play.

The Court pointed out that Section 23 was very concrete, and did not state general, abstract principles of the kind found in the other charters. Because of its specific character, it comprised a unique set of constitutional provisions, with no parallel outside Canada[18].

Section 23 is of historic importance for Canada; it remedies school systems considered deficient by the authors of the 1981 Constitution. The gap is filled by a single measure applying to all ten provinces.

The Supreme Court confirmed its decision on Act No. 101[19] in the Mahé judgment[20]. It repeated that Section 23 of the Charter was intended as a remedy and that this was the spirit in which it should be interpreted broadly and liberally[21].

The main, guiding principle which emerges from the Mahé judgment[22] is that the Supreme Court gives linguistic minorities speaking an official language the right to manage and control the language of instruction, the content of the curriculum and the minority schools. The extent of management and control may vary with the number of pupils actually enrolled. They will be absolute when "the number justifies it"; they will be relative, i.e. there will not necessarily be a homogeneous school board or a homogeneous school, when the number of pupils enrolled is too small.

Speaking for the Court, Chief Justice Dickson defined the minimum level of Section 23 of the Charter when he said that Section 23 required, at minimum, that instruction be provided in the minority language; if there were too few pupils to justify a programme that could be described as minority language instruction, Section 23 did not require that such a programme be established.[23]

---

[18]   Ibid. p. 79.

[19]   Mahé v. Alberta (P.G.) (1990) 1 R.C.S. 342.

[20]   O.A.P.S.B. v. Quebec (P.G.), supra, note 17.

[21]   Supra, note 19.

[22]   Ibid.

[23]   Ibid. p. 367.

He defined the upper level when he said that the phrase "minority language educatioinal facilities" established an upper level of management and control.[24]

Every case must necessarily be assessed separately, since the Supreme Court does not specify "justifying" figures. It does, however, mention two factors which are to be taken into consideration: (1) the services appropriate to the number of pupils should be determined, as should (2) the cost of the planned services. In this connection, it specified that the most important point was, perhaps, that setting up wholly separate schools boards was not necessarily the best way of realising the aim of Section 23. What was, however, essential to realising it was that the language group should have control over those aspects of education which concerned or affected its language and culture. To a great extent, this degree of control could be secured by guaranteeing the minority representation on a joint schools board and by giving its representatives exclusive control over all those aspects of the minority's education which concerned linguistic and cultural matters.[25]

Section 23 of the Charter thus constitutes a general right to instruction in the minority language, its purpose being, as the Supreme Court affirmed, to preserve and promote the language and culture of the minority throughout Canada.[26]

In the Mahé judgment[27], the Supreme Court also considered equality rights and religious rights. It found that neither Sections 15 and 27 of the Canadian Charter nor Section 93 of the Constitution Act of 1867 were incompatible with Section 23 of the Charter.

Undoubtedly, as Professor Pierre Foucher wrote in an article, the Mahé judgment is the "judgment of the decade in the field of language rights"[28]. Firmly rooted in the logic of Section 23, but uncertain until it was confirmed by the Supreme Court, recognition of the right of management and control represents - although the extent of its exercise may vary - a definite step forward for the French-speaking minorities. Moreover, the positive obligation of

---

[24]   Ibid. p. 370.

[25]   Ibid. p. 375-376.

[26]   Ibid. p. 371.

[27]   Ibid.

[28]   P. Foucher, "L'affaire Mahé: le jugement de la décennie en droits linguistiques", (1990) Forum constitutionnel 10, pp.10-11.

legislating, imposed by the Supreme Court on the provinces less sympathetic to language equality, is a source of hope for all the country's French speakers.

B. English and French at parliamentary, legislative and judicial level

Speaking for his colleagues in the Manitoba language rights case, Chief Justice Dickson said that the importance of language rights was founded upon the essential role played by language in the existence, development and dignity of every human being. It was is language which enabled us to formulate ideas, to structure and order the world around us. Language was the bridge between isolation and community which enabled human beings to define their rights and obligations towards each other and so live together in a comunity[29].

In 1867, language rights were enshrined in Section 133 of the Constitution Act. This section deals with legislative, parliamentary and judicial bilingualism in Quebec and in federal government[30]. French was not protected in any of the three other provinces which existed at that - surprisingly, not even in New Brunswick[31]. This was remedied in 1982.

French was, however, protected in Manitoba when it joined the Federation in 1870. Sir Georges-Etienne Cartier dreamed of making it a second Quebec. Section 23 of the Manitoba Act of 1870 essentially repeats for Manitoba the provisions contained in Section 133 for Quebec. However, Manitoba passed a law in 1890, removing this protection. Two lower courts declared the measure invalid, but Manitoba chose to ignore their judgments. It was not until 1979 that the Supreme Court of Canada had occasion to decree that Manitoba must comply with Section 23[32], since it had no right to strike out this constitutional guarantee unilaterally. In June 1985, the Supreme Court declared, in its judgment on language rights in Manitoba, that Section 23 was mandatory and that laws passed only in English were invalid; it added, however, that these laws would have temporary validity from the date of the judgment until the minimum period needed to translate, re-adopt, print and publish them had expired.

---

[29]   *Renvoi sur l'article 23 de la loi de 1870 sur le Manitoba (1985) 59 N.R. 321 (C.S.C.), p. 345.*

[30]   *See the judgments in Jones v. P.G.N.B. (1975) 2 R.C.S. 182 and P.G. (Qué.) v. Blaikie no.1 (1979) 2 R.C.S. 1016; P.G. (Qué.) v. Blaikie no.2 (1981) 1 R.C.S. 312.*

[31]   *See R. Patry, "La législation linguistique fédérale", Editeur officiel du Québec, 1981. The Acadians were, however, as the author emphasises, very numerous.*

[32]   *P.G. Manitoba v. Forest (1979) 2 R.C.S. 1032.*

In 1982, the Constitution underwent enormous changes in respect of language rights. Sections 16 to 22 of the Constitution Act of 1982 supplemented Section 133 of the Constitution Act of 1867. New Brunswick agreed to be bound by the sections of the Charter concerning official languages. This provides appreciable linguistic protection for the Acadians. Section 23 of the Manitoba Act remained intact.

Sections 16 to 20 go much further than Section 133, taking in a number of very important services as well, and establishing institutional bilingualism. It is to be hoped that other provinces will follow New Brunswick's example.

Section 16 lays down the principle of equality of the two official languages at federal government level. This gives the French-speaking minority in Canada a very high degree of constitutional protection.

Although both languages are official at federal level, the same is not the case at provincial level, where asymmetry prevails.

This question has been a focus of attention in Canada since the Laurendeau-Dunton Commission, the federal Act of 1969 on official languages, and Quebec Acts Nos. 63, 22 and 101.

Section 16 of the Canadian Charter of Rights and Freedoms provides:

16. (1) English and French are the official languages of Canada and have equality of status and equal rights and privileges as to their use in all institutions of the Parliament and government of Canada.

   (2) English and French are the official languages of New Brunswick and have equality of status and equal rights and privileges as to their use in all institutions of the legislature and government of New Brunswick.

   (3) Nothing in this Charter limits the authority of Parliament or a legislature to advance the equality of status or use of English and French.

In 1867, language minorities did not have the protection they enjoy today. What an enormous change there has been! Having made such a good start, however, we should not be content to leave things there: the struggle for protection of language rights at provincial level must continue.

In the Acadians' Society of New Brunswick case[33], the Supreme Court found that the principles of natural justice and Section 13 (1) of the Official Languages of New Brunswick Act entitled a litigant in a New Brunswick court to be heard by judges capable of conducting the proceedings and following the evidence regardless of the official language used by the parties. This right is not founded, however, on Section 19 (2) of the Constitutional Charter. The Court declared that the rights guaranteed by Section 19 were of the same kind as those protected by Section 133 of the Constitution Act of 1867 .

Judge Beetz remarked that these rights belonged to the speaker, drafter or author of the procedural documents produced in court, and gave the speaker or drafter the power, guaranteed in the Constitution, to speak or write in the official language of his choice. Furthermore, neither Section 133 of the Constitution Act of 1867, nor Section 19 of the Charter guaranteed, any more than did Section 17 of the Charter, that the speaker would be heard or understood in the language of his choice, or gave him the right to be.[34]

The judge in such cases must, however, take reasonable steps to understand the language used in the pleadings, in the interests of natural justice. It is up to him to decide honestly and as objectively as possible to what extent he can understand the language in which the proceedings are being conducted.

The Court offered no definition of "reasonable steps". Simultaneous interpretation might be one such measure. It has left the door open for clarification in a later case.

The Court makes an important distinction between classic funadamental rights and language rights. The latter are the product of political compromise while the former are derived from long-established principles. This is why the two kinds are interpreted and applied differently. According to the Supreme Court, courts should be slow to alter language guarantees which result from political compromise. Judge Beetz suggested that the courts should treat them more cautiously than than they would when interpreting legal guarantees.[35]

---

[33]   Société des Acadiens du Nouveau-Brunswick v. Association of Parents (1986) 1 R.C.S. 549.

[34]   Ibid. p. 574.

[35]   Ibid. p. 578.

In the Acadians' Society case, Chief Justice Brian Dickson asked, in his dissenting opinion, what use the right to express oneself in one's own language was if the people one was addressing could not understand it?[36]

Mrs. Justice Wilson shared this view.

In the Acadians' Society judgment[37], the Supreme Court took care to point out that legislatures also have a part to play in protecting language rights. The legislator must legislate in order to introduce bilingualism. The judiciary and the legislature both have parts to play.

V. FUNDAMENTAL RIGHTS

Since the end of the Second World War, there has been a strong movement in favour of incorporating charters of rights and freedoms in constitutions. The example originally set by America in 1789 has been followed by several countries since 1945. Canada has not escaped the trend. Indeed, having passed through various stages, and adopted legislative charters, it acquired a genuinely constitutional Charter[38] of individual rights in 1982. Having a strong judiciary, it has firmly followed the American line - and this is, for us, a very good thing.

In 1982, a Charter of Rights and Freedoms was incorporated in the Canadian Constitution. This Charter protects individual rights first and foremost. It safeguards the collective rights of the aboriginal peoples and of the Catholic and Protestant communities.

The classic fundamental rights, democratic rights, the right to freedom of movement, legal guarantees, the right to equality and language rights are all protected.

---

[36] Ibid. p. 566.

[37] S.A.N.B. v. Association of Parents, supra, note 33.

[38] Part I of the Constitution Act, 1982. Under section 52 of the Constitution Act of 1982, any law incompatible with the Charter is null and void.

A. Freedom of religion

Canada has no state religion, as Judge Taschereau pointed out in the Chaptut v. Romain judgment[39]. In the Big M. Drug Mart judgment[40], the Supreme Court declared, in passing, that to impose a state religion would contravene Section 2 of the Charter.

In the same judgment[41], the Supreme Court concluded that Section 91 (27) of the Constitution Act of 1867 gave Parliament power to legislate on Sunday observance, but that the Sunday Act violated the principle of freedom of religion laid down in Section 2 (a) of the Charter and that Section 1 of the Charter could not make such an act lawful. In passing, it spoke of the interaction between Sections 93 and 2, but added that it was not required, for the time being, to give a ruling on this point.

B. Sex equality

The Canadian Charter of Rights and Freedoms provides constitutional protection for equality of the sexes. Section 15 of the Charter prohibits discrimination based, inter alia, on sex, and Section 28 expressly provides:

Notwithstanding anything in this Charter, the rights and freedoms referred to in it are guaranteed equally to male and female persons.

Women outnumber men in Canada, but can actually be said to have constituted a minority group until now in more respects than one. They have not been equal, but have been a "minoritised" majority.

Happily, Sections 15 and 28 of the Canadian Charter of Rights and Freedoms of 1982 have now rectified this situation. In our opinion, because of its wording, which begins with a derogation clause, Section 28 operates independently of the other articles in the Charter. It is a substantive, and not simply procedural article. It was added after the compromise of November 1981, and has its own raison d'être. It prohibits all discrimination between men and women. It covers all the rights mentioned in the Charter, and not only those which are in force.

---

[39]   *Chaput v. Romain (1955) R.C.S. 834.*

[40]   *R. v. Big M. Drug Mart (1985) 1 R.C.S. 295.*

[41]   *Ibid.*

Section 15 provides, for its part, for social promotion programmes to make it possible, inter alia, for women to achieve equality in practice.

Section 28 applies to the whole Charter. I do not believe, for example, that any cultural group could use Section 27, which protects the multicultural heritage, to perpetuate a patriarchal or matriarchal system which violated the Charter.

C. Collective rights

The Constitution of 1867 includes a number of collective rights. Case law has stressed that the protection provided by Section 93 applies to Catholics and Protestants as groups, as "classes"[42]. The same case law has seen a "racial" category in Section 91 (24)[43]. Controversy continues, however, over Section 133. According to Chief Justice Laskin, Section 133 gives people a "constitutional right" to use either language[44]. Before he became a judge, Professor W.S.Tarnopolsky wrote that language rights seemed to lie in a kind of border zone[45]. Professor Pierre Carignan places them firmly in the category of collective rights[46].

Canadian lawyers have not so far concerned themselves greatly with the definition of collective rights.

In the Greater Hull School Board case, Judge Le Dain said that what the term "collective rights" suggested was that the interests of the entire class of people or community in respect of denominational education should be taken into account, and not the interests of the individual taxpayer.[47]

---

[42]   On this subject, see the Mackell judgment, supra, note 8.

[43]   See Judge John Beetz's reasons in P.G. Canada v. Canard (1976) 1 R.C.S. 170, p. 207.

[44]   See the Jones judgment, supra, note 30, p. 193.

[45]   W.S. Tarnopolsky, "Les droits à l'égalité", in G.-A. Beaudoin and W.S. Tarnopolsky (eds.), "Charte canadienne des droits et libertés", Montreal, Wilson et Lafleur (1982), p. 52.

[46]   P. Carignan, supra, note 7, pp. 70-71.

[47]   Supra, note 9, p. 599.

Professor Pierre Carignan has defined collective rights as follows:

> Writers on the law describe rights as collective either because they belong to communities or because of they must be exercised collectively.[48]

Judge W.S.Tarnopolsky has remarked that :

> The assertion of group rights [...] is based upon a claim of an individual or a group of individuals because of membership in an identifiable group.[49]

D. Multiculturalism

In 1982, also for the first time, the words "multicultural heritage" appeared in the Constitution. Section 27 of the Constitutional Charter provides that:

> This Charter shall be interpreted in a manner consistent with the preservation and enhancement of the multicultural heritage of Canadians.

It will be noted that the words chosen are "multicultural heritage and not "cultural rights".

It will be recalled that, following the work of the Laurendeau-Dunton Commission, Prime Minister Trudeau made a statement on multiculturalism in the House of Commons on 8 October 1971, in which he said that, although there were two official languages, there was no official culture, and no ethnic group had precedence. He added that multiculturalism in a bilingual context seemed to the government the best means of preserving Canadians' cultural freedom.

Several Supreme Court judgments have already dealt with Section 27, as have a considerable number of judgments by other courts.

The scope of this article is subject to discussion. The words "rights and freedoms" do not appear in it! Professor Hogg has suggested that this article may be pure rhetoric[50], but Professor (now Judge) Tarnopolsky believed that

---

[48]   *P. Carignan, supra, note 7, p. 44.*

[49]   *W.S. Tarnopolsky, "The effect of Section 27 on the Interpretation of the Charter" (1984), 4:3 Crown Counsel's Review 1 to 3.*

[50]   *P.W. Hogg, supra, note 3, p. 72.*

it had real substance[51]. Professor Magnet wrote that Section 27 "requires a little dynamism"[52].

The courts have occasionally based their judgments on this article, as the Supreme Court did in the Big M. Drug Mart judgment[53], when it ruled that the Sunday Act violated freedom of religion and was not compatible with maintenance and enhancement of Canadians' multicultural heritage, as provided for in Section 27.

The purpose of Section 27 is plainly to indicate that Canada, although a bilingual country at federal level and in some provinces, has nonetheless a multicultural heritage.

Professor Magnet concludes his study of Section 27 of the Charter as follows:

This article allows the Charter's discipline to be relaxed in cases where the full exercise of individual rights would threaten the survival of certain cultural communities. Thus Section 27 makes it possible to orientate development of the Charter to match the special demands of the dual nationality and cultural pluralism which are, perhaps, the most striking features of a cultural tradition which is genuinely unique.[54]

It can therefore be said that the Constitution Act 1982 changed the fate of the ethnic minorities.

Section 15, which concerns equality rights, prohibits various forms of discrimination, particularly those based on national or ethnic origin. This article can be taken in conjunction with Section 27.

---

[51] W.S. Tarnopolsky, "Les droits à l'égalité", in G.-A. Beaudoin and W.S. Tarnopolsky (eds.), "Charte canadienne des droits et libertés", supra, note 45, pp. 550ff.

[52] J.E. Magnet, "Multiculturalisme et droits collectifs: vers une interprétation de l'article 27", in G-.A. Beaudoin and E. Ratushny (eds.), "Charte canadienne des droits et libertés", 2nd edition, Montreal, Wilson-Lafleur, (1989), 1058 p., pp. 817-866, on page 819.

[53] R. v. Big M. Drug Mart Ltd., supra, note 40.

[54] J.E. Magnet, "Multiculturalisme et droits collectifs: vers une interpretation de l'article 27", supra, note 52, p. 866.

The possibility of combining Sections 2 and 27 of the Canadian Charter of Rights and Freedoms can be used to protect an ethnic minority's religion.

In the Edwards Books judgment[55], the Supreme Court ruled on the closing of shops on Sunday. It recognised the validity of an Ontario law, the Retail Business Holidays Act, which was intended to provide a uniform weekly day of rest. This act was passed in pursuance of the legislative powers given Ontario by Section 92 of the Constitution Act of 1867. The Court added that Section 2 of the Ontario Act struck a blow at the religious freedom of retailers whose day of rest was Saturday, but that this was justified by Section 1 of the Charter.

In the Edwards Books case, Chief Justice Dickson noted that freedom of religion had both individual and collective aspects[56]. He added that Section 27 of the Charter might be taken into account in interpreting freedom of religion.

This means that the provinces may legislate to introduce a uniform weekly day of rest without infringing the Charter. The Court referred to other countries where Sunday was also the day of rest: France and Japan, for example. The French Constitution states, however, that France is a secular country, while Japan is not a Christian country[57].

VI. THE RIGHTS OF THE ABORIGINAL PEOPLES

The aboriginal peoples had little protection in 1867. The 1867 Constitution gave the central Parliament full legislative authority over the "Indians and the land reserved for the Indians". Protection of the aboriginal peoples derived from the Royal Proclamation of 1763 and the treaties concluded with the British Crown. This protection was, however, extremely relative. In fact, although the provinces could not interfere with these treaties in their general legislation, the federal Parliament was allowed to go against them by Section 91 (24) of the Constitution Act of 1867[58]. Such was the opinion of the courts.

---

[55]   R. v. Edwards Books et al (1986) 2 R.C.S. 713.

[56]   Ibid. 781.

[57]   The Court did not rule on the inequality between small shops with seven or fewer employees and other shops, because Section 15 was not yet in force when the case began.

[58]   "In Re Indians" (1939) S.C.R. 104.

Parliament defined the term "Indians" in the Indian Act[59]. In 1939, the Supreme Court ruled that the Eskimos were covered by Section 91 (24).

The Constitution Act of 1982 uses the word "métis" for the first time in the Canadian Constitution.

Although the rights of the aboriginal peoples are far better protected than they were in 1867, they have still to be satisfactorily defined. The whole country has now realised this. The aboriginal peoples - the first majority to become a minority in this country - have a constitutional means of having their rights defined and protected in Sections 35 and 35 (1) of the Constitution Act of 1982.

The first constitutional amendments introduced in Canada after up-dating of the Constitution in 1982 were made in June 1984 and concerned the aboriginal peoples' rights[60].

Section 25 of the Charter states that the Charter does not detract from the rights and freedoms of the aboriginal peoples of Canada. The aboriginal peoples enjoy special status.

In the Sparrow judgment[61], the Supreme Court developed the the Constitution Act of 1982. The Sparrow judgment is highly important: it is to Section 35 of the Constitution Act of 1982 what the Oakes judgment is to Section 1 of the Charter.

Chief Justice Dickson and Judge La Forest drafted the judgment with the unanimous (6-0) approval of the Court, and laid down the framework for interpretation of Section 35 (1).

The Court took the view that the exercise of a right provided for in Section 35 (1) of the Constitution Act of 1982 might be restricted.

In its justification test, the Court ruled out two principles - the concept of "public interest" and the presumption of validity. Concerning these two principles, it said that the justification founded upon "public interest" was so vague that it offered no useful guideline, and so general that it could not be used

[59]   Indian Act, L.R.C. 1985, c.1-6.

[60]   Particularly on inequality between men and women among the aboriginal peoples.

[61]   (1990) 1 R.C.S. 1075.

as a criterion to determine whether a restriction imposed on certain constitutional rights was justified.[62]

It added that, although the "presumption" of validity was now obsolete, given that the ancestral rights in question had constitutional status, it was clear that the importance of the aims of conservation had long been recognised in legislation and government action.[63]

Finally, when subsistence fishing and conservation measures were the issue, absolute priority should be given to the aboriginal peoples' right to fish. In this connection, the Supreme Court explained that the constitutional right stated in Section 35 (1) required Her Majesty to ensure that her regulations respected this priority, but that this requirement was not intended to undermine Parliament's authority and responsibility to introduce and administer general conservation and management plans for salmon fishing. The aim was, rather, to make certain that these plans treated the aboriginal peoples in a way which ensured that their rights were taken seriously[64].

Under a constitutional amendment in force since 1984, sex equality applies to the aboriginal peoples[65].

A Royal Commission, chaired by Judge René Dussault and Dr. George Erasmus, has been set up to study and report on the situation of the aboriginal peoples. One of the issues it is considering is self-government for them.

VII.   THE AMENDMENT PROCEDURE

Education and culture (other cultural matters) are protected under the constitutional amendment procedure, and specifically by Sections 38 and 40 of the Constitution Act of 1982. If seven provinces, comprising 50% of the population, were to decide to transfer this sector to the central Parliament, the constitution would be amended accordingly. A dissenting province might still

---

[62]   Ibid., p. 1113

[63]   Ibid., p. 1114.

[64]   Ibid., p. 1119.

[65]   Proclamation of 1983 amending the Constitution of Canada, 21 June 1984, Gazette du Canada, Part II, 11 July 1984, volume 118, p. 2984.

choose, however, to keep its jurisdiction in this area, and would then be entitled to "just compensation" from the federal authorities. This provision is of vital importance for Quebec, the only place where French-speakers are in the majority. Although they are in a minority nationally, it allows them to oppose the centralisation of education, insofar as it concerns them in Quebec, and to keep their legislative competence without suffering considerable economic loss.

Section 40 is worded as follows:

Where an amendment is made under subsection 38 (1) that transfers provincial legislative powers relating to education or other cultural matters from provincial legislatures to Parliament, Canada shall provide reasonable compensation to any province to which the amendment does not apply.

CONCLUSION

Minorities were already constitutionally protected in 1867. The Constitution Act of 1982 developed and expanded this protection, particularly for the aboriginal peoples. We must pursue this process.

What of the derogation clause provided for in Section 33 of the Canadian Charter of Rights and Freedoms? Democratic rights, freedom of movement, language rights, religious rights the rights of the aboriginal peoples and, in my view, sex equality lie outside the scope of this clause. Otherwise, however, Section 33 applies and can be used to waive application of Sections 2, 7 and 15 of the 1982 Charter. We are against using this clause. In our opinion, the restrictive clause included in Section 1 of the Charter is sufficient.

The Canadian Charter of 1982 is not concerned with social and economic rights. However, these rights are covered by the provincial charters which all the provinces have and which have semi-constitutional status.

Our Charter is partly based on the U.S. Bill of Rights and this, the last great "Enlightenment" text, was clearly founded on the notion of individual rights. This is the case of most rights and freedoms in Canada.

We must, I think, be cautious in dealing with collective rights. They exist in some states for certain purposes. In Canada, such rights are incorporated in Sections 91 (24) and 93 of the Constitution Act of 1867. They seem to be justified.

Constitutional charters are designed primarily to protect the citizen against the growing power of the state. This was certainly Thomas Jefferson's intention[66], and many American judges, from William C. Douglas on, have agreed[67].

Charters also exist to protect minorities against parliamentary majorities. Majorities are fickle and, if left to their own devices, can very easily interfere with the rights of minorities. This is why minorities must be protected.
Canada is composed of several peoples. The words "aboriginal peoples" appeared in the Constitution for the first time in 1982.

In 200 judgments given on the Charter since 1984, the Supreme Court has revealed its true character. Once again, its drafters were obliged to use such expressions as "where the number...so warrants", "reasonable limits", "minority language educational facilities", to take only three examples of terms which remain ill-defined.

The Court will also have to decide whether or not the Charter protects certain implied rights. This was the case in the United States. It may also be the case in Canada - particularly since, in the Press in Alberta judgment of 1938[68], the Supreme Court had already begun to speak of rights implied by the Constitution.

The Canadian Supreme Court, which is strong and independent, and which crowns the Canadian judicial system, has sought, in interpreting the Constitution, to improve the protection of minorities, particularly in respect of language and of rights and freedoms generally. It has given the rights of the aboriginal peoples its attention. The remarkable work which it has done in a few short years commands admiration.

---

[66] *The author of the Declaration of Independence and third President of the United States declared: "Nothing then is unchangeable but the inherent and unalienable rights of man". S.K. Padover, "Thomas Jefferson on Democracy", New York, The New American Library (1939), p. 68.*

[67] *W.O. Douglas, "Go East Young Man. The Early Years. The Court Years 1939-1975", "The Autobiography of William O. Dougalas", New York, Random House (1980). Judge W.O. Douglas's dictum, "Keep the government off the backs of the people", is well-known.*

[68] *"In Re Alberta Statutes" (1938) R.C.S. 100, p. 134.*

Canada has made two attempts to improve its constitutional system since 1982 - in the Meech Lake Accord, which lapsed on 23 June 1990 because it had not been ratified by all the provinces, and the Charlottetown Accord of 8 August 1992, which was accepted by our political leaders, but rejected by the Canadian people in the referendum held on 26 October 1992. Had they succeeded, these two initiatives would have improved the constitutional protection of minorities.

Germany

PROTECTION OF MINORITIES
IN FEDERAL AND REGIONAL STATES

by

Professor Helmut STEINBERGER
Professor at the University of Heidelberg (Germany)
Director, Max-Planck Institute
for Foreign Public International Law

The structure and organisation of Germany as a federation of individual states does not rely on ethnic, religious or linguistic differences of its constituent states, but on the historical diversity of regions as well as on the territorial division of the allied post-war zones of occupation.

The federal rules protecting minorities are very few. Efforts to include a clause on minority protection in the Basic Law have been made within the Commission on Amending the Basic Law, composed of members of the Bundestag and of the Bundesrat, but have not as yet been approved by the legislature. Proposed articles for the Federal Basic Law for the protection of minorities as outlined by the constituent states of Sachsen, Brandenburg and Niedersachsen use the terms "national and ethnic" (Sachsen), "ethnic, cultural, religious or linguistic" (Brandenburg) and "cultural minorities" (Niedersachsen).

Federal law happens to use the term "minority" or equivalent terms, e.g. s. 6 of the Federal Electoral Law provides for an obligatory exception from the 5 % blocking clause to parliament in favour of "national minorities".

Protocol N° 14 to art. 35 of the German-German Unification Treaty of 1990 refers to "Sorbish nationality ... culture ... tradition ... people". The Unification Treaty itself uses the term "Sorbes" and "Sorbish population" in Appendix I, which is a constituent part of the treaty. The Basic Law does not contain any reference to an official language. However, Appendix I to the Unification Treaty provides for the right to use the Sorbish minority language in public affairs and therefore constitutes an exception to s. 184 of the Federal Constitution of Courts Act, in favour of the Sorbish minority. This exception, which relates to the use of language in court only, resulted from the process of unification, and has taken into account that the "Sorbish privilege", set by art. 40 of the former east-German constitution, should be continued. The treaty is part of federal law.

At the federal level, since 1965 the Danish minority has had the benefit of a special participatory body attached to the Ministry of the Interior.
Art. 25 of the constitution of Brandenburg provides for the right of the Sorbish people to use their language in public affairs. This gives effect to the above protocol referring to art. 35 of the Unification Treaty.

The term "minority" or equivalent terms are more often used in state law, e.g. in constitutions of some constituent states where minorities reside, as in art. 5 of the new constitution of Schleswig-Holstein of 1990 (using the terms "minorities and ethnic groups"), in art. 25 of the constitution of Brandenburg of

1992 (using the term "Sorbish people" to describe an ethnic minority) and in art. 6 of the constitution of Sachsen of 1992, using the term "national minorities".

Further examples are found, in common legislation, s. 3 of the Electoral Law of Schleswig-Holstein ("minority"), s. 58 and 60 of the Schools Act of Schleswig-Holstein ("minority") as well as in draft laws in matters of public concern such as elections, schooling, media and culture.

In the above mentioned texts, neither the federal or state constitutions nor the statutes define the term "minority" or the equivalent terms used. But the texts imply both German citizenship (expressly stipulated in the proposed article of Sachsen for the Basic Law in view of the protection of minorities) and a lasting presence on the national territory, because the texts were outlined in consideration of the minorities already existing on the German territory, i.e. the Danish, Frisian and Sorbish minorities.

The only exception in this connection is the article proposed by Brandenburg as an amendment to the Basic Law, because this proposal is aimed at the protection of aliens settling on German territory.

The principle of affirmative action whereby minority interests are promoted by public authorities is not expressly provided for in the Basic Law, but is recognised by the proposed articles for the Basic Law and by the constitutions of Schleswig-Holstein (art. 5), Brandenburg (art. 25) and Sachsen (art. 6). These provisions tend to improve the legal status of minorities and prescribe an explicit public obligation to promote them in the fields of language, religion and cultural identity and tradition.

Except for a limited federal power concerning framework legislation on tertiary education (art. 75 (1a) of the Basic Law), legislative and executive powers over the schools lies with the constituent states pursuant to arts. 70 and 30 of the Basic Law. These have been implemented by various state laws, including laws licencing schools.

The constitutions of those states where minorities reside guarantee both protection and promotion of their minorities. Education is regarded as a component factor of the linguistic and cultural life of minorities (art. 5 of the constitution of Schleswig-Holstein, art. 6 of the constitution of Sachsen). Art. 25 of the constitution of Brandenburg refers expressly to an active promotion of private and public schools, which are to be promoted with regard to the minority language and culture.

Schooling laws specify the recognition of independent schools which teach in minority languages and provide for public allowances especially for them (ss. 58 and 60 of the Schools Act of Schleswig-Holstein, s. 2 of the Schools Act of Sachsen and the draft Schools Act of Brandenburg). In the Eastern states of Germany, three years after reunification, most of the relevant laws have been drafted or are the subject of legislative procedures.

The above mentioned constitutions and existing and draft Schools Acts provide both for the study of and for the education in the languages of the Danish, Sorbish or Frisian minorities, not only in private schools, but also in public schools in the areas of settlement of the minorities (eg, s. 2 of the Schools Act of Sachsen).

State constitutions refer to an active promotion of minorities by affirmative action in cultural matters, an obligation which is to be implemented by public authorities in the administrative process. For example, art. 25 of the constitution of Brandenburg prescribes bilingual topographical information in the settlement area of the Sorbish minority.

Like s. 6 of the Federal Electoral Law, s. 3 of the Electoral Law of Schleswig-Holstein and s. 7 (6) of the Electoral Law of Sachsen provide obligatory exceptions from the 5 % blocking clauses to parliament in favour of minorities. It only facilitates eligibility, without guaranteeing a minimum membership in the respective legislative body.

Art. 26 of the constitution of Brandenburg provides for an active participation of the Sorbish minority in the legislative process, as far as they are concerned.

Consultative and participatory bodies in favour of minorities are part of the governments of those constituent states concerned; in Schleswig-Holstein at state level there exists a consultative body in favour of the Frisian minority as well as a state agent for minority affairs; a body for participation even in legislative affairs is outlined in art. 26 of the constitution of Brandenburg.

Italy

FEDERALISM AND PROTECTION OF MINORITIES

Regional aspects in Italy

by

Professor Sergio BARTOLE,
Professor at the University of Trieste (Italy)

Italy is not a federal State. It can be defined as a regional State : the powers of the central government are counterbalanced by the powers assigned to the regions (and to the local government). However, one cannot say that the Italian Republic is an association of regions, because the regions did not take part in the establishment of the Italian State. Instead they were created by the State at a later stage of its history through a devolution of functions to newly established regional authorities. Like the other institutions of the local government (Comuni and Province), the regions are autonomous (not sovereign) bodies which have legislative and administrative functions. These functions are different from the sovereign powers of the State because they were developed on the basis of a decision of the central authorities of the State.

Since the regional powers are committed and not proper to the regions, these cannot be deprived of them without a revision of the Constitution. Therefore we can say that the autonomy of these bodies is founded on and guaranteed by the Constitution. Nevertheless the constitutional rules outline only the chief elements of the regional organisation and functions, leaving to the State Parliament some discretion as to their implementation. This is a further difference between Regions and member States of a federation, as the central State and the regions do not have equal constitutional position and guarantees.

The regions have a representative government. As a matter of fact their legislative assemblies consist of elected counsellors. A region is a self-governing institution because the people living in the territory under its rule can participate in the government of their own affairs through the election of the regional representative body as far as those affairs fall within the competence of the region itself.

When the Constitutional Assembly decided the creation of the regions in 1947, the regional reform was not directly aimed at the protection of linguistic minorities. Linguistic minorities are not a main problem of the Italian Society. They are established only in some border regions of Italy : a German speaking group in the province of Bolzano; a French speaking group in the Valley of Aosta; a Slovenian speaking group in the eastern part of Friuli-Venezia Giulia (especially in the provinces of Trieste and Gorizia) and the Ladinian speaking group living in the provinces of Bolzano and Trento. Notwithstanding the limited dimension of the phenomena, the Constitutional Assembly immediately realized that the regional institutions could be helpful in dealing with the problem of the protection of minorities. Besides, the implementation of the De Gasperi-Gruber Agreement required Italy to follow this way, and internal political obligations bound Italian authorities to a similar arrangement in Valle d'Aosta. The presence of the German speaking group and of the French speaking group in the territories of Trentino-Alto Adige and Valle d'Aosta suggested giving these two regions a special constitutional status, and taking into account the protection of linguistic minorities within the organization of these regions. As a matter of fact the provisions concerning both these regions were adopted by constitutional statutes in 1948 (the statute concerning Trentino-Alto Adige was modified in 1971) and the space left to national Parliament discretion for their implementation is much more limited than it is when other regions are at stake.

Both the above-mentioned constitutional statutes provide for the use of the languages of the minorities, for the preservation and development of their cultural identities, for the protection of their traditional social and economic distinctive features. In Trentino-Alto Adige some of these provisions interest the Ladinian speaking group as well, but the main stage of the protection of this minority is set up at a sub-regional level. Also the protection of the Slovenian minority is implemented at a sub-regional level, especially at a municipal level. Therefore we can say that the general principles of the Italian legal system do not carry out the protection of the linguistic minorities through the regional institutions only, but imply the resort to all the institutions of the local government for that purpose according to the dimension of the concerned minority. The Slovenian speaking group is a very limited minority in relation to the dimension of the population of the Friuli-Venezia Giulia region. This region has a special constitutional status as well, but this status was adopted because of the economic and social problems of a border region and the presence of the Slovenian minority was not really determinant for that decision. In the constitutional statute concerning Friuli-Venezia Guilia we do not find provisions which are similar to those concerning the German and French minorities contained in the Trentino-Alto Adige and the Valle d'Aosta statutes.

In conclusion, it can be said that in the Italian legal system there is a link between the protection of the minorities and the institutions of the local and regional self-government. But only the statutes concerning Trentino-Alto Adige and Valle d'Aosta take care of the protection of the minorities directly, while in other situations the implementation of the protection of the minorities is shifted to a sub-regional level.

The purpose of the general regional reform was the conversion of the centralised Italian State into a State with large regional autonomies, but we believe to be pertinent to the matter in hand only an analysis of certain legal provisions relating to the regions, that is to say of those concerning the above-mentioned two special regions. Therefore, the next pages will deal with Trentino-Alto Adige and Valle d'Aosta, and some final remarks will be made as to the local self-government in Friuli-Venezia Giulia with regard to the situation of the Slovenian minority.

The Trentino-Alto Adige region is divided into two provinces, which are given a special constitutional status and a peculiar autonomy that is very similar to the autonomy of the regions. The splitting up into two separate bodies is aimed at insuring the German speaking minority (which mainly lives in the territory of the province of Bolzano) a territorial self-government, and, therefore, at implementing its protection within Trentino-Alto Adige, that is in a regional frame as required by the De Gasperi-Gruber Agreement.

Both the Trentino-Alto Adige region and the province of Bolzano have legislative powers (namely a primary function, a concurrent function and a supplementary function) and administrative powers. No Italian region has judicial powers. The distinction between the three legislative functions is based on the different limits bounding the regional autonomy in the exercise of each of those functions. The peculiar limits of the primary functions are the general principles of the Italian system of law, the international obligations of the Italian State, the guidelines of the economic and social reforms and the national interests (with the enclosed interests in the protection of linguistic minorities). With regard to the concurrent function, there exists not only the above-mentioned limits but the limit of the principles laid down by special national statutes as well, and the supplementary function is bounded by the limit of each of the national statutes for the implementation of which it has to provide. The legislative and the administrative functions must be exerted exclusively with regard to the regional or provincial territory and to the fields (or matters) assigned to the region and to the province by their constitutional statutes. As to these fields, we can say they concern the organisation of the local institutions in the case of the region, and the local economic, social and cultural activities and the local environment and territorial planning in the case of the province.

The Province has a concurrent legislative function in the field of public education. There are schools for the Italian speaking and German speaking students where the teaching language is their own language respectively. The administrative staff of these schools is under the direction of the province while the teaching staff has a state employee status. Both the province and the State concur in the appointment of the heads of the administrative and teaching staff.

The most important governing bodies of the province are the provincial legislative council, the executive board and the President. The legislative council is elected by the people who have been resident in the province for four continuous years. The provincial counsellors are members of the legislative council of the Trentino-Alto Adige region together with the counsellors of the legislative council of the Trento Province. In the executive board and in the presidency of the legislative council, the presence of representatives of both linguistic groups is required : special provisions ensure their rotation in the main offices of both the bodies. Similar rules have to be applied in the minor local self-government authorities.

In the Trentino-Alto Adige region German is given the same constitutional status as Italian. In the province of Bolzano, the German speaking people can use their language in the relations with the public authorities. The offices of the State Administration in the Bolzano province must have German and Italian speaking employees according to the size of the respective linguistic groups which is ascertained on the basis of personal statements in the last census.

The powers of the Trentino-Alto Adige Region and of the Bolzano Province, and the minority rights of their inhabitants can be enforced by the constitutional court.

The provisions concerning the representation of linguistic groups in the bodies of the Bolzano province and of the local minor self-government, the staff of the State authorities and the teaching in the nursery and primary schools are also applied with regard to the Ladinian language in the territories where the Ladinian group is settled.

Valle d'Aosta as well is a region with special autonomy. The provisions concerning its functions and organization were adopted by a constitutional statute.

The region has legislative (primary and supplementary) functions in many fields of local relevance : their list is in some way similar (but more restricted) to the list of the matters assigned to the competence of Trentino-Alto Adige. In the statute there are no rules concerning the distribution and the rotation of the offices between Italian and French speaking groups. However, French bears in this region the same constitutional status as Italian. The State employees have to be born in Valle d'Aosta or to know French. In the schools of the region the same time is devoted to the teaching of French as to the teaching of Italian, and French is also used as a teaching language.

In Italy, the statutes concerning the election of the two chambers of Parliament do not have special provisions on the representation of the recognised linguistic minorities which however may and do have representatives within Parliament. Nevertheless, special rules allow the political parties of the linguistic minorities settled in Valle d'Aosta, the Province of Bolzano and in Friuli-Venezia Giulia to arrange electoral alliances with other political parties in such a way that in any case one (or more) of them can be represented in the European Parliament.

The local branches of the state-owned radio and television company provide daily programs for the German and French minorities.

The principles of the Italian system of law imply, therefore, an implementation of the constitutional protection of linguistic minorities which may vary with regard to the different situations of linguistic minorities, according to the peculiarities of the areas where they live. Moreover the link between the regional and local self-governments and the protection of minorities is not always similar.

On the above-mentioned basis, the protection of the Slovenian minority in Friuli-Venezia Giulia can be analyzed. In the provinces of Trieste and Gorizia, where this minority is settled, there are schools for the Slovenian speaking children and the Slovenian language is taught and used as teaching language. In the little "comuni" of both provinces where the Slovenian group reaches a important percentage of the population, the Slovenian language can be used in the relations with the public authorities directly and in the meetings of the self-government bodies. Otherwise, and in the judicial procedures, a system of translation by interpreters is provided. The Fruili-Venezia Giulia region and the local self-government authorities are given powers to implement the policy of the protection of the minority, especially through financial aids to the preservation and development of its ethnic and cultural identity. The Slovenian names of the localities are recognised and place name signs in the minority language are installed. The local branches of the state-owned radio and television company have special daily programs for the Slovenian minority.

Spain

**MINORITIES AND
THE STATE OF REGIONAL AUTONOMY
IN SPAIN**

by

**Mr Luis AGUIAR DE LUQUE
Director of the Constitutional
Research Centre, Madrid, (Spain)**

CONTENTS

0. **Presentation of the problem**

1. **General aspects of "the State of regional autonomy"**

2. **Axiological principles of "the State of regional autonomy"**

2.1 The constitutional right to autonomy

2.2 The equality principle

    a)   in terms of individuals
    b)   in terms of the Autonomous Communities

2.3 The solidarity principle

3. **The components of "the State of regional autonomy"**

3.1 Statutes of Autonomy

    a)   Legal status
    b)   Drafting Statutes of Autonomy
    c)   Content of Statutes of Autonomy

3.2 The competences of Autonomous Communities

3.3 Institutional organisation of Autonomous Communities

3.4 Linguistic pluralism

4. **Participation of Autonomous Community authorities in State decision-making**

5. **The Autonomous Community constitutional model in practice**

0. Presentation of the problem

One of the major challenges facing the drafters of the Spanish Constitution in 1978 (and consequently one of the most critical problems in the transition to democracy) was no doubt the matter of the State's territorial organisation.

This problem, which mainly originated last century in the failure to achieve political, legal and economic unity in multicultural Spain, was greatly exacerbated, especially in Catalonia and the Basque Country, by the centralistic rigidity and intransigence of the Franco era. Consequently, in late the 70s, restoring the democratic system was seen as going hand-in-hand with solving this problem. The fact that immediately after the first democratic elections (June 1977) the Government of Adolfo Suárez gave priority to restoring the regional autonomous institutions, even before the process of formulating a constitution was properly under way, shows the urgency of the problem and the link between autonomy and democracy.

The first outcome of this process of reorganising the country launched by the 1978 authors of the Constitution was described as the "Estado de las Autonomias" (literally the "State of Autonomies" or "the system of Autonomous Communities"), a model of political organisation broadly based on two premises. The first premise is that Spain is a unitarian cultural, historical and social entity ("the Spanish Nation, the common and indivisible homeland of all Spaniards"), given concrete form by the Spanish State, a legal and national organisation which is unitary in both domestic and international terms. Concurrently, the autonomy of certain entities is recognised as a principle for structuring the State termed the "right to autonomy", a right which the nationalities and regions enjoy to set up structures of self-government (Article 2). Needless to say this right is meaningful only within the limits expressly defined in the Constitution itself. For example, the first Additional Provision of the Constitution stipulates that the general updating of the "Fuero" system "shall be carried out ... within the framework of the Constitution", an expression which the Constitutional Court interpreted in judgments 123/84 of 18 December 1984 and 76/88 of 26 April 1988, pointing out that the "Fuero" system "is not the result of an agreement between territorial authorities which preserve rights predating and outweighing the Constitution, but rather it is a rule which is issued by the constituent authority and has general force within the scope of the Constitution and extends also to prior circumstances in history."

However, it would be a mistake to consider the "Estado de las Autonomias", as a model for the territorial distribution of competence which was completed and perfected at the same time as the Constitution. In fact the material delimitation of regional autonomy established in the Constitution is relatively narrow, being confined to setting out procedures for acceding to autonomy and leaving extensive scope for manoeuvre around the governing principle. This is why Professor Cruz Villalón, in a statement very frequently quoted by Spanish experts, affirmed that the Spanish Constitution launched a process of deconstitutionalising the form of the State[1], and also why Professor Rubio Llorente has said that Title VIII of the Constitution (concerning the territorial organisation of the State) is the product of history, and not a system.

The purpose of this **memorandum** is to briefly analyse the most significant aspects of this complex (and largely dynamic) phenomenon which we have defined as "Spanish system of Autonomous Communities", in so far as it may be a constitutional model for the study of cultural minorities. However, this paper will not go into the following subjects: defining the concept of "minority", its possible applications to the Spanish reality, the applicability of the concept to historic nationalities, the status of minorities in Spanish law and the internal contradictions of such status, since the historical demand for the principle of equality before the law contradicts "the right to be different", the basic nucleus of the affirmation of what are known as the rights of minorities.

In any case we should stress that the Spanish Constitution contains an exhaustive declaration of the fundamental rights and public freedoms (Articles 10 to 52), as well as the principle of equality before the law stated in general terms in Article 14 of the Constitution, that the combination of the two aforementioned ideas give the individual a status based on the "dignity of the person", proclaimed by Article 10.1 as the "foundation of the political order and social peace" and that we can consequently consider that the rights of minorities are sufficiently protected by the Spanish constitutional system despite the absence of a specific concrete provision on the subject in the Constitution itself[2].

---

[1] Cruz Villalón, P., "La estructura del Estado, o la curiosidad del jurista persa", Rev. de la Facultad de Derecho de la Universidad Complutense, no. 4, 1981.

[2] In view of the very broad nature of the declaration of rights, the lack of a specific mention of minorities in the Constitution is offset by a certain implicit recognition of the right to be different. Nevertheless, this lacuna has made it difficult for minority groups to assert the rights which they enjoy and to secure implementation of the procedures to safeguard them. The Constitutional Court has repeatedly

1. General aspects of "the State of regional autonomy"

The Spanish system of Autonomous Communities, the result of a hard-won agreement acceptable both by Catalan and Basque nationalists[3] and upholders of the unitarian conception of the State, is not, as one might think, a closed model arising out of a pre-agreed conception delimited according to plan. Article 2 of the Constitution, which sets forth the premises forming the basis of the model (see above) and Title VIII, which further develops them, are rather an "ad hoc" response drawn from a wide variety of sources (the 1931 Spanish Constitution, the Italian regional model, the specific dynamics of political life during the constitution drafting process with a number of "pre-autonomies" already in operation, etc) caused by hesitation on the part of the authors[4]. This is borne out by the wide varieties of texts used throughout the drafting process, which initially began with uniform, general territorial decentralisation (preliminary draft Constitution of January 1978) and ended, as far as possibilities for self-government are concerned, with a system of differentiated autonomy which ultimately benefited Catalonia, the Basque Country and Galicia.

As we have mentioned, the end result was an intermediate formula between the Federal State, formally with a greater degree of autonomy for the federated entities, which have a homogeneous and constitutionally guaranteed basic position) and the centralised State, with at most a mere administrative

---

corrected this deficiency through what legal theories have defined as the constitutional protection of collective or diffuse rights. More specifically, judgment 214/1991 of 11 November 1991 accepted the standing of a person of Jewish stock to defend her honour which had been attacked in her capacity as a member of the Jewish social group: "In her dual capacity as a citizen and a member of a community, in this case the Jewish community, which suffered a full-scale genocide at the hands of national socialism and ... we must inevitably conclude that the interest mentioned in the appeal should be considered legitimate for the purposes of redressing the right to honour of our country's Jewish community, of which the appellant is a member".

[3] *The abstention from the constitutional referendum advocated by the PNV (Basque Nationalist Party) was an expression of the party leadership's resignation vis-à-vis a formula which they could not reject but which they also could not formally accept (J. Pradera, "La liebre y la tortuga", Claves de razón práctica, no. 38, 1993).*

[4] *J. Pérez Royo has written on this subject "there were enormous political fluctuations concerning Title VIII and consequently the formation of the right to autonomy and the Senate, so that points of contact between the first draft and the final text of the Constitution hardly coincided at all". 'La reforma imposible", Claves de razón práctica, no. 20, 1992.*

decentralisation. The aim of the Spanish system of Autonomous Communities is to solve the problems both of the traditional demands for political autonomy from regions with a more obviously autonomous destiny (particularly Catalonia and the Basque Country) and of achieving functional decentralisation to encourage better relations between government and governed and greater efficiency in State action, thus making the whole new institutional system more democratic.

In order to achieve such objectives and take account of the two dimensions to which they give rise, the Constitution lays down a series of elements and rules which should be properly defined from the outset.

- The right to autonomy is generally applicable throughout the country and is implemented by means of a process of setting up Autonomous Communities (ACs), based on substantial participation by the populations concerned; in other words any region of the country can potentially declare itself to be an AC or else join one of the existing Communities.

- Two procedures have been provided for setting up ACs. The first is general in nature and basically takes account of the will of the entities that make up the traditional local system (municipalities and provinces). The other is theoretically more complex: it requires formal evidence of a more deep-seated autonomous destiny and the holding of a referendum for the population involved. This latter procedure was considerably simplified for Catalonia, Galicia and the Basque Country.

- At the same time two levels of autonomy are established, in that ACs which achieve autonomy through the latter of the two procedures (in practice these are Catalonia, the Basque Country, Galicia and Andalusia) can exercise legislative and executive powers in important fields and thus accede to high levels of autonomy satisfying (or at least attempting to satisfy) the more conspicuously nationalistic sectors of Catalonia and the Basque Country; the other level, the so-called general or common system, apparently did not allow the Autonomous Communities to exercise legislative powers for an initial 5-year transition period (the Constitution's ambiguity on this point prompted Professor Tomás Ramón Fernández to say, in a rather hasty, premature interpretation, that this second type of AC could on no account exercise legislative powers; subsequent practice has not confined this

- 399 -

interpretation[5]), and the areas in which powers could be exercised were qualitatively and quantitatively inferior; nevertheless, once the 5-year period has elapsed these latter communities can increase their powers to levels similar to those enjoyed by the others.

This treatment, which in theory is standard and uniform but in practice comprises two different systems and is geared to solving two very different types of problem (J. Pradera speaks of the "political" problem of the Basque Country and Catalonia and the "administrative" problem of the need to decentralise[6]), is not without certain practical difficulties, and not only because of certain ambiguities in Title VIII of the Constitution. Above and beyond its openness, the territorial organisation established by the 1978 Constitution is susceptible of two different interpretations, one being more federalistic in that it advocates a uniform level of competences for all ACs (especially now that the 5-year transition period has elapsed), and the other more asymmetrical in that it recommends transferring the *de facto* differences in the desired levels of autonomy in the various nationalities and regions into the system for determining the Autonomous Communities' levels of autonomy and competences. Moreover, we must take account of the difficulties of rationalising administrative activities in a two-tier structure. However, subject to the further explanations set out below, it would be unfair to deny that the authors of the Constitution created an operational framework capable of addressing the problem of Spanish minorities in the context of the political situation obtaining in the late 70s.

2. Axiological principles of "the State of regional autonomy"

2.1 The constitutional right to autonomy

The word "autonomy" recurs several times in the Spanish Constitution with reference to situations presupposing the possibility of exercising certain specific powers of self-regulation, which obviously all widely differ in scope. For instance, just as the right of the nationalities to autonomy is enshrined in the aforementioned Article 2, Article 27.10 recognises the autonomy of the universities, Article 72.1 starts by declaring that the Parliamentary Chambers shall establish their own rules of procedure and then goes on to grant them

---

[5]   Tomás Ramón Fernández Rodríguez, "La organización territorial del Estado" in *Lecturas sobre la Constitución española*, Vol. I, Madrid, 1978 (1st edition).

[6]   J.Pradera, op. cit.

autonomy to approve their own budget, and Article 140 secures the autonomy of the municipalities. Countless further examples are to be found in ordinary legislation (including Article 6 of the Organic Law on the *Defensor del Pueblo* (Ombudsman), Article 2 of the Organic Statute on the State Counsel's Office, etc). We must base our analysis of the extent of autonomy in the nationalities and regions on the common idea underlying all these expressions, which basically boils down to the concept of autonomy with self-regulatory powers[7], but which also necessitates criteria differentiating the autonomy of the territorial entities set out in Article 2 from all the other aforementioned types of autonomy. This difference no doubt derives from the importance of the fields in which the autonomy faculty is implemented, but even more so from the nature of the powers which can be exercised in this way and which, in the case of ACs, include powers relating to the citizen's legal situation and powers of innovation, in short the production of legally binding norms.

The autonomy enshrined in Article 2 for the benefit of the nationalities and regions is consequently a right granted to certain well-defined communities ("bordering provinces with common historical, cultural and economic characteristics, island territories and provinces with a historical regional status", Article 143.1), which might be incorporated into the category of institutional safeguards which C. Schmitt used to define certain principles set out in the Weimar Constitution[8], but, if we go further, the right to autonomy is a structural principle of the State as a whole, or in the words of Sánchez Agesta "a general organisational principle"[9] which adjusts the nature of the State established in 1978. The Constitutional Court itself acknowledged when it stated that "ACs ... enjoy qualitatively greater autonomy than the administrative autonomy granted to local entities, as they also have legislative and governmental powers which give a political character to their autonomy" (judgment 25/1981 of 14 July 1981).

However, we should also point out that this right to political autonomy enshrined in the Constitution and the self-government which arise out of its

---

[7]   *García de Enterria, E., y Fernandández, T. R., Curso de Derecho Administrativo, Vol. I, Madrid, 1980, pp. 250 et seq.*

[8]   *Schmitt, C., Teoría de la Constitución, Madrid, pp. 197. The application of the concept of institutional safeguards to our subject is studied by Parejo Alfonso, L., Garantía institucional y autonomías locales, Madrid 1981, pp. 115.*

[9]   *Sánchez Agesta, L., Comentarios a las Leyes Políticas (directed by O. Alzaga), Vol. I, Madrid, 1983, p.122.*

implementation can in no case be approximated to the right of disposal which the State possesses *per se*. "Autonomy is not sovereignty", in the words of the Constitutional Court in judgment 4/1981 of 2 February 1981, given that it is a power bestowed by the Constitution and therefore not an inherent one, in other words restricted to a field of competence limited by the Constitution and which actually, from the legal point of view, has an impassable limit, the unity of the State considered as a principle structuring the new State through the oft-quoted Article 2: "The Constitution is based on the indissoluble unity of the Spanish nation".

2.2 The equality principle

Equality is a fundamental principle of the legal order which is set forth several times in the Spanish Constitution with various adaptations of content: for example, in Article 1 it is set out in a general manner as one of the higher values of the legal order, Article 9.2 presents it as one of the criterion on which the public authorities should base their action, in Article 14 equality is mentioned from the angle of equality before the law, and lastly it also appears as a criteria determining the substance of several rules relating to the fundamental rights (Arts. 23, 31 and 32, i.a.). However, its extrapolation to the field of autonomy, where it is shown in two different lights, namely as regards individuals and in respect of relations between ACs, does pose considerable problems. Let us consider these two dimensions separately.

a) At individual level, Article 139.1 states that "all Spaniards have the same rights and obligations in any part of the territory of the State", which, according to one approach, might be interpreted as a mere extension to the field of autonomy of the principle of equality before the law set out in Article 14. However, the Constitutional Court was quick to grasp that the said Article 139.1 involved much deeper complications than those deriving from the other Article in question which appears under Title I and which is indubitably one of the most complex articles from the angle of constitutional interpretation. The problems stemming from the proclamation of the principle of equality as a right[10] are here compounded by the problems arising out of the legislative pluralism of regional autonomy as practised in Spain, so that an excessively rigid interpretation of Article

---

[10] *The principle of equality before the law is not unanimously considered as a subjective fundamental right, and case law has varied. In any case its inclusion in Art. 14 means that it is protected by the amparo appeal, which means that it is indisputably protected by a legal remedy.*

139.1 would in practice render the legislative powers of the ACs meaningless; after all, as the Constitutional Court stated in its judgment 37/1981 of 16 November 1981, "it is obvious that this principle can in no case be interpreted as conveying a strict, monolithic uniformity in the legal order, to the effect that the same rights and obligations must be recognised under the same circumstances in any part of the national territory". Nevertheless, Professor I. de Otto later remarked[11] that the problem subsisted, albeit in mitigated form, despite the aforementioned judgment, because the rejection of "monolithic uniformity" does not block the way to a "certain" uniformity, which would in any case reduce the scope of the ACs' competences; according to Professor de Otto, the optimum interpretation would probably be that the declaration of equality set out in Article 139 does not prevent the various legal systems of the Autonomous Communities from regulating matters in different ways and establishing a legal position for Spaniards which varies in accordance with the territorial area but prohibits differentiated treatment within each of the regional legal systems. This does not mean that the individual aspect of the equality principle is meaningless in the autonomy framework, with the emergence of legal positions which vary radically according to the AC in question, a hypothesis which the Constitutional Court has explicitly ruled out (judgment 37/1987 of 26 March 1987). However but the safeguard against such an eventuality is set forth in Article 149.1.1 which reserves exclusive jurisdiction for the State in the "regulation of the basic conditions guaranteeing the equality of all Spaniards in the exercise of their rights and in the fulfilment of their constitutional duties", not in the aforementioned Article 139.1.

b) Secondly, even though it is not included in the text of the Constitution, a second strand of the equality principle which directly concerns ACs is implicit in the Constitution, and derives from both the general principles (particularly the recognition of the right to autonomy in Article 2) and Article 138.2 ("The differences between the Statutes of the various Autonomous Communities may in no case imply economic or social privileges"). The problem stems from the existence of two different means of acceding to autonomy, which presupposes the creation of two types of ACs with very different levels of jurisdiction, and it is also very much in line with the direction implicitly taken by the Constitution. Nevertheless it

---

[11]   De Otto, I., "Los derechos fundamentales y la potestad normativa de las CCAA en la jurisprudencia del Tribunal Constitucional", *Revista Vasca de Administración Pública*, No. 10, Vol. II, 1984.

is true that in the text of the Constitution as finally approved, and as highlighted by the Committee of Experts[12] in 1981, this distinction was based solely on political caution and attempted to tackle Spanish regional heterogeneity by providing facilities for transitional stages, though these would in no case be given sufficient legal force to depart from the aforementioned equality principle. As the Committee of Experts pointed out in its report, "we must insist that the Constitution does not impose two categories of ACs; the only stipulation it actually makes, and with considerable prudence, is a transition period aimed at giving most of the territories the specific powers of the single model". The constitutional practice in the ensuing years (1982/1993), which will be analysed later, has confirmed that this interpretation of the constitutional model for the territorial organisation of power prevailed, and currently, with the formulation of the Organic Law on Transfers which standardises the upper limits on competences (L.O. 9/1992 of 23 September 1992) and the subsequent transfer process, the transitional period of inequality is over (at least in theory).

2.3 The solidarity principle

Although the Constitution proclaims equality (see previous paragraph), it is obvious that there are also *de facto* situations characterised by profound economic and social inequalities between the different nationalities and regions. This being the case, the right to autonomy is accompanied by a duty to show mutual solidarity, which is described in Article 2 of the Spanish Constitution as one of the elements defining the Spanish State and further developed in Article 138, which entrusts the State with the defence of the material implementation of this principle.

If solidarity is to be effective, very specific instruments must be implemented requiring the State to construct the bases for its existence. These instruments include the "interterritorial clearing fund" (Article 158.2 of the Spanish Constitution), which is a specific part of the State budget earmarked for investment expenditure, and such capital is distributed in accordance with the criteria established by the law regulating it (Law no. 29/1990 of 26 December 1990).

---

[12] *This refers to the committee of university professors under the chairmanship of Professor García de Enterría, mandated by the Government of L. Calvo-Sotelo in April 1981 to prepare a report to guide and rationalise the second phase of the autonomy process.*

3. The components of "the State of regional autonomy"

3.1 Statutes of Autonomy

a) Legal nature

According to Article 147.1 of the Spanish Constitution, Statutes of Autonomy are the basic institutional rules governing the ACs and are a vital factor in their creation and organisation, in that when a regional entity adopts such Statutes it automatically accedes to AC status. As legal theorists have affirmed, although the Statutes can in no case be considered as the Constitution of a federate state on the grounds of its origin (since the concept of autonomy as hitherto set forth is very different from that of sovereignty), nevertheless from the functional angle there are great similarities, because it is the Autonomous Community's supreme norm, from both the logical and the prescriptive angle, which determines, inter alia, the body and procedure through which the Community's legislative power is exercised, the subjects covered by its activities and the extent of the Autonomous Community's other powers[13].

From the very outset a multitude of political and doctrinal positions have attempted to define the legal character or the nature of Statutes of Autonomy. These statements can be broken down into two basic positions. Some consider that the Statute of Autonomy is a norm which is part of the State's legal order since Article 147.1 stipulates that "the State shall recognise them and protect them as an integral part of its legal order", with, moreover, the force of an organic law (Article 81: "Organic laws are those ... approved by the Statutes of Autonomy"); others consider Statutes of Autonomy as norms with a unique, contracted character which expresses not the legislative will of the State but an agreement reached between the central legislative power and the populations involved, in a sort of "constitutional contract", to the extent that the draft is prepared by a specific Assembly representing the affected provinces (Article 146), or, if necessary, the text is ratified by referendum (Article 151) and its reform "shall be in accordance with the procedure established in them" (Article 147.3). Experts are nowadays unanimous that Statutes of Autonomy are State norms with all the consequent legal effects, though this does not prevent them having a very special position since firstly, for the aforementioned reasons, they have a special passive force vis-à-vis other State laws and a certain

---

[13] See Pérez Royo, J., _Las fuentes del derecho_, Madrid, 1984, pp. 135 and 136.

hierarchical superiority over the laws of the Autonomous Communities of which they are the foundations, and secondly they have a delimited physical framework which strengthens their special force and explains the relationships between the different Statutes of Autonomy, which are by no means peaceful.

b) Drafting Statutes of Autonomy

As already mentioned, the Spanish Constitution lays down widely differing procedures for drafting Statutes of Autonomy which give rise to clearly differing levels of autonomy. Nevertheless, the common factor in all these procedures is the prior initiative phase, a simple expression of the desire for autonomy unbound by any statutory text, which can also take on a variety of forms depending on the level of autonomy aspired to and which consists (today it is fair to say "consisted", now that the map of Autonomous Communities is completed) in the primary decision to establish the constitution of the Autonomous Community. There are three basic procedures for the said initiative: an initiative under-taken under ordinary procedure by the Provincial Deputations and two thirds of the municipalities involved; an initiative undertaken by the *Cortes* by means of an Organic Law which can replace the aforementioned expression of desire for autonomy for reasons of national interest; and lastly, an initiative taken under the so-called special procedure by the aforementioned local bodies, though with greater majorities (three quarters of the municipalities) and ratification by referendum (the Basque Country, Catalonia and Galicia being exempted from the latter requirement under the Constitution), resulting in higher levels of autonomy.

When the initiative phase is completed, the procedure for drafting the Statute *stricto sensu* varies between the first two possibilities and the third one. The latter method, used by the aforementioned regions (Basque Country, Catalonia and Galicia), and later also followed by Andalusia on completion of an extremely complicated process, requires the Congress's Parliamentary Commission on Constitutional Affairs to monitor the progress of the draft (prepared by an Assembly made up of regional parliamentarians and representatives of the local authorities), ratification by regional referendum and ratification by the *Cortes*. The ordinary procedure followed by the Asturias, Cantabria, La Rioja, Murcia, Valencia, Aragon, Castilla-La Mancha, the Canary Islands, Navarra (with some distinctive features), Estremadura, the Balearic Islands, Madrid and Castilla-Léon more simply requires parliamentary follow-up to the draft prepared by the same methods as in the previous procedure, whereafter it is merely approved as an Organic Law.

c) Content of Statutes of Autonomy

Statutes of Autonomy usually begin with general considerations of either a programmatic or structural nature (territorial framework of the Community, use of languages if appropriate, anthem and other symbols of identity, etc) and go on to dead with regulations on the main institutions of the Autonomous Communities and their mutual relations, the powers taken on by the Community, which are defined by subject and also the type of public action (legislative or executive); these themes (institutions and powers) make up the core of the Statute. Frequently, the Statute also specifies the Autonomous Community's financial foundations, and concludes with a description of the procedure for amending the Statute.

Moreover, this model content coincides with all the subjects which Article 147.2 of the Constitution reserves for the Statute of Autonomy: "name of the Community", "the delimitation of its territory", "the name, organisation and seat of its own autonomous institutions" and "the competences assumed within the framework of the Constitution". Nevertheless, some disputes have had to be settled by the Constitutional Court, which has found that the content of Article 147.2 refers solely to a "reserva estatutaria relativa" (a field which is in principle governed solely by the Statute of Autonomy), which may very well be complemented by the State laws provided for in Article 150 in connection with powers (Article 147.2.d) and also by regional laws, where the organisation and seat of the specific institutions are concerned (Article 147.2.c). The hypotheses set out in sub-paragraphs a) and b) of the same Article regarding the name of the Community and its territorial delimitation are somewhat different because, as concrete concepts, they must be considered as subjects which have to be regulated exclusively by the Statute (judgment 89/1984 of 29 September 1984).

3.2 The competences of Autonomous Communities

The formula used in the Spanish legal system for apportioning competences does not tally with the traditional criteria of most systems which have opted for the federal or regional version of political decentralisation: these are based on a single list of competences attributed to either the State or the regional entities, leaving all remaining competences to the other authority (this is the so-called "residual clause"). On the contrary, the starting point in the Spanish Constitution is a heterogeneous, not a systematic, criterion which has left a great deal of scope for complementary legislation. The Constitution grants a great deal of freedom to the Statutes of Autonomy, within the limits of the Constitution, to acquire the powers which are deemed necessary to achieve the desired degree of autonomy. This shows that the Statute of Autonomy is the prime law-making corpus when it comes to determining the competences of a given Autonomous Community. Nevertheless, the distribution of competences can exceptionally be modified by the central authorities through extraordinary mechanisms such as those set out in Article 150 of the Spanish Constitution (organic laws on delegation or transfer of competences).

Formally, the Constitution devotes two articles to this question: Article 148, which enumerates the matters falling under the jurisdiction of all Autonomous Communities, and Article 149, which enumerates the competences of the State, areas in which the Communities have no jurisdiction. In addition to these two lists, the central authority adopts principles of prevalence or supremacy of central power (in cases of conflict of concurring competence, State law prevails), of the complementarity of State laws, and also the residual clause, whereby competence in respect of matters not attributed to the ACs by their respective statutes fall to the State (Article 149.3).

However, closer inspection of the Constitution enables us to qualify this initial outline. Firstly, we must point out that Article 148 only takes in the form of a guideline which in no case obliges the Communities to remain within the strict framework of their competences. Secondly, the Constitution assigned two very practical and different functions to Article 149.1: firstly, Article 149.1 establishes the matters which fall under the exclusive jurisdiction of the State, and consequently the State is not authorised to transfer them to the autonomous bodies (apart from selective use of the provisions of Article 150 of the Spanish Constitution); but secondly, Article 149.1 provides possible new frameworks of competence for ACs with a higher level of autonomy or special autonomy in matters not reserved to the State, by means of a number of rather vague formulae which have on several occasions had to be interpreted by the Constitutional Court. In this connection we must bear in mind that the State has exclusive competence in some matters, in terms of both legislation and enforcement (international relations, defence, nationality, immigration, emigration, aliens and the Administration of Justice), that in other cases it only has legislative powers (including the power to issue standard-setting regulations, cf. Constitutional Court judgment 35/82), which empowers ACs to take responsibility for enforcing and organising services, and lastly that in yet other cases the State has only the competence to lay down principles - basic legislation[14] - while the ACs are empowered to legislate and further develop and implement these basic principles - constituting autonomous legislation.

3.3 The institutional organisation of the Autonomous Communities

The question of institutional organisation is one which, together with that of competences, has revealed the largest number of lacunae and ambiguities in Title VIII, as the Spanish Constitution refers solely to the organisation of the privileged ACs, stating that it shall be based "on a Legislative Assembly elected by universal suffrage in accordance with a system of proportional representation which assures, moreover, the representation of the various areas of the territory; a Government Council with executive and administrative functions and a President elected by the Assembly from among its members and appointed by the King..." (Article 152.1 of the Spanish Constitution). The other ACs found no explicit organisational schema in the Constitution, which initially had very far-reaching effects since it seemed to imply that legislative assemblies were exclusively reserved for ACs which were from the outset authorised to attain the maximum level of autonomy allowed by the Spanish Constitution. However, it very quickly became obvious that it was inconceivable to refuse the so-called "second-rank" Autonomous Communities the right to form a Parliament because autonomy is based precisely on political decentralisation, in other words the right of an entity to pass its own laws. This fact was confirmed by the report of the Committee of Experts on Autonomy, the autonomy agreements and the Constitutional Court. It is therefore not surprising that when the institutional model laid down in Article 143 of the Constitution was implemented throughout the country, the result was that the corresponding Statutes were approved according to the procedure laid down in Article 144. This maximalist tendency enabled all ACs to closely mimic the State by adopting an institutional micro-model similar to the national institutions, a model of micro-parliamentarianism

---

[14]   *The Constitutional Court case law has considerably changed where the formal characteristics "bases" of the State are concerned. The position maintained in the first few years via two very influential judgments (Nos. 32/81 and 1/82) was inconsistent with a purely formalistic approach to the basic laws, as it held that the bases of the State were to be found in legislation in the strict sense of the word, and even implementing regulations, which gave rise to some uncertainty of the law vis-à-vis the apportionment of powers. Subsequently, judgment 69/88 in particular partly modified this doctrine by stressing the formal status of all post-constitutional basic norms and, even more importantly, requiring that the formal basic law explicitly set out the extent of all or some of these norms, or at least enable such status to be inferred without much difficulty (Judgments 80/88, 182/88,248/88 and 13/89, i.a.).*

with conventional institutional powers (Parliament elected by universal suffrage, Government answerable to the Assembly, etc), complemented with the special features of the Spanish parliamentary system (constructive motion of censure - i.e motions of censure must be accompanied by proposals for alternatives).

Consequently, all the Autonomous Communities today have a single-chamber representative parliamentary institution which is elected by direct universal suffrage on the basis of a proportional system, has the specific rights of a parliament apart from parliamentary immunity, and is responsible for the legislative function. This Assembly, as the regional expression of democratic legitimacy, elects the President of the Autonomous Community, who is the supreme representative of the Community and directs the Government Council, an organ which exercises the executive and administrative functions within the Community; this means that the Government Council, headed by the President, is politically answerable to the Assembly; the particular right of dissolution appertains only to 4 executives (in Catalonia, the Basque Country, Galicia and Andalusia)[15]. The Judiciary, on the other hand, is considered as appertaining to the central government despite the different territorial constituencies.

3.4 Linguistic pluralism

One of the most important aspects of Spain's cultural wealth is linguistic variety, the result of the coexistence of Spanish and the various regional languages, a subject which is also relevant to any discussion of the rights of minorities. Article 3 of the Spanish Constitution further develops a principle set forth in the Preamble ("The Spanish Nation proclaims its will to ... protect all Spaniards and peoples of Spain in the exercise of human rights, their cultures and traditions, languages and institutions") and addresses this question by declaring that Spanish is the official language; this implies the right to use it and the duty to know it, and also the official status of "all the other languages of Spain ... in the respective autonomous communities, in accordance with their Statutes". Lastly, the third sub-paragraph of this provision emphasises the cultural asset of linguistic variety and consequently the implicit requirement on public authorities to respect and protect it.

This is not the only article of the Constitution which proclaims the linguistic variety of Spanish society: the matter is also dealt with in Article 20.3 governing

---

[15] *The reason for this particularity is the guarantee on the 4-year parliamentary mandate so that a common date can be respected for the elections in the Autonomous Communities.*

- 410 -

the State-run mass media and Article 148.1.17 on the competences of the Autonomous Communities. In any case, it would be worth commenting on the first of these articles, which in fact lays down the general, basic regulations on linguistic pluralism in the Constitution.

Firstly, the official status of the Spanish language, beyond the general right to use it, particularly as a means of communication between the citizen and the public authorities, also implies the equally general duty to know it, which establishes it as the common means of communication between all Spaniards, established throughout Spanish society. On the other hand the "other languages of Spain" have an official status subordinate to the declarations made thereupon by the various Statutes of Autonomy and limited to the territories identified by the territorial scope of the corresponding Autonomous Community. In any case, a declaration of "joint official status" implies that every citizen is entitled to express himself in either of the Autonomous Community's official languages (Spanish or regional language) in his contacts with public authorities having powers limited to the Autonomous Community in question.

Several Statutes of Autonomy have availed themselves of Article 3 of the Constitution to proclaim the joint official status of more than one language in their respective Autonomous Communities (principally Catalonia, Basque Country, Galicia, Valencia and the Balearic Islands), and a number of legally binding regulations issued by both the State and the Basque, Catalan, Valencian or Balearic Autonomous Communities have developed specific mechanisms to give substance to the defence and promotion of the cultural asset of linguistic pluralism.

From the perspective of the State, the main regulations on this issue have been directed towards arbitrating on the means of linguistic communication between the citizen and the public authorities, which in principle corresponds to the idea of the official status of Spanish and the "co-officiality" of regional languages. In this context we might particularly stress Section 36 of Law No. 30/92 on the Legal System governing Public Departments, in connection with relations between the citizen and Government departments[16], Section 231 of Organic

---

[16]   *"The language of procedures undertaken by the Central Government shall be Spanish. Notwithstanding this affirmation, persons applying to the departments of the Central Government established within the territory of an Autonomous Community may also use the official regional language. In such cases the procedure shall be implemented in the language chosen by the person concerned ...".*

Law 6/85 on the Judiciary[17] and Section 540 of the Law on Criminal Procedure in connection with relations between the citizen and the judicial system.

Legal rules issued under Autonomous Community legislation may expand the communication function of such Communities languages by using the implicit argument that their use must be protected and promoted on account of the social predominance of Spanish within the ACs, a hegemony and domination which are in fact often more rhetorical than real. The euphemistic "Law on Linguistic Normalisation" laid down regulations on the subject in Catalonia, the Basque Country and Galicia. At one stage, appeals were lodged against these regulations with the Supreme Court, which subsequently declared them consistent with the Constitution.

In the light of these principles it is fair to say that sound legal guidelines have been laid down for the language problem in Spain, though in practice this does not prevent occasional conflicts. In fact this is not at all surprising in view of the multiple ramifications and impacts of the language theme, from the regulations on the right to education and the role reserved for indigenous language teaching in the curricula, through to the conditions stipulated for competitive examinations for civil service posts, including knowledge of the indigenous regional language: all these regulations show the degree of sensitivity of language issues. Nonetheless, case law is beginning to create extensive doctrine and the constitutional principles are becoming sufficiently specific, which allows us to conclude that the degree of protection afforded to linguistic minorities is satisfactory.

4. Participation of Autonomous Community authorities in State decision-making

The territorial division of the State into ACs must necessarily be integrated into the organisation of the State, for reasons not only of efficient administration but

---

[17]   "In all legal proceedings judges, law officers and other officials of the Courts shall use Spanish, the official State language ... They may alternatively use the AC's specific official language, unless one of the parties has an objection on the basis that he/she does not know this language, in cases where this might interfere with the right to a fair trial. The litigant parties, their "procuradores" ("protectors") and their "abogados" ("attorneys"), as well as any witnesses and experts, may use the official language within the territory of the AC where the proceedings are taking place ...".

also of the desirability of reinforcing the legitimacy of the central structures and offsetting the centrifugal tendencies peculiar to decentralised structures.

The Constitution defines the Senate as "the chamber of territorial representation" (Article 69), an institution formally conceived as an instrument facilitating consultation and the participation of the ACs in the State structure. Nevertheless, the two-chamber structure of the Spanish Parliament is perhaps the aspect of the Constitution which, from the technical angle, has prompted the greatest criticism, most of which has centred on the vagueness of the official definition of the second chamber as quoted above.

The Senate has a twofold composition: on the one hand 200 senators are elected by direct universal suffrage by means of elections held in the provincial constituencies (commonly known as provincial senators), and, on the other the ACs (or the Legislative Assemblies of the ACs, to be more exact) each appoint a "basic" senator and an additional senator per million inhabitants of their respective territories, which in practice means some fifty senators, usually referred to as "senators of the Autonomous Communities". The numerical difference alone shows the inadequacy of this form of Autonomous Community participation in the central institutions.

A second constitutional instrument aimed at enabling the Autonomous Community authorities to participate in central decision-making is the ACs' right to initiate legislation and constitutional reform in the central Parliament.

Nevertheless, it is within the Government and the day-to-day administration that the requirements on proper organisation have necessitated closer co-operation and participation by Autonomous Community authorities in the Central Government's decision-making process. Section 4.1 of Law No. 12/1983 on the Autonomy Process set up the "Sectoral conferences of councillors from the ACs and the Minister(s) concerned, with a view to exchanging opinions and jointly considering the problems facing each sector and the action envisaged to tackle and solve them". Following this example, a great many joint bodies have been set up in the last ten years, by means of legislation and also under bilateral agreements facilitating the participation of Autonomous Community governments in State decision-making.

5. The Autonomous Community constitutional model in practice

As stated above, the definitive form of the Spanish Constitution stipulates that the territorial organisation of power can have "differentiated systems of autonomy, which in the final analysis enhanced the possibilities of autonomy in Catalonia, the Basque Country and Galicia". However, realities have forced us to interpret this stipulation very differently.

Once, or even before, the Constitution was adopted (prejudging to a large extent the final text[18]), the Statutes of the Basque Country and Catalonia were drawn up. Far more laborious negotiations impeded progress in the drafting of the Galician Statute of Autonomy, which was adopted and promulgated in December 1980. The three aforementioned ACs have attained levels of autonomy comparable to those of Federate States within a Federal State.

However, the other areas of the country were expeditious in their drive to become ACs, with an eye to a physically more limited set of competences but nevertheless a genuine legislative power and a specific institutional organisation, ie an autonomous Parliament elected by direct universal suffrage. On the other hand, some of these regions are also beginning a long, complex process of achieving levels of autonomy similar to those of the Basque Country, Catalonia and Galicia. The strength of the political parties involved and their negotiations between them have enabled some of these regions (Valencia and the Canaries) to halt the process in exchange for certain concessions. This has not been the case in Andalusia, which, after a hurry of events which we need not go into in this memorandum, acceded to levels of autonomy similar to those of the three initial ACs. Cracks are appearing in the model. The initial objective, which was never explicitly declared but was nevertheless implicit in the intentions of the drafters, to give a large measure of autonomy to Catalonia, the Basque Country and, by analogy, to Galicia, while establishing basically administrative decentralisation for the rest, has been replaced by a territorial organisation of power which is different, but only transitionally, as virtually all the ACs set up by virtue of Article 143 of the Constitution have signalled their wish to increase their powers after the five-year period laid down in Article 148.2. Adolfo Suárez, the then Prime Minister, gave a clear account of the situation in his speech during a political debate in the Congress of Deputies, starting on 20 May

---

18 *I say "prejudging the final text" because in both the Basque Country and Catalonia the draft Statutes were prepared in parallel to the drafting of the Constitution, so that as soon as the latter was published on 27 December 1978, both the said Statutes were submitted to the Bureau of Congress, on 29 December.*

- 414 -

1980 (it is important to note that three months had elapsed, since the Andalusian referendum on autonomy, the veritable turning point in the Spanish autonomy system, according to Pérez Royo[19]): "from this angle it would seem difficult to deny that the distinction, which has been completely exaggerated for emotional reasons, between the two channels for exercising a single initiative for acceding to autonomy, has lost virtually all its initial meaning" (my underlining). The Committee of Experts meeting from April 1981 onwards used strict technical considerations to defend the new interpretation of the Constitution: "it is vital to stress that the Constitution does not in fact provide for two different types of Autonomous Community; the only stipulation which it very cautiously makes is the transitional period" (Report of the Committee of Experts on Autonomy, 1981). The "State of the Autonomies" established by the Constitution is thus replaced by a model for the territorial organisation of power which is very close to that of the Federal State (considered solely from a practical point of view as safeguarding general political autonomy for all nationalities and regions tending towards medium-term standardisation of spheres of competence).

Nevertheless, we cannot overlook the fact that this legal equality in powers, which might be the final stage in the federalisation of the State, very obviously has an element of political distortion, the undeniable, overriding aspiration towards national identity in Catalonia and the Basque Country, which takes concrete form in the so-called "hecho diferencial"[20], a *de facto* hypothesis which is inherently difficult to express in legal terms and transform into specific powers, apart from those deriving from the linguistic specificities of both Communities, a circumstance which can also be extended to Galicia, the third of the four ACs based on Article 153 of the Spanish Constitution.

In short, it would be fair to say that the "State of the Autonomies" is currently facing two problems relating to constitutional development: how to provide a practical vision of the increase in the competences of the Autonomous Communities conceived in the light of Article 143 of the Constitution, an increase which is dealt with by Organic Law No. 9/1992 and is currently envisaged by the various Statutes of Autonomy, and secondly, the search for

---

[19] *Pérez Royo, J., "La reforma imposible", op. cit.*

[20] *The expression "hecho diferencial" ("differential fact"), which is frequently used in political discussions in moderate nationalist circles, particularly in Catalonia, refers to the distinctive features of Catalonia and the Basque Country to justify differential treatment by the central State departments. These features and their consequences have never been given any practical substance.*

formulae for fleshing out and organising the aforementioned concept of "hecho diferencial".

Efforts to solve the former problem, that of the increase in the powers of ACs based on Article 143, are proceeding satisfactorily: Hugs would appear to be settling, not quite effortlessly, into a rather convoluted constitutional procedure which might nonetheless eventually prove effective: cf. the Autonomy Agreements signed by the Socialist Party and the People's Party, the subsequent drafting of an Organic Law on transfers, the current reform of the various Statutes of Autonomy and, lastly, the current negotiations in the Technical Committees on Transfers concerning the transfer of a multitude of services, the results of which will be enshrine in the corresponding Decrees on transfers.

Although it could make its presence felt in legislation or in other types of political activity, the second problem lacks a specific constitutional basis and goes beyond the subject of this **memorandum**.

Switzerland

FEDERALISM AND PROTECTION OF MINORITIES IN SWITZERLAND

by

Professor Giorgio MALINVERNI
Professor at the Law Faculty,
University of Geneva (Switzerland)

CONTENTS

a. Principles
b. Scope of cantonal powers

3. Inter-cantonal agreements

B. Application of the law

III. FEDERALISM AND ACHIEVEMENTS OF AUTONOMY

IV. FEDERALISM, MINORITIES AND BASIC RIGHTS

A. Protection of linguistic minorities

1. The territoriality principle
2. Official languages

B. Political rights

CONCLUSION

FOREWORD

Switzerland is widely known as a composite state where several minorities have long co-existed. Moreover, each Swiss citizen can safely be said to belong in one way or another to a majority and to a minority as well. To give but one example, a French-speaking Protestant resident of Valais belongs to a denominational group forming a majority at federal level but a minority at cantonal level and speaks the canton's majority language, a minority language at federal level.

The principal demands and aspirations of minorities are equal treatment with the majority and some degree of autonomy as a means of preserving their cultural heritage.

The autonomy and self-determination aspired to by minorities are nevertheless only principles which must be given effect in everyday political affairs. Federalism is no doubt an excellent means of applying and fulfilling these principles, by virtue of its ability to foster pluralism and accommodate national differences. Its flexibility makes for a certain balance between the desire of the majority and the aspirations of minority groups to autonomy.

Swiss federalism does not basically differ from that of other states but is conspicuous in having ensured decades of peaceful co-existence for many minorities. This brief study sets out to examine the typical institutions and chief mechanisms of Swiss federalism.

I.   PROTECTION   OF   MINORITIES   THROUGH   STATE INSTITUTIONS

A.   Representation of minorities within the federal institutions

Minorities in Switzerland are protected primarily through their representation in the central bodies of the state.

1.   Federal parliament

The federal parliament is bicameral. The people's representatives sit in the first chamber (National Council) and the representatives of the cantons in the second chamber (Council of States).

For the purpose of electing the 200 National Council representatives, the territory of the Confederation is divided into 26 constituencies corresponding to the boundaries of the 26 Swiss cantons (Article 73, Federal Constitution). The 200 seats are allocated to the cantons according to their respective populations under the proportional representation system (Article 72 (2), Federal Constitution). The procedure for allocating seats (rule of the largest remainder) has the effect of favouring the representation of the smaller cantons in the lower house. Elections are then held by direct universal suffrage. Each voter elects the members for his constituency, ie his own canton. There are from one to 35 members per canton depending on its population. Elections are conducted by proportional representation, so that minorities can be represented. The very small cantons with a population under 1/200th of the total Swiss population, which would be deprived of all representation by the proportional system, are nevertheless entitled by statute to one representative, who is elected by majority vote (Article 72 (2), Federal Constitution). As a result, the small cantons are in fact over-represented in the National Council because their single member, unlike those of the other cantons, represents over 1/200th of the population.

The second house of parliament, known as the Council of States, has 46 members, two per canton and one per demi-canton. The method of election is freely determined by the cantons. The membership of the Council of States distinctly favours the small cantons, which have two representatives on the same terms as the large ones. This also means that the minorities are protected and well-represented.

The two upper house representatives are frequently elected in such a way as to represent the various facets of the canton, eg the two language groups, the two denominations and the two main political tendencies. As the Council of State members vote without instruction (Article 91, Federal Constitution), these tendencies can be expressed at the time of voting.

It would be mistaken to believe that the federal element is represented solely in the Council of States. The National Council is also substantially "federalised"; since as already explained, its members are elected in the cantons. In Switzerland, moreover, the political parties are organised very much on a cantonal basis and a political career at federal level is very difficult to achieve without support from the cantonal sections of the parties.

2.   Federal government

The government, known as the Federal Council, is also made up in such a way as to represent the various components of the state.

Accordingly, to ensure that as many cantons as possible are represented in the Federal Council, Article 96 (1) of the Constitution stipulates that not more than one member may be chosen from the same canton.

According to an unwritten rule the seven members of the Federal Council must furthermore include two or sometimes three councillors representing the French and Italian-speaking minorities. At present the two minorities, which together make up less than 25% of the total Swiss population, are over-represented in the federal government with three out of seven members of the federal executive.

According to another unwritten rule observed since the early 1960s, the four main political parties share the seven government seats in a ratio, called the "magic formula", of two seats each for three parties and one seat for the fourth. These four parties, which are known as the governing parties and represent some 90% of the political forces in parliament, include three centre parties and one left wing party. Although the three "middle class" parties would be well able to govern on their own and leave the minority Socialist Party in opposition as is the case in other countries, they have elected to give it a share of responsibility for national affairs as part of the government. Thus a substantial political minority is involved in government. Only the very small political minorities, in particular the extreme right and the extreme left, are not represented within the executive.

3. Federal Court

Concern for equitable representation of minorities is also perceptible in the composition of the country's supreme judicial body, the Federal Court. Article 107 of the Constitution provides that in electing the Federal Court judges and their substitutes, the Federal Assembly shall ensure that the three official languages of the Confederation are represented. In practice, the composition of the Federal Court also reflects the various political tendencies in Switzerland, and judges are elected in such a way that all regions of the country are represented.

It will have been observed that the guiding principle underlying the composition of all federal bodies is proportionality, as they must reflect the political and linguistic components of the nation in proportion to their importance. Compliance with this principle understandably entails a search for compromises between the interests of the various communities constituting the nation (democracy of concordance).

B. Cantonal self-government

Another institutional means of protecting minorities in Switzerland is the autonomy of the cantons in all matters of self-government. Article 3 of the Constitution provides that the cantons are sovereign insofar as their sovereignty is not restricted by the Federal Constitution and that they accordingly exercise all rights not delegated to the federal power.

As space does not permit a detailed description of all fields within the cantons' sphere of competence, only the chief ones will be mentioned.

1. Constitutional law

a. The cantonal institutions

As decentralised public authorities, the cantons are free to adopt whatever forms of organisation they consider appropriate and to allocate the cantonal power to such bodies as they may see fit to establish. Thus each canton has its own constitution. Cantonal self-government is furthermore recognised indirectly by Article 5 and 6 of the Constitution and has enabled them to retain to some extent the political institutions handed down to them: assembly-based democracy (Landsgemeinden) in the cantons of early Switzerland; representative democracy in the former aristocratic cantons; direct democracy in the cantons where democratic ideas triumphed in the mid-19th century.

Article 6 of the Constitution simply requires the cantons to have a republican and democratic government. While all have adopted the collegial system of the central government, there is nothing to prevent them from choosing another political system, eg parliamentary or presidential government. All cantons have their own distinctive versions of four main bodies: the electorate, the parliament, the government and the judiciary.

i.   The cantonal electorate

Within the limits imposed upon it by federal law, each canton establishes its own definition of the categories to be granted political rights, ie the right to vote, elect representatives and sign public proposals for legislation or reform (initiative populaire) or petitions for referendum in cantonal affairs (see Article 74 (4) of the Constitution). Consequently, there are fairly significant differences between cantons.

These firstly concern age, ten cantons having fixed the age of civic majority for cantonal affairs at 18 and the rest at 20 years.

The differences also relate to nationality; Jura canton, for example, gives foreigners resident in the canton for ten years the right to vote.

Two cantons allow their expatriate citizens to belong to the cantonal electorate, while residence in the canton is a condition laid down by the other cantons for enjoyment of political rights.

In the vast majority of cantons, the electorate avails itself of its rights through secret ballot. Five cantons, however, have preserved to this day a typical institution of early Switzerland, the Landsgemeinde. This is a general assembly of citizens which meets once a year outdoors and conducts all cantonal elections except the election of the parliament, which is by ballot. It is also empowered to revise the cantonal constitution and pass legislation. Voting is by show of hands.

ii.   The cantonal parliament

All cantons have a parliament but its official title varies (Grand Conseil, Kantonsrat, Landsrat). The number of representatives in each assembly ranges from 60 to 200.

The method of election in nearly all cantons is that of proportional representation, the general rule (except in Geneva and Ticino) being that the cantonal territory is divided into several constituencies made up of the communes, circumscriptions (= cercles) or districts. Some cantons nevertheless have the majority system (Grisons, Uri, Appenzell Inner and Outer Rhodes).

Cantonal parliaments also have varying terms of office, usually four years but in some cases less (Grisons: 2 years) or more (Fribourg: 5 years). Grounds of incompatibility also vary greatly from one canton to the next.

There are further essential differences between the parliaments of Landsgemeinde cantons, which necessarily have limited powers, and those of the city cantons such as Geneva, Basel or Zurich, which are modern parliaments on the model of national parliaments.

This diversity stems from the specific history of each canton but also reflects the extent of citizen rights and the party system, which includes the single party (one canton) multiparty systems (in 15 or more cantons) the bipartite system with a dominant party.

iii.   The cantonal government

Each canton has a governments, whose official title varies.   The cantonal governments are all collegial bodies like the federal government, but their membership varies from five to seven according to the canton. They are usually elected by majority vote, but two cantons (Zug and Ticino) use the proportional representation system.

The age of candidacy also varies from one canton to the next.

While professionalism is the rule for the members of cantonal governments, some small cantons have citizen part-time governments whose members continue to hold another occupation.

iv. The cantonal courts

The cantons have considerable autonomy as to their judicial order. Except for the Federal Court and a few special appeals boards, all the Swiss judicial authorities are cantonal (see Article 64 and 64 bis of the Constitution). The salient feature of this judicial order is its great diversity. Civil, criminal, administrative and special or extraordinary courts must be differentiated separately for each canton. For instance, in addition to the ordinary civil courts some cantons have a special civil authority dealing with employer-employee disputes (conciliation boards). Some have the institution of trial by jury for serious criminal offences, others not.

There is also a variety of cantonal administrative courts. Twenty or so cantons have recently set up an administrative court ruling on the lawfulness of most administrative decisions. In cantons not yet having adopted this institution, appeals are made to the cantonal government or to specialised appeals boards.

b. Local structures

These are invariably governed by cantonal law, either stringently or with some scope for autonomy.

Where their internal structures are concerned, the communes can be divided into two main categories. While they all have at least two bodies, ie the local electorate and the local government, some also have an assembly. The bipartite structure (consequently without an assembly) is typical of the smaller communes; the tripartite structure is more commonly found in the large ones.

Owing to the importance of communes as the lowest tier of authority in the Swiss legal order, the right to preserve their autonomy is secured to them but the scope of this right is for the cantons to determine.

Subject to Article 43 (4) and (5) of the Federal Constitution, cantonal law determines the composition of the local electorate. In Neuchâtel canton, for instance, foreigners resident in the canton for five years and in a commune for one year may vote in matters affecting the commune, while they are not granted this right in the other cantons.

c. **Other territorial authorities**

The characteristic structure of the Swiss state comprises the Confederation, the cantons and the communes. However, within this three-tier state, there occur in a few cantons other authorities which will merely be mentioned in passing, eg the districts which come next above the communes in certain cantons. The circumstances of Grisons canton are true public authorities whose bodies hold considerable judicial, political and administrative powers.

2. **Political rights**

Political rights also vary considerably between cantons.

a. Mandatory referenda are normal in all cantons for review of the cantonal constitution (see Article 6 (2) (c) of the Federal Constitution), but some cantons apply this requirement to still other official acts. Fifteen prescribe it for the passing of ordinary legislation and some even for parliament orders, and 19 for expenditure over a certain amount (financial referendum) and for the conclusion of inter-cantonal agreements or treaties (treaty referendum).

Optional referenda may be held in respect of legislation in the 11 cantons which do not have a mandatory referendum for this purpose; 18 cantons also prescribe it for expenditure over a certain amount, and five do so for inter-cantonal agreements.

The time allowed for requesting a referendum is from one to two months depending on the canton.

b. The "initiative populaire" form of consultation exists in all cantons but the number of signatures required varies. Furthermore, cantonal law lays down the conditions of its success and in particular the time within which the lists of signatures must be lodged with the competent authority. Cantonal law also regulates the formulation of the question to be put to electors, especially where the government counters it with its own proposal.

c. Only seven cantons apply the right of revocation, enabling a faction of the electorate to move the dissolution of parliament, the dismissal of the executive or the removal of any official.

3. Taxation law

The Swiss cantons enjoy extensive autonomy as regards taxation. Except where taxes are levied solely by the Confederation, eg turnover tax (Article 41 bis (1) of the Federal Constitution), the cantons have freedom to define the purpose, basis and rate of cantonal taxes and the persons on whom they are levied. They also have free use of their tax yield.

In particular, the cantons levy a direct tax on personal income, on the turnover and capital of corporate bodies, private assets and capital gains. They collect excise on vehicles, property conveyance dues, entertainment tax, foreigners' residence fees, estate duty, etc.

Cantonal autonomy in taxation matters means that cantonal taxes are highly diversified.

4. Federal law restrictions on cantonal self-government

In all fields mentioned above, cantonal self-government is of course not absolute, is to be exercised strictly within the limits prescribed by federal law. The chief restrictions are as follows:

-   As regards political institutions, Article 6 of the Federal Constitution requires the cantons to ensure that political rights are exercised in a republican, ie representative or democratic manner. In order to take effect, their constitutions must be accepted by the citizens of the canton and be open to review when the absolute majority of citizens so request (Article 6(2)(c) of the Federal Constitution). In other words, the cantons must arrange consultation by "initiative populaire" in constitutional matters. They are also required to have their constitutions guaranteed by request to the Confederation, which is not granted unless the cantonal constitution complies with federal law in general.

    Furthermore, Article 43 determines to some extent who may vote in cantonal and local elections and other forms of consultation. Likewise, Article 44 settles some of the conditions under which foreigners may acquire or forfeit citizenship of a canton or commune.

    Nor is the fiscal autonomy of cantons absolute. Apart from the need to respect the Confederation's sole power to levy certain taxes, established federal practice requires that their own taxes are prescribed by a law in the strict sense. Lastly double taxation is prohibited by the Federal Constitution, (Article 46(2)), as are certain ecclesiastical taxes (Article 49(6)). Article 42 quinquies gives the Confederation responsibility for harmonising federal, cantonal and local taxes.

Needless to say, in the exercise of cantonal powers, whatever their nature, the cantons must observe the basic principles of the rule of law, such as separation of powers, legality, independence of the courts and the fundamental rights of the individual.

II. PROTECTION OF MINORITIES THROUGH THE MAKING AND APPLICATION OF LAW

A.   Law-making

1.   Participation by the cantons in the federal process of decision

The Swiss cantons form one of the Confederation's basic entities, or even the chief entity alongside the Swiss people, and as such are actively involved in the process of central government decision.

a. Accordingly, every full or partial revision of the Federal Constitution must be approved by the majority of the people and by the majority of cantons. Thus the constitutional power in Switzerland consists of the people and the cantons (Article 123 of the Federal Constitution). This dual majority is also required to ratify international treaties of very high importance such as those dealing with collective security and instituting supra-national communities (Article 89(5)). It can therefore be said that in Switzerland no domestic or foreign policy decision is possible without the assent of the majority of the cantons.

The dual majority requirement has two implications.

Firstly, those cantons which constitute minorities, eg linguistic minorities, may oppose a project accepted by the majority of the population if they are supported by a few other cantons.

Secondly, as the vote of each canton is determined by the majority of its citizens and as each canton has one vote, irrespective of its population, a minority of the population can block a project accepted by the majority of the population if that minority is distributed throughout most of the cantons.

The constitutional history of the Confederation includes instances where a proposal to revise the Constitution did not come into force because it was rejected by the majority of the cantons.

b. The cantons also form an entity of the Confederation in that a law passed by the federal parliament can be subjected to referendum at the request of 8 cantons (Article 89). Thus cantons representing minorities may possibly defeat at referendum a law to which they object, thanks to this provision.

c. Each separate canton may furthermore submit a proposal to the federal parliament for the adoption of a law or constitutional provisions (Article 93(2)).

Lastly, according to firmly established practice, whenever the federal government has a federal act in preparation, before submitting the bill to parliament it applies the procedure known as consultation which serves to obtain the opinion of various entities or groups affected by the bill. These include political parties, trade unions, the various pressure groups and of course the cantons. If a bill is not favourably received by the cantons, the federal government generally refrains from putting it to parliament or amends it before doing so. As a referendum can be requested by a minority of the population (50,000 citizens) or of the cantons (8), its likelihood compels the federal government to take account of the opinions expressed by the entities consulted.

## 2.	Apportionment of responsibilities between the confederation and cantons; legislative autonomy of the cantons

### a.	Principles

Under Article 3 of the Federal Constitution, matters within the competence of the Confederation must be specified in the Constitution. In other words, if the Confederation is to intervene and legislate in a given area, it must be identified in the Constitution. Otherwise it rests with the cantons, so that they have their own powers in all matters for which the Confederation lacks competence. The extent of cantonal powers nevertheless varies according to the nature of the federal power.

Where the Confederation has sole competence, as in national defence (Article 18 to 22), customs (Articles 28 and 29), rail transport (Article 26), post and telecommunications (Article 36), currency and bank notes (Articles 38 and 39) and foreign affairs, the cantons hold no power in their own right.

In those areas where the Confederation has been assigned parallel competence above and beyond questions of principle, such as private law, intellectual property, prosecution for debt and bankruptcy (Article 64), criminal law (Article 64 bis), public labour law (Article 34 ter), the cantons no longer have undivided powers if the Federal Government has made full provision by enacting exhaustive legislation on the subject, pending which they hold such powers on a provisional basis only.

In fields where the Confederation holds parallel powers in respect of the principles only, ie power to enact outline legislation, eg on regulation of forests (Article 24), hunting and fishing (Article 25), spatial planning (Article 22 quarter), the cantons hold indefinite powers of their own, though only as regards regulation of the details.

In spheres where the Confederation and the canton are assigned corresponding powers, the two may enact concurrent legislation.

Lastly, the cantons have sole power in matters over which the Confederation has no authority.

b.   Scope of cantonal powers

-    In the private law sphere, the Confederation adopted a Civil Code in 1907 and a Code of Obligations in 1911, so that the private law sectors in which cantons can legislate are very limited and consist of those few areas in which they have a delegated competence under either code (Section 52.1 and 55.1 in the last chapter of the Civil Code; Section 686 of the Civil Code). On the other hand, the cantons have retained competence in respect of civil procedure insofar as proceedings take place before the cantonal courts, and the rules of civil procedure vary accordingly between cantons.

-    Criminal law was also unified by the adoption of the Swiss Penal Code in 1937, so that the cantons no longer have the authority to define certain acts as crimes or offences, although Section 335.1 of the Penal Code concedes their power to legislate on petty offences not covered by federal legislation. The cantons have nonetheless retained competence in respect of criminal procedure insofar as trials are held before the cantonal courts, and the rules of criminal procedure vary accordingly between cantons.

- Public law differs in that the cantons have retained considerable legislative autonomy depending on the public law field, so that wherever the Confederation has only an enacted outline legislation the cantons hold some degree of legislative power. Such areas are spatial planning, regulation of forests, hunting and fishing and routine naturalisation of aliens. To take just the foregoing example, it can be pointed out that as set forth in Section 12 of the Federal Act on the acquisition and forfeiture of Swiss nationality, Swiss nationality is acquired under normal procedure, through naturalisation in a canton and a commune. An alien therefore becomes Swiss by acquiring citizenship of a canton. Section 15 of the same act merely lays down the minimum requirements stipulated for securing Swiss nationality, while the naturalisation procedure is arranged by the cantonal authorities.

The cantons may also legislate in areas where both they and the Confederation are competent, namely their own political institutions, the political rights of citizens at cantonal level, the judicial order, procedural law and taxation law.

Lastly, there are fields where the cantons may legislate exclusively; these are education, public works, public health, culture, church-state relations and worship, law and order, fire prevention, building regulations etc.

3. Inter-cantonal agreements

In those areas where they hold legislative power, the cantons may also conclude mutual agreements known as inter-cantonal concordats. These are the chief instrument of what is commonly termed co-operative federalism.

Though such use of them is rather uncommon in practice, these agreements may enable cantons comprising minorities, for example linguistic minorities, to settle certain questions by common agreement without the federal authorities intervening.

B.   Application of the law

The fact that certain matters rest with the Confederation does not completely remove them from the influence of the cantons. In Switzerland, legislative activity is the only field to which the principle of apportionment of powers between central and cantonal government applies absolutely. It is less rigidly adhered to in the field of judicial and executive activity.

In matters where legislation rests with the Confederation, it shares judicial power with the cantons. This is particularly so as regards private law and criminal law. Although the Civil Code and the Penal Code were enacted by the Confederation, disputes in private law and criminal law are settled initially by the cantonal courts. The application of federal law by the cantonal courts can result in differing interpretations of the same rule and have repercussions on the sometimes dissimilar settlements adopted by these courts in respect of litigation referred to them. One frequently mentioned example is abortion, for which Section 118 of the Penal Code provides prison sentences. While this provision is stringently enforced by certain cantonal courts, it has become virtually obsolete in other cantons, so much so that debate has arisen over the expediency of finding a federal solution, ie adaptable to each canton, to the problem of termination of pregnancy. This example shows that even in branches of law which have been unified there is room for some cantonal autonomy in the interpretation of the law.

These considerations also apply to the application of the law by the administrative authorities. Indeed, there are fields where the Confederation not only legislates but also takes decisions and has them enforced by federal officials, eg railways, postal services and customs. Elsewhere, however, legislation passed by the Confederation is carried into effect by the cantons in what is called executive federalism. In some cases, the Constitution explicitly provides for the enforcement of federal law by the cantons, for instance in the fields of civil defence (Article 22 bis (2)), nature conservation (Article 24 septies (2)), protection of animals (Article 25 bis (3)) and national highways (Article 36 bis (2)).

Legal practice and theory nevertheless concur in acknowledging that the federal legislator, even where not expressly authorised to do so by the Constitution, may delegate power to execute federal laws to the cantons. Executive federalism has moreover become a basic principle of Swiss federalism, enabling the cantons to retain some autonomy even in areas covered by federal legislation. The extent of this autonomy depends on the thoroughness of the federal legislation and the exactitude of the rules therein.

III. FEDERALISM AND ACHIEVEMENT OF AUTONOMY

Federalism is a type of political structure enabling minorities to achieve some degree of autonomy while averting secession. The constitutions of several federal states provide the possibility of establishing new federated states within the supreme state, but the Swiss Federal Constitution contains no such rules.

Nonetheless, there is no impediment to a minority incorporated into a canton achieving autonomy by forming a new canton, as witness the creation of Jura canton.

In 1815 the Jura districts with their predominantly Catholic French-speaking population were attached to the mainly Protestant, German-speaking Bern canton, although historically the Jura districts, at least in the North, had always had special links with France and the Basel area rather than with Switzerland.

This minority expressed its wish to become an independent canton on several occasions. However, this necessitated a curtailment of Bern canton's territory. In 1970 the population of this canton agreed to a change in its constitution to allow the organisation of plebiscites in the Jura districts possibly resulting in the formation of a new canton. Under the newly adopted provisions, three plebiscites were held in succession.

During the first plebiscite on 23 June 1984, the population of the seven Jura districts in Bern canton voted by a small majority for the creation of a new canton (the northern districts in favour; the southern districts against).

The principle of a new canton being established, its boundaries remained to be defined. This was done in the second plebiscite on 16 March 1975, when each district was asked whether it wished to separate from or stay with Bern canton. The three northern districts chose separation, the four southern ones the perpetuation of the status quo.

In a third and final plebiscite held in October 1975, eight communes on the dividing line between the northern and southern districts voted to join the new canton while six others expressed the wish to remain part of Bern canton.

The reception of a newcomer by the Confederation still had to be approved by the majority of the Swiss people and cantons. Approval was given at a constitutional referendum held on 25 September 1978. 82% of electors and all cantons voted in favour of creating the new Jura canton. The object of the referendum was to amend Article 1 of the Federal Constitution containing the list of Swiss cantons.

The creation of this new canton thus took place in compliance with two major principles, the first being the democratic principle: the majority of the population of Bern canton in 1970 accepted the principle of ultimate separation from the Jura districts and resultant loss of territory, while the majority of the Jura population chose separation. The second essential principle on which the whole operation was founded is the federalist principle: the Jura districts did not become a new canton in law until the majority of the Swiss people and cantons agreed to amend Article 1 of the Federal Constitution.

The case of Jura canton shows how a minority formerly incorporated into a larger political unit was able to fulfil its aspiration to autonomy by becoming a canton. Had it not formed itself into a fully independent canton, it might have assumed demi-canton status like three Swiss cantons which are divided into two. In one case, the division was carried out to enable the two denominational communities to lead separate lives.

IV. FEDERALISM, MINORITIES AND BASIC RIGHTS

The Federal Constitution of the Swiss Confederation contains no special provisions on minorities. Minorities can avail themselves of the basic rights secured to all citizens. Under Article 4 of the Constitution, these rights must be exercised without discrimination of any kind.

In two areas, however, minorities receive special protection. Firstly, certain guarantees are secured to linguistic minorities. Secondly, minorities of any kind have the opportunity to take part in the process of political decision.

A.   Protection of linguistic minorities

1.   The territoriality principle

Article 116 (1) of the Federal Constitution provides that Switzerland shall have four national languages, German, French, Italian and Romansh. This constitutional provision does no more than to set the official seal on an existing situation, ie the division of Swiss territory into four language zones, the German-speaking region (some 75% of the population), the French-speaking region (about 20%), the Italian-speaking region (about 5%) and the Romansh region (less than 1%).

The French and Italian language minorities are concentrated in certain cantons where they make up the bulk of the population.

Article 116 (1) of the Constitution establishes the principle of territoriality. This is designed as a constitutional guarantee of Switzerland's linguistic plurality. Relying on this provision, the Confederation can take such measures as it deems necessary on behalf of languages which are in a minority or endangered. For instance, Article 116 (1) was the basis for the adoption by the Confederation of the Federal Act on subsidies to Grisons and Ticino cantons for the preservation of their culture and language.

The territoriality principle also enables linguistic minorities to make use, in their own cantons where they form a majority, of their own language in official relations with the authorities and in schools.

2. Official languages

Of these four national languages, only three are official, viz German, French and Italian. Romansh, not being widespread enough, has not found sufficient favour with the constitutional power to be elevated to the status of an official language. However, the current preparations for a revision of Article 116 of the Federal Constitution include the question of Romansh as a further official language.

The recognition of three official languages in the Constitution has the effect of conferring on the minorities, particularly the French-speaking and Italian-speaking ones, the right to communicate in their own language with the political, administrative or judicial authorities at federal level. Another implication of the official languages principle is of course that these authorities are required to communicate with the minorities in their own language. Likewise, the three official languages are used for the publication of federal acts and for the conduct of Federal Parliament debates, with simultaneous interpretation. Within the federal administration, the three official languages can be used internally and in contacts with members of the public. Lastly, applications can be made to the Federal Court in each of the official languages, and its judgments must be set out in the language of the decision appealed from.

The territoriality principle and the official languages principle are also applied mutatis mutandis at cantonal level in the three bilingual cantons of Bern (French-speaking minority), Fribourg and Valais (German-speaking minorities). Each language may be used in relations with the cantonal authorities.

Grisons canton is the only trilingual one, with a German-speaking majority and two minorities using Romansh and Italian. However, the application of trilingualism is not all-embracing. Locally, the communes have a very wide degree of autonomy and consequently settle the official language problem in their own way. Matters are complicated by the fact that Romansh is not a single language but has five separate dialects. Efforts towards unification have resulted in a standard language, "Rumantsch Grischun", thanks to which it is hoped that a language threatened with extinction will be preserved.

As demonstrated above, at the level of the federal authorities the language minorities are duly represented in the Federal Council, the Federal Assembly and the Federal Court without the need to introduce a quota system.

B.   Political rights

Political rights, particularly those of initiative and referendum, constitute the second area in which minorities enjoy special rights.

-    The right of initiative enables 100,000 citizens to request the amendment of the Constitution (Article 121 of the Federal Constitution). This institution allows a religious, linguistic or other minority of the population to put forward at constitutional level a set of regulations in its own favour. As has been explained, this right can be exercised in constitutional as well as legislative matters by each canton (Article 93 (2)). It also enables any one canton inhabited by a minority (eg the Italian-speaking Ticino canton) to propose an amendment to the Federal Constitution or the enactment of a law on an issue concerning that minority. In order to take effect, the statutes proposed must of course be approved by the majority.

The right of initiative also applies in all cantons and can be exercised by their resident minorities.

-    The right of referendum enables 50,000 citizens to request that any law passed by Parliament should be submitted to the people for approval. Here too, any minority considering itself disadvantaged by a law can therefore attempt to defeat it at referendum by collecting the required number of signatures. The same right can also be exercised by a minority of cantons (Article 89 (2)).

CONCLUSION

A few observations may be made to round off this succinct study.

In Switzerland, the solution to the problem of minorities lies chiefly in the fact that the country is primarily and essentially a political reality and much less a cultural entity. As a state, it is founded on common political convictions and ideals such as federalism, democracy, rule of law and determination to share these values. They are respected as long as they remain unchallenged by minorities, whatever their nature. On the other hand, when a state is not defined in terms of common political values but first and foremost by its linguistic and cultural characteristics, minorities have far more trouble in gaining acceptance.

Secondly, Switzerland is composed of older political entities, the cantons. These are historical realities which cannot always be defined in terms of their linguistic or denominational characteristics, three being bilingual and one trilingual. The cantonal boundaries thus do not coincide with the boundaries of the three language regions or indeed with the denominational communities. Because Switzerland is divided into cantons, not into three regions corresponding to the language regions, it cannot be split up into cultural, religious or linguistic entities. In other words, the political divisions of the country do not correspond to its cultural demarcations. As minorities are part and parcel of the cantons, the language regions are not the sole context of diversity but merely a further context.

This interweaving of the political and administrative boundaries with the linguistic and cultural boundaries makes it very hard for any group to predominate. As a result, Switzerland consists of a large number of minorities which offset and counterbalance each other. As pointed out earlier on, each Swiss citizen belongs to a minority in one way or another. This intricate patchwork is definitely more conducive to the protection of minorities than the clear differentiation and geographical localisation which often apply.

Sales agents for publications of the Council of Europe
Agents de vente des publications du Conseil de l'Europe

AUSTRALIA/AUSTRALIE
Hunter Publications, 58A, Gipps Street
AUS-3066 COLLINGWOOD, Victoria

AUSTRIA/AUTRICHE
Gerold und Co., Graben 31
A-1011 WIEN 1

BELGIUM/BELGIQUE
La Librairie européenne SA
50, avenue A. Jonnart
B-1200 BRUXELLES 20

Jean de Lannoy
202, avenue du Roi
B-1060 BRUXELLES

CANADA
Renouf Publishing Company Limited
1294 Algoma Road
CDN-OTTAWA ONT K1B 3W8

CYPRUS/CHYPRE
MAM
The House of the Cyprus Book
PO Box 1722, CY-NICOSIA

DENMARK/DANEMARK
Munksgaard
Book and Subscription Service
PO Box 2148
DK-1016 KØBENHAVN K

FINLAND/FINLANDE
Akateeminen Kirjakauppa
Keskuskatu 1, PO Box 218
SF-00381 HELSINKI

GERMANY/ALLEMAGNE
UNO Verlag
Poppelsdorfer Allee 55
D-53115 BONN

GREECE/GRÈCE
Librairie Kauffmann
Mavrokordatou 9, GR-ATHINAI 106 78

IRELAND/IRLANDE
Government Stationery Office
Publications Section
4-5 Harcourt Road, IRL-DUBLIN 2

ISRAEL/ISRAËL
ROY International
PO Box 13056
IL-61130 TEL AVIV

ITALY/ITALIE
Libreria Commissionaria Sansoni
Via Duca di Calabria, 1/1
Casella Postale 552, I-50125 FIRENZE

LUXEMBOURG
Librairie Bourbon
(Imprimerie Saint-Paul)
11, rue Bourbon
L-1249 LUXEMBOURG

NETHERLANDS/PAYS-BAS
InOr-publikaties, PO Box 202
NL-7480 AE HAAKSBERGEN

NORWAY/NORVÈGE
Akademika, A/S Universitetsbokhandel
PO Box 84, Blindern
N-0314 OSLO

PORTUGAL
Livraria Portugal, Rua do Carmo, 70
P-1200 LISBOA

SPAIN/ ESPAGNE
Mundi-Prensa Libros SA
Castelló 37, E-28001 MADRID

Llibreria de la Generalitat
Rambla dels Estudis, 118
E-08002 BARCELONA

Llibreria de la Generalitat de Catalunya
Gran Via Jaume I, 38, E-17001 GIRONA

SWEDEN/SUÈDE
Aktiebolaget CE Fritzes
Regeringsgatan 12, Box 163 56
S-10327 STOCKHOLM

SWITZERLAND/SUISSE
Buchhandlung Heinimann & Co.
Kirchgasse 17, CH-8001 ZÜRICH

BERSY
Route du Manège 60
CP 4040
CH-1950 SION 4

TURKEY/TURQUIE
Yab-Yay Yayimcilik Sanayi Dagitim Tic Ltd
Barbaros Bulvari 61 Kat 3 Daire 3
Besiktas, TR-ISTANBUL

UNITED KINGDOM/ROYAUME-UNI
HMSO, Agency Section
51 Nine Elms Lane
GB-LONDON SW8 5DR

**UNITED STATES and CANADA/
ÉTATS-UNIS et CANADA**
Manhattan Publishing Company
468 Albany Post Road
PO Box 850
CROTON-ON-HUDSON, NY 10520

STRASBOURG
Librairie internationale Kléber
1, rue des Francs-Bourgeois
F-67000 STRASBOURG

Librairie des Facultés
2-12, rue de Rome
F-67000 STRASBOURG

Librairie Kléber
Palais de l'Europe
F-67075 STRASBOURG Cedex

Council of Europe Press/Les éditions du Conseil de l'Europe
Council of Europe/Conseil de l'Europe
F-67075 Strasbourg Cedex